THE MEMOIRS OF
ROBERT AND MABEL
WILLIAMS

THE MEMOIRS OF ROBERT AND MABEL WILLIAMS

AFRICAN AMERICAN FREEDOM, ARMED RESISTANCE, AND INTERNATIONAL SOLIDARITY

ROBERT F. WILLIAMS AND
MABEL R. WILLIAMS

EDITED BY
AKINYELE OMOWALE UMOJA,
GLORIA ANEB HOUSE, AND
JOHN H. BRACEY JR.

The University of North Carolina Press
Chapel Hill

Designed by Lindsay Starr
Set in Dante MT Pro and PF Fuel Grime
by Jamie McKee, MacKey Composition
Manufactured in the United States of America

Cover art: *Top:* Photograph of Robert and Mabel Williams by John H. Williams, courtesy of the Freedom Archives. *Bottom:* Robert and Mabel Williams with food canning factory workers in Shanghai, c. 1963, Robert F. Williams Papers, Bentley Historical Library, University of Michigan.

Library of Congress Cataloging-in-Publication Data
Names: Williams, Robert F. (Robert Franklin), 1925–1996, author. | Williams, Mabel R., author. | Umoja, Akinyele Omowale, editor. | House, Gloria, 1941– editor. | Bracey, John H., editor.
Title: The memoirs of Robert and Mabel Williams : African American freedom, armed resistance, and international solidarity / Robert F. Williams and Mabel R. Williams ; edited by Akinyele Omowale Umoja, Gloria Aneb House, and John H. Bracey Jr.
Description: Chapel Hill : University of North Carolina Press, [2025] | Includes bibliographical references and index.
Identifiers: LCCN 2024059218 | ISBN 9781469680125 (cloth) | ISBN 9781469680132 (paperback) | ISBN 9781469680149 (epub) | ISBN 9781469680156 (pdf)
Subjects: LCSH: Williams, Robert F. (Robert Franklin), 1925–1996. | Williams, Mabel R. | African American civil rights workers—North Carolina—Monroe—Biography. | African American radicals—Biography. | African Americans—Civil rights—North Carolina—Monroe—History—20th century. | Black power—United States—History—20th century. | Monroe (N.C.)—Race relations—History—20th century. | BISAC: SOCIAL SCIENCE / Ethnic Studies / American / African American & Black Studies | HISTORY / United States / 20th Century | LCGFT: Autobiographies.
Classification: LCC E185.61 .W376 2025 | DDC 305.896/07307567550922—dc23/eng/20250303
LC record available at https://lccn.loc.gov/2024059218

For product safety concerns under the European Union's General Product Safety Regulation (EU GPSR), please contact gpsr@mare-nostrum.co.uk or write to the University of North Carolina Press and Mare Nostrum Group B.V., Mauritskade 21D, 1091 GC Amsterdam, The Netherlands.

publication supported by a grant from
The Community Foundation for Greater New Haven
as part of the *Urban Haven Project*

CONTENTS

ILLUSTRATIONS

PART I. WHILE GOD LAY SLEEPING

PART II. WE WANT TO SEE EVERYBODY RISE

PREFACE

AFRICAN AMERICAN FREEDOM, ARMED RESISTANCE, AND INTERNATIONAL SOLIDARITY

> One thing I am really happy about is at last the Iron Curtain of secrecy has been lifted on our role in the civil rights movement. You know for many years, while Robert was alive, the news of our struggle was suppressed. . . . The powers that be did not want the example of Black people really struggling for true equality, true liberation, and did not want the example of Robert Williams out there. So, I'm very happy and very proud the real story's being told.
>
> —Mabel Williams, interviewed by Walter Turner, KPFA FM (2004)

On August 6, 2016, the younger son of Robert and Mabel Williams, Pastor John Chalmers Williams, supported by his wife, Lisa, and his brother, Franklin, hosted a meeting to continue the revolutionary legacy of his parents. John's health was challenged, and he was committed to passing on the contributions and perspectives of Robert and Mabel to new and future generations of Black freedom fighters. In the years preceding the gathering, the Black Lives Matter movement had emerged after the killings of Trayvon Martin in Sanford, Florida, and Michael Brown in Ferguson, Missouri. Mabel Williams had joined the Ancestors in 2014 and entrusted John with the publication of Robert's and her memoirs, as well as the circulation of family photographs, recordings, and memorabilia, to enrich young activists' understanding of the lessons of the Williams family's remarkable journey during the 1950s and 1960s. John invited two eminent activists, Dr. Muhammad Ahmad (aka Max Stanford) and Professor John Henry Bracey, to join the Williams family in sharing the Williams legacy and challenging the suppression of their story from the dominant narrative of the Black freedom struggle. Both Ahmad and Bracey had been inspired by the Williamses when they built the Revolutionary Action Movement (RAM)—a national network of revolutionary nationalists established in the early 1960s.[1] Robert Williams served as the RAM international chairman while in exile in Cuba and China. Others in attendance at this meeting included former political prisoner Claude Marks of the Freedom Archives, Charles Ferrell of Detroit's Charles H. Wright Museum of African American History, and scholar-activist and author Professor Akinyele Umoja.

One immediate outcome that emerged from this gathering was that Bracey and Umoja agreed to lead the effort to publish Robert Williams's manuscript, "While God Lay Sleeping." Robert began writing his final memoir after his return to the United States from exile in 1969. Both Mabel and John Williams had worked on editing Robert's memoir, which he completed a year prior to his death in 1996. Mabel, John, and Lisa traveled to Beijing in 1999 during the celebration of the fiftieth anniversary of the Chinese Revolution. The Williams family residence in Beijing was dedicated as a national museum and symbol of the Chinese Revolution's solidarity with the Black freedom struggle. After their return, Mabel was motivated to begin to document her memory of the family's saga. The decline of Mabel's health and then John's prevented them from physically bringing the tasks to fruition. The family entrusted Bracey and Umoja with the editing and submission of the manuscript to a publisher approved by the family.

After his initial review, Professor Bracey was adamant that Robert's manuscript be published together with Mabel's memoir. Bracey's perspective was that the project would be strengthened and made more complete by her voice and recollections. Motivated by Bracey's insistence and advocacy, Umoja and

1. The Revolutionary Action Movement began as a student organization on the Central State College campus in Ohio in 1962. By 1964, it had expanded to a network of Black radicals from Cleveland, Philadelphia, New York, Chicago, Detroit, and Northern California. See Akinyele O. Umoja, "From One Generation to the Next: Armed Self-Defense, Revolutionary Nationalism, and the Southern Black Freedom Struggle," *Souls: A Critical Journal of Black Politics, Culture and Society* 15, nos. 3–4 (Fall 2013): 218–40; Robin D. G. Kelley, *Freedom Dreams: The Black Radical Imagination* (Boston: Beacon, 2003), 75–76; and Muhammad Ahmad, *We Will Return in the Whirlwind: Black Radical Organizations, 1960–1975* (Chicago: Charles H. Kerr, 2007), 95–98.

the Williams family recruited scholar-activist Professor Gloria Aneb House specifically to edit Mabel's manuscript. House was a friend of Robert and Mabel Williams and a veteran of the Student Nonviolent Coordinating Committee (SNCC) and the Provisional Government of the Republic of New Afrika, organized by Black Power advocates in 1968 who declared their independence from the United States and formed a governing body to represent their sovereignty movement. The Provisional Government of the Republic of New Afrika elected Robert Williams, then in exile in China, its president.[2]

The Williams family provided Bracey, House, and Umoja with Mabel's uncompleted manuscript, and the editors sought out additional source material on Mabel, such as interviews, to offer a more complete rendering of Robert's and her journey in the Black freedom struggle and internationally, in her own words. The editorial team used Mrs. Williams's interviews with Claude Marks and Lincoln Bergman of the Freedom Archives and with Wanda Sabir from the *San Francisco Bay View National Black Newspaper* and also her conversation with historian David Cecelski for the Southern Oral History Program Collection at the University of North Carolina's Center for the Study of the American South to supplement her story in her own voice. Mrs. Williams also had conversations with historian Pero Dagbovie, who provided notes and documents from those encounters to the editorial team. All material that originated from interviews and other supplementary material is cited in footnotes.

THE FREEDOM FIGHTERS

This volume includes the testimonies of two African American freedom fighters, Robert Franklin Williams and Mabel Ola Robinson Williams. Both stories begin in Jim Crow North Carolina, with Robert and Mabel each sharing vivid memories of terror and segregation, as well as the family and community resilience that not only enabled them to survive but also paved the way for a shared lifelong commitment to radical Black Nationalism and internationalism.

In his memoir, Robert Williams describes growing up in the vibrant and nurturing community of Monroe, North Carolina, and the challenges and restrictions that he faced as an ambitious, talented, and socially conscious young Black male in the violently segregated and unequal United States of the 1940s and

2. For background on the Provisional Government of the Republic of New Afrika, please see Edward Onaci, *Free the Land: The Republic of New Afrika and the Pursuit of the Black Nation-State* (Chapel Hill: University of North Carolina Press, 2020); and Akinyele Umoja, *We Will Shoot Back: Armed Resistance in the Mississippi Freedom Movement* (New York: New York University Press, 2013), 186–88.

1950s. His resistance to the limitations imposed on him and his fight for dignity motivated his rise as one of the most controversial figures of the civil rights movement and emergence as the most visible advocate of armed self-defense in the southern Black freedom struggle. Williams organized the Guard, a paramilitary armed defense group, to thwart Ku Klux Klan invasions into Monroe from 1957 until 1961. The Monroe resistance movement, led by Williams, became a significant example for the freedom struggle and the fight to eliminate segregation during the 1950s and early 1960s. Forced underground and into political exile due to trumped-up charges of kidnapping and interstate flight, the Williams family (Robert and Mabel and their sons, Robert Jr. and John) received political asylum in Cuba during the early years of the revolution there and later in China during the Great Proletarian Cultural Revolution and before détente with the United States in the early 1970s. Even in exile, Williams was a symbol of resistance for the Black Power movement and rebellion in the United States. He returned to the States in 1969. While residing in Michigan, he fought extradition to North Carolina before his return to the state of his birth in 1975 to address the court. The kidnapping charges were dropped by the prosecutors. Williams completed his manuscript in 1995, the year before his death.

Williams's accounts in his memoir of activism and confrontation with Ku Klux Klan violence and white supremacy in Monroe in the late 1950s and early 1960s are especially particularly riveting. He also revisits his conflicts with the more conservative leadership of the national NAACP over his open advocacy of armed Black resistance to racist white violence. Williams's description of the ordeal that forced him into exile and his family's going underground and flight to Cuba and then to China in the 1960s is particularly suspenseful and captivating, as he offers a candid view of both the Cuban and Chinese Revolutions. An insider to the extent that he lived in both countries, admired both Fidel Castro and Mao Zedong, and offered solidarity with communist revolutions, he was nonetheless an outsider: an exiled, African American radical who shared unique reflections on problems internal to both socialist societies. His account of his travels through postcolonial East Africa during the 1960s also provides the complex perspectives of a descendant of African heritage coming "home." Williams's description of his return to the United States in 1969 includes a nuanced and somewhat contradictory story of the political repression that awaited him but also details how he was sought out by political and commercial elites for his firsthand knowledge about Communist China and his intimate engagement with the country's leaders. Williams also addresses his advocacy for human rights and social justice in Michigan and North Carolina, which he pursued until his death.

Mabel Williams's memoir, *We Want to See Everybody Rise*, parallels much of

Robert Williams's story of Monroe and the couple's international experiences but is distinguished in several ways. Mrs. Williams offers memories of being a Black female growing up under Jim Crow. She also describes elements of their saga unexplored by her husband, from the couple's earliest days together through the civil rights struggle in Monroe and their exile in Cuba and China, visiting Vietnam, and return to the United States. She recounts in interesting detail the development of the Monroe movement's newsletter, *The Crusader*. Her comments concerning Robert's relationship with Nation of Islam spokesperson Malcolm X and their meetings with Mao Zedong and Ho Chi Minh are particularly memorable. Mrs. Williams's account of her activism through her Christian faith reveals the spiritual foundation of the couple's social justice orientation.

Neither memoir explores the family's domestic life during exile. There is no commentary on the everyday challenges the family must have faced as the boys, Bobby and John, navigated foreign languages, cultures, and educational systems in Cuba and China. Moreover, in their discussions of the southern civil rights movement and the politics of the Third World nations that harbored them, the Williamses do not discuss family life, gender roles, or the role of women in political struggle—issues that preoccupied the progressive movements of their time. Yet Robert Williams's readiness to intervene personally and through legal challenges to defend African American women in the Monroe community demonstrated his commitment to fight for Black women's safety and dignity.

In an interview with Professor Pero Dagbovie, Mrs. Williams explained, "We agreed that our [personal] relationship would not be disclosed [in the memoirs]."[3] The Williamses had every reason to be guarded about their private lives, given the relentless US government surveillance and repression to which they were subjected before, during, and after their exile. The way they lived and worked together as freedom fighters reflected the culture of the southern civil rights movement, where daily resistance to racial oppression fostered a collective, mutually responsible consciousness, a sense of partnership within and among families.

Mrs. Williams stated in an interview with Professor Cecelski that she was not only a housewife but also an "active participant" with her husband in their political work.[4] She could have remained in the United States with her children,

3. Mabel Williams quoted in Pero Dagbovie, "God Has Spared Me to Tell My Story: Mabel Robinson Williams and the Civil Rights–Black Power Movement," *Black Scholar* 43, no. 1/2 (Spring 2013): 85.

4. Mabel Williams, interview by David Cecelski, August 20, 1999, Interview K-0266, Southern Oral History Program Collection (#4007), Center for the Study of the American South, Southern Historical Collection, Wilson Library, University of North Carolina at Chapel Hill, https://dc.lib.unc.edu/cdm/compoundobject/collection/sohp/id/12844/rec/1.

yet she chose to stand with her husband, venturing into cultures, politics, and dangers for which she had little preparation. The two memoirs give us the story of an extraordinary partnership in which Mrs. Williams was, in many ways, her husband's equal in revolutionary determination, bravery, and resilience.

FROM THE SOUTH TO THE WORLD

The human rights struggle that Robert and Mabel Williams led in Monroe in late 1950s and early 1960s is probably best known for its advocacy of the right of Black people to defend themselves from racist violence and terrorism. Robert Williams and the Monroe movement openly called for the freedom movement to "meet violence with violence." Armed self-defense was certainly practiced in Black communities throughout the Jim Crow South, but no other civil rights activist openly proclaimed this position and organized national and international solidarity for the resistance fight in the late 1950s and early 1960s. The efficacy and example of the Monroe movement and Williams's open advocacy of armed self-defense was embraced by grassroots Black workers, students, and street forces, as well as by radical white allies, but opposed by accommodationist and "mainstream" civil rights activists. In Robert's hometown of Monroe, the local white power structure and white supremacists attempted to neutralize him with support of the Federal Bureau of Investigation's counterintelligence program.

The Williamses were also effective in organizing a national campaign to expose the arrest, conviction, and sentencing of two African American male children, nine-year-old James Thompson and eight-year-old David Simpson for the "crime" of being kissed on the cheek by Sissy Marcus, an eight-year-old white girl. James Thompson and David Simpson were arrested and beaten by Monroe police, convicted of molestation of Sissy Marcus, and sentenced to incarceration at the state reformatory in 1958 until they reached the age of twenty-one. Williams utilized his national network to develop a legal defense, fundraising, and a media campaign to expose this human rights violation, which led to the pardon of the two boys in 1959, a year following their conviction.

Robert and Mabel Williams were extremely successful in communicating their perspectives to a national and global audience. In 1959, the Williamses and their neighbor Ethel Azalea Johnson established *The Crusader*, a newsletter that became the vehicle to coordinate material aid for the Monroe movement and to support the advocacy of armed self-defense. The Williamses continued to make an impact on the Black freedom struggle through the publication and distribution of *The Crusader* even while in exile in Cuba and China. Robert and

Mabel added another major media vehicle in Cuba—*Radio Free Dixie*. This radio program was produced by Robert and Mabel with support from participants in the Cuban Revolution and broadcast to the airwaves in the United States to a loyal audience from 1961 to 1965.

Another fundamental aspect of the Williamses' legacy was their commitment to revolutionary solidarity and internationalism. While often describing himself as a Black Nationalist and separatist, Robert Williams maintained a practice of aligning himself with socialist movements and anti-imperialist and anti-colonial national liberation struggles globally. Robert was a contributor to *The Militant*, the paper of the Socialist Workers Party in the 1950s, before his emergence to national recognition as a civil rights activist. He was an early supporter of the Cuban Revolution, exhibited by his being a founding sponsor of the Fair Play for Cuba Committee, a US-based activist network in support of the Castro-led revolutionary government. Williams organized a Fair Play for Cuba delegation to visit revolutionary Cuba in 1960. The delegation included writer Leroi Jones (later known as Amiri Baraka), novelist John Oliver Killens, and historian John Henrik Clarke. Williams wrote a letter to Fidel Castro in 1960 inviting the Cuban revolutionary leader to visit Monroe and in solidarity planted a Cuban flag in his front yard and praised the Cuban Revolution in *The Crusader*.

Robert and Mabel both describe the hostility and potential for race war in Monroe as a result of Ku Klux Klan violence on August 27, 1961, on nonviolent activists in town to protest segregation. That evening, Monroe's Black residents prepared to defend the predominantly Black neighborhood of New Town from an anticipated white supremacist invasion. In this tense environment, angry armed Blacks apprehended a white couple driving through New Town and took the motorists to Robert Williams. He decided to offer the couple shelter in his family's residence until daybreak. After their departure the following morning, Robert Williams was charged with kidnapping the couple for whom he had provided shelter. He also received phone calls threatening to lynch him in the town square. Robert and Mabel and their two sons fled North Carolina—for which he was also charged with unlawful interstate flight.

Mabel Williams acknowledged that the successful escape of the family from lynch-level hysteria and a witch hunt in North Carolina was due to the solidarity of national and international friends and allies who supported the Monroe freedom movement. Inside the United States, this network included grassroots civil rights activists, Black Nationalists, and Black and white radical-Left comrades. The Williams family also received refuge in Canada, living underground with help from the *Crusader* network north of the US border. Robert Williams's history of solidarity with Castro and the Cuban Revolution was obviously a significant factor in the family receiving political asylum in Cuba. Robert traveled to Cuba and organized opposition to US intervention in the Castro-led Cuban Revolution in its early days of seizing power. Mabel Williams's reflection also informs readers that some Cubans were aware of the Monroe movement through the distribution of *The Crusader* before the family's exile there. In his memoir, Robert reveals that the spouse of Cuban revolutionary leader Juan Almeida Bosque helped Williams escape from pursuit in Canada to safety in Cuba.[5]

The support offered to the Williams family by Cuba and China was a symbol of the solidarity of the socialist regimes with the Black liberation struggle in the United States. Robert Williams also lobbied heads of state to express solidarity with the Black freedom struggle. The most notable was his successful solicitation of Mao Zedong's 1963 statement "Calling Upon the People of the World to Unite to Oppose Racial Discrimination by U.S. Imperialism and Support the American Negroes in Their Struggle against Racial Discrimination." In its preamble, Chairman Mao noted the efforts of Williams to motivate the Chinese revolutionary leader to make a public statement: "Mr. Robert Williams, the former President of the Monroe, North Carolina, Chapter of the National Association for the Advancement of Coloured People, has twice this year asked me for a statement in support of the American Negroes' struggle against racial discrimination."[6]

Drawing on the activist skills they had honed in Monroe, Robert and Mabel used their political asylum to lobby international arenas on behalf of the Black freedom struggle around the world and to promote solidarity between pro-socialist and anti-imperialist national liberation movements and the civil rights and Black Power movements. Mrs. Williams highlights the couple's meeting with Ho Chi Minh in Vietnam in 1965 at an international conference in Hanoi opposing US imperialism. Speaking as the chairman-in-exile of the Revolutionary Action Movement, Robert addressed the gathering opposing US imperialism

5. The editors could not identify the name of Juan Almeida Bosque's spouse or other family members. A security policy of the Cuban Revolution was not to reveal the identities of family members of their leadership, to evade attack from their enemies. Almeida's family members were not detailed in the press even after his death. See "Fidel Castro Loses His Right-Hand Man as Juan Almeida Dies from Heart Attack," *Daily Mail*, September 14, 2009, https://www.dailymail.co.uk/news/article-1212991/Fidel-Castro-loses-right-hand-man-Juan-Almeida-Bosque-dies-fatal-heart-attack.html.

6. Mao Zedong, "Calling Upon the People of the World to Unite to Oppose Racial Discrimination by U.S. Imperialism and Support the American Negroes in Their Struggle against Racial Discrimination," August 8, 1963, as printed in *Peking Review*, August 16, 1963, https://www.marxists.org/subject/china/peking-review/1963/PR1963-33a.htm.

and aggression in Vietnam as well as educated his audience on the historic and contemporary fight of "the captive people of the free world of racist America."[7]

In his memoir, Robert Williams points out to audiences that the saga of the Williams family and its conflict with white supremacy did not end in defeat but in victory. The Williams family survived being hunted by a lynch mob and a federal counterintelligence campaign meant to capture or kill Robert Williams. They received international support and solidarity, ultimately returning to the United States in 1969, where the trumped-up charges against Robert were finally dropped in 1975. Robert Williams stated that Black youth are often taught that Black radical leaders end up assassinated, incarcerated, or in permanent exile, but Robert and Mabel Williams both retired and transitioned as Ancestors, surrounded by family and community in the United States.

THE MEMOIRS

The book presents both memoirs in full, with editing and brief annotations for clarity and context. Robert's memoir, *While God Lay Sleeping*, is divided into seven periods of his life: (1) growing up in Monroe and early adulthood; (2) life in the US Army, challenges as a veteran on the GI Bill, and reenlistment in the US Marines; (3) formally joining and leading the desegregation movement in Monroe; (4) flight and exile to Cuba; (5) political asylum in China; (6) return to the United States; and (7) activism in later life.

Mabel's memoir, *We Want to See Everybody Rise*, follows a similar pattern: (1) early years of her life and growing up in the Jim Crow South; (2) meeting and marrying Robert Williams and her political transformation into activism; (3) the Monroe movement; (4) the repression of the Monroe movement and flight of the Williams family from the United States; (5) exile in Cuba and China and travels to Africa; (6) return to the United States; and (7) life after exile and later years. In Mabel's memoir, brief contextual background added by the editors appears in italics, and material that originated from interviews and other supplementary material is cited in footnotes.

Together, the two memoirs strive to continue the mission of the Williams family to break "the Iron Curtain of secrecy" of the contributions of their father and mother, Robert and Mabel Williams, to the Monroe movement and to their advocacy and practice of armed resistance and internationalism. The story of

7. Robert F. Williams, "Speech Delivered at the International Conference for Solidarity with the People of Vietnam against U.S. Imperialist Aggression for the Defense of Peace, Hanoi, Democratic Republic of Vietnam, November 25–29, 1965," *The Crusader* 6, no. 3 (March 1965): 1–5.

Robert and Mabel challenges the popular narrative of the civil rights movement and provides new generations with alternative political strategies and perspectives. The civil rights movement is generally taught and promoted as a nonviolent one and in a liberal framework. The Williamses' story includes the involvement and perspectives of grassroots activists and radicals who played critical roles in the movement. Robert and Mabel Williams also publicly identified with anti-colonial movements internationally and were supportive of and called for solidarity from the socialist world, including Communist Cuba and China. Their actions and ideas promulgated through their newsletter, *The Crusader*, and through broadcasts from Cuba on their show, *Radio Free Dixie*, inspired and influenced a new generation of radicals and the emerging Black Power movement. The Williamses' advocacy of armed resistance and Black international solidarity became cornerstones of the Black Power ideology of revolutionary nationalism. Robert Williams would become a symbol of this new radical militance within the Black freedom struggle. Our hope is that the book continues the Williams family mission to break the silence and erasure of their experience and its significance to the Black and global fight for human rights and liberation.

A note on language: Quoted racist language and inferences that may offend some readers have not been deleted from the memoirs. By including them, the Williamses intended to reveal the ways in which oppressive, racist hostility from whites pervaded the social environment and negatively impacted African Americans' lives in the South, 1960s–80s.

Akinyele Omowale Umoja
Gloria Aneb House
In memory of John H. Bracey Jr.

ACKNOWLEDGMENTS

It is an honor to have been given the responsibility of editing the memoirs of two heroes of our people's historic fight for liberation. We consider it a blessing to have been entrusted with this task by the Williams family. We salute the memory of Pastor John Chalmers Williams, the son of Robert and Mabel, who initially recruited John Bracey and Akinyele Umoja to undertake this project. Pastor Williams stated that his intention was to share his parents' experiences and perspectives with a new generation through publication of their manuscripts. To that end, he undertook the Robert and Mabel Williams legacy project.

Pastor Williams, a Black liberation theologian in the Afro-Christian tradition, described himself as a "Maoist-Baptist." His own story is an important part of the Williams family saga that should be documented and shared in the future. He emphasized these essential aspects of his parents' ideology:

1. Self-defense is a deterrent to white supremacist terror.
2. Demonic forces need to know there are consequences.
3. Judgment is a spiritual principle. We need to be on the "right side."
4. We don't advocate senseless and untargeted violence. God is not pleased when innocent blood is shed.
5. The focus is love of humanity. The revolutionary movement often lost sense of this focus and became reactionary.

After Pastor Williams joined the Ancestors, we could not have continued this work without the assistance and encouragement of his soulmate and loving wife, Lisa, and his younger brother, Franklin. Lisa assisted us with family information and photos to complete the project. In this regard, we also appreciate the assistance provided by grassroots activist and organizer Kwasi Akwamu, who offered his expertise to prepare photos for the book.

We started on this journey with the remarkable revolutionary historian Dr. John Bracey as part of the editorial collective. Dr. Bracey joined the Revolutionary Action Movement as a college student and young activist in Chicago in the early 1960s. His insight, mentorship, and leadership in this project were crucial. One aspect of Bracey's legacy to Africana studies and scholar-activism was his role as an ally to Black feminists and his advocacy of Black women's history. From our initial meeting, Dr. Bracey insisted on the inclusion of Mabel Williams's voice. He urged publishing the two manuscripts together as the best way of telling the Williamses' story to future generations. His insistence led to the recommendation from Lisa Williams that Dr. Gloria Aneb House be added to the editorial collective, given her relationship with Robert and Mabel and her history of scholar-activism.

Dr. Bracey joined the Ancestors on February 5, 2023. He was a coeditor of this project, and this book serves as his last publication. We are proud to have served on this team with him. The blessing and advice of Dr. Bracey's comrade and friend Dr. Muhammad Ahmad (aka Maxwell Stanford Jr.), a longtime associate of the Williams family, was also essential.

We must thank Professor Pero Dagbovie of Michigan State University for providing notes and materials he collected from Mabel Williams. Professor Dagbovie's gracious assistance in supplying materials and interviews collected from Mrs. Williams helped complete her manuscript.

We are greatly indebted to the participation of the Freedom Archives in this project. Freedom Archives founder and codirector Claude Marks was involved in the project from the very beginning of our work. The interviews that Claude and Lincoln Bergman conducted with Mabel Williams were indispensable to the completion of her memoir. Freedom Archives primary sources are available online (including issues of *The Crusader*). Those sources and the production of the audio documentary *Robert F. Williams: Self-Respect, Self-Defense, and Self-Determination* (2005) were critical for increasing our knowledge of the Williamses' saga. Special thanks is due to the archives codirector Nathanial Moore for his assistance and contributions. We are also thankful to journalist and artist Wanda Sabir for her 2004 interview with Mabel Williams published in the *San Francisco Bay View National Black Newspaper* and to historian David Cecelski for his 1999 interview with Mrs. Williams, found in the Southern Oral History Program Collection of the Center for the Study of the American South at the University of North Carolina at Chapel Hill. Finally, we wish to express our appreciation to Debbie

Gershenowitz for her excellent guidance and collegiality throughout the University of North Carolina Press production process.

We pray that Pastor Williams and his family, as well as their many friends and fellow movement activists, will be pleased with the efforts we have made to fulfill this legacy mission.

Akinyele O. Umoja
Gloria Aneb House

TIMELINE

1925 Robert Williams is born on February 26.

1931 Mabel Robinson is born on June 1.

1945 Robert is drafted into the US Army and released from service in 1946.

1947 Robert and Mabel Williams are married.

1948 Robert Franklin Williams Jr. (aka Bobby) is born on January 29.

1950 John Chalmer Williams is born on April 27.

1954 Robert enlists in US Marines, is discharged the following year, and returns home to Monroe.

1957 Robert assumes the presidency of the Monroe, NC, chapter of the NAACP.

The desegregation struggle in Monroe gains momentum.

The Black community begins protracted fight to desegregate the Monroe swimming pool.

Robert and other armed African American men defend Dr. Albert Perry, Monroe NAACP vice president, when the Ku Klux Klan attempts to raid his residence.

1958 Two African American boys, James Thompson and David Simpson, are imprisoned in a reformatory in the "Kissing Case."

1959 Robert leads national campaign to win gubernatorial pardon for the two boys involved in the "Kissing Case."

The NAACP national office suspends Robert from the presidency of the Monroe chapter because of his advocacy of armed self-defense against white supremacy violence. The community elects Mabel Williams to the local presidency to replace her husband.

The Williamses and their neighbor Ethel Azalea Johnson begin production of *The Crusader* newsletter.

1960 Robert cofounds the Fair Play for Cuba Committee, a US-based organization to build solidarity with the Cuban Revolution.

Robert joins an African American delegation to Cuba.

1961 Swimming pool protests are reinitiated and the first attempt is made on Robert's life.

Organizers from the Student Nonviolent Coordinating Committee arrive to carry out a nonviolent challenge to segregation in Monroe.

Armed exchange between whites and the Guard leads to false charges of kidnapping and US government pursuit of Robert Williams.

The Williams family begin exile as guests of the Cuban government.

1962 Robert writes and publishes *Negroes with Guns*.

1962–65 The Williamses broadcast *Radio Free Dixie* and publish *The Crusader* from Cuba.

1963 Mao Zedong issues statement supporting the African American struggle.

The Williamses are invited to attend the National Day Celebration in China.

1964 Robert is named international chairman of the Revolutionary Action Movement, a national network of Black revolutionary nationalists and internationalists.

1965 The Williamses are invited to North Vietnam to attend the International Conference for Solidarity with the People of Vietnam and meet Ho Chi Minh. Robert delivers a major address in solidarity with the people of Vietnam at the conference.

1966 The Williams family moves to China as guests of state.

1968 Robert and Mabel visit East Africa.

Robert is elected president-in-exile of the Republic of New Afrika, a provisional government of Black Nationalists demanding self-determination, sovereignty, and reparations.

1969 Officials in England arrest and imprison Robert as he attempts to make a connecting flight back to the United States. He carries out a hunger strike in protest.

The Williams family returns to the United States.

1971 Franklin Hamilton Williams (Robert's son) is born December 27.

1972 The Williamses settle in Baldwin, MI, near the historic African American resort community of Idlewild.

1975 North Carolina drops the kidnapping charges against Robert.

1970s–1990s The Williamses assume leadership roles in the cultural and political development of the Idlewild community.

1991 Son Robert Jr. dies.

1995 Robert completes his memoir, "While God Lay Sleeping"

1996 Robert F. Williams dies.

1999 Mabel, son John, and daughter-in-law Lisa are invited to Beijing for the celebration of the fiftieth anniversary of the Chinese Revolution.

Mabel begins work on her memoir.

2014 Mabel Williams dies.

2016 Son John Chalmers Williams dies.

THE MEMOIRS OF ROBERT AND MABEL WILLIAMS

PART I

WHILE GOD LAY SLEEPING

ROBERT F. WILLIAMS

CHAPTER 1

WHILE GOD LAY SLEEPING

It was a hot and sultry autumn. Autumn in North Carolina can sometimes emit heat like a furnace. The little town of Monroe, where I was born, was loyal to its southern traditions in almost every aspect. It was predominantly white, Protestant, and racist. It was so reactionary that when a Catholic priest appeared on the scene, seeking converts to establish a church, local bigots who met him on Main Street spat in his face. They told him that his kind was not wanted there and that the wages he paid his "nigger" cook would spoil all the "niggers" in the town. The racists were horrified by rumors passed that the newly arrived Catholics were having small groups of Blacks and whites meeting together.

It was Friday and exceptionally humid. For as long as I could remember, Friday was a day that had special meaning in our house. Aside from signaling the end of the week, there was a certain heightened atmosphere spawned from the realization that the rigors of the week had all but passed. It was a time of approaching leisure and rest. The souls of Black people belonged to the insensate white bosses during the week, but the weekend, in a limited way, offered a fellowship of respite from a communion of dismal bondage. In our house, which stood on the crest of one of Boyte Street's many dusty hills, Friday was a day when everything accommodated prayer meeting. My mother either went to a neighbor's house, or she played host to neighbors in our home.[1] My mother was

1. Emma Carter Williams was Robert Williams's mother. Emma Williams was a devout member of Elizabeth Baptist Church in Monroe who didn't allow alcohol, tobacco, gambling, or card games in her home.

liberal enough in her religious beliefs to allow us a certain amount of Christian autonomy. I was the fourth of five children. None of us were ever forced to attend prayer meeting, and we never volunteered. The only demand made on us was for quietness and respect for the sessions.

Gently I gathered the mail I was to deposit at the post office and set out to beat the 5:30 deadline. The prayer meeting had already started in our living room. Someone had finished reading scripture, and as I left the yard the group raised one of its perennial hymns. As I quickened my pace down the street, I could hear them singing "What a Friend We Have in Jesus."

The community where we lived was called New Town. It was in north Monroe and contained the town's largest Black section. We were completely surrounded by poor whites, with the exception of a grove of a wooded area to our northwest. Parents of Black youth cautioned us to take a shortcut to town to avoid being exposed to young whites who made sport of attacking defenseless Blacks who ventured passage through their territory. Taking a shortcut meant passing through a railroad shop area and a series of tracks where freight trains shifted and reconnected. This maze of tracks was fraught with danger. Because there had been deaths and maiming, we were instructed to exercise extreme care in crossing. We were besieged by white hostility on the north, the east, and the south and by a bush land of nothingness on the west. It was indeed sad that mothers were forced to demonstrate a greater fear for the well-being of their children from white racists than from the hazards inherent in negotiating a busy railroad yard.

I crossed over a long line of standing freight cars that bore the names and markings of many faraway places. As I descended from one of them, I saw the slightly stooped figure of a man standing near a boxcar. His bulky figure startled me. He was drinking from a whiskey bottle. He looked like a white man. Drunken white men always struck terror in the hearts of little Black children. He lowered his bottle and spoke to me in a heavy, coarse voice. I recognized him; he was not a white man. It was Mr. Curtis, who worked in the engine shop the same as my father. His railroad cap was backwards on his huge head, and the front of his sooty and greasy overalls were wet with urine. He wove and rocked from excessive drink, slightly raised his head, and grimaced like a dog about to howl. He started to sing in a graveled voice. Like a man who had tasted too much of the bitter cup of life, the words seemed to come naturally. He was singing a blues song called "Trouble in Mind." As I moved on down the line, I could hear him singing: "Troubled in mind, I'm blue . . . but I won't be blue always, 'cause the sun's gonna shine in my back door someday."

This dismal encounter left me possessed with a sense of sadness. I remembered that it had been said that he was one of the railroad men who traded heavily in script issued through Fitzgerald and Company, commonly called "the grab." Sometimes he was known to draw only a dollar after two weeks of work. Legally, they had to pay the minimum of a dollar to avoid some type of peon law.

I made the post office in time and entered the usual state of anxiety as I faced the long wait for my order to be filled by the Johnson Smith Novelty Company. As I crossed the street to the opposite side of the post office, I was startled by the screams of a woman who sounded desperate and in deep pain. I could also hear great laughter rising from small groupings of whites that congregated to watch a sordid spectacle. Some Blacks, too, had stopped to watch. Their emotions seemed harried with shame and horror. Even at the tender age of twelve it was already obvious to me that on many occasions whites felt moved to laugh while our people had reason to cry. The chief of police, who was a giant of a man and a hard-core racist, was dragging a drunken Black woman along the pavement to his car. He tugged her as if he might have been pulling a log or a sack of potatoes. His weather-beaten face reflected deep hatred and contempt. His nose was huge and crooked on the end in a fashion similar to that common to birds of prey. His strenuous efforts caused his police shirt to be wet with perspiration. Chief Helm's propensity for kicking Black men and slapping Black women had earned him a well-deserved reputation for his brutal treatment of Afro-Americans. A mere approach by him struck terror in the hearts of our people.

As the woman's poignant screams echoed up and down the street, Black men shook their heads and walked away in silence. The chief wore one of the biggest revolvers that I had ever seen. It sagged at his side in cowboy style. He threw the paining and screaming woman into his car and sped away toward the jail. Nausea gripped me, and I felt empty inside. Everything seemed futile. I left the scene wondering in the innocent way of a child why Black men were impotent and seemed so useless in moments like these. With both my hands in my pockets and straining to keep from crying, I started to walk the mile or so back home. The hymn "What a Friend We Have in Jesus" kept forcing its way back into my mind.

Among Black folks, Monday was commonly known as Blue Monday. It always meant the beginning of a new cycle of facing up to the pain and frustrations of being Black in America. In those harsh days of precarious survival, it seemed that life was divided into short units. It seemed that destitute Blacks lived from week to week. Oftentimes, a week contained only three significant days. They were Friday, Saturday, and Monday. Sunday was sometimes colorful, but at sundown a sense of quiet, sullen apprehension crept over the community. It was a most unwelcome prelude to Blue Monday. One had to mentally prepare himself to meet "the man," the white man. White insurance men and a sundry array of bill collectors invaded the ghetto. Monday was a day when neighborhood clotheslines weighed heavily from all manner of laundry. Industrious mothers did the family wash, and all too frequently clothes from across the track hung on the sagging lines. Black women worked their hands to the bones for a pittance. Some Black women went to white homes to do the washing, cook, and nurse children of the master race.

This Blue Monday morning, my mother was laboring in a washtub. She was vigorously rubbing clothes on a rub board. Occasionally she paused and wiped the perspiration from her face to keep it from her eyes by bending her arm and lowering it in a gentle motion from her forehead to her lips. I stood at a huge black washpot and stoked the fire under it. The clothes had to be boiled to assure cleanliness. The sun had risen to a scorching position. The carefree song of birds permeated the air.

My uncle Charlie entered the yard and approached my mother. "Hi there, Emma. At it again?" he drawled. His shirt bore evidence of heavy sweating. Myriad beads of perspiration clung to his face.

"Hey, Charlie," she responded in a not-too-pleased voice. "Been in the liquor barrel again, huh Charlie? You got started early today. Didn't you? If you don't change your ways, you're going straight to hell!"

I had heard this dialogue all too often before; therefore, I braced for the battle of words that was bound to ensue.

Uncle Charlie was a veteran of the First World War. He had attended Wilberforce University, had studied law, and was a principal of a rundown rural elementary school. He was known as one who kept intimate and frequent company with the bottle. His speech was militant. Uncle Charlie had encountered a score of minor brushes with the law and had done much better in the courtroom than in his physical clashes with bigoted policemen. His medium stature bore no resemblance to the rugged physique common to those whose laborious drudgery paralleled that of beasts of burden. He kept his reddish hair tightly waved, and his ruddy complexion was no darker than that of whites who were constantly exposed to the burning sun. The upper portion of his cheek bore a small nick. He was said to have brought this slight scar back from the army. Its history was never told.

We lived in the southern Bible belt. Even Blacks who lived less than chaste lives dared not deny God. Uncle Charlie did. He was a professed atheist, a first-magnitude iconoclast. He seemed to relish riling Christians, and my mother was no exception. Today, they were at it again.

"You drunken infidel, it's no wonder that God don't strike you down in your tracks," she said.

"Now Emma, there you go again! You niggers are always on your knees praying and talking about a white God punishing somebody. You mean your God would punish me for a little drinking? Don't you think that's rather harsh dealing for a power that's just? If he would take such drastic measures for such a small infraction, why the hell doesn't he curse the white folks for what they are doing to good niggers?"

"Oh Charlie, you ought to be ashamed of yourself. You'd better fear God; someday we all will have to answer for our sins. You ought to be ashamed to talk like that in front of that boy. I sure don't want him to grow up an infidel like you. God is a just God!"

"Emma, you don't really believe that hogwash, do you? If there is a God who can hear you niggers praying on your knees, why in hell don't you niggers pray for your just God to set the niggers free? Are you niggers scared to pray for freedom? Yeah, because you think he is white too, you think he meant you to be meek, humble and long-suffering and to serve the white folks. You niggers scared to pray for freedom from his white folks because you think he may think you're getting too uppity for the places he put you in to serve. Well, to hell with that! Before I'd bend my knee to a creator like that I'd rather burn in hell with the devil."

"You leave this yard right now, Charlie, and don't come back until you're sober!" my mother demanded. It was evident that she feared that somehow Uncle Charlie's words might provoke the wrath of God.

"You niggers have been shouting and screaming prayers loud enough to make a deaf man hear. If you've got a God, he must be somewhere sleeping!" Uncle Charlie retorted.

He shook his head in frustration as he left the yard. I was sorry to see him go. I liked to hear him talk. He was provocative and audacious.

CHAPTER 2

X-32

THE PRELUDE

I was fourteen now, restless and subject to migraine headaches. The school I attended was segregated and dismal and inspired more daydreaming than serious study. It was pure torture to get up in the mornings, and I disliked it more and more. The library had many empty shelves, and the books had very little meaning. The science room was as sparse as the library. The best-equipped department was for home economics. There, the Afro-American girls were being trained to work in the white folks' kitchens. The red brick building was brand new, but not an imposing one. The campus was bare, dusty clay, and not a single tree stood on it. When the old building had burned, all the athletic equipment had burned with it. Rumors had it that Blacks who had become disgusted at the state's consistent refusal to remedy overcrowded and hazardous conditions had deliberately burned it. Football was out, and basketball was too colorless to generate any worthwhile interest. The teachers did all they could to make the best of what they had to work with.

The superintendent, W. R. Kirkman, was a grumpy old white man whose periodic visits terrorized teachers and students alike. The sight of his car arriving on the yard charged the atmosphere with fear and dread as the word was passed that "Supe's coming." There was a mad shuffle and frightful demands by the teachers that we all get in our places and remain quiet. Superintendent

Kirkman would storm into the building with his hat on and correct and bawl out teachers right in the presence of students. His grumpy and mean voice could be heard roaring up and down the hallways. He was feared and hated. No one dared to rebel.

Despite the daytime white abuse and hatred of our race, the darkness of night brought an influx of prowling white men in quest of Black sex. Black men complained among themselves but never gave physical vent to their frustrations and anger. It was diligently enforced law that any Black man caught being intimate with a white woman suffered death or flogging at the hands of vindictive white men or extravagantly heavy penalties from kangaroo-type, racist courts.

Once, while watching a court session from a balcony reserved for "colored" (commonly called "the buzzard's roost") with a buddy who had grown up with me, I witnessed a case involving an interracial fracas. Testimony showed that a group of Black men, riding a watermelon truck, had stopped at a rural gas station and had been attacked by white ruffians without provocation.

Witnesses testified that the whites were responsible for the altercation. The redneck judge dismissed the case. He peered over his wire-rimmed glasses and announced to the owner of the country store that he wanted to ask him a question.[1] He said it puzzled him as to how the store owner had allowed that many "darkies" to congregate in one place. He stated in an instructive voice: "Don't you know that when you allow that many 'darkies' to congregate in any one place, there is bound to be trouble?"

It was disgusting to see the racist attitude of a court that held the life-or-death fate of such a despised people in its grasp. How revolting it was to watch the insensate railroading of Blacks through the kangaroo court–type session. My buddy "Cad" Roddy and I left this antiquated old courthouse, shaken by white justice for our people. The imprint was deep.

Cad, John Gaither, who was another one of my neighborhood buddies, and I frequently roamed and played in the wooded area that bordered the northeast corner of New Town. One day we descended from the wooded area onto a paved road called Morgan Mill Road. Four white hunters were standing by their parked car with shotguns in their hands. As we approached them, we could hear one remark that some "nigger" boys were coming. When we started to pass, they pointed their guns at our feet. One of them shouted, "We like to see niggers dance. Dance, niggers, dance, or we blow your damn feet off!"

1. In rural areas of the South, the "gas station" often consisted of a lone gas pump installed on the front property of a small store.

Cad exploded with anger. He exclaimed, "If you wanna see somebody dance, go getcha damn mama!"

Such brashness stunned them. The shock mentally disarmed the white hunters. They were at an impasse. We walked on up the road to our destination with adrenaline pumping in an anticlimax.

A tall Black man who seemed to have had too much to drink came up our street. He labored under a slight stagger and yelled like a town crier: "You niggers better stay in the house tonight 'cause it's gonna be hell in this town."

"How come?" asked Mr. Crowder, our next-door neighbor who was sitting on his front porch in his spotless undershirt.

"'Cause that mean nigger Boyce Richardson done cut Chief Armfield's collar off his uniform and the white folks is boiling mad!"

"What happened, man, what happened?" Mr. Crowder implored in an impatient voice.

"Boyce and his little boy was sitting on the curb on Main Street eating watermelon and the chief come up and done kicked Boyce's ass."

"What happened den, boy?" asked Mr. Crowder anxiously.

"That crazy nigger Boyce Richardson done cut the collar slap off old man Armfield."

"Mr. Armfield oughta knowed better 'n kick Boyce Richardson. That nigger'll fight a circle saw. What'd they do to Boyce?"

"The whole force come and got him. I heard they 'bout beat 'im to death when they got 'im to the jailhouse. De crackers is some kinda mad uptown. Dey say de gon lynch 'im and run all the 'no-good' niggers outta town tonight. Dat's why I'm making it in befo' nightfall."

Mr. Crowder called across the yard to my father, who was preparing to go into the night shift, "John, did you hear what that fellow said?"

"Yeah!" my father answered without comment, as if to discuss the matter would enhance the possibility of night terror.[2]

My father gathered his hat and lunch and tried to sneak a pistol in his overall jumper unnoticed. He admonished us to stay in the house as he left for the "roundhouse." He lacked the timbre and pugnacious attitude of Uncle Charlie and Uncle Arthur, his brothers. He often said that either one of them would fight at the drop of a hat.

The streets were as deserted and silent as a cemetery. The older people who had experienced the ferocity of racist violence unleashed exuded such hysteria

2. John L. Williams was a laborer (boilermaker's assistant) for the Seaboard Air Line Railway Company, a major employer in Monroe, North Carolina, in the 1920s.

that they unwittingly infected their children with deep-seated fear. To be so terrorized was to feel a chill deep inside that left me numb and helpless. It is one of the greatest traumatic experiences in the world for a child to need the protection of a parent and to find that parent impotent and paralyzed by vicious and unjustified racial intimidation.

In the ensuing weeks, an idea for starting a secret organization impregnated my mind. It was to be called the X-32. It was to have thirty-two members, and I was to be Captain X. Its objective was to be a highly disciplined night attack force of young neighborhood vigilantes. We worked diligently making white hoods to conceal our heads. Each white hood had X-32 imprinted on its front with black shoe polish. We designed a pennant-type flag of black felt emblazoned with X-32 in white shoe polish. After recruiting a hard-core cadre, we took to the woods every day after school to practice formation running, discipline, and methods of attack. We initiated a loyalty oath that brooked no insubordination, resignation, or breach of secrecy or dropping out.

After intensive training in nighttime camouflage, stone throwing, stick fighting, and methods of handling possible exigencies, we were ready to make war on white philanderers who fancied Black women after dark. We also extended our targeted objectives to include certain Black panderers. At last, we were going to feel the power of vengeance and the glory of strength and courage in the midst of impotence and shameful submissiveness. It was exhilarating to have our own army with a mission to bring terror to the terrorists.

Our first target was the grumpy superintendent of schools. He was to appear at a night affair in the school auditorium. It was always considered a big deal to have "Supe" attend an affair at the Winchester Avenue School in the ghetto. We didn't attend. We waited in the darkness at the edge of the schoolyard. It had been customary for the principal and superintendent to linger behind the crowd to count the door receipts. As a group of women and children stragglers set out for their homes, we passed them running in single file on our way to the building. Our flag and masks terrified them, and they screamed, shrieked, and scurried into the night. A door was unlocked at the end of a long corridor. The hallway was dark, but we could see a screen of light coming from the office more than halfway toward the other end of the structure. We tiptoed quietly. In front of the formation, I collided head-on with a figure. When the man glimpsed our weird hoods, he exploded in a fit of hysteria. He let out a howl and scream that bore no resemblance to anything ever uttered by a human. He scampered down the hallway, roaring like an express train. His reaction had caught us completely unprepared. We too experienced a state of shock. We took off in the opposite direction in a mad rout that caused a pileup of entanglement. We scrambled to our feet and scattered in the night. The next day we learned that our abortive encounter had been with the principal instead of the superintendent. We were pleased to know that he had not suffered a heart attack.

We got to recognize the white men and their cars that made frequent night incursions into our community. We also knew Black women who catered to them. The worst offender was a redneck who worked on the railroad. He had come to Monroe from Georgia. He had a notorious reputation for lauding his interracial exploits over Black men who worked around him. He was a racist from his heart, and his every action manifested only contempt for Black people. He drove a Cord automobile and thought as much of it as he would if it had been solid gold. We looked forward to springing an ambush on Mr. Clarkston with a passion surpassed only by the anticipation we experienced in waiting for summer vacation to begin. Night after night we vainly patrolled the alleys and dark sectors of the streets hoping to catch him in range. We saw him a few times, but our plans were frustrated. He moved too fast for us to catch him.

Finally, one Saturday night, we saw old Clarkston make his pickup. It was in a place sometimes called "the Neck" and sometimes called "Fourteen." I suppose these names grew out of some local legend, but I had never heard the full story. The Neck was dark, and the streets were deserted. It was a perfect place for an ambush. We knew old Clarkston would be back soon to return his illicit "colored" lover. We knew the girl he had picked up. She had grown up in the neighborhood, and it was commonly known that she was quite free with her body. Among other things, she was labeled a "nymph." She had a light-brown, smooth complexion and tempting body-build.

We dispersed our assault forces to their stations. We waited in silence and concealment. Not many cars rolled through the Neck at night, and the Cord was dead-on for identification. It had a low-slung profile and was the only car on the road with wide headlights. Its engine had a sound distinct from all other vehicles.

Tenseness filled the night. Clarkston was rolling head-on into our ambush. As soon as the young woman got out of the stopped car, on signal, we released a broadside barrage of stones and bottles. The attack made a fierce sound in the night. It was a sound of stone on metal and breaking glass. For a while the car seemed to run wild from one side of the street to the other. When it came under control, it sped into the night like an airplane. A trail of dust hovered over the street, giving an appearance of a mighty commotion. We ran to our staging area to regroup. We had a seizure of laughter and satisfaction. In the following months we carried out a series of diverse raids. To some people, nighttime became terror. Our antics attracted too much attention, and our parents forbade us to go out at night. We then decided to lay low and let things cool off.

We placed our little army in mothballs, sworn to an oath of silence and a pledge to remobilize whenever the situation warranted it. The X-32 was never reactivated. Of the old officer gang, in years to come, two became dentists, one a policeman, one a federal civil servant; a journeyman welder and all traces of the others vanished into the vastness of time. So far as I know today, I was the only one of the group who advocated a military-style stance in the much later civil rights movement.

Left to right: unidentified relative; Robert's father, John Lemuel Williams; and Robert's sisters, Jessie Williams (Link) and Lorraine Williams. Courtesy of the Williams family.

CHAPTER 3

GROWING UP TO THE SOUNDS OF NEW TOWN

Through the week when nights were as quiet as a lonely desert, I would lie in bed and listen to the after-midnight freight trains rumbling through the eastern edge of New Town. The huge steam engines always seemed to leave lonely echoes that lingered in their wake as they faded into the distance. The train whistles made me restless. I wondered what distant cities they were destined for and why destitute men called "hoboes" rode them. Most always they were racked with hunger, sooty and ragged men in quest of a better promise. Sometimes the hoboes detrained in Monroe to beg for leftover food or just cold bread. Despite the fact that they never engaged in violence against the townspeople, their presence aroused much fear. My father worked the night shift, and this fact engendered a special fear in my mother. When they came to our house, begging in the night, her Christian tenets would not permit her to turn them away. She would ask them to stand back from the door as she passed food out to the floor of the porch.

For some reason, night trains were a romantic part of community life. One engineer became a legend in his time. We never knew his name, but the whole community knew when he was passing through. He was such a master of the train whistle that he would play the tune of the song "Happy Days Are Here Again" as he passed through. He was known by all as "Happy Day." Everybody liked to hear him come roaring through the town with his whistle going.

On Friday and Saturday nights, I could lie awake and listen to distant laughter and music. Contrary to the complaints of the Christian neighbors that these disruptive "ballers" should be driven from among "decent" people, I burned with a desire to be in their number. They seemed to enjoy life immensely. Miss Polk's house served as a way station for desperate and sometimes highly talented musician wanderers.

Though New Town claimed some of the most prosperous Black citizens, as far as city facilities went, we were the scorned and neglected by the city fathers. The army of WPA workers had not yet reached our ghetto with their construction of sewer lines. Outhouses constituted a central part of the Black homestead. Miss Sis Polk's house was a block away across a vacant lot. This Saturday night, true to routine, Miss Polk's joint was jumping. Barrelhouse music engulfed the neighborhood like a dense fog. I stole out of bed and slipped out of the house, as often it was necessary to do on a mission to the outhouse. I could hear the piano, hot and spicy, rolling out the blues. A washboard, a harmonica, and a guitar complemented the piano and at times seemed to challenge its blue notes.

The down-home blues drew me like a magnet. I soon found myself standing beside Miss Sis's house. I was standing in a crowd peering into her window. The house was jam-packed. The ones outside could not get inside. The aroma of frying fish drifted out of the kitchen window and stoked the appetites of all who stood or passed. A big dark man was at the piano. His face was a mass of perspiration. He closed his eyes and pounded the keys of the piano as if all the adversities of his life were being transferred through his fingers. Occasionally he would reach for a glass on top of the piano and drink a liquid so white and colorless that it was almost invisible. It was what was called stump liquor or white lightning. A sweating thin brown man played his guitar so melodiously that it seemed to sing a crying and tortured lyric. The washboard man was so short that I could barely see him. His skin was lighter than the others', and he wore overalls that looked too big for his underdeveloped body. Miss Sis's house was really jumping. The painted women with their cheap cosmetics danced more with their bodies than with their feet. The women clung to their men as if they may have been Siamese twins. The dancers rolled their stomachs together and rocked from side to side. Occasionally some happy soul would bellow, "Mercy, mercy, mercy!"

An outsider looking in on these poor souls could easily be mistakenly led to believe that they had not a worry in the world. A drunken voice yelled from the crowd, "Let the good times roll, cause I'm laughing just to keep from crying!" In my young innocence, I thought that Miss Sis's house was a happy house, a haven for Black people that bordered on paradise.

I was a child peeking into an adult world without realizing that this was the Black man's momentary escape hatch to a sanctuary, devoid of the white man's hatred that created a Black man's hell. As if in a state of ecstasy, someone cried out, "Play it, Key! Play me some low-down dirty blues!"

The house was rocking. It was really rocking. The old, battered piano was taking an awful pounding. Key Frances's fingers were moving so fast that my eyes had to strain to keep up with them. As many nights as possible thereafter I kept my rendezvous with what seemed to be a ritual. The high life at Miss Sis's house made me feel the impatience of a boy in a hurry to become a man.

CHAPTER 4

THE WORLD THROUGH THE RADIO

When I was fourteen, I became a newspaper delivery boy. Delivering the *Charlotte News* gave me status and some money to boot. Money had been scarce since the beginning of the depression. Two years before, I remember that my father had sent me in quest of change for a five-dollar bill. I visited four stores and many homes in vain. All summer of 1941 I stayed busy with my paper route. Mr. Sam Roddy ran a store about halfway down the block from our house. Railroad men gathered there to exchange tales, play checkers, and commiserate with each other. There was very little recreation and entertainment for Black people, and respected railroad men didn't dare be caught coming out of a "barrelhouse." Some were very poor readers, and after I had finished my daily paper route, they often inveighed on me to read and explain the news to them. I liked the way they praised my smartness.

After becoming a Sunday school dropout, I spent my Sundays listening to the big console radio. It was an Atwater Kent radio that had come to our house after the death of my uncle Charlie. The radio always brought him back to my memory. It was a sad memory. He was the first person I ever saw die. The extended family was called to his house one morning just after my father had come from work. My aunt Cora was trying to make Uncle Charlie comfortable on his dying bed as I arrived there with my father. The others were huddling around a coal heater and talking in whispered voices.

Uncle Charlie was weakly gasping for breath. I was standing at the foot of the bed, and his deep-set eyes seemed glued to me. In a short while, he gasped no more. Aunt Cora shook her head, closed his eyes with her hands, and pulled the sheet up over his head. His wife, Aunt Lizzie, let out a hurtful screech, then moaned, "Oh Lord! You took Charlie; take me too." When I played his radio that had fallen to us, often times I felt grief well up within me. It was almost a ritual for me to listen to the New York Philharmonic over CBS every Sunday. In the environment I grew up in, it was incongruous for a young Black boy to enjoy classical music. I liked all kinds of music, and though seeming strange, I exposed myself to whatever was available.

The old Atwater Kent also had a shortwave band. Many were the late Saturday nights that I listened to the great big bands broadcasting from the Cotton Club in that faraway world of New York. I dreamed that someday I would see the Promised Land of Harlem in the Big Apple. And as the popular song explained, we all concurred in "going to the Apple to live on Lenox Avenue . . ." The Blacks who had migrated to New York sometimes, mostly on holidays or when a relative died, returned on visits back home dressed like millionaires. They drove modern cars as flashy as the white folks did down home. Some even assimilated the New York brogue. They showered the old folks with lavish gifts accompanied by a pretentious air that provoked envy and fired the desire of emulation.

It was Sunday, December 7, 1941. I was scanning the dial of the old Atwater Kent. The program was interrupted. The shocking announcement was, "The Japanese have bombed Pearl Harbor." I ran to the kitchen where my mother was putting the finishing touches on our Sunday dinner. I shocked her with the news of Pearl Harbor. She wiped her face on her apron and sat down at the table. She shook her head and seemed dazed. She had seen the men come back from the First World War, gassed and maimed forever. Before I was born she had bought a large framed picture of colored solders in formation while one stood caressing his wife in front of a cottage fronted by a white picket fence. The Black soldier was bidding his wife goodbye. A caption at the bottom stated, "THE COLORED MAN IS NO SLACKER." My mother was thinking of her three sons.

I picked up my papers early the next day. Everybody wanted a copy of the "extra" announcing the bombing of Pearl Harbor. The other shoe of war had been dropped. The premature announcement that Hitler had set the world ablaze when he went into Poland was now a truism. The summer before as we sat on our back porch, Grandma Pearl had looked at the long columns of ants crossing the yard and stated that this was God's warning of impending war. The older people had a propensity of interpreting nature's latent messages.

Some years earlier, we would go to a nearby street that descended down what we called "Slick Hill." In the heat of the summer night, we would romp and play under a streetlight. To avoid the intense heat of his bedroom, Mr. Bob

Anthony used to sleep on a pallet on his front porch. In a loud voice, he would cry out that he could hear the cannon bombing all the way to Japan. He insisted that when he was coming down the railroad tracks one night, he met a little brown man who was a hobo. He said that the little brown man was a "Jap" and that he had told him that war was coming between the US and Japan. Along with the adults, we had laughed at him. Derisively, he had become known as "Jap Anthony." He angrily stated that we could laugh at him all we wanted to but to mark his word that we boys would someday have to fight the "Japs." He looked Japanese but seemed too big in stature to be one. He wore oversize overalls all the time, and the rupture that caused a big bulge between his legs added to his strange appearance.

CHAPTER 5

WAR FEVER RISES

War fever struck America. The nation shifted into high gear, and mobilization was the order of the day. Men were registering for the draft all over the nation. Volunteers were swarming into the service. Rationing books were fast becoming a part of our daily lives. My mother was spending more and more time in solitary prayer. She was praying for her sons. Because of the war, more opportunity for training and employment became available to our people. The National Youth Administration (NYA) had come full circle. The Roosevelt administration was pushing for the full utilization of the nation's potential. In the summer of 1942, at the age of seventeen, I joined the NYA. Black youths were supposed to be trained on an equal basis with whites. I was assigned to a group that was to be trained as stonemasons. Eight of us teenagers were assigned to a rock quarry. We were told that we would have to dig stones and later we would be taught to lay them while constructing an armory.

We were laboring in a place called Bakers, which was six miles from Monroe. The white boys were sometimes digging and sometimes playing on another side of the quarry. The Carolina heat was exhausting. Because we were at a depth with very little air circulation, our clothes stayed wet from perspiration. There was great thirst and need for water. George Banner, one of the eight of us, asked the white supervisor for a drink of water. He brought us a battered and dirty old bucket of water and gave us an old Coca-Cola bottle that still contained some residue of the oil that had been used to lubricate the jackhammer. One of the

Black boys asked, "Why have the white boys got a clean new bucket and dipper for water and we've got to drink from this old dirty stuff?"

"You damn boys are here to work, not to ask questions. If you don't wanna drink, git your asses back to work!" the white man exclaimed in a hostile manner.

"Well, we don't want no water bad enough to drink out that bottle!" Fulwood, another one of our group, stated.

"I don't want no lip out you niggers. You do what I say or your ass is fired, you understand?" shouted the supervisor.

I threw my pick down and climbed out of the quarry. I had had enough. I had not canvassed the others to ascertain their possible reaction. To my surprise, when I looked behind me, they were all climbing out in single file. Cad Roddy, my neighbor and close friend, asked, "What're we gonna do now? It's six miles to town, and they won't take us back on the truck!"

I told them we had feet and we were going to walk back to town. Without a single complaint, we filed down the highway. After we had walked about a mile, one of the boys said, "Here come that old white man in the truck!"

The man pleaded with us to get on the truck and come back to work. He said he would give us a new bucket and dipper just like the white boys had. We declined. We went to the courthouse, where the director's office was located. Mrs. Armstrong, a grandmotherly type of old white woman, asked why we were there at that time of day. I gave her a rundown of the situation and informed her that we had quit. She begged us to go back and that she would straighten the situation out. We could see that she was very nervous. We told her we had been promised training but were only being used as laborers. We told her we would not go back ever. Fulwood's mother was a teacher. She wrote a letter to Washington. Some days later we were told that the supervisor had been fired. After this incident, all the newly recruited Black boys were taught construction skills as they constructed the armory.

Summer had come and gone. I was back in high school. As more and more boys donned service uniforms, the war became a part of all our lives. I had an exact replica of a small radio that I had bought at a novelty store. I asked my young homeroom teacher, Miss Holt, if I could turn my radio on so the class could hear President Roosevelt speak. She answered in the affirmative and asked whether I had the radio with me, and if so, it would be a good lesson for the class to hear the president's speech. I removed the little radio from a bag. The room was solidly silent. Thelma Mitchell, a good-looking girl, was seated in front of me. I passed the radio to her and asked her to turn it on. Thelma fumbled with the dial while everyone anxiously waited for the speech. When she turned the dial, the front of the radio opened up. The facsimile of a huge snake sprang out. Thelma let out a hysterical-sounding shriek as she covered her face with her hands. In a flash, I realized I had overplayed my hand. My male friends laughed. Miss Holt bristled from shock and anger. She commanded me to leave the room immediately and not to return until she sent for me.

CHAPTER 6

NATIONAL YOUTH ADMINISTRATION

My mother and my older sister, Jessie, were very upset when I informed them that I had signed up to go to a National Youth Administration training center in Rocky Mount, North Carolina. I promised my mother that after I finished training in a trade, I would return and complete high school. My sister told my mother that if I quit school, then I would never finish.

My old friend Cad Roddy, Benny Montgomery, and I ended up in the same training center barrack. Cad trained as a welder. Benny and I trained in machine shop. We could not imagine then that mild-mannered Benny would in later years return from the Battle of the Bulge shell-shocked and would die in the electric chair for killing his white boss. The NYA was a highly disciplined camp with Black boys from all over the state.

The NYA camp was situated at the edge of town. The Rocky River ran just a few feet from the back of our barrack. My shop instructor was a good-hearted old white man. He owned a machine shop in Rocky Mount. He taught us in the evening and considered it his contribution to the war effort. He had caught some flak from the local bigots for training us as machinists. He insisted on quality work and constantly drilled us on the fact that we would be among the first of our race to fill such skilled jobs and that we had a duty to our people to do a good job. After training we were to be assigned jobs at navy yards that were short of skilled help.

On Saturday nights, most of the youth split up into small compatible groups and headed for the juke joints in town.[1] We constituted a great windfall of new kids on the block, and the young wild girls were easy pickings for us. I was pretty much a loner, which had its advantage, until I learned the side that manifested the disadvantage: we were not very popular with the local boys. They resented what they considered our intrusion.

It was another Saturday night. We always anxiously looked forward to Saturday night. The boys had shined themselves up for a night on the town. They asked me to come along. I told them that I would be on later, after I had finished writing some letters. It was a ruse to split from the herd. I later made my way into town. The dingy little joint called the Cozy Corner was really jumping. As far as I could ascertain, I was the only one from the NYA camp there. The music was loud and hot. The place was filled with the smell of barbecue, hamburgers, and the Saturday night staple, fish. A line of tables stretched across the front near the grill. Beer and wine lined the tables. A jukebox was in the far corner blasting across the small but crowded dance floor. I had just come in and was standing at the jukebox, looking for an appropriate selection. A short, rather plump girl with an attractive brown face approached me and asked if I could dance. I gave her an affirmative answer and reached for her hand. Her hand bore evidence of hard work. Rocky Mount was a tobacco center, with many warehouses and processing plants. Upon approaching the town, the smell of tobacco was strong enough to give a newcomer a nagging headache.

The lights over the dance floor were dim. Now the music was a slow drag. As she danced close to me, she asked my name. Hers was Cleo. After the dance, we went to a table where she already had a half-finished bottle of beer. I ordered two more beers, told her where I was from, and talked about my training. I was fantasizing that I had scored and that the glory of the night was all mine.

Cleo leaned forward, bent over, and fumbled with her shoe. She struggled with her shoe for such a long period that I became curious. Suddenly, a tall, rather rough-looking man was standing at the table. His face bore a mark that gave the appearance of a healed-over cut. Perhaps it was a battle scar from some previous encounter. He was armed with a switchblade knife. "Cleo!" he called out in an angry voice. In desperation, instantly my mind computed my options. She sprang to her feet.

1. A juke joint was an informal nightclub with music, alcohol, and often dancing and gambling.

The tall man swung at her with the long, shiny knife. She stepped backwards, snatched a beer bottle from the next table, threw it, and struck him in the head. My option was to leave in a hurry.

When I hit the street, the night was filled with an awful commotion. I could hear the sound of loud voices, breaking glass, and cars being stoned. The boys from the NYA were withdrawing from a donnybrook and were fighting a rear-guard action against the locals. One of our fellows recognized me and shouted, "Man, they're jumping us! You'd better come on and get your ass out of town!"

Police cars were rushing to the street. We made a detour to a darkened street and ran the mile to the camp. The fight had only caused some bruised knuckles, blackened eyes, and slight injuries. There was some summary investigation. Shortly thereafter we were dispersed to other centers. I was transferred to Elizabeth City State Teachers' College to finish my machinist training.

The teachers' college was resplendent with young, lonely, and beautiful female students. However, I soon learned that beauty was no substitute for substance of nourishment. The food was so skimpy that in most cases it had to be supplemented by care boxes from home. Too often the breakfast diet consisted of greens, dried apples, tomatoes, and grits or powdered eggs. The entire food situation bordered on a starvation diet. The NYA boys had grown accustomed to an adequate government-supplied diet. The boys bitched and bitched until somebody wrote a letter to Washington. A government-employed white woman came to investigate. She asked one of the boys how often we got milk, eggs, butter, and meat. He looked at her and laughingly asked, "Lady, is all that stuff sompin' you s'pose to eat?"

"You mean you're not being served these things in your diet?" she asked incredulously.

In unison, a number of the boys chimed in, "No ma'am, we ain't seen nothing like that since we been here!"

"Well, I'm here to see that you get a regulation diet that's mandated by the government."

"We shore glad to see you, miss, before we starve to death!" a voice intoned from the crowd.

Results from the lady's inspection were slow in materializing. Meanwhile, we supplemented the emaciating diet as best we could. On a number of occasions, I wrapped Luden's cough drops in peanut butter for a snack before bedding down for the night.

The government finally moved. It was a move that we did not relish. We were given specially designated tables in the dining hall. The NYA youth were fed government-issued food similar to what soldiers would be fed. The college students across the imaginary line could see and smell our food. It was an awkward feeling to eat to one's content before hungry people. In keeping with her religious belief, my mother had always taught her children that it was a sin to eat before hungry people without offering to share with them. It took me quite a while to override my conscience. It was a state college, and I wondered why the state was indifferent and irresponsible toward its obligation to those its duty was to protect and educate. It was a segregated institution, and the racist state of North Carolina grudgingly provided a flagrantly flawed education system. Racism generates contempt and hatred on the part of the victim as well as its perpetrator. Sometimes the boys slipped food from our tables to the girls.

The only redeeming factor in our narrow little hapless world was the abundance of lovely girls. Once a week our social life consisted of a school-sponsored dance. At one of these dances, I met a very pretty girl named Lois Wilkins. It was a relationship that lasted a number of years through correspondence.

It was a happy day when graduating time arrived. It was a time of war, and the government needed skilled workers. We were told that all that desired were to be placed in naval shipyards. I opted to find my own employment. My oldest brother, John, had already been drafted and was serving in the army field artillery. My other brother, Edward, whose age was nearer to mine, was employed at a defense plant in Detroit, Michigan.

I, too, went to what President Roosevelt had pegged as the "arsenal of democracy." The war had created all kinds of opportunity for employment. It was easy to land a job. I became an employee of the Ford Motor Company at its huge Rouge plant. It was a sprawling complex that staggered my imagination. It was said to be the workplace of 80,000 men and women. I was assigned to a boring mill in the rolling mill. At eighteen, I was the second Black person to be assigned to machine production in that plant. The rolling mill was so noisy that one could hardly engage in conversation. The noise even heightened when the long sheets of rolled steel, white with heat, rumbled down the conveyer belt. My shift started in the early afternoon, and we worked long hours into the night. After being in the plant for extended periods of time, when I was able to witness a sunset, the entire world seemed foreign and strange to me.

CHAPTER 7

MARE ISLAND, CALIFORNIA, WORK CHALLENGE

The Kaiser Shipyard was recruiting skilled workers for California on the West Coast. It promised first-class transportation, available housing, and high wages for relocating. I saw Kaiser's offer as an exciting opportunity and a chance to travel across the nation. It brought me great joy having passed the physical and being accepted. I became more excited by the hour in anticipation of a new life and a new world. Two anxiously hectic weeks passed. I had given notice to Ford and was now released from work. After I waited what felt like a lifetime, the Kaiser recruiter finally summoned me to the State Employment Office. I responded with a joy that one experiences much too rarely in life. As I confronted the recruiter, he nervously thumbed through some papers on his desk. His face was red and masked with a half frown. He looked up and pronounced, "I'm sorry, your application has been rejected."

"Why?" I asked in disbelief, as my dreams exploded.

"There seems to be some problem that bars you."

"But you told me with my training I was a sure bet."

"I say again, I'm really sorry about the whole thing."

"I've got a right to know what happened!" I insisted.

"Yes, I believe you have a right to know. It is no fault of Kaiser. They are willing to accept you, but the machinist union has a closed shop, and they are refusing to accept Negroes."

"What kinda shit is this? A war is going on and the damn sons of bitches are more interested in beating us down than they are in defeating the enemy!" I exclaimed. "What the hell am I supposed to do?" I asked angrily.

He seemed to ponder the situation for a while, then in a somewhat reluctantly cautious voice informed me that a navy recruiter was soliciting volunteer workers for Pearl Harbor. The navy man had set up in the same office. He suggested I go over and talk to him.

The navy man was hospitable. The deal was that recruits who signed on would do a stint at the Mare Island Navy Yard for six months with an option thereafter to move on to Pearl Harbor. Volunteer workers would be housed in government dormitories at Vallejo, California. They would be provided with meal tickets until the first pay and would be given a railway Pullman ticket. It sounded better than the Kaiser deal. There was no union at the navy yard, and although I belonged to the militant Local 600 at Ford, for the first time I felt a measure of hostility toward organized labor.

Twenty of us arrived at Vallejo around nine in the evening. The night was damp and foggy. I had contracted a splitting headache. A community of dormitories was arrayed on a hillside. In front of the office a lighted sign proclaimed the name to be HILLSIDE DORMITORIES.

The dormitories looked rather spartan and colorless. We were checked in assigned small, cubicle-type rooms. I spent most of the night unpacking and wondering what my fortune would be. I anticipated that California would be a vastly different world from what I had known.

We were transferred by bus to the ferry docks. Vallejo was a strange-looking place. As we rode along the streets, it seemed more of an Oriental city than that part of America I had known. The Filipino influence was highly visible in business and culture.

We were conveyed to Mare Island Navy Yard on a ferryboat that I considered to be vastly overloaded. After a bout of pushing and jockeying for space and being arrayed like sardines in a can, the little ferry traversed the somewhat rough water and made it to the island. The navy yard was an imposing complex. A number of huge warships were in dry dock, being repaired and refurbished. I had never before seen an oceangoing vessel out of the water. They dwarfed the tradesmen who toiled feverishly from scaffolding along the sides of the mighty ships. There was something about a warship in dry dock that provoked an eerie sense of wonder. Where had it been? Where had it fought? What were its battle scars, and how many of its crew had been buried at sea?

There seemed to be a scarcity of Black people in Vallejo, which meant that I could not expect too much of a social life. Luckily, in my second week there,

I met Forrest De Coven. He was a short Black man who wore a processed hairdo. Forrest was friendly and jovial. He had been in Vallejo some months before I arrived. He knew the city and the places among the Filipinos where Blacks were welcomed. We went out for a night on the town. It was a world strange and different to me. The night was chilly and damp. The air carried the smell of seafood being cooked. The jukeboxes blasted up and down the street with American music peculiar to the Oriental and Spanish cultures. This unfamiliar scene gave me a quaint sense of longing. It reminded me that I was a long way from home. Suddenly, I began to realize that Pearl Harbor was even farther. I was beginning to wonder what I had got myself into. I was supposed to do a six-month stint at Mare Island and then on to Pearl Harbor. A war was being fought and skilled workers were needed at Pearl Harbor. Rumor had it that life was rugged there. I kept remembering that I was experiencing, because of the war, an employment breakthrough that my race had never attained before.

Forrest had been a child actor and at some time had appeared in movies with the actors from "Our Gang," the children's television show. He invited me to visit his place of residence. He lived in a modest hotel residence in a not-so-affluent sector of town. Forrest had casually mentioned that he shared a room with his girlfriend. We entered the rundown old stucco building. We walked a long, dingy corridor. Music mingled with the myriad sounds of household noises and loud voices. Cooking odors permeated the entire structure.

Forrest fumbled in his pocket for his keys. He said, "This is where I live with my 'old lady.'" He held the door slightly ajar and called to the woman inside:

"Honey, I am back, and I have a friend with me!"

The voice from within responded in a tone that seemed irritated. "How could you have the gall to bring somebody to this junked-up place?"

"Aw, honey, it's OK. Everything is hunky-dory," he intoned.

"Hell, it may be all right with you, but I've still got some pride left!"

I was shocked by the size of the woman. It was even more shocking to see that she was white. She had a good-looking face, framed by long black hair. I supposed that she weighed in the neighborhood of 300 pounds. He introduced her as Pearl. She never warmed up to me. She seemed ill at ease in my presence. I suppose she saw a like attitude in me. Being southern-born and -bred, I had never been in the presence of an interracial couple, and they were a striking example of an incongruous pair to me.

I was constantly experiencing severe headaches. After a medical exam, I was informed that I was suffering from an obvious case of sinusitis. I had been in

Vallejo a mere three months, and the doctor informed me that the climate was averse to my sinus condition. This meant that Pearl Harbor was out of my future. The unknown factor of the East loomed in my life again. I looked forward to seeing my family and friends again. I was homeward bound.

CHAPTER 8

BACK TO MONROE

RESISTANCE FROM BLACK MPS

Monroe, North Carolina, was as dusty, hot, and sooty as ever. Being a railroad junction, the Black section of the town was always infested with soot. It was a sleepy town that had started to stir faintly. The war was ushering in some radical changes, though race relations remained the same. The railroad was now employing Black women to do the heavy dirty work that had once been reserved for Black men. Many of the young men with whom I had grown up were no longer there. They had been drafted into the armed services. An army camp, Camp Sutton, had been constructed in Monroe to bolster the war effort. Because of its strong army engineer and quartermaster training facilities, many Black soldiers were stationed there.

The ghetto was overrun with Black soldiers. The war had drained off local young men, and now many women went wild over the new wave of lovelorn men. Despite the war and the fact that young Black men were being called on to serve their country, racism was still a way of life.

It was a situation that engendered mixed emotions—to see military police in uniform, yet with only billy clubs to maintain law and order. White MPs were armed with .45s, while the Blacks carried sticks. Whites were authorized to roam and police the entire town. All persons who dared get out of line were fair game for their police action, and they seemed to move with great zeal and dispatch when they saw an opportunity to club a Black soldier.

There was a restaurant near the Seaboard Railway Station. It was called the New York Cafe, and the owner was commonly referred to as "John the Greek." The spacious dining area in the front portion of the building carried a sign near the entrance that read "For white only." Black people were relegated to a run-down kitchen area at the back door. It was, in essence, a hole in the wall. There were six ragged stools at a bar that separated the stoves from Black patrons. The place never closed. As a result, soldiers and civilians mingled there most of the time. In wake of a number of fights, the military command assigned Black MPs to the area. Whites were giving them such a hard time that they had to be armed. The military notified white citizenry that the post was short of white MPs and that armed Blacks were being assigned to the area and that they would be authorized to take whites into custody and hold them until white MPs could reach the scene. This act created great consternation in the white community. It was like the renewal of a Civil War edict. Local blue-collar bigots swore that no "nigger" would ever enter a white-owned establishment to take one of their race into custody.

It was a damp and misty Saturday afternoon when some drunken white soldiers started a vicious brawl in the New York Cafe. A drunken white woman ran out to the sidewalk, screaming that the soldiers were fighting inside. Four black MPs hurried to the front door. John the Greek was standing at the entrance. He stretched his arms to block their passage. In a hostile voice, he exclaimed, "You colored boys can't come in here!"

The big Black MP sergeant bristled. "What the hell you mean, we can't come in there? We're on duty and our orders say we can go anywhere soldiers are making trouble!"

The proprietor angrily motioned them back and further stated, "Niggers can't come in the front door of this establishment!"

Another bigot came menacingly forward with a baseball bat. He said, "John, maybe we ought to teach these uppity niggers to respect white folks and our southern way of life!"

The Black MP's lips seemed to tremble, and his face displayed overriding anger. He pulled his .45 from its holster and pointed it straight at John the Greek's face. John looked stunned and backed away.

As the MPs ushered a number of huffing white soldiers to the street, two military trucks bearing white MPs and an officer arrived on the scene. The Greek danced from one foot to the other in a show of great emotion. A number of white civilians made a spate of exaggerated charges against the black MPs. The captain was informed that local law required "niggers" to enter the back door of such places. The white captain was cool and diplomatic. He informed the bigots that they were short of MPs and until such time that whites were available, they would have to suffer the consequences of military orders. Many Blacks stood in view and earshot of the locally unprecedented affair. This dramatic incident gladdened the hearts of the downtrodden Blacks. They had never dared to dream that such would occur in their powerless lifetime. Rumor of the confrontation spread through our community like wildfire. It was uplifting to a people who had always been trampled underfoot without recourse. Ours was a meekly, conforming people without power or the benefit of law and police power.

Frequently fights were developing among drunken soldiers. There were a number of racial fights in the main sector of town. Although my mother had been glad to see me return from so far away, I could tell that she was suffering some apprehension relative to my being there. The war and the camp had changed the town. I am sure my father concurred with her misgivings. They inquired as to why I didn't go north where I could utilize my NYA training as a machinist. It was the fate of young Black Americans that if they were in quest of halfway decent work and better wages in civilized society, they had to migrate north. Faraway, unfamiliar places beckoned me once again. Subconsciously, I was in quest of a dream that had eternally eluded our people.

CHAPTER 9

OFF TO THE "BIG APPLE"

One hot summer day I ran into Cad's cousin Charlie Roddy, a boyhood friend. Charlie was a rambler. He was streetwise. He suggested we go to New York. He had been there before. He had kept out of the draft because he been classified as 4-F. The thought of New York fascinated me. I had heard glorious tales about New York. I kept recalling the song that proclaimed, "I'm going to the Apple to live on Lenox Avenue." A few days hence, I bid my father and mother farewell.

They seemed saddened that I was leaving but relieved that I would be out of the racist cauldron of the South. This was an emotion felt by many Black parents who dared think of what white hate could do to their sons in Dixie. In a few days, Charlie and I were off to the "Big Apple" with just a few dollars between us.

We arrived in New York well after midnight and took the subway from the Port Authority up to Harlem. It was the first time I had ridden a subway train. My heart beat with anxious expectation. I thought going to live in Harlem would be like being a child transported to fairyland.

About 2:00 a.m., we ascended from the underground to the surface. My puzzled eyes scanned the bleak buildings and the dirty streets. "When are we going to get to Harlem?" I asked.

"You're already in Harlem. This is it, the Big Apple!" he smilingly informed me. "What did you expect?"

"I just thought it would look different!"

Still experiencing a sense of despair, we settled into a sparsely equipped hotel with bath and toilet facilities some distance down a barren hallway. This was a

Robert Williams wearing a zoot suit, popular among young men of color in the post–World War II period. Courtesy of the Williams family.

sorely disappointing Harlem, but I knew I had to make the most of the Apple. There was no turning back. A few days there, and survival became an adventure.

My childhood buddy from our X-32 gang, Cad Roddy, had already settled in New York a month before and lived uptown with his aunt. We visited him in what was a swank Sugar Hill apartment. We convinced Cad to pull up stakes and move downtown with us. We got a room on Lenox Avenue and went in quest of work. Charlie's previous experience resulted in his being employed right away in a hotel. He stood for the rent, and at least we were sheltered.

Charlie developed a habit of absenteeism, and sometimes we did not see him for days. He started showing up with wads of money and expensive jewelry. He finally admitted that he had some kind of hustle with some racketeers. Eventually, his absence became complete, and we were still without employment and were now at the mercy of our landlady. She was a kind, motherly type who after three weeks kindly informed us that she could not carry us any longer. With no money and no jobs, we had to go.

I had the address of Dora, a schoolmate and childhood sweetheart, who lived in Brooklyn. Into the rain of the night we went desperately in search of her. After a tiresome, wet quest, we finally located 577 Warren Street, and after what seemed an eternity, Dora finally opened the door. She closely scrutinized us but without instant recognition. She finally broke into a smile and exclaimed, "Where in the hell did you people come from on a night like this?" She invited us in. "You guys are soaking wet and look like you're living high on the hog!"

"We got caught in the rain trying to find you," I said shyly.

"Trying to run that old downhome jive on me, huh," she intoned as she mocked us with friendly laughter.

"We're doing OK," Cad said in a deceptive voice.

"You old buzzards look hungry. When did you eat last?" she asked.

"We ate before we came here," Cad stated falsely.

"Well, I got a big pot of soup I just made. If you don't want it I'll have to throw it out," she said.

"No, don't waste it. We don't want you to have to throw food away," I declared.

We spoke of old times in Monroe as she warmed the soup. We ate like hungry dogs. Dora agreed to take us in, and once settled, we desperately went in quest of employment. Dora informed us that the B&O Railroad used extras on the waterfront and paid daily wages. Two days later we signed up and started work. Life was now somewhat more secure. The work was rugged. It consisted of unloading freight barges, towed over to New York from New Jersey by tugboats. It was hard work, but it was a break that came our way just in the nick of time. As the days went by, we became accustomed to the toil and sweat of the waterfront.

The immediate vicinity where we lived was a tight-knit community. Stella, a tall, brown-skinned woman originally from Georgia, was the nerve center of community gossip. She occupied the first street-level apartment and constantly sat in the window observing the activity of the neighborhood. She was commonly referred to as "that big-mouth Georgia woman." She had an extra loud voice, and it very seldom fell silent. We often sat on the stoop to catch a cool breeze and to receive Stella's rundown of the latest happenings. Every morning she conducted an exchange of gossip from our stoop to the one across the street. An old woman we came to know as Miss Dukes was her gossip buddy. Miss Dukes constantly proclaimed herself to be a Pentecostal Christian, a denomination I had never before heard of. Aside from her ceaseless gossip, Miss Dukes never missed an opportunity to attempt to convert Cad and me to her religion.

On April 12, 1945, I was airing myself on the stoop at 577 Warren. It had started as an ordinary day until Stella burst out of her apartment crying and screaming. Her words were almost unintelligible. She was half choking with severe emotions. "Mother Dukes!" she screamed in a loud, broken voice.

"Girl, what in the world is wrong with you? What's happened?"

"Oh Lord! They just announced on the radio that the president is dead!"

"Dead?"

"Yeah, dead!"

"Lord have mercy, you mean President Roosevelt is dead?"

"Yeah, it's the God's truth! Turn on your radio!"

Up and down Warren Street, radios started to loudly blast. The stoops came alive with solemn and weeping people. An old woman stood on the sidewalk crying. She kept remotely repeating, "Lord have mercy! What we poor people gonna do? The only one of the white folks who cared anything about us done gone!"

A middle-aged Black man came down the street. He was visibly disturbed as he shouted, "You niggers' asses gonna ketch hell now. Old Lady Roosevelt ain't gonna be in the White House no more!"

A cloud of sadness seemed to settle over everything. I felt weak and subsequently sat down on the step. There was so much sadness around me that I could no longer restrain my tears. I had never given much thought to the presidency other than the fact of its being enmeshed in Hoover bashing.

Because I had been classified as a skilled worker in the defense industry, I had been given an exemption from the military draft. After I left California, I had to change my draft registration to my new address. Three months after moving to Brooklyn, I was summoned to the draft board. When I arrived there, the center was bustling with activity. The fat white woman who sat at the desk to which I was directed was thumbing through my dossier. She gave me a contemptuous look and instructed me to sit. After a brief period of interrogation, in which I attempted to explain that I had left my defense job at Mare Island for medical reasons, it was more than obvious that the cards were stacked against me. The draft board woman said in a voice bordering on hostility, "You must know that there is a government edict that all able-bodied men must either work or fight!"

Somewhat riled, I wanted to match her attitude. "Work or fight! It's all the same to me, lady. I just as soon go to fight as to work!"

Even though I was displaying an exaggerated bravado attitude, it felt good to proclaim that I really didn't give a damn, one way or the other.

CHAPTER 10

WARTIME ARMY INDUCTION

Two weeks after my tough-guy act at the draft board, I was back in Monroe depositing my personal belongings and bidding farewell to my parents. My mother was very upset and full of prayer for me. My oldest brother, John, was already in the Army 350 Field Artillery Unit deployed to combat in France. I went into military service at the age of twenty, in July of 1945. Germany had already surrendered, but attention had shifted toward an invasion of Japan. That feat was expected to be bloody.

After being processed at Fort Bragg, North Carolina, I was among a group of all-Black recruits designated for training at Camp Crowder, Missouri. Two railway coaches assigned to us were attached to the rear of six railcars bearing white recruits. We traveled through South Carolina and had a short stopover in Atlanta, Georgia. We were allowed to visit the "colored section" of the spacious Atlanta station. However, when we arrived at the Birmingham, Alabama, station, we could see the white soldiers dismounting and queuing up for donuts and coffee. A Red Cross unit was serving them from a mobile canteen. Somebody yelled, "Free donuts and coffee, boys! We're in luck."

The young Black men, in our newly issued soldier's uniforms, scurried for the doors. A burly white train conductor who stood watch on the platform raised his hands, signaling us to halt. In a gruff southern drawl, he asked, "Where in the hell you boys going?"

Slaughter, who had been placed in charge of the group, declared we were going to get some donuts and coffee.

The conductor scowled, "Not here you ain't. Don't you boys know that it would be a insult for these white ladies to have to serve nigras? You boys just turn around and march right back on the train."

A chorus of disgruntled curses rose from the group as we meekly submitted to the outrageous affront. We Black soldiers watched forlornly out of the dingy coach windows, thirsty and weary, as the white soldiers observed the disgraceful spectacle approvingly. One of the soldiers, whose white skin afforded him the special privilege of receiving a cup of hot coffee, came to the window of our coach and slowly poured a cup of coffee on the ground. He contemptuously gave out a mocking laugh and drawled, "Night fighters ain't gonna be served no coffee in broad open daylight, 'cause it will turn 'em into monkeys!"

Slaughter retorted, "You goddamn peckerwood, I hope the Japs blow your balls off!"

Sensing more trouble brewing, the conductor summoned an officer. The officer ordered an end to the bitter exchange and commanded the whites to return to their coach.

Our coach was dark now with only an occasional ray of light flashing in the window as we passed sleeping towns and villages. It was a weary and sleepless night. For as long as I could remember, trains that passed in the night seemed to permeate the stillness of the night with a melancholy refrain. The incident at Birmingham left a bitter imprint on my heart and soul. I thought of the anguish and brutal misery involved in the savage slave trade relative to the ocean passage. Anger was beginning to seize me. I wondered how a so-called civilized nation could do what America had done to us, then force us to go to the other side of the world in a life-and-death conflict, supposedly to save "democracy." To add insult to injury, Western democracy cloaked itself in the color of Christianity. I remembered the arguments between my Christian mother and my atheist uncle Charlie. My mother assured Uncle Charlie that there is a just God who sees everything and will smite the transgressors. Uncle Charlie would always shoot back that if there is a just God, he must be asleep, else he would never tolerate what mean white folks were doing to the "niggers." As our coach shimmered down the track, casting a hypnotic spell on all who listened to her sound, in my mind, I retorted: If God is sleeping, for our sake, he had better wake up soon.

The following day we arrived at Camp Crowder. The Birmingham experience still nagged at me in a way that I felt sure would haunt me all the days of my life. The main entrance to Camp Crowder looked good. Flowers lined the well-manicured grass that bordered the long boulevard, which led to the barracks area. It was a good-looking residential billet area for soldiers. The barracks were all-white and well-kept two-story structures. It was a good feeling to know that from a military standpoint, we were going to be well housed.

The buses on which we were being conveyed to our place of billet soon left all of the attractive barracks behind. It seemed that the sun had instantly buried its bright light behind a cloudbank. Bright hope had suddenly turned to dim despair. "What the hell is this?" a loud voice asked.

"Hell, this is where you are going to live, better known as 'Shanty Town.' This is where darkie soldiers billet," the Black bus driver informed us.

The whole chain of events was indicative of the Black man's blighted sojourn in America. There was always some surprising event lurking in the background to add insult to injury.

The barracks for the so-called colored soldiers were a shame and disgrace. They were long single-story structures with outer walls covered with black tar paper. There were no glass windowpanes, only hinged tar-paper flaps that swung outward. It was more than obvious that these buildings had not been used in quite a while. The interior was layered with heavy dust and reeked of strong musty odors. We feverishly went to work and by bedtime and exhaustion, we had transformed the ghastly place to one more acceptable for human habitation.

After a few days of processing, our segregated group of young Black men was formed into the 29th Battalion. Our commanding officer was British. Occasionally, when he wanted us to exert ourselves more, he would tell us how his fellow officers pulled strings to avoid being assigned to a "colored" outfit. Lieutenant Cannings took pride in telling us how he volunteered to serve with Black troops. He exerted great effort to be accepted as one of the boys. He wanted to learn ghetto slang, and when no other officers were around, he went all-out to imbue himself with Black culture. The word "spook" was a code word that Blacks often used among ourselves. Sometimes when Lieutenant Cannings was strolling around the area and met some of our men, instead of saluting, some soldiers would greet him with, "Hi, spook!" He would respond in kind, not really knowing that he was being referred to as a Negro.

We were being trained as linemen, and the instructors never let us forget that we were the benefactors of a white man's trade. We were expected to show gratitude. Most of us would have preferred some other training.

CHAPTER 11

SEEDS OF CONFRONTATION

After basic training, I was assigned to a signal corps outfit. The commanding officer was an ex-paratrooper redneck. He wore his cap low over his eyes and had special hard heels on his boots for effect. He screamed and cursed and had a habit of turning beds over when men overslept. He had the outfit cowed down. On Sunday morning, while the white pole climbers relaxed in their barracks, eating goodies from the PX and reading comic books, we were sent out to move and haul the heavy poles that they had left scattered throughout the training area.[1] We experienced additional humiliation when we were forced to collect their garbage and clean their areas.

Our executive officer was Jewish. He was on duty on Sunday morning when we were being assembled to police (clean) the white work area. He fumbled nervously with the roster and looked rather stark. He gave us a great shock when he told us that he was not advising us what to do but that we were American soldiers the same as the whites and that they should clean up their own mess. His words sparked resistance in us. They loaded us on the trucks as usual. Now, we were grumbling for being forced into such a disgraceful and dirty detail on a Sunday morning.

By the time the trucks reached the work area, not a single soldier remained aboard. Lieutenant Tillsbury was summoned back to camp. He had us rounded

1. The PX is the post exchange on US military bases, a retail store for military personnel and their households.

up and flew into a cursing rage. He threatened us with court-martial if we persisted in our work refusal. Sheepishly, we went to the field of shame. There was an old saying, that when it rains, it pours. The world I had known had never accepted Black people as individuals with human emotions. Unless we were half-dead, we were never to be too sick to work, and there was never a stressful situation that injured our lives.

I had received a "Dear John" letter, and the girlfriend I had been engaged to since childhood was going to get married, so her aunt informed me. Civilians were being encouraged to write lonely soldiers. Jewel's aunt, who was rather young herself, had struck me at the wrong time with the wrong message. It was years later that I learned that there had been animosity between the two of them; however, the damage was done. Meanwhile, this could be said to have been the straw that broke the camel's back. My attitude changed, and my buddies wanted to know what was wrong with me. To make bad matters worse, I kept my hurtful ordeal private. I felt that I was going to explode.

It was Monday morning, and the sound of reveille was loud and clear. Everybody in the barrack was scrambling out of his bunk. That morning, I felt the accumulation of a lifetime of powerlessness, emasculation, and dehumanization break the bonds of our eternal submissiveness. I had become an angry human being. This was the moment, no matter how fleeting, that I was going to stand tall. I was going to buck the system and to hell with the consequences. We were a handicapped and cruelly stunted people. We were no more than a silent shadow, not seriously seen or heard.

Everyone was up and ready for duty. I lingered motionless in bed. My buddies became alarmed. They crowded around my bunk and asked if I were sick. When I explained that I was not sick, they seemed puzzled. Fearing for my well-being, they pleaded for me to get up.

I could hear the roll call in front of the barrack. It was still dark. Someone answered for me when the sergeant called my name. The sergeant had the men count off. A man was missing. He called the roll again; this time the deceptive voice failed to answer. Now it was known that I was the absentee. I remained motionless, awaiting the confrontation.

Sergeant Jackson was a heavyset Black man. He came and stood at the head of my bunk. "Soldier, are you sick?" he inquired.

"No," I replied.

"Well, what the hell is wrong with you, then?"

"Sergeant, I just don't feel like getting up this morning—and when I don't feel like getting up, I don't!"

Sergeant Jackson bellowed, "This is the army, and no living ass sleeps in this man's army. Get the hell up! I don't want to put you on report. You know Lieutenant Tillsbury will turn the bed over and kick your ass!"

"Well, he'll get the chance this morning."

Sheer terror gripped Sergeant Jackson's face. It was obvious that he had never before been confronted with such a situation, and he was at a loss as to how to defuse such an explosive encounter. His tone of voice receded to more of a plea than a command. In exasperation, he gave up and hurried off to the orderly room.

I heard Lieutenant Tillsbury coming. His hobnailed boots gave off a sound like a storm trooper. Sergeant Jackson and the executive officer came with him. Lieutenant Tillsbury stood at the side of my bunk looking down into my face. "Are you sick, soldier? Do you need to go on sick call?"

"No!" I responded.

"I know I didn't hear you right. Soldier, you couldn't have said what I think you said, 'cause if I heard you right, I'm just about to kick your ass outta that bed!"

"Lieutenant, if you kick me, we're going to lock asses and go to hell together this morning. I am as much man as you, and if you don't believe it, try me!"

He was visibly shaken by the grimness that masked my face. His intimidating brashness faltered. He was embarrassed. His tone and his attitude changed. After standing motionless and silent for a moment, he told me to report to the orderly room after getting up.

Later that morning, I was confronted by a group of officers headed by the battalion commander, who reasoned with me in a fatherly manner. He explained that if the army allowed its men to get away with such conduct, there would be no army. It was absolutely essential that the army maintain discipline at all times, and inasmuch as other soldiers had witnessed my conduct, they could not afford to let me slide.

At my special court-martial, I was sentenced to three months in the stockade for insubordination and was told that I could shorten my time through good behavior. I told the court-martial board that it really did not matter because I had been in prison all of my life, that having been born Black in America, I was born a prisoner. That pronouncement shook them up.

CHAPTER 12

PRISON SPIRAL INTO TENT CITY

The stockade was a place of all kinds of attitudes and dispositions. The warden was a Major Stonebreaker. I thought it was a joke when I was first told that his name was Stonebreaker, but I learned that his name was really Stonebreaker, and it appeared that he was trying to live up to his name.

As prisoners, we were assigned to work in a fenced-in woodyard. It was wintertime and very cold in that part of Missouri. The prison system had placed discarded barrels inside the work compound wherein we could burn most of the wood we cut to keep warm. Some crews cut wood while others congregated around the fires, told jokes of their past, and shared their dreams for the future. Often it seemed the prisoners were engaging in a game of who could relate the tallest tale; however, there was much deriding of the men from the Deep South. Southern life was so ridiculed that none of the group wanted to admit being from the South. White guards policed the fenced-in compound where we worked.

The guards who patrolled from raised guardhouses and along the fences crowned with barbed wire were at a loss in trying to control the activity within. On occasion, some of the white soldier guards displayed sympathy and solidarity with the Black prisoners. Unnecessary talking, playing, and smoking were banned. Some looked the other way while we broke the rules, while other guards were forcefully tough. They cursed, threatened, and sometimes wrote prisoners up, but the men stood together covering for each other. On a few occasions, we became unruly and defiant to such an extent that Warden Stonebreaker was summoned and became so frustrated that he ordered us to remain locked in the work compound through our lunch hour.

Perhaps half a mile from our woodyard was a German prisoner of war camp. Oftentimes, we could hear music and songs in German emanating from their camp. It appeared that they were much more comfortable than we were. A detail of German prisoners was marched daily by our work compound. They served as attendants in white officers' clubs. As the days went by, they started to identify with us. They would smile and give a clenched-fist salute, and we responded in kind. Eventually, we started to find packs of cigarettes scattered in the woodpile. The Germans were stealing cigarettes from the officers' clubs, and as they returned to their camp after dark, they would throw the packs over the fence so we would find them the next morning when we came to work.

One day when we came to work in the woodyard, there were no cigarettes. There was loud music, great laughter, and joyful sounds coming from the prisoner of war camp. A friendly guard informed us that the Germans were shipping out for home. Later that day we watched as an army of blue uniforms marched by us. Many of them smiled, saluted, and waved goodbye to us. It was a scene of mixed emotions. The Germans were happy to be going home, but we were losing the friendly faces we had known outside our group. This was the end of the forbidden smokes.

Routinely, after lunch, we were allowed to rest a few minutes in our barrack. We were allowed to lie on the floor beside our bunks but would be punished if we were caught lying on the beds. One day, I overslept and missed roll call during formation. The men had hurried so frantically to make the formation that they had not noticed that I was still sleeping. Such an offense was always punished severely. I was taken before Major Stonebreaker, and he sentenced me to one week in Tent City.

Tent City, no doubt, was the nearest thing to a concentration camp on US soil. It had very high double fences. The fences were about eight feet apart and were topped with rolled barbed wire. Its interior was about 200 feet square. Overlooking the compound were towering guardhouses on the east and west sides. Thirty-caliber machine guns were mounted on tripods that allowed them to protrude out of the windowless structures. The prisoners inside the barbed wire were the only troops exposed to racially integrated living conditions at Camp Crowder. All the guards were white. A white soldier who had been in the notorious Alcatraz prison informed me that Tent City was much harsher than that had been.

Tent City consisted of two-man pup tents, a hole in the ground, and straw for bedding. We were issued two thin blankets and a mess kit. Each day, just before dark, a truck brought K rations, and individually packaged food was thrown over the gate. Only a small detail of inmates was allowed at the gate to fill our canteens with water. Upon confinement, we had been strip-searched for matches, cigarettes, or any other contraband. Tent City was only operated in the dead of winter. It was meant to break the spirit of soldiers who would not submit; however, it conditioned many to become more defiant. All that I had seen, all that I had experienced as a child growing up in a cruelly segregated America, climaxed with great embellishment with the Tent City ordeal.

One night, because of the bitter cold, none of us had been able to sleep by midnight. In contempt and defiance of the guards, many of us crawled out of the tents and started exercising in front of them to keep from freezing. The guards frantically yelled through their bullhorns for us to return to our tents. Shortly after midnight, we could see the bright lights of a convoy moving toward us. We braced for a showdown that we were sure was to come. The convoy stopped at the gate, and two soldiers dismounted and proceeded to tug at the locks on the gate. Though they labored feverishly, their work was in vain. They were unable to budge the locks. After repeated conferences and a long delay, another detail arrived with soldering torches. The locks had been frozen beyond operation. When the gate was opened, a medical officer announced by bullhorn that we were all to prepare to return to the stockade. The medics had insisted that we be moved to warmer quarters, stating that if we remained under those extremely cold temperatures and conditions, we possibly would not survive the night. We were moved to heated barracks, and Tent City was closed permanently.

CHAPTER 13

PHIL GRACE

DEFIANCE TO FREEDOM

The stockade had an isolation section. Prisoners who fouled up were sent there. The cells were dark. Day could be distinguished from night only through a small round hole that let in a ray of sunlight during midday. There was no mail call there, and the diet consisted of one loaf of bread and a pitcher of water daily. It was necessary to hang the bread on a suspended wire to keep it from the rats. A big white lieutenant from Georgia who was a boxer would be sent in to intimidate noisy and unruly inmates. He was the enforcer who beat the men into submission. A young corporal, assigned to the bread-and-water distribution detail, was told by Phil Grace, an inmate from Chicago, that the next time he came to bring his daily fare, he had better have his mail and bread with some butter on it. Phil threatened that if he did not come with these demands, he was going to kick his ass. The prison grapevine was humming with the news that Phil had "broken bad." The following day was a time of great supposition. We were very sorry for what we knew Phil had coming to him. As had been customary, we saw the big boxer go to the isolation section. The men were as silent as could be. We wanted to hear what was transpiring.

We could hear Phil cursing. He was a habitually prolific curser. He used all of the wicked, scurrilous words of the Chicago ghetto. He often bragged about how bad he was and how many men he had messed up. We thought of him as just a slick windbag. Now we thought that his big mouth had gotten his ass into a situation of deep grief.

We heard the lieutenant screaming for the guards to unlock the cell door and let him out. The lieutenant's screams were those of a man in deep pain and frantically desperate for survival. The guards scrambled to make way for his speedy exit. When the big white boxer was pulled out, he was splattered with blood and was bleeding profusely. Somehow, Phil Grace, who was Chicago ghetto slick, had concealed a razor blade and taken it into isolation. He had positioned it between his fingers, and with the palm of his hand open, he had seized the initiative before the boxer could go into action. Great joy swept over the compound. The men were highly elated, and some jumped for joy. Phil Grace was a hero who had matched his extensive bragging with deeds. He was for real!

Three days after the incident, Warden Stonebreaker brought in a board of high officers; they met with Phil Grace and issued him a dishonorable discharge. They gave him a black suit with sleeves and legs too short, a bus ticket, and twenty-five dollars in cash. As he left, he cursed Major Stonebreaker for everything he could think of and challenged him to a duel. He yelled to us that we were fools to stay in the white man's army. He said he was Chicago-bound and that as soon as he made it to the South Side, he would "lay a chick and drink a Bloody Mary" for us. That was the last we saw or heard of Phil Grace. He was now a legend among us, and in a strange way, in the following days we all missed him and his big mouth.

The following month, Camp Crowder was closed, and we were dispersed across the country. I was sent to Fort Lewis, Washington. The army was in a period of transition. I was assigned to a casual company with nothing much to do. Demobilization was underway, but my name was way up the list. I got in a lot of sleep, and that served to allay the anxiety attendant to waiting. Rather than a discharge, I was given leave. I was happy to be going, but I was already dreading the thought of having to come back.

In the two weeks before my furlough, I started to experience a series of dreams that bordered on what I thought to be some strange vision. A dream kept recurring wherein a very beautiful girl was always there. Mostly during my daytime naps, this girl appeared for more than a week. She was unknown and yet seemed so familiar. When I explained it to my barracks acquaintances, they laughed and told me that I was really going batty. They joked that I was more due for a "section 8" than a furlough.[1]

1. Section 8 is a military discharge for someone mentally unfit for service in the US armed forces.

CHAPTER 14

FURLOUGH ENCOUNTER

It was late spring when I left Tacoma, Washington, by train. I looked for the strange girl I had dreamed so much about at every stop. I would go through the train stations, searching for the familiar face among the travelers. Most of the travelers were servicemen being transferred or on their way home. I had a long layover in Chicago. I desperately searched the crowd that milled about the station. I even visited some nearby bars. I had finally come to realize that the whole affair was but a dream and nothing more. The nagging question now was why such a dream had recurred so many times.

I was sadly disappointed when I hauled my heavy duffel bag aboard the southbound train from Chicago. The coach was full of drinking and joyful soldiers. Seats were scarce as I made my way through the coach. Near the end of the car, this very pretty girl with her head buried in a magazine, ignoring the other soldiers' overtures, looked up at me and smiled. She spoke and asked whether she didn't know me. I stated that perhaps she did. I told her to slide over. She had sat next to the aisle and placed her belongs on the inside seat to reserve the seat to herself. We introduced ourselves. Her name was Helen Edwards. She lived in Chicago and was going to Columbia, South Carolina, to visit her grandmother.

As we approached Chattanooga, Tennessee, the conductor announced that the train would be there for thirty minutes. I convinced Helen to leave the train and walk with me through the station. When the five minutes' notice of the train's departure was given, I asked Helen to remain outside the entrance to the coach. I told her that I had a big surprise. I could tell she was greatly puzzled. I rushed aboard the coach and hurried off with our luggage. She wanted to know what I was doing. Her voice reflected anger. I explained in a commanding voice, as my heart pounded with anxiety, that we were stopping over there so that we would have more time together. The train pulled away as she pouted childishly.

A taxi driver drove us to a cozy little Black-owned hotel. At that time, stringent segregation was still in force. Eventually, her anger and shyness vanished, and we fondly exchanged our life stories. By the time we left the next day, we were engaged to be married. She insisted that I go with her to Columbia to meet her grandmother. I promised her that after I had visited with my mother for a day, I would come to her.

My mother wanted to know what was so important that I would leave after one day at home. When I explained that I was engaged to a girl that I was going to visit for a few days, she asked how long I had known this girl. When I told her that I had met her on the train, Mama became very upset. She exclaimed that being in the army must have driven me crazy. My older sister concurred. Their negative reaction dampened my enthusiasm.

Helen's grandmother, Mrs. Bailey, lived alone on a dusty street in a small house with a fenced-in yard. Though the house was old and weather-beaten, it was immaculate inside and was filled with objects that reflected character. It was obvious that she was highly religious and that she memorialized her relatives and friends with a great array of photographs. Mrs. Bailey was a feisty little woman who delighted in relating her many experiences. She told me that the previous month a white policeman who resented a Black man having a new car had stopped him on a phony traffic violation and shot him dead right in the presence of his screaming, hysterical wife. The expression on her aged face related evidence of the distraught emotion that lingered in her heart. Bubbling over with consternation, she declared that if it had been her man and her, she would have come out of the car with the pistol blazing that was subsequently found in the car. She said that day she would have gone to judgment with her man. Her attitude gave me cause for admiring her.

I visited Helen in Columbia twice before returning to Fort Lewis. Four letters arrived from Helen before I was discharged the following month. But after the four letters, I never heard from her again. As a civilian, I had a great urge to visit her grandmother. I never made it. Helen seemed to have disappeared as mysteriously as she had appeared. I always wondered what happened to her.

CHAPTER 15

CONFRONTING JIM AND JANE CROW AT THE EMPLOYMENT OFFICE

Monroe, my hometown, had not changed much. Camp Sutton had closed, and the soldiers had gone. The streets flourished with local ex-soldiers who had come home wearing ruptured duck patches affixed to their army uniforms, showing that they had been honorably discharged from the military. We had returned to our racially segregated community after a military service that left our lot pretty much the same as it had been for many generations. There was a shortage of employment, so the government had initiated a program we called the 52/20 Club. It constituted a stipend of twenty dollars given to each veteran weekly for a period of fifty-two weeks. In my community, we congregated in the local barbershop, where we renewed old acquaintances, a tightly knit camaraderie. Individuals had been to all corners of the world, and each one had different experiences to draw from. Unemployed, short on money, and having hardly any place of amusement where we would be welcome, we entertained ourselves.

Veterans who were sustained by the 52/20 Club had to report to the local employment office weekly with a list of at least three places we had visited in pursuit of work. All the workers in the employment office were white, and their attitudes bore witness to the fact that they resented Black ex–service personnel receiving any service-connected benefits. With the passing of each week, the caseworkers' tone of voice became more and more hostile. The office supervisor was the worst offender. She was an Amazon-type with peroxide-bleached hair.

She had a very nasty attitude and talked to what she called "cullud" veterans as if we were no more than dogs. She had a tendency of discussing her golf game with other workers while Black persons were forced to wait out her contempt. Her name was Kate Cason, and her attitude had become a daily barbershop topic of conversation. Everyone who could would maneuver to avoid having her take care of his or her report. Sometimes we waited in the hallway until she had become busy so as to avoid her desk.

On one occasion, when I went in to report for my 52/20, Mrs. Cason called me to her desk. Evidently, she had heard me make a comment concerning the fact that the whites were displaying a slave master attitude. I had spoken loud enough to the Black veterans deliberately so that the white office workers could hear my comment.

When I obeyed her offer to sit at her desk, I could tell that she was greatly upset and had pegged me as someone who needed to be put back in his place. With a scowl on her puffy white face, she informed me that she had a job for me.

"Good," I said. "What kind of job is it?" I asked, surprised because virtually no jobs worth having were available to Black applicants.

"It's a good job for you," she said gleefully.

"Where is it located?" I asked, puzzled.

"At the Pure Oil Service Station," she informed me.

"How much does it pay?"

"It pays eighteen dollars a week," I was told.

"No! I want to keep looking for a better-paying job," I said.

Her face became drawn. Her mouth quivered, and the tone of her voice became even more caustic. "You know the law says that your claim becomes void when you refuse gainful employment. If you refuse this offer of gainful employment, I'll have to deny processing your claim."

"That's not gainful employment. I'll lose money by taking that job!" I explained, pointing out that the 52/20 Club accorded me twenty dollars a week. The job paid two dollars less, and I would have to get to the job, buy lunch, and acquire extra clothes.

She went into a spiteful tirade. "The trouble with you nigra veterans is that you think the world owes you a living." Her words and manner angered me.

"We don't think the world owes us a living any more than you do. We would just like a job sitting on our asses just like you!"

She became hysterical and jumped up from the desk. She shook with rage. "I don't have to take that kind of talk from you. I'll call Chief Jesse Helms, and he'll throw you out of here!" she shouted.

Chief Jesse Helms, father of the man who was later to become Senator Jesse Helms, had a reputation of manhandling Blacks.[1] The mention of his name struck terror in the hearts of Blacks who engendered the wrath of local gentry. He had been a policeman so long it seemed he had become immune to law and the Constitution.

I told her to go on and call him if that was what she wanted to do. She was shocked by my attitude. I am sure that she realized that I was not intimidated by her action, and to call in Chief Helms was going to create the type of incident that could expose the errant conduct of the white office workers toward Black veterans. She backed down. The Black veterans who had witnessed the action gave me a "thumbs up" and made it known that they were with me. It was obvious that they were elated that their feelings had been openly expressed.

I appealed the local decision to the state employment office in Raleigh. Also, as a writer, I filed a self-employment claim, which was approved. This entitled me to a hundred dollars a month instead of twenty dollars per week. To the local white gentry, I had become a Black pariah, and I now had the extremely dangerous label "uppity nigger." To the local Black veterans, I had become a hero. Later that year my life changed drastically: my mother died, and I became attracted to a local teenage girl, Mabel Robinson, and we were married.

1. Jesse Helms (1921–2008) was a conservative Republican senator from North Carolina. He served in the US Senate from 1973 until 2003 and was considered an opponent of civil rights and African American voting rights. For a biography of Senator Helms, see William Link, *Righteous Warrior: Jesse Helms and the Rise of Modern Conservatism* (New York: St. Martins, 2008).

CHAPTER 16

PURSUING HIGHER EDUCATION

I exhausted my GI unemployment, after which I enrolled in West Virginia State College under the GI Bill. While there, I fell under the spell of Dr. Herman G. Canady and President John W. Davis, who greatly enhanced my tendency toward Black consciousness.[1] Dr. Canady was my psychology teacher. He was as much an entertainer as an educator. His classes were always overflowing. Students filled all the seats and sat on the floor, carefully absorbing his wisdom delivered in a comical vein. He never taught from the textbook but insisted that we study the book on our own. His exams were always based on the formal course outline. He contended that we needed Black psychology to face the life before us. He often reminded his students that surviving as a Black man in the white man's America was pure hell.

As often as possible, Dr. Davis attended the students' Friday night forums. In the forum, we discussed world events as related in the news media of the week. Like myself, many of the students were veterans. During this time, there was a vicious controversy swirling around the great artist Paul Robeson. Paul had appealed to the US government to intervene in the South to protect the human rights of the Afro-American people. The government's reply was that the violent racial situation in the South was a local matter that the national government

1. Dr. Herman Canady (1901–70) was the chair of the psychology department at West Virginia State College and a pioneer in the study of African American psychology. John Davis (1889–1980) was president of West Virginia State College from 1919 to 1953 and was also active in civil rights advocacy.

could not become involved in. It was said to be a matter of states' rights and not a national issue.

This official reply had created great tension in many Black communities. Attitudes became even more inflamed when Paul Robeson declared that if those were the only conditions that could give the government cause for direct intervention, then perhaps we should make it a national issue. The nation had not been accustomed to this kind of talk coming from a Black man, most of all a famous Black man who white America felt should have been more than appreciative of the fact that his talent had raised him high above the downtrodden masses. Many timid and Uncle Tom Negroes joined the chorus of condemnation, hoping to curry favor from their white benefactors.

Our campus reflected the great debate that Robeson had sparked. Many Negroes declared for the pleasure of bigoted white America that Paul did not speak for the Negro. They publicly insisted that he spoke only for himself. The more militant and racially conscious among us declared that Paul spoke our very same sentiments. We were elated. He was our hero. We defended him with words and pledged to prepare ourselves for any action that might result.

One veteran stood in the forum and related how he had defended this country once and would most surely do it again. He said he wanted to repudiate Paul Robeson's "irrational" declaration. He received a lukewarm ovation from the audience. In the wake of his speech, members of the crowd became very noisy as they commented among themselves. I had gotten the floor during the distraction and had started to speak. Dr. Davis rose to his feet, waved his hands frantically, and called excitedly for the students to listen to what I was saying. His manner telegraphed his elated approval.

In a spirit of fervent disapproval of the former speaker, I declared that a Black person who had fewer rights than a common street dog in this country should be ashamed to brag about how he had defended America. I explained that such an attitude approximated that of the slaves who had to be driven from their masters' plantations by a woman with a bullwhip, referring to Sojourner Truth. I further stated that Paul Robeson had soared to heights that many of us would call heavenly, and yet his concern and love for his wretched people had resulted in his risking it all for the uplifting of us all. I insisted that we should love the country enough to get rid of not only the Hitlers in Germany but also the ones in America. I said that I was willing to fight the enemies abroad as well as the ones at home and that Paul spoke for me when he uttered those glorious words. There was thunderous applause when I finished, and I felt pleased to have said what I felt needed to be said. My words had reversed the tendency of the meeting. Dr. Davis ended the session with the words, "Young ladies and gentlemen, you do not have to be brilliant to outsmart the racist white man; all you have to do is do just the opposite of what he advises you to do!" This remark brought the house down.

West Virginia State's literary magazine, *The Quill*, had a rule that freshmen could not serve on its staff. I submitted some of my writings to them and they waived the rule, making me the first freshman to serve. A Scottish poet, Dr. Edward G. Davison, who visited our campus, saw some of my work in *The Quill* and requested to meet me. He looked at some of my other poems and informed me that he had detected a political strain and that if I really wanted to succeed in the field, I would have to forgo that tendency. He said that he would recommend me for a scholarship to study writing at the University of Colorado and that I should go out there, even if I had to thumb my way.[2]

By this time, I was married and already the father of a son. I was struggling to stay in school and keep my family together. I never made it to Colorado. My molding in Black institutions, however, had its own virtue and merits.

During the summer of 1950, at the age of twenty-five, I attended North Carolina College at Durham (now North Carolina Central University). There, I shared a student room in the city with my childhood friend Cad Roddy. While there, I was invited by Professor Ray to sit in his graduate course on literature.

After the summer at NC Central, I transferred to Johnson C. Smith University in Charlotte. The transfer there enabled me to live in Monroe with my wife and now two sons. It was a rugged daily commute from Monroe to Charlotte, riding in the back of the bus, which the law and white culture required. Sometimes the white bus drivers' attitudes could be downright hostile.

The word was out that the Celanese Company was going to build a giant plant in Rock Hill, South Carolina, that was merely about thirty miles from Monroe. The foundation was already being constructed, and laborers as far away as Monroe were being recruited. We were told that Afro-Americans were to be given equal opportunity as white workers. In the summer of '51 a group of us military veterans who had enrolled in college under the GI Bill commuted daily to the Celanese site as construction workers. We soon learned, to our consternation, that we had been misled about equal employment opportunities pertaining to the construction of the plant. A number of us who filled a truck each morning were all assigned to a pick and shovel detail. We worked digging ditches for the foundation of the huge structure. The foreman and timekeeper were white, and evidently they both were semi-illiterate. In order to keep our time straight for the payroll, a white man who had been so extensively exposed

2. "Thumb my way" refers to hitchhiking.

to the sun that his skin was as dark as some of ours would bring the time sheet to the ditch and have us fill in our own. We later learned that he was concealing his lack of education from the front office. What a cruel twist of fate: Black college men, striving and dreaming for a better life, were forced into a category commonly thrust upon the uneducated, while white illiterates rose to clerical positions on the sweat and anguish of the disinherited. Our pay was a paltry seventy-five cents an hour.

I spent the next year at Johnson C. Smith, after which I decided to leave the seemingly impenetrable walls that always loomed before the Black man to constrain his potential human development and social mobility. In quest of that ever-illusive self-satisfaction, I followed my destiny to Los Angeles, California.

Robert Williams during his tour as a US Marine, c. 1954.
Courtesy of the Williams family.

CHAPTER 17

BOOT CAMP

MARINE CORPS EXPERIENCE

My sojourn in Los Angeles was disappointing and short-lived. My search for employment was in vain. I ended up in a run-down hotel. Despite the fact that the rooms were cheap, I soon ran out of money. I was in a strange environment without even moral support. I was too far out in an unfriendly land and had burned the bridges behind me. I was trapped.

On display in the local employment office was a poster that announced JOIN TODAY AND LEAVE TOMORROW! It also guaranteed that enlistees would be assigned according to their aptitude testing if they signed up for four years. The pitch sounded great. I felt like my situation could be compared to a prizefighter trapped on the ropes who was miraculously saved by the bell. I had studied and practiced creative writing and had contributed to small publications. I signed up for the Marine Corps, and my testing showed an aptitude for information services. To me this meant that after my basic training, I would be sent to Quantico, Virginia, and given college-level training in journalism. As the poster promised, the next day I joined a contingent of men destined for boot camp at San Diego.

I arrived in a group of twelve about eight in the evening at the San Diego Recruit Depot on January 20, 1954. We were all anxious, a bit curious, and somewhat proud to have been accepted to serve with the world-famed US Marines.

By this time, the Marine Corps was integrated, and I assumed it would be unlike my segregated army experience.

This was the first time that most of the youngsters assigned to the group had been away from home. They had no idea what to expect or how to conduct themselves.

Being senior in age, twenty-eight, I had already crossed the States four times and had spent a tour of duty in the US Army. I felt that I had some idea as to what military life was all about. We stood grouped like a grazing herd of cattle in front of the military police hut. As civilians, we were not accustomed to forming military lines and controlled discipline. Above the noise of our milling and talkative, restless bodies, a gruff voice fell out of the night. It stabbed at us caustically. Complete silence and fear reigned. The voice and white helmet belonged to a marine-hardened corporal. "I'm Corporal Douglas," he stated. "You will speak only when you're given permission to speak, and you will address me as sir when given an order or when moving from one place to another. You will always move on the double. Is that clear?"

"Yes sir!" we all replied in unison.

With the suddenness of a pouncing cat, the corporal's hands sprang out to a gum-chewing recruit's collar. He tightened his grip and drew the frightened recruit forward.

The lad was in a panic. "Swallow that gum, you goddamn shit bird, before I deck you," he demanded in a ferocious voice. The kid gave a remote gulp that attested to his swift compliance to the order. The corporal shook him up a bit and shoved him back in file.

After some tense moments of much verbal conditioning, we were taken to receiving barracks for preliminary processing and billeting. We formed a long line with other recruits along the walls of a corridor. The gruff-voiced corporal ordered us to form a ladder [a military training drill requiring trainees to run up a ladder]. The recruits were unaware that a staircase was referred to as a ladder, so disorder prevailed.

"All right! As you were, you goddamn eggheads!" he shouted.

Closed out of the lines that had formed tightly under the influence of panic, three miserable recruits stood trapped in the open aisle. The corporal charged like a raging bull and planted his boot in a sequence of rumps. In an atmosphere of panic and apprehension, we had ladder drills and fall-out drills until taps sounded.

Reveille went before dawn. The barracks were a beehive of activity. We made morning chow before the sun had risen. As the sun burned its way through the morning's chilly mist, we were far into our schedule for the day. We were issued

Health and Comfort supplies, which consisted of toilet articles, stationery, and the Said Book, the marines' guidebook.

After the noon hour, our heads were shaved. We looked so grotesque that an uninformed outsider might have confused us with a Hollywood set of men from Mars. During unfilled moments of processing, we cleaned the barracks and toilets. We worked in almost complete silence and resembled a camp of mummies.

Four days aboard and we were assigned to a training platoon. We were given positions in the platoon according to height and were billeted by squads. The drill instructor [DI] did not like the way we moved with our heavy loads of gear. "Are you a bunch of dead pussies or marine recruits?" he demanded.

A youth of Latino lineage chuckled.

"Come here, laughing boy!" the big, rugged-looking DI demanded in a threatening voice. The lad moved toward the senior DI instructor reluctantly and fearfully. The junior DI moved instantly behind the youth. When the lad came within the range of the DI's arms, they both collared him. "See sumpin' funny, laughing boy?" the senior DI yelled.

"No sir!"

"Well, why did ya laugh, then?"

"I wasn't laughing, sir. "

"Boy, you gonna make me out a liar?"

"No sir! I just got sumpin' in my throat!"

"Boy, when I say you was laughing, you was laughing, understand?"

"Yes sir!"

"Yes sir, what, boy?"

"I was laughing, sir!"

The drill instructor's hand cracked on the recruit's face like a popgun. He jabbed him in the midsection, and the lad reeled back against the bulkhead. The youth scurried back into the group like a frightened dog. The incident served notice on us that discipline was more than just a term. It was more in the vein of a stamp of an iron fist. Through the haze of amazement, the DI's voice snapped, "Fall out!"

We ran over each other in a wild stampede for the street.

The rainy season had set in around San Diego. When reveille sounded, it was cold and raining and great pools of water stood all over the camp area. The ponchos, which had been issued to us, were left, neatly folded, in our locker boxes as we were marched in formation through the cold, relentless rain. By the time we reached the mess hall, we were all soaking wet. Shuddering, we stood like machines, marking time in ankle-deep water at the entrance of the mess hall. Our feet rose and fell in the water in perfect unison that mocked the idle of a heavy diesel engine.

The long-overdue command to halt was finally given. The senior DI walked between the double files. Hysteria swept over the recruits. We feared an extemporaneous inspection. The disciplinarian stopped about the middle of the two files. "You cold, boy?" he shouted at a trembling recruit.

"No sir!"

"Well, how come you're trembling, then?"

"I don't know, sir!"

"You like the corps, boy?"

"Yes sir!"

"You wanna go home?"

"No sir!"

"Do we treat you all right here?"

"Yes sir!"

"Do you know anything to say besides 'yes sir,' boy?"

"No sir!"

"Don't you like the rain?"

"Yes sir!"

"Are you getting wet?"

"Yes sir!"

The palm of the DI's hand ricocheted off the recruit's face. He stood fast in the unyielding position of attention.

"It never rains on a marine! Do you understand that?"

"Yes sir!" the undaunted youth replied.

The rain descended relentlessly as night tightened its grip on the San Diego area. We sat like one large family in a barracks that seemed far from civilization. We were cleaning our rifles and spit-shining our shoes when the DI came in. A voice called, "Atten-tion!"

We rose to our feet and froze in our tracks. He shouted, "I want to hear the 'Marines' Hymn.' I want to hear it loud and clear. Do you understand?" he shouted.

"Yes sir!" we replied in unison. Like little children singing piously in Sunday school, we exerted our lungs.

CHAPTER 18

WE WERE PROUD MARINES

We were in full dress greens, and we were exceedingly happy. No longer were we referred to as "shit bird" or "eggheads." We were proud marines. This was the day of graduation. The band was there and all of the big brass, all the way up to the commanding general. I was a part of a platoon that was said to be one of the sharpest ever to come through San Diego, and we had been given an honor flag to prove it. We stood out on the vast parade ground. We were mechanically erect and rhythmically snappy when we passed the reviewing stand. This was our last time in the field as a unit. After this day, we would be dispersed throughout the Marine Corps. We were glad to have completed the great ordeal, but we had become attached to each other as a unit. Farewell was like the breakup of a big family.

Our last night in the barracks was like a child's restless anxiety on the eve of Christmas. This was the longest night in all of boot camp. After much turning, tossing, and sleep talking, the reveille of reveilles went. No one was hard to arouse this morning. In a matter of seconds, the entire platoon had hit the deck, and the mad scramble for the early use of the toilet facilities was on. The barracks became a relative anthill.

In full dress greens and anxious to go, we fell into the company's sheet with our orders and duffel bags. The senior DI gave us the command "Right shoulder, seabags [duffel bags]!" We marched in platoon formation with the bags over our shoulders. About halfway to our destination, which was the bus stop at the base theater, our shoulders began to weaken under the strain of the heavy bags. Our knees began to buckle, and it was hard to keep in step. The smaller guys staggered along like overloaded barflies. We dared not even think of resting.

When the bus pulled off, elements of the second battalion were on the drill field. The band was playing the "Marines' Hymn." The formation was sharp. Last week at this time we were standing the same inspection, but it was all over now, and we were going home and to our next duty station. We were singing the "Marines' Hymn" when the bus pulled through the gates of the fenced-in depot that bore a striking resemblance to a prison. The depot faded into the distance.

I passed through Los Angeles en route to North Carolina, my native home. It was a splendid feeling to be in the outside world again. It seemed like ages since I had mingled freely among civilians. The colorful movement in Union Station looked like a wonderland to me. After a two-hour wait, the train pulled out. A boisterous couple sat in front of me. They passed a whiskey bottle between them. I listened to their toasts and jokes until I fell off to sleep.

The little town of Monroe had not changed. People were still complaining about a shortage of work and consequently not enough money. My twenty-one days of leave were flying. Five days had been used en route. After many days of frustrated overtures, I reached reconciliation with my estranged wife. We spent three days honeymooning, and I caught a train for Camp Pendleton, California. I encountered a snafu in connections and therefore turned in a day late at Pendleton. I was placed on restriction for fourteen days.

Despite the fact that life was rugged at Camp Pendleton, I was developing a strange kind of affection for the Marine Corps. Up until now, I had realized the first racial equality in my life. At last, I had started to feel that I was an American and was experiencing a pride in being a part of the nation. Since high school I had started to see the flag as a symbol of white supremacy and oppression. It had represented a walled society that relegated my people and me to a subhuman status. Now, I even entertained some idea of becoming a career marine. The walls that had restricted and stunted my life no longer loomed before me. A seemingly hopeless past had given way to a hopeful future with unlimited success possibilities.

CHAPTER 19

DISILLUSIONMENT

The recruitment pitch had promised to assign me according to my aptitude. My aptitude testing showed that I was qualified for information services. I dreamed of the day that I would be sent to Quantico, Virginia, for journalism training. Day after day, men were being sent out on assignment. After weeks of anxiety, I was summoned by the commanding officer, who informed me that I was going to be given the best job in the Marine Corps. When I happily inquired as to what that job was, he sheepishly informed me that I was going to be trained as a supply sergeant and that I would remain on the base. My dreams exploded in my head like a concussion bomb. Struggling to contain my disappointment and anger, I informed him that when I enlisted, I had been promised training in information services. He strained to muster a benevolent expression on a face that hypocrisy betrayed and again informed me that the Marine Corps was generously giving me the best position in the corps. I informed him that I didn't want the best position, I just wanted to go to information services. He summarily dismissed me. I had once again been cast into America's purgatory. In the flash of a moment, my dreams had exploded, and my life had been shattered. Dejectedly, I retreated to the barracks and sought refuge on my bunk. My mind was swirling with disgust, anger, and hatred. All the bitterness of my life welled up in my heart. I am sure that if I had been in possession of a hydrogen bomb, at that moment I would have sacrificed my life to explode it. My esprit de corps was gone, and I knew that big trouble was coming.

I was assigned to a barracks of so-called misfits. The marine who slept next to me was Jewish and obviously had some mental problems. He had converted to the Jehovah's Witnesses religion and was being completely ostracized. He adamantly refused to salute the flag and refused to make formations. Because I befriended him, everything that he was guilty of became the basis for accusations against me. The cadre set out to make our lives a living hell. Eventually, I concluded that my last and only refuge was the chaplain.

I felt certain that the chaplain, who was Catholic, would be sympathetic. The chaplain was a big man with a deceptive appearance. He looked like the fatherly type, but he exuded an air of strict adherence to the status quo. After I had related my entire story to him, his face hardened, and he gave me that indifferent look that is all too familiar when white men cast aside their humanity to sternly remind Black men of our impotence in a world in which we have no natural claim.

In a stern voice, he informed me that it was his duty to tell me that there were no Black marines in information services. He further stated that if I kept pushing to go to Quantico, I was going to get into very serious trouble. I left the building completely crushed. Once again, I remembered my uncle Charlie's words, the words that had come back many times like a heavenly refrain, that if there was a God, he must be sleeping and could not hear the mournful prayers of wretchedly oppressed Black people.

Two weeks after my meeting with the chaplain, I was ordered to pack my seabag and get ready to move out. I had been assigned to one of a convoy of buses ferrying men to the docks of San Diego, en route to Korea. There was a huge transport ship waiting at the dock. A band was playing as we went up the gangplank. There were many women and children who had come to see their loved ones off. I had just been assigned a hammock when a sergeant major came and instructed me to get my gear and follow him. He was white. He was friendly and seemed too much of a gentleman to be a marine. He whispered to me, "Keep this under your shirt. You've been classified as a security risk and ordered off the ship. Be careful. I think it's a damn shame! Good luck, marine!"

They had already raised the gangplank, and now they were lowering it again. When I started down the gangplank, many of the marines who were standing along the railing to wave a last goodbye to those who had come to see them off gave out a thunderous ovation. They screamed, "You lucky stiff!"

CHAPTER 20

MABEL'S VISIT

The next month my wife was coming to Oceanside to visit me. The day before she arrived, we were to have a dress parade because some high brass was coming to inspect the troops. The gunnery sergeant told me, "Since you refused to salute the flag and are an enemy of the country, you are barred from the parade." After the parade, the sergeant returned and informed me that my wife was arriving the next day, but I would be unable to see her because I was being placed on restriction for being absent from the parade. After being dismissed, I immediately went to see the chaplain and explained what was going on. He interceded on humanitarian grounds.

The following week, during a morning policing of the barracks, a hostile little corporal from Texas gave me an order to wash the windows. He went away and returned shortly and said, "Professor, you go clean the head"—the toilet. I left the windows and went to clean the head. After a few minutes, he came into the head and said that he had given me an order to wash windows and that I had disobeyed his order.

I declared, "When two or more orders are given, regulations require me to obey the last order and disregard the first."

"Oh, you're a smartass shit bird!" he fumed and wrote me up and put me on report for a court-martial. The summary court-martial landed me in the brig. A prisoner who was getting out of the brig slipped a letter out for me addressed to President Eisenhower. Two weeks later the warden's office was buzzing with military brass. A formation was called. I learned from infuriated officers that all letters to the high command had been sent up through channels.

Despite my breach of regulations, an answer had arrived from Washington, and military law required that Washington's response had to be read before the entire formation. The men were highly elated when an officer from the inspector general's office read Washington's response to me and made himself available to all men and me who had complaints that we wanted to register. My sojourn in the brig was cut short.

When I returned to the company, I was sent to the hospital and locked in a padded cell. When I protested, I was told that this was a regulation formality that applied to all troublemakers who could not adjust to military life. I was held incommunicado, and the isolation gave me a feeling of desperate helplessness. It seemed that the world had vanished from existence and that I had entered the twilight zone of impending doom. I had read that the Russians maintained a system of committing individuals who pressed for human rights to mental hospitals. This was America, land of the free, where human dignity was supposed to be the foundation of democracy. The dignity of the individual was supposed to be a cardinal difference between America and Russia. It was what America so brazenly boasted to the world—that in the USA, the human persona is sacrosanct.

Lucky for me the psychiatrist who attended me was Jewish and had some understanding of racism. Insensate men who presided over a punitive, vicious system that treated Black men as if they were game for sport and entertainment at a turkey shoot could not sway him. For them it was like shooting fish in a barrel. How could they miss? Everything was to their advantage, and they made the most of it. That was the American equation: the weight of the white man balanced against that of the Black man.

CHAPTER 21

MILITARY INTELLIGENCE RECORDS

Years after these incidents occurred, I was able to obtain records under the Freedom of Information Act. Some excerpts from those records state:

> On 23 February Tech Sgt. Kenneth Curney informed reporting agent that subject had been admitted to the U.S. Naval Hospital, Camp Pendleton on 21 February 1955 with a diagnosis of Passive-aggressive Reaction, #3212, and advised that subject was being given a series of psychiatric examinations and evaluations, but that he was granted liberty from 1630 to 0800 the following morning. On 28 February T. Sgt. Curney advised that he called Dr. R. Werman LTJG MC, USNR, Psychiatrist U.S. Naval Hospital, in an attempt to determine the facts concerning subject's medical case, at which time, Curney advised, Dr. Werman commented that subject stated that he was being called a Communist and that he was being unjustly treated. It was Dr. Werman's opinion that subject was getting "pushed around."
>
> . . . Character of Investigation. ESPIONAGE AND SUBVERSIVE ACTIVITIES: Surveillance of subject and wife had no questionable literature in hotel room or luggage and furnished a list of names found in address book of subject's wife. Subject admitted to U.S.N. Hospital, Camp Pendleton 21 Feb. with diagnosis Passive-aggressive Reaction 3212 and a board of medical survey recommended subject for discharge as unsuitable for service (see encl [2]). Mail cover revealed subject sent two letters and a telegram

to the President of the U.S. between 30 Mar. and 13 Apr. 1955, sent a letter to NAACP Headquarters, Washington, D.C. and received two letters from members of the U.S. House of Representatives on 25 and 26 Apr. T. Sgt. Curney stated that subject's name had come up last November, at which time he interviewed [redacted] Staging Regiment, who became suspicious of subject due to his expressing himself in a radical manner and constantly complaining of racial discrimination. T. Sgt. Curney stated that after [redacted] reported the matter and after he made his preliminary investigation, a period of time elapsed before he re-contacted [redacted] and, upon re-interview, no further complaints and appeared to be a model marine, and requested that the investigation be discontinued.

As a result of an authorized search of subject's effects by TSGT Curney on 12 January 1955 without subject's knowledge, enclosures (1) through (26) were obtained. The above evidence was photostated at the Motion Picture production unit, Marine Corps Base, Camp Pendleton, at TSGT Curney's request and took place in his presence. The original of all these enclosures were returned to subject on 21 January 1955 and all enclosures were initialed by TSGT Curney.

TSGT Curney stated that a perusal of subject's effects revealed that he considers himself a poet, author and song writer. The tenor of some of subject's articles and poems, as well as subject's wife's letters, follows somewhat the Communist Party line.

Enclosure (5), an unmailed and undated letter by subject, indicates he requested sanctuary in the base brig as a protective measure and carries the usual discriminatory complaints and the threat of appealing to civil authority and aid of American newspapers to relieve subject's oppression.

Enclosures (6), (7) and (8) are samples of subject's poetry which tends to follow the Communist Party doctrine.

Enclosure (9) contains a vocabulary and the following title: "The Red Maelstrom, A Day of Judgment." It should be noted that a portion of the above phrase appears on page 1 of enclosure (10).

Enclosure (10) is an article written by subject entitled "The Lost Heritage" in which subject portrays in unfavorable light treatment of recruits undergoing training at the U.S. Marine Corps recruit Depot, San Diego, California, and the ruthlessness of the drill instructors there.

Enclosure (11) is a copy of the frontispiece of a book of Russian poems, indicating subject's interest in Russian poetry. Enclosure (11a) which was found inside the book, indicates it was purchased at the Marlboro Book Store in New York City.

> Enclosures (14) and (15) are subject's UAW-CID Local #22 membership cards in Detroit, Michigan for 1948 and 1949, which indicate his possible employment and residence in that area during the years in question.
>
> Enclosures (19), (20) and (21) indicate that subject attended West Virginia State College in 1949 and 1950; North Carolina College at Durham in June 1950; and Johnson C. Smith University at Charlotte, North Carolina in 1951 and 1952.
>
> It should be noted that among subject's effects sighted by reporting agent was a booklet entitled "The Quill" mentioned in enclosure (2), which was published by the West Virginia State College in May 1950 and marked Volume #5. This booklet contained a short story and poem written by subject for which subject was highly praised in the forward [*sic*] by a member of the teaching staff at instant college. A perusal of the books mentioned in enclosure (2) revealed one entitled "Educational Psychology" wherein various sections pertaining to the psychological effects of racial discrimination upon negroes, the causes and the complexities thereof, were underscored in pencil.
>
> In view of subject's confinement and his past disciplinary record, it was not deemed advisable to obtain a Statement of Personal History, National Agency Check forms or Fingerprint Card from him under any type of pretext. Therefore, undeveloped leads set out below are based on information contained in subject's service record book and information developed through search of his effects. After subject is restored to duty the possibility of obtaining the above-mentioned background data will be considered.

Despite all the bitter, negative experiences I had encountered growing up in white supremacist, oppressive America, I had never imagined, until I obtained my files, that a single private citizen could become the victim of such a detailed, personal investigation, vicious lies, and distortions by constituted authority. On April 19, 1955, Agent F. V. Frost reported to G-2:[1]

> No others in Monroe or Charlotte, N.C. could give any information that subject had ever engaged in CP [Communist Party] activities or was sympathetic towards Communism. No known contacts of subject in Monroe or Charlotte are known to be sympathetic toward Communism. Informant states, considered to be reliable, intelligent, capable and loyal to the

1. G-2 is military intelligence.

United States. Subject has been away from Monroe, N.C. for the most part since about 1944. He had been back to live for perhaps two years in that time, and has been home once on leave since joining the Marine Corps. Would recommend subject as a loyal citizen as far as subject is known to him. Other informants believe subject to be reliable, however states subject does appear odd, in one way and that is, he writes poetry.

CHAPTER 22

REQUEST MASS AND SEPARATION FROM THE CORPS

One night while strolling alone through the company area, I met an Afro-American marine sergeant. He was a veteran of many battles in the Pacific. He had the medals to prove it. He said he knew of my problems but could not afford to get personally involved because he would be eligible for retirement in another eighteen months and could possibly jeopardize his standing. He informed me that he was going to give me some information that could help me but that if I should see him again, I was to please not speak to him. He scanned the area, lowered his voice, and told me that there was a little-known right in the corps that very few marines had ever heard of. He explained that marines were the president's special troops and that there was a procedure called Request Mass. He informed me that I should write a letter of complaint, addressed to the commandant, seal it, and write "Private Request Mass" on the envelope. He said that I should present it to the sergeant major, and he would be duty bound, under regulations, to pass it up through channels. He wished me good luck and disappeared into the night. I thanked him, went back to the barrack, and wrote my letter. I followed his detailed instructions.

When I presented the Request Mass to the company sergeant, he became very nervous and asked me what my problem was. I told him it was a private matter and that it could not be solved there and that I wanted an audience with the commandant. He tried his best to dissuade me. Later in the day, the company commander summoned me to his office. He was nervously mopping the sweat from his face, and his attitude was completely different from what it had been toward me. He tried in vain to persuade me that he could handle any problem that I had. He said that if I didn't withdraw the Request Mass that he would have to deliver it to the battalion commander. He even made a pitch to curry sympathy from me. I informed him that I would not withdraw my complaint.

When I made it to the battalion commander, he, too, was all smiles and mustered his best condescending attitude. The regimental commander repeated the act. He explained that this was a serious request and that he could solve my problem if I allowed him to. My spirit soared again in light of the fact that I had bargaining power.

A few days after the Request Mass had started through channels, the commanding officer again summoned me to his office. This time he was desperate. My Request Mass had reached General Goode, the base commander. He had consented to grant me an audience in three days. It seemed that the CO was straining every muscle in his body to muster a pleasant, friendly mask on his face. His trembling hands betrayed his vain attempt to conceal his panic.

In three days' time, the CO was driving me by jeep to see the commanding general. He shook with fear and asked me if I was not nervous to go before the general. I replied to him, "No, he's just a man like me!"

He confessed, "I'm always nervous when I go before such high brass."

I was left sitting on a bench outside the "old man's" office as the captain went in for a brief conference. The captain came back looking scared and anxious as he informed me, "General Goode will see you now."

Facing the general, I saluted, stood at attention, and waited for a response from the "old man." He fumbled through papers on his desk without looking up at me. I suppose he kept me standing frozen at attention for a good ten minutes that seemed to span an eternity. He finally looked up from his desk with his eyes glaring in cold contempt toward me. "At ease!" he finally blurted out, then added, "All you want is to go to information services, right, marine?"

"Yes sir!" I intoned.

"You don't have any problem that I can't solve, marine. You've started a process of Request Mass and only you can rescind it. If you insist on going through with it, the Marine Corps will have to fly you all the way to Washington for an audience with the commandant. If that happens, it will mean that an enlisted man had a problem that we could not solve on this base. That will be a black mark on the record of every officer here at Camp Pendleton. You wouldn't want to do that, would you, marine?"

"No sir!" I responded.

"If all you want is to go to Quantico, I can arrange that for you, but before I can do that for you, you will have to withdraw your Request Mass. Do you want me to send you to information services?"

"Yes sir!"

"Then sign this petition for withdrawal," he said as he pushed the already prepared order to the edge of the desk before me.

I signed, feeling at peace and that progress was again an avenue toward contentment and pride in belonging to the US Marine Corps.

As soon as my signed withdrawal was secure in his hands, a scowl appeared on General Goode's face. His lips quivered with anger, and he growled, "You're an ex-doggie (soldier) and ex-doggies don't make good marines! You're a troublemaker. You don't belong in the corps, and I am going to see to it that you are drummed out!"

I knew then that I had been had. I had fallen for an age-old trick. It was a perennial trick that the white man had used throughout history to deprive people of color of property and their birthrights. Historically, the white man has manifested a high-intensity talent for deception in dealing with gullible Third World people who sought honesty where none existed. The broken promise and the forked tongue were the greatest weapons for conquest in the devious white man's arsenal. I could imagine that my feelings were parallel to those of the African who boarded the slave ship, beguiled by feigned generosity and benevolence. I felt that my feelings must have approximated those of the Native Americans and the Aborigines who gambled their birthrights on the promise of men who had less respect for them, and for themselves, than they had for common street dogs.

In three weeks, I was taken before a board of old white naval officers who rigged a situation wherein I was given an undesirable discharge. All of this was done in violation of the existing naval regulations. I was placed under guard, escorted to a private compartment on a railway car, and shipped to North Carolina with a notation that I could not remain in California. All of this was consummated despite the fact that the medical examiner had recommended a general discharge and one of my former platoon leaders had submitted a written statement that he thought I could make a worthwhile contribution to the corps if allowed to remain in service. In addition to the termination, it was stipulated that I was not to be given any more GI Bill money for education. The whole affair was geared to the fulfillment of the promise that I had come into the corps a (Black) ditchdigger and that I would go out a ditchdigger. The intent was that I would go home a broken and hopeless Black man of even less value than what a Jim-Crowed society decreed my people from birth. I went home, not broken but driven by anger.

CHAPTER 23

RETURN TO DIXIE TO JOIN THE STRUGGLE

Once back in civilian life, I tried in vain to get the discharge changed. I tried in vain to get more GI Bill money for school. Though I had experience in the auto and aircraft industries, Douglas Aircraft in Charlotte, North Carolina, turned me down and even tried to have the federal attorney indict me because I used my honorable army discharge in applying for employment there instead of my more recent "undesirable" [discharge], which I was attempting to get reversed.

It appeared that my government and my country had declared war on me. But after much reflection, I came to feel that my country had declared de facto war on me at birth, when I had been born Black. I wasn't going to drop dead! I wasn't going off into a corner to cry and self-destruct. No matter how isolated, no matter how feeble my response, I was going to fight back. Someday they would hear from me again. They would have to deal with me, even if my life was to be lost in the effort.

Monroe, North Carolina, was the county seat of Union County. The population of Monroe was about 11,000, of which approximately one-third was Black. It is located fourteen miles from the South Carolina border, and its spirit was closer to that of South Carolina than to the liberal atmosphere of Chapel Hill, which people tend to associate with North Carolina. At that time, there were no trade unions in the county, and racism was rampant.

At the time of my return, there was also a small and expiring branch of the National Association for the Advancement of Colored People. The Union County chapter was a typical southern branch. It was small, not very active, and dominated by and largely composed of the "upper crust" of the Black community. Before the *Brown v. Board of Education of Topeka* Supreme Court desegregation decision of 1954, the NAACP was not a primary target of local segregationists. In many places in the South, including Monroe, racists were not too concerned with the small local chapters. But the Supreme Court decision drastically altered this peaceful coexistence attitude. The Ku Klux Klan and the White Citizens' Councils made it their business to locate any NAACP chapter in their vicinity and to find out who its officers and members were. Threats of violence and economic sanctions were applied to make people withdraw their support. Under this tremendous pressure, chapters, already small, dwindled rapidly, resulting in many even ceasing to exist.

The rank discrimination I had experienced in the Marine Corps had left me bitter with a feeling that I wanted to join the ranks of forces struggling against racial oppression. As soon as I got home, I attended an NAACP meeting and joined. At the very first meeting I attended after joining, members were being selected as delegates to the state conference of branches. My name was suggested as a delegate to represent the group. It was voted down with the weak excuse that I was too young and that someone more mature should represent the branch. It was a lame excuse bordering on a not-too-complimentary joke.

CHAPTER 24

VOTED PRESIDENT OF THE NAACP

Within a year, with only six members left, I was voted president of the branch. Soon the six members bowed out, fearing white animosity that was spurring economic sanctions and sometimes vicious violence in many parts of the South. I was left with a branch with no members. I soon realized that I had become the victim of a cruel joke. The branch was slated for death, and I was to preside over its last rites. The old NAACP hands did not want the national office in New York to think that fear was overriding their devotion to the cause of social justice. They did not want to be stuck with the stigma of having chickened out.

As I approached the Black professionals who had operated the organization many years before, their attitude was negative. I was told that if I could get Dr. Creft, the oldest and most affluent Black medical doctor in the area, to renew his membership, other professionals would do likewise. It was more than obvious that I had a catch-22 situation on my hands. I failed to get a single old member to reenlist. My spirit flagged, and I burned with contempt and disgust. The one positive thing that I had brought out of the Marine Corps was the philosophy of aggressiveness in battle and to shun surrender. The thought of failure in attempting to organize a fighting branch was more than I could accede to. I was determined to revive the organization. But the burning question was how?

Religiously inclined parents tended to discourage their sons from frequenting pool halls. They taught that the halls exerted a bad influence and that they constituted a breeding place for shiftless hustlers. Having been raised in that atmosphere, I never learned to shoot pool and only on a few occasions had I experienced the inside of one. The local community pool hall was adjacent to a restaurant. One day after leaving the restaurant, I passed the door of the pool hall, and the noise indicated a sizable, jovial group of young men inside. I ventured in. Feeling somewhat awkward, I shouted in a loud voice, "I am the new president of the NAACP, and from this day forward these white people are going to catch hell in this town! I want you guys to join up and help me!"

I was surprised that complete silence fell over the room. They had halted their games. One fellow who was about to make a shot froze, looked up at me, and asked, "Man, you mean *we* can join that thing?"

"Yeah," I answered.

"How much, man?" he wanted to know.

"Two dollars!" I replied.

I signed six members right there on the pool table. Others stated that as soon as they got two dollars, they too would join. Some joined, using their wives' names for fear of economic retaliation. Some used chosen fake names and gave my home address. That situation apprised me of the fact that I had been wasting my time on the wrong people. I left the building fired with the confidence that I had struck a winner. The branch was certainly going to experience a rebirth with militancy and with muscle.

The following month I called the first meeting with thirty new members. None of the former cadre attended. When I opened the floor for nomination of officers, the group unanimously agreed that inasmuch as I had single-handedly reconstituted the branch, they felt it to be imperative that I have the most gung-ho officers to work with me. Subsequently, I was given the authority to appoint officers. When I explained that NAACP procedure required an election, someone in the audience said to hell with procedure—we were not organizing a Sunday school; we were organizing to fight. It was more than obvious that the most oppressed segment of the community expected vigorous action and that they were in no mood to create a goody-goody debating club to follow in the footsteps of the old guard. Without much prompting, I agreed to their wishes and appointed all veterans of the military, with the exception of the branch secretary, who was a woman, Mrs. Ethel Azalea Johnson, a local political activist.[1] Dr. Albert E.

1. Ethel Azalea Johnson (January 31, 1916–June 26, 1985), often referred to as "Azalea," was the "co-founder, editor, business manager, and columnist of *The Crusader*"; see Rhea Estelle Lathan, "Crusader: Ethel Azalea Johnson's Use of the Written Word as a Weapon of Liberation," in *Women and Literacy: Local and Global Inquiries for a New Century*, ed. Beth Daniell and Peter Mortensen (New York: Lawrence Erlbaum, 2007), 59–69. Johnson left Monroe in the early 1960s and engaged in radical organizations like the Revolutionary Action Movement

Perry Jr., an ex–army officer and a practicing medical doctor, became the vice president. John W. McDow, an auto-body man who was self-employed, became treasurer. Matthew Williams, another veteran, became board chairperson. His task was to set up a board. We went to work immediately and soon became known as the "big four."

The local library had always been segregated. That was our first target. The library was under the local city recreation department. I called Wally Mars, the chairman of the department, and informed him that the branch wanted the library integrated immediately. He told me that it wouldn't bother him a bit if "nigras" used the library. He said that he didn't read there anyway.

The very next day, fate presented me with a golden opportunity. A veteran, James Byrd, who was enrolled in a local junior college, approached me seeking some answers to a school-related assignment. I suggested that we had a library in town and that he should use it for needed information. He asked me if colored people could use the library. I told him that yes they could, but no person of color ever went there. I did not tell him that the system didn't serve Blacks for fear that the truth might spook him. I told him that I would drive him there. He readily agreed.

I stood in the middle of the floor as he approached the desk. The white patrons in the library gave full attention to our appearance. The librarian seemed momentarily stunned. It was obvious that she was straining to maintain her composure. Byrd explained that he had a school assignment and that he needed to look up the structure of the state government. Nervously she brought him a volume and opened it to the page that contained the information he was seeking. I could see that she was anxious to help him to the extent that his time there would be shortened.

He took some notes and thanked her, and we started for the door, surrounded by complete silence. As we made our way to the sidewalk I shook his hand and congratulated him. "For what?" he asked.

"For integrating the library—you are the first one of us to use it!" I informed him.

"You're joking!" he exclaimed.

"No. You have made history!"

---

and the Workers World Party. She remained a lifelong friend of the Williamses until her death in Baldwin, Michigan. See Paula Marie Seniors, *Mae Mallory, the Monroe Defense Committee, and World Revolutions* (Athens: University of Georgia Press, 2024), 1–2, 9–54; and Muhammad Ahmad, *We Will Return in the Whirlwind* (Chicago: Charles H. Kerr, 2007), 100–101, 103–4, 113–14.

"Damn, man, that was a helluva joke!" he stated, smiling broadly, exuding a rare kind of pride that Black people had seldom had occasion to experience. In looking back, it was really a small victory but a much-needed one. When the news spread through the community, it perked the people's pride and gave them courage and the impetus to struggle against bigger barriers. It was shocking to us that Afro-Americans had met with violence in Virginia and other southern communities endeavoring to integrate libraries when our effort had come without travail.

Yale and Towne Corporation had constructed a modern plant just at the outskirts of the city. No Blacks were hired in skilled capacities, and the word had been brazenly passed that none would be hired. We knew that our fledgling group did not have the clout to force the issue, but our teenage members were full of fire. They voted to protest, if no more than to show our disapproval. Our local Black high school students had been skirmishing over community turf control. That internal hostility, commonly associated with gang presence, evaporated as soon as their restlessness was channeled toward constructive endeavors.

On Highway 74, in front of Yale and Towne Corporation's factory, twelve youths staged a protest line. It was something that had never been seen before in that area. They carried placards charging the company with racial discrimination. The sight of pickets attracted great attention from passersby. Some racists who passed shouted angry racial epithets. The young people were stoic and became more emboldened. As never before, they were worthy of notice. It turned out to be a mighty training exercise.

In the summer of 1956, three young Black boys lost their lives swimming in unsupervised ponds. It was shocking to the entire community. There was a white swimming pool at a place called Lake Lee. This pool had been constructed by the Works Project Administration with federal funds. Blacks were barred from swimming there. Blacks were allowed in the area only to caddy for white golfers at the exclusive, white-only Monroe Country Club adjacent to the pool. In the heat of summer, whites could be seen basking in the cool fun of the pool. The pool was enclosed within the confines of a cyclone fence. It was an attractive center of a forbidden world.

The tragic loss of the Black children had caused us to take a closer look into the matter of the pool. Our NAACP branch designated Dr. Perry, John McDow, and me to approach the city council with a request that time be set aside wherein Black children could use the pool. We asked for three days a week. The city council replied with a resounding "NO." We asked then for two days. Council members' response again was negative. We told them that we were willing to settle for one day a week, just one day, set aside for our children, and the answer was the same—no! When we asked why not, even for just one day a week, they informed us that they could not allow our children to swim because it would be too expensive. When we asked why it would be too expensive, the reply was that the water would have to be changed each time the "nigras" had used it. I informed them that in that case, segregation was a luxury that they could ill afford.

Father John Garrone, a Catholic priest who was white, owned a station wagon. He started taking Black youth to nearby Charlotte to swim in a so-called Negro pool. Some of the city officials of Charlotte saw this priest swimming in the so-called Negro pool with the children and wanted to know who the white man was. The Black supervisor explained that he was a priest who brought some Black children to swim. The city officials angrily stated that they didn't care whether he was a priest or not, he was white, and they had segregation of the races in Charlotte, so they barred the priest from the so-called colored pool. Again, the children were without a safe place to swim.

CHAPTER 25

DECISION TO PICKET THE SWIMMING POOL

I called a meeting of our branch of the NAACP and reported our experience at the city council. The meeting was charged with anger. I asked the group to support direct action against the pool. The vote was unanimous in favor. The young people were thrilled. Now we were really going to shake things up. For total effectiveness, we needed the element of surprise; subsequently, the group gave me the authority to start the protest without further consultation. I could call the group to action whenever I deemed the time to be appropriate. This was done in order to neutralize the usefulness of any informer who may have infiltrated our group. It was customary for the racist power structure to plant informers in Afro-American communities. Through the spying of these traitors, the bigots were informed of all "secretive" activity in Black communities. This system gave them the advantage of being able to preempt or weaken freedom activity.

Eight high school youths volunteered for the protest action. I stressed that no youth from families directly dependent on local whites for survival should engage in the protest action.

At a Sunday branch meeting, I explained to the group and the youths that we would start practicing for the protest the following Monday, the next day. They were told that Monday would just be a practice day but that they should meet at my house at 2:00 p.m. with swimming trunks and towels to do a dry run that would approximate the real thing. By two o'clock, they were all there and anxious to prepare for the time when they could really go into action. I gave them the proper preparatory instructions and then explained to them that it was not a dry run. This was the real thing, and I informed them of the necessity of conducting it in this fashion in order to catch the whites off guard. The news hyped them up, and they beamed with pride, joy, and anticipation. It seemed that a spirit of self-confidence burst forth from within them that had been pent-up and restrained all of their young lives. They had a sense of the history that had been and that would never be again. Above and beyond their predecessors, they had overcome the fear that had paralyzed their forefathers.

We called two taxis, and Dr. Perry arrived at the same time as the cabs. When the young people saw Dr. Perry, they greeted him with great elation. It was obvious that they felt up to any task. They had never before been blessed with adults willing to lead them into such an explosive conflict and willing to risk whatever price the stand would cost. I felt a great pride in them, and their gallant action gave me cause to realize that the greatest negative factor in the dehumanization of Afro-Americans was the lack of bold, thoughtful, and determined leadership. It was more than obvious that this was why white America singled out our people with such qualities for extermination. White America was cognizant of the fact that a united people with solid leadership could not be subjugated in a nation determined to maintain itself in splendor.

We arrived at the pool and quickly lined up at the attendants' counter. We had our towels and trunks in our hands, and it was obvious why we had come there. We caught them off guard. A white youth who was standing near the counter ran frantically to the poolside, screaming, "Niggers have come to get in our pool!" Whites started jumping out of the pool as if it had caught fire. The attendant asked us what we wanted. I told him that we had come to swim. He stated that "nigras" could not swim there. I proceeded to explain to him that the pool had been constructed by the federal government and that we had as much right to swim there as any other American. "Not here!" he retorted. After much wrangling, when they saw that we were not leaving, the white swimmers began to leave. When they were all gone, we were informed that the pool was closed for the day.

News of the incident spread over the town like wildfire. When we arrived back in New Town, our protesters danced for joy. Many of the people in the community congratulated us. The telephone rang incessantly from anxious parents and individuals wanting to know how the operation went. The young demonstrators insisted that we repeat the feat the following day.

When we arrived at the pool the following day, the number of swimmers, despite the summer heat, was greatly reduced. There was a reception of hard-hat rednecks. They stood a few feet away from the entrance to the pool and waited in silence. A white woman who wore a hard hat confronted us. Her face was full of anger, and it was a sure thing that she was a plant to provoke trouble. She directly confronted me and shouted, "You niggers ain't gonna swim here, and you better leave now!"

The protesters stood silently behind me in line without wavering.

"If you don't leave, nigger, I'm gonna slap your Black face!"

I pointed my finger in her face and said in a voice loud enough for the men in hard hats to hear, "If you slap me, lady, it will be the last face you will ever slap on this earth!" I looked straight into her eyes. She looked back at her back-up bigots, and they appeared frozen in place. They failed to move to her support, and she started to back away from me. The bigots had never before seen a Black man with the nerve to talk that way to a white woman. The raw courage seemed to unnerve them. We went back to the pool every day for the balance of the week, and each time we arrived, the authorities closed the pool.

CHAPTER 26

WHIPPED-UP HYSTERIA AND A KLAN PETITION

The unfriendly media started to cover the story in a way that was sure to bring out the worst element of the racist town. In the past, it had been customary for whites to control Black communities just by dropping a hint of impending terror. This time was no exception. The bigots raised their traditional and savage specter of imminent violence and terror.

Placards and leaflets started to infest the town like natural growth that erupts in the season of spring. Ads appeared in the local press and whispers abounded that the Ku Klux Klan was moving into Monroe and was becoming active in a big way. The Klan had come out of the closet.

Afro-American women, some of whom were members of our NAACP branch, worked in local white homes. They began to bring us information about homes wherein they had detected Klan regalia. A South Carolina bigoted preacher called "Cat Fish" Cole was making frequent trips and holding meetings designed to inflame local white supremacists.

The local press announced a petition campaign, sponsored by the KKK, wherein a table had been set up on the courthouse square; the petition demanded that Dr. A. E. Perry and Robert Williams, members of the "Communist inspired NAACP," be driven from the town, never to return again. The local press claimed that the Klan had collected 3,000 signatures during the first week.

I went to the square. A man was attending a table and collecting signatures. I approached the table and inquired what the petition was all about. Because I was a Black person, the bigot seemed somewhat uncomfortable in explaining the meaning of what he was doing. "It is a petition to drive that Dr. Perry and Robert Williams out of town."

"What have they done?" I asked with an innocent voice.

"Nigras and white folks have always lived in peace here, and now they are trying to stir up trouble. They are Communists, and the Communists are out to destroy our country."

"Do you know this fellow Robert Williams?" I asked solemnly.

"No, but I know he's trying to make trouble for all of us!"

"Don't you think it is dangerous to try to drive people out of town that you don't even know?"

He nervously fidgeted with the papers on the table. He was sensing that I was in opposition to the petition campaign.

"For your information, I am Robert Williams, and I want you to know that you've got a right to circulate your petition, but you're going to meet with some serious trouble when and if you ever try to enforce it!"

The Klansman turned red in the face and lost his voice. He seemed devastated as I walked away.

CHAPTER 27

GROUP ORGANIZED FOR SELF-DEFENSE

The following week, while we were holding a meeting at the Community Center, Dr. Perry's wife called and asked him to hurry home. She was frightened because she had received a call wherein an individual who identified himself as a Klansman had threatened to blow up the house. Dr. Perry was a young Catholic physician who had attended the needs of the community regardless of whether the people could afford to pay. He was very popular and well liked in the community. He was selected as a special target because whites considered him an "uppity nigger" and his living standard was better than most. Because he was a medical doctor, the bigots thought him to be the only Black capable of leadership.

We closed down the meeting. I suggested that we go home, arm, and meet at "Doc's" house. I went home, got my Luger, and hurried to Perry's house. I was shocked when I arrived at his modern ranch-style home with its spacious, well-kept lawn. Cars were everywhere, parked along the road and in the driveway. Men were milling all around the exterior of the house, and many were inside. I later learned that when Dr. Perry's wife, Bertha, called my wife and informed her of the threat, Mabel called Azalea Johnson, and they both proceeded to call other wives to inform them and ask them to pass the word to others. When I approached the group, they gave out loud applause. The men were armed with sundry weapons. In times past, such a threat from the Klan would have sent Black people fleeing to their homes in fear, extinguishing all lights and cringing in terror. No one counted, but it we estimated that perhaps sixty men had turned up.

I explained that such an undisciplined group with so many arms constituted a dangerous situation. Voices in the group called for organization. I was caught off guard when there was a clamor that since I was president of the NAACP, it was only natural that I assume leadership of the armed group. Reluctantly I accepted the position, and we began to make our plans for self-defense.

Both the local and Charlotte media reported that Klan meetings were drawing hundreds of bigots in the county. Finally, they reported thousands in attendance at the rallies. Things were moving very fast. Klansmen started making forays into our community. Within a few weeks, as many as eighteen Black women had been struck by objects thrown from cars that passed in the night. John McDow and I were sitting in his car in front of my house one night when we saw a carload of young white boys pass by and throw a bottle from a car that struck a Black woman. We chased the car and got the license number. At our insistence through the NAACP, the boys were brought to court. The judge asked them why they were in the Negro community at night. They explained that they were just playing and were out for some fun. He fined them fifty dollars and explained that as explosive as the situation was, it was extremely dangerous for them to be over there, and the next time they wanted to have fun, they should realize that it would be safer for them to strike a policeman on Main Street.

Tension rose to the point that Klan motorcades invaded our community with some shots fired from cars that stretched for almost a mile, bumper to bumper. On one occasion a Black woman was forced to dance at pistol-point under a streetlight in a Black community. A group of Black ministers appeared before the county officials and appealed to them to stop the Klan from terrorizing Black women and children. The authorities informed the pleading Black ministers that the Klan had as much right to organize as our NAACP, and they flatly refused to take any action against the terrorists. Our group asked the preachers to please not beg the racist officials to stop the Klan again because we would stop them ourselves.

By now we had about 200 Black men under arms. I dressed up the titles of their occupations so that there would be no indication that we were Afro-Americans, and I applied for and got a charter from the National Rifle Association. During the swimming pool protest, we had already established a newsletter called *The Crusader* to get our side of the story out. It became a national and international publication. We started to equip the armed group with military surplus. We sent an appeal out through the newsletter, soliciting funds to buy army rifles. The response was terrific. Vehicles started to arrive by night laden with heavy rifles. We also received money to purchase more ammunition. After we had exchanged gunfire with the Klan, we started to fill sandbags and got steel helmets and gas masks. I had learned from my military experience how to make Molotov cocktails (gas bombs).

Dr. Perry lived on a dead-end street. The way in was the only way out. The women and children in that vicinity gathered many glass bottles. We filled them with gasoline and stuck rag wicks in the tops. We lined the gas bombs along both sides of the street. The idea was that if the Klan carried out the threat it had made to wipe us out, the bombs would be available to be thrown to create a wall of fire. The police had reported the fact of our bottles to the *Monroe Journal*. In an attempt to denigrate us, the *Journal* reported that we had made torches because we feared that the city was going to turn off the power and the "colored" folks were afraid of the dark. We were to be the butt of a racist joke, but little did they [the police and local white racists] realize that we had created an extensive death trap. We had been the first to introduce the Molotov cocktail to the civil rights movement.

We appealed to Luther Hodges, then governor of the state of North Carolina, to protect our community from the violence of the night-riding Klan. His response was that the Klan had not been disorderly or broken any law. We appealed to President Eisenhower. There was no response from Washington. It was more than obvious that there was no Fourteenth Amendment for us. We may as well have been a people without a government. It was an extremely demoralizing and hopeless feeling, to be completely outside the realm of protection by constituted authority. We had less force of law from government than common street dogs. I had grown up listening to the horrible experiences of old Black men who congregated around the neighborhood store. Their lives bore tragic scars of the Black man's ordeal of living in racist America. They had not dealt with the problem of the white man's brutality. They had coped through acquiescence. Now a new generation had come on the scene, and I had been designated to be their leader. I had an opportunity to make a difference, and I was determined to turn things around no matter what the cost might be. Deep down in my heart I knew that timidity would invigorate oppression and tyranny.

In the summer of 1957, we formed a defense perimeter around the area encompassing Dr. Perry's home in the wake of continuing threats from the Klan. We slept out of doors behind sandbags while some men walked guard. We never relaxed our vigil. We established a communication system by telephone and gunshots. The system was so set up that in case of Klan sightings, shots would be fired, men would arm themselves and rush to the defense area, and our wives would start serial calling on the phone. Becoming alarmed at our extensive organizing and the growing strength and militancy of our movement, the racist forces united against us.

In midsummer 1957, the KKK made one big attempt to crush our rebellious spirit. A mammoth motorcade of armed, hooded Klansmen invaded our community and headed straight for the area where Dr. Perry lived. We met fire with fire. Our returned gunfire caused them to break rank, and they scurried to get out of our community. These night riders, who had traditionally struck terror in the hearts of our people, had shown the yellow side of their bellies and had fled in terror from a confrontation wherein their intended victims had managed to create a level playing field in the game of violence. The philosophy of the deadly deterrent worked wherein constituted authority and law had failed. They had no stomach for evenly matched combat. They stopped raiding our community. After this clash, the same officials who had stated that the Klan had as much right to organize and demonstrate as our NAACP passed a city ordinance in an emergency session banning the night riders from Monroe without a special permit from the chief of police.

At the time of our clash with the Klan, only three black publications, *The Afro-American*, the *Norfolk Journal and Guide*, and *Jet* magazine, reported the fight. *Jet* carried some pictures of the self-defense guard. Our fight occurred two weeks before the famous clash between the Lumbee Indians and the Klan.[1] We had driven the KKK out of our county, and it went into the Indian Territory, where it was also repelled. The national press played up the Indian–Klan fight; evidently, they did not consider that incident a great threat. The Indians were a tiny minority, and the nation could laugh at the incident as a sentimental joke, but the media did not want Black people to get the impression that this was an effective way to deal with the Klan. The white press maintained a complete blackout concerning the Monroe fight.

1. On January 18, 1958, hundreds of men from the Lumbee nation conducted an armed raid at a Ku Klux Klan rally in Maxton, North Carolina. The raid was in response to cross burnings and racial intimidation of Indigenous and Black people in Robeson County. The armed Lumbees dispersed the white supremacists at the KKK rally, leading to a decrease in racial violence against Native Americans in the county. "Battle of Hayes Pond: Routing of the KKK," Museum of the Southeast American Indian, University of North Carolina at Pembroke, accessed October 24, 2024, https://www.uncp.edu/resources/museum-southeast-american-indian/museum-exhibits/battle-hayes-pond-routing-kkk; Malinda Maynor Lowery, *Lumbee Indians in the Jim Crow South: Race, Identity, and the Making of a Nation* (Chapel Hill: University of North Carolina Press, 2010), 181.

CHAPTER 28

DR. PERRY'S CASE

After violence had failed to crush our spirit and destroy our movement, the racist terrorists shifted their efforts to the courts and utilized kangaroo law. Dr. Perry, our NAACP chapter's vice president, was indicted on a trumped-up charge of performing an abortion on a white woman. The night he was arrested, he had answered a phony emergency call to his office, which was located on the outer edge of the downtown area. Some Blacks who happened to be passing by saw him being taken into custody. They sounded the alarm, and the word swept through the Black community like wildfire. Consequently, throngs of Afro-Americans marched on the police station and the jail.

When I arrived on the scene, an angry throng had filled the police station and the crowd spilled out into the street, blocking it. Another group had descended on the jail and were threatening to break down the doors unless "Doc" was released. I made my way through the crowd in the police station and asked the nervous chief, A. A. Mauney, why Doc had been arrested and what the charges were. Chief Mauney informed me that the charge was criminal abortion. I asked him the amount of the bond, and he told me that it didn't matter because we wouldn't be able to make it. I asked him a second time, and he informed me that the bond was $7,500. That was a very high bond, deliberately set so that Dr. Perry would have to remain in jail overnight. There were many reports that Klansmen were waiting on the outskirts of town and obviously planned to lynch him.

I asked Chief Mauney for permission to use the telephone. He nodded and pointed to it in the affirmative. The crowd was reaching a zenith of anger and was becoming more menacing. I called J. Ray Shute, a white Unitarian who had become a friend and was responsible for my converting to the Unitarian religion. He was also a local developer, considered to be one of the city fathers, and was considerably wealthy. I explained to him what had happened and that the town was about to burst into flames. He asked to speak to the chief. Chief Mauney said that Mr. Shute wanted the two of us to come to his house and to bring the bond for him to sign.

When we arrived at the Shute home, Chief Mauney was afraid to ring the doorbell. As Mr. Shute invited us in, Mauney removed his hat and lined up behind me. His entire demeanor had changed. His arrogance had faded, and his hands trembled as he passed the bond papers to be signed. Mr. Shute sat at his desk and read the charges, looked up at the chief, and said, "I'm tired of all this racial trouble around here. It is getting so the colored people can't live in peace because of the bigots. I want it stopped. Do you understand?"

"Yes, Mr. Shute, I'll do what I can," he meekly replied.

Dr. Perry was immediately released, and the tension was defused. I am certain that it would have been a very bloody night if he had not been released.

While awaiting trial and being under bond, Dr. Perry's political activities were greatly curtailed. Our group had suffered a grievous blow, which spread some demoralization among our people. But despite the bigots' shift in tactics, we managed to keep our group together. The local people mounted a massive drive to raise funds for Dr. Perry's legal defense.

Even though Dr. Perry was a Catholic physician who had refused to perform even legal abortions or to file sterilization permits for the county welfare department on grounds that such was contrary to his religious beliefs, and notwithstanding a long, fierce legal defense, he was tried, convicted, and sentenced to five years on a chain gang. He lost his license to practice medicine and was barred from his home in Monroe after his final release.

CHAPTER 29

THE INTERNATIONALLY INFAMOUS KISSING CASE

In the late fall of 1958, I received a telephone call from someone who identified himself as the mayor of Monroe. He chided that since I was so good at causing problems, he wanted to see how good I was at solving one. He informed me that a couple of "colored juvenile delinquents" had been jailed for molesting a white girl. He asked me to get their mothers to sign an authorization so they could be sent to reform school.

When I went to see the mothers of the boys, I found to my surprise that the so-called juvenile delinquents were only eight and nine years old. The two, David "Fuzzy" Simpson and James Hanover Thompson, had been playing with a little white girl who sat on the older boy's lap and kissed him on the cheek. When she innocently informed her mother of their childish play, the mother became hysterical and began scrubbing the little girl's face with soap and water. Her father loaded his shotgun and rushed out to kill the boys. The police got there first and arrested the two children, charging them with "attempted rape."

Instead of convincing the boys' mothers to agree to sign them into the reformatory, I telephoned some of my fellow officials in the local NAACP and informed them of the problem, and they all agreed that we needed to intervene on the children's behalf.

We found out that a hearing was being conducted the next day, and we proceeded to the courthouse in the afternoon. When we attempted to enter the courtroom, a police officer blocked our entrance to the door and informed us that the hearing was over and that the only thing that was left to do was the sentencing.

I asked where the children's mothers were and how they held a hearing without them or their accusers being there. The policeman mockingly informed me that the judge did not believe in mixing the races, so he had held a "separate but equal" hearing with the white child and her parents that morning.

Judge J. "Hamp" Price sentenced the two Black boys to the state reformatory to remain there until they reached twenty-one. This meant twelve- and thirteen-year sentences. Once we learned of the judge's actions, I contacted Kelly Alexander, a mortician from Charlotte who presided over the North Carolina State Conference of NAACP Branches, seeking help for the boys. Alexander refused to help with what he referred to as a "sex case" that the organization could not afford to get mixed up in. We then appealed to the national executive director, Roy Wilkins, who responded in a similarly negative way. They both were more concerned with not involving the organization in a "sex" issue than they were in seeking justice for the two unjustly imprisoned young boys.

Fortunately, James had an older sister who lived in Brooklyn, New York. She contacted her ward representative, and because the facts had been vaguely conveyed to her, she had him contact me to ascertain what had happened. He found the story to be unbelievable. Being a local official of the Brooklyn NAACP, he asked if I had contacted the national office. When I informed him that I had indeed and what had transpired, he became outraged and said that he was going to personally contact Roy Wilkins.

When he called back, he was greatly upset. After a few curse words, he asked me if we had a local lawyer. When I answered in the negative, he asked me if we wanted a lawyer. I explained that we could not afford to hire a lawyer. He asked me again if we wanted one, and I told him yes. He said one would call me soon.

We reported the events surrounding the case in our newsletter, *The Crusader*, and a few days after learning of the refusal of the NAACP to help, Conrad Lynn, a militant Black lawyer from New York, volunteered to help us and take the case. Some organizations there were going to join in to raise funds to help pay for legal fees. George Weissman, also from New York, called and asked if he could come with Lynn.[1] I gladly agreed, and the next day we joyously welcomed them to Monroe.

1. George Weissman (1916–85) was a journalist and member of the Socialist Workers Party.

When they arrived, however, James and Fuzzy had already been tried, convicted, and sent to the Hoffman boys' reformatory. Conrad Lynn went to talk with Hamp Price, the judge who had passed sentence on the boys. Judge Price told Lynn that he had held a "separate but equal" hearing. When asked what he meant by that, Judge Price told him how on the morning of the trial, he had called in the white mother and daughter, the mother had made a statement, and they were sent home. And then in the afternoon the two "Negro" mothers were summoned to the court and their boys were brought in. The judge then stated to Lynn, "I told them what the girl's mother had told me, and since they were guilty, I sent them up."

The story slowly began to get widespread coverage by outraged reporters in both the US and the overseas press. Eventually, after the foreign press started printing stories with captions like BLACK CHILDREN ARRESTED FOR A KISS, even the national networks and the *New York Times* were obliged to report the story. The eyes of the world were focused on Monroe and the famous "Kissing Case," and reporters from around the globe began to converge on Monroe.

When Joyce Eggington of the *London News Chronicle* asked for my help in interviewing and photographing the two boys in prison, I told her it would be impossible for a journalist to see them. Pretending to be a social worker, we went with James's mother to the Hoffman boys' reformatory in Southern Pines, North Carolina. I hid a Brownie camera in a bag of fruit we were taking for the boys. Miss Eggington said to the guards that she thought that we could have a more relaxed visit if the guards were not present. They agreed and reluctantly left the room. The moment they were gone I pulled out my camera and began to snap pictures of them. A surprised Miss Eggington, after the initial shock of seeing me with the camera taking pictures, suggested that she put the roll of film in her pocket so that we could possibly get it out safely should the camera be discovered later. Fortunately, we were able to get the camera and the pictures out without being discovered.

A few weeks after our return to Monroe and Miss Eggington's return to England, the *London News Chronicle* ran a front-page story on the "Kissing Case," including the interview with the boys in the reformatory interspersed with the pictures I had taken of them.

After this story appeared, a groundswell of protest committees were formed in other countries, and criticism of the system of justice, which allowed this travesty, was widespread and vocal, so much so that the Voice of America began to discuss the "Kissing Case" in some of its broadcasts. But even the best propagandists of the State Department and its information services could not think of logical excuses for the jailing of eight- and nine-year-old children.

The news spread across Europe. A protest petition, bearing 10,000 signatures from elementary school children in Holland, was sent to Mrs. Eleanor Roosevelt at the United Nations. Only then did the US media start to express concern about the "Kissing Case." Some insensitive US papers raised the Communist specter. They accused the student petition sent to Mrs. Roosevelt as being Communist propaganda until a European paper identified the source as being orphans in a Catholic school.

Now that the "Kissing Case" was becoming a cause célèbre, with interest being generated both far and near, the national office of the NAACP became intensely interested. The national leadership informed me that they were coming into the case and that we should dismiss Conrad Lynn. I explained that the national office did not understand our local sense of loyalty and that Conrad had come to our rescue when our backs were against the wall. Our branch could never be counted on to be so ungrateful as to stab him in the back. We held out for Conrad. Because of the worldwide publicity, the NAACP wanted the case so bad in order to save face that the organization offered to pay Conrad Lynn and keep him on as cocounsel. It was also suggested that if I shifted the case up to the NAACP, there was a possibility that I could be offered the job of the soon-to-be-retiring field representative. My answer was to stay put and finish the work that I had started. Gloster B. Current, then NAACP director of branches, told me that I was unwittingly getting tied up with "Reds." He stated that many years previously, Lynn had been expelled from the United States Communist Party and that George Weissman was a character of the Socialist Workers Party. My response was that I didn't give a damn if they were from hell. They had come in a time of need when our situation was desperate, and we were not playing political games—our survival was on the line.

After recognizing the futility of trying to get us to dump Attorney Lynn, the NAACP accepted Conrad, and together they got a state-level hearing. This initial progress was due to the mounting widespread political pressure exerted on the state of North Carolina. The hearing was set in the adjacent county of Anson. The NAACP sent a battery of lawyers. Malcolm Seawell, the North Carolina attorney general, came personally to argue for the state. There were two rows of newsmen who came from newspapers as far away as Europe to cover a juvenile case of a childhood kiss. Judging by all the fanfare, anyone who unwittingly happened upon the scene might have thought that some vicious serial killer was facing the bar.

The Anson County courtroom was overrun with lawyers and newsmen. Local authorities lost the ability to enforce their traditional regimen of racial segregation. North Carolina was truly under the world spotlight. With so much media present, the bigots wore their best faces of deception. They were on their best conduct and out to convince the world that theirs was a just civilization based on Christian precepts that required separation of the races because God had created them differently. They had often advanced the theory that if God had meant the races to commingle, he would have made them the same color and given them the same intelligence.

When the court commenced, North Carolina attorney general Seawell sprang a surprise. He bellowed out, "I want Robert Williams to take the stand." A momentary ruffle of disapproving "ahs" and murmurs revealed astonishment. I was sitting next to Attorney Frank Reeves of the Washington bureau of the NAACP. He nudged me in the side and told me that I did not have to take the stand. It was more than obvious that the attorney general had an agenda that encompassed much more than a simple hearing bearing on the legal ramification of the incarceration of the little boys. The battery of NAACP lawyers agreed with Reeves that I was not a party to the case and had no right to be called. I was certain that they thought I would not be able to cope with the obvious intended grilling by Seawell. I stood up and informed them that if Seawell wanted me on the stand, it was OK with me.

The attorney general seemed thrilled that he had me in what was to be the hot seat. He confronted me with a cold stare like a prizefighter ready to demolish an inferior foe. His first question was, "Where were you the night before Christmas?"

Instantly, I ascertained where he was leading, and I responded, "I was up in free New York!"

"What were you doing in New York?" he asked, somewhat flustered red.

"I was up in New York trying to bring some justice to this social jungle called Dixie," I said with vigor.

Ted Poston of the *New York Post* and Conrad Lynn gave out loud, defiant laughs. Seawell tried to continue with a straight face.

"Do you know Carl Braden of Louisville, the Communist who burned his house down to collect insurance?[2] Isn't he one of your supporters in this case, and don't you both belong to the Communist Committee to Combat Racial Injustice?"

He asked a series of questions in rapid succession. I knew he was attempting to smear my activity before the world press. This was his tactic to demonstrate

2. Carl Braden (1914–75) was a white radical labor organizer who engaged in solidarity with the African American freedom struggle. Braden was imprisoned in 1961 for nine months for refusing to answer questions posed to him by the House Un-American Activities Committee, established by the US House of Representatives to investigate "subversive" political activity, particularly Communism, during the Cold War.

that the "Communists" had mounted a conspiracy to slander North Carolina. Evidently, he felt if he could reveal a connection, he would be able to whitewash the evil shame of the state and justify the treatment of James and Fuzzy by using the psychological, mystic, everything-is-fair game in dealing with "Communist conspirators." "Communist," from his point of view, was a magic word that could be relied on to turn logic and truth upside down.

"Yes, I know Carl Braden. He was a good man who had his home burned down by bigots and was framed like Dr. Albert E. Perry!" I responded, taking the wind out of his sails. Seawell was devastated. His planned ambush had failed. With a red face, he dismissed me in an atmosphere of courtroom laughter.

Two weeks after the farce of a court hearing and the folly of North Carolina laid bare before the world, the NAACP was informed that the boys could be released to better housing in another city.[3] The NAACP secured an apartment in Charlotte, twenty-five miles from Monroe. The boys' mothers were given new furniture and better housing. The boys were taken to Charlotte, well-scrubbed and with all new clothing. The press greeted them with a photographic occasion. The state of North Carolina, in conjunction with the NAACP, made a pitch to stage a show of humanity. Both of them, in collusion with the local press, quietly kept the red-baiting rumors humming, even inferring that I had received large sums of money as a result of my involvement with the case. They also told these lies to the mothers of the children in an attempt to alienate them from me.

3. Simpson and Thompson were pardoned by North Carolina governor Luther Hodges, who also refused to apologize for their incarceration.

CHAPTER 30

VIOLENT ATTACKS ON BLACK WOMEN THAT DEMANDED A RESPONSE

In 1959, Mrs. Georgia Mae White, an Afro-American mother of five who worked in a Monroe hotel as a maid, was kicked down a flight of stairs into the hotel lobby by a white guest named Brodas Shaw. This railroad trainman claimed he kicked Mrs. White down the stairs because she had been making too much noise while working in the corridor and had disturbed his sleep.

When we asked for an indictment, the chief of police, A. A. Mauney, flatly refused our request. Finally, when we threatened to take legal action by bringing NAACP lawyers in, he relented and placed the man under a seventy-five-dollar bond. When this violent bigot failed to appear in court for his trial, the case was dismissed.

That same day there was another Afro-American woman in court, Mrs. Mary Ruth Reed. Mrs. Reed was eight months pregnant. She was the victim of an attempted rape by a white man, Lewis Medlin. He had come to her home, drove her out of her house, and beat her because she refused to submit to his advances. He caught her while she was trying to escape down a dusty country road, knocked her down, and crawled on top of her. Her seven-year-old son armed himself with a fallen tree limb and came to the aid of his screaming mother by hitting her assailant over the head. She escaped and ran to a neighbor's house. Her neighbor, a white woman, gave her aid and called the police.

The white neighbor accompanied Mrs. Reed to court to testify on her behalf. In the days preceding the court session, Mrs. Reed's relatives wanted to take vengeance on Lewis Medlin. I dissuaded them. The men in our rifle club wanted to go shoot up the house of the violent, would-be rapist. I disagreed. They pleaded with me to allow them to drive out and throw dynamite on his porch. Some of them begged me with tears in their eyes to let them spray his house with machine-gun fire. I dissuaded all of them and consoled them with the information that a woman Jewish lawyer from New York, a friend of Conrad Lynn, had volunteered to come down and prosecute the assaulter in court.

The courtroom overflowed with Afro-American women. They had come to see justice done. They were silently showing their support for Mary Ruth Reed, her white neighbor, and the white woman lawyer from New York. Everyone was aware of the fact that it required a lot of nerve for Mary's white neighbor to appear there on her behalf. She testified that she had seen the defendant chasing Mrs. Reed and that Mrs. Reed had come to her house in an excited, hysterical state, without shoes and with her clothes torn from her.

During the trial, Lewis Medlin's attorney arranged for the defendant's wife to sit by his side, as if she were also involved in the case. The only defense his attorney presented on Medlin's behalf consisted of denigrating statements against Mrs. Reed. He appealed to the judge's racism by dramatically stating, "Judge, Your Honor, you see this man with his wife at his side. This white woman, this pure flower of life. Judge, Your Honor, the white woman is God's greatest gift to man. Do you think that this white man would leave God's lovely creature for that!" And he pointed at Mrs. Reed with contempt and disdain.

Angry groans permeated the courtroom. The judge struck his gavel and frowned impatiently as he announced, "Case dismissed."

The white woman lawyer from New York had only been able to introduce herself to the court and to proclaim that she was Mrs. Reed's attorney. All of the pent-up emotions that had dogged the Black women throughout their lives seemed to surface in their violent outcries. Pandemonium reigned, and violence was on the verge of being released.

The court officials had to speedily dispatch Lewis Medlin through the judge's chamber and out of harm's way. A wrath I had never known before or faced on the part of those I had led was now directed at me. I was reminded of the fact that I had trusted in the white folks' law, that I had kept Lewis Medlin from being punished, that I had opened the floodgates on them, and that the court had given white men a license to do to them whatever they wanted to with impunity. "Now what are you going to say!" one shouted.

CHAPTER 31

"WE WILL MEET VIOLENCE WITH VIOLENCE"

There was a reporter there from the Associated Press, and he turned to me with pad and pencil in hand, anxious to hear and record my response.

My response was, "In a civilized society, the law is a deterrent against the strong who would take advantage of the weak, but the South is a social jungle, and it has become necessary for us to revert to the law of the jungle! From this day forward, we must become our own judge, jury, and executioners. We must create our own deterrent, and from this day forward we will meet violence with violence."

The AP reporter rushed out of the courthouse. The white woman lawyer went across the street to the Bluebird Ice Cream Parlor, hoping to be served a sandwich. The manager of the Bluebird asked her to leave and to "go back with the niggers" because they served only white people there. Her spirit was broken by the intensity of the traumatic experience. She flew back to New York, and we never heard from her again.

That night, I was awakened at midnight by a call from the Greensboro, North Carolina, bureau of the Associated Press. The reporter apologized for calling me at that late hour, but he wanted to check with me before filing his story. He reminded me that I had made an angry statement at the Union County Courthouse about 5:00 p.m., and he wanted to give me time to cool off. He read the statement back to me and asked if I wanted to retract it. I told him that what

I had said earlier I would say again that midnight, and if he called me six years from then I would say the same thing. He said, "OK. That was a rather violent and provocative statement, and I wanted to be sure that you meant it."

The following morning was like I had set the entire world ablaze. The southern radio stations were blaring all day.

The television joined the clamor, and it seemed that I was being misquoted from every quarter. The meaning of my statement was being distorted in an extreme way to turn the wrath of all white America against me. Some bigoted southern press and radio stations trumpeted in shrill tones that "extremist Negro leader advocates murder of white people." Some even stretched the point to the extent that I had advocated the "killing of white babies in their cradles."

The telephone was ringing so intensely that it seemed that it was going to jump off the table. All kinds of people wanted to interview me, hoping that they could goad me into making irrational statements. It was customary for southerners to label Black people who dared to defend themselves against whites as "crazy niggers." They hoped I would speak in a manner that would add validity to their racist mindset.

CHAPTER 32

DISAPPOINTING RIFT WITH THE NATIONAL NAACP

Roy Wilkins, the executive secretary of the NAACP, called. His was the voice of an angry and pressured man. He wanted me to come to New York, go on national television, and apologize to the white people of America. He explained that many white people contributed to the NAACP and were very much disturbed by my violent statement. I told him that I did not speak for the NAACP, but for Robert Williams as a man. He retorted, "You are a branch president, and we are bound too close for your statement not to affect us. We are a nonviolent organization, and as a branch president, your violent statement will be attributed to the whole organization. We are too close to be separated in a situation like this."

I responded by asking, "If we are so close, why didn't the organization come to my aid when Nationwide Insurance Company canceled my coverage on the grounds that I was too much of a risk to hold an insurance policy with it?"

Roy said that he would give me time to think about the apology and that he would get back to me later in the day. As promised, he did call back later. My answer was the same. His tone of voice gave evidence that he was highly peeved and impatient with my attitude. He informed me that the national office had decided to suspend me as branch president and that the action would be verified in writing by telegram. Immediately after our conversation, however, the news media networks announced that I had been suspended for advocating violence. Members of our local branch were furious. The prevailing attitude was that New

York had done nothing that voluntarily demonstrated support for our branch. In fact, it was stated that Wilkins had labeled me a dictator because of the way the branch was run. Some months earlier, during the state convention, a group of the old guard with the support of the state president, Kelly Alexander, met with the principal speaker, Thurgood Marshall, and attempted to solicit his support in removing me from office on the grounds that I was provoking race war.[1] During Thurgood's speech, he stated that he would rather see militant leadership make honest mistakes than to see them do nothing. He took the wind out of their sails and left them frustrated because he not only had refused to side with them but before the entire conference had given some credence to our militancy.

Meanwhile, on the local front, I convinced the chapter that we should not renounce our charter, as some members were suggesting. They insisted that they would remain affiliated with the NAACP only if my wife would agree to accept the office of chairperson. The state field representative, Charles McClain, paid us a visit and, feeling the futility of trying to get us to adhere to New York's line, contacted the national office. He then informed us that my suspension was not permanent but merely for a term of six months. It was now OK for my wife to act as chair until the end of my suspension.

The next day, in an interview with the *Carolina Times*, I again pointed to the lack of protection from the courts. I said, "These court decisions open the way to violence. I do not mean that Negroes should go out and attempt to get revenge for mistreatment or injustices . . ."

I made this statement again on the same day, over a Cincinnati radio station, and later that evening in a telecast interview in Charlotte. I again made it clear that I spoke of self-defense when the courts failed to protect us.

The right of self-defense seemed such an elementary human right and so natural and obvious to me that I could not understand the intense fallout and the great notoriety it engendered across a nation so violent as the United States. Every schoolchild knows that violence gave birth to America.

Two years previously, when we had exchanged gunfire with the KKK in self-defense, not a single white newspaper in America reported the incident. We were merely serving notice that violent racists, who dared attack us, could no longer expect to escape with impunity. The announced belief in such a simple

1. Thurgood Marshall served as an informant to the FBI about radical forces within the NAACP. Marshall encouraged the FBI to investigate Robert Williams "because he will seek to arouse the people in the North Carolina area to take action which could become violent and cause racial tension and unrest." Thurgood Marshall FBI file quoted in Timothy Tyson, *Radio Free Dixie: Robert F. Williams and the Roots of Black Power* (Chapel Hill: University of North Carolina Press, 1999), 155.

principle had sent shock waves across the nation. The aspect that I had not considered was that establishing a principle born out of our experience, which could and would set an example to others, was greatly feared by the power structure. It also shook up the NAACP and set off a debate that forced the organization to make an official renunciation of the right of Afro-Americans to self-defense against racist violence.

Attorney Conrad Lynn, who acted as our legal representative pro bono, researched the NAACP's constitution and discovered that there was no provision in it to justify the national office's fearful action. Subsequently, I requested a hearing before the national board of directors. On June 3, 1959, I appeared for a hearing before them in New York City. The hearing turned out to be a trial with me being the defendant.

I was disgusted to learn, for the first time, that Wilkins and other obsequious Negroes were being bent by the white influence personified by white men who sat there silently but wielded total power by eye contact and facial expressions. This even included the chairperson of the National Council of Negro Women, a Negro woman, scolding me for the statement I had made relative to my anger spawned by a rape attempt on a pregnant Black mother who had been ridiculed in a racist kangaroo court.

I had really expected the Black woman board member to be sympathetic toward a Black man dedicated to the defense of Afro-American women and children. I was wrong. I was in a hostile environment and was made to feel that I was a thug who had committed some repulsive criminal act. I returned home crushed with only the consolation that the branch was still intact and my wife had been confirmed as president. The national office had proclaimed to the world that as far as the organization was concerned, I was a pariah. I felt the whole affair with the national office was tantamount to proclaiming to the southern bigots that I was "free meat."

I did not think of doing anything more immediately about the suspension. There was a more important matter at hand. As a result of the trial, I was more convinced than ever that one of our greatest and most immediate needs was better communication within the race. The real Afro-American struggle was merely a disjointed network of pockets of resistance, and the shameful thing about it was that Blacks were relying on the white man's shallow and most times slanted reports as their only information about these isolated occurrences. I went home and concentrated feverish efforts toward developing a newsletter. The newsletter would be our voice in broadcasting to the entire world the Afro-American bitter ordeal of pain, suffering, dehumanization, and struggle in the so-called free world.

CHAPTER 33

THE BIRTH OF *THE CRUSADER* NEWSLETTER

After much hard, late-night work on the part of dedicated volunteers and many fundraising fish fries, parties, and contributions, the funds were raised to start our new project. The first crude issue of *The Crusader* came off the newly purchased mimeograph machine on June 26, 1959. It caught on like a firestorm. Not only did it cover Monroe, but it also spread across the nation and drew readership and support from at home and abroad.

Letters and telegrams urging me to take my NAACP suspension case to the national membership started arriving from all over the country. Subsequently, I decided to appeal the national board's decision to the Fiftieth Anniversary National Convention, scheduled for New York in July. In order to combat the emerging sympathy toward me, the national office found it expedient to issue a special convention pamphlet attacking me. The pamphlet attempted to intentionally confuse my statement that Afro-Americans should meet violence with violence as a means of self-defense with the advocacy of lynch law. Through carefully contrived inference, the national office contributed to the erroneous impression played up by the racist press—that I was agitating for race war and the indiscriminate slaughter of white people. My suspension was upheld by the convention delegates, many of whom either felt or were pressured into seeing that the vote was a question of publicly supporting or disavowing the NAACP national leadership. But on the real issue at hand, delegate sentiment forced the national leadership to support the concept of self-defense. The preamble to the resolutions passed by that convention, though not widely known, read, "We do not deny but reaffirm the right of an individual and collective self-defense against unlawful assaults."[1]

We were the stepchildren of the NAACP because of our militancy. We refused to allow the national office to tone us down. We had become a part of the civil rights movement because we wanted to end the brutal dehumanization of our people. We were convinced that to challenge such a brutally savage system would instigate violence more widespread and vicious than we had been subjected to prior to our new spirit of resistance. We, in the South, had personally felt the blows of a most inhuman racist tyranny. We could see no special dignity or human value in granting our oppressors impunity in maiming and murdering our people. Many timid Afro-Americans denigrated our self-defense stance as foolhardy and suicidal. There was an ever-present chorus of frightened Blacks across the country that constantly reminded us that to meet violence with violence would place the entire race in jeopardy. We, on the other hand, felt that Black Americans were being victimized and killed anyway. This had been our historical plight in bigoted America. We felt that our human dignity required us to fight back. Many Black men concealed their unmanly timidity in a newly adorned cloak of pacifism. They had instantly developed split personalities. Black men who never hesitated to use violence against other Black men, and even against their women and children, suddenly started to preach of the glorious virtue and power of nonviolence and love. Many Blacks wanted to absorb the injury of unmitigated violence until such time that brutal bigots tired of flailing us. We vehemently disagreed and set out on our own course.

The national office of the NAACP was determined to stay within the good graces of the numerous influential, wealthy white northern supporters and contributors who were disturbed by our militancy. It maintained a hostile attitude toward our branch. We had a charter, and that was all.

1. The preamble appeared in Gloster Current, "Fiftieth Annual Convention: A Jubilee for Civil Rights," *The Crisis*, August–September 1959, 408–9.

CHAPTER 34

INTENSIFIED LOCAL STRUGGLE

BID FOR LOCAL SCHOOL INTEGRATION

Since we had been wounded by New York's public repudiation, I knew that local bigots expected us to restrict our activity. They felt us to be in an untenable position, but they were wrong. We were more determined than ever to intensify our struggle for civil rights as we saw the need locally. I had learned from the Marine Corps that the best defense was an offense and that one of the greatest weapons in combat is the element of surprise. Our two sons, Robert and John, volunteered to become the subjects in a move for school integration.

When Mabel and I went before the school board to personally plead our case, there sat the superintendent, W. R. Kirkman, who had held that seat for as long as I could remember. It riled me no end just seeing him there. As I waited for my opportunity to address the body, I remembered how Kirkman had for many years terrified our "Negro" school with his tyrannical tirades against the Black teachers and how they transferred their fear to their young students. When granted the opportunity to speak, I reminded him of how he had approached our classrooms with his hat on and roared like a vicious lion. That night, I spoke to him the way he had spoken to our teachers. He was greatly humiliated to have a Black man address him that way in an official meeting. He seemed greatly shocked and disbelieving to be made to realize the very negative lifelong impression he had left on the minds and souls of those he had held in such contempt. The school board stalled and pigeonholed our request, but the confrontation was worth the trouble. They had gotten the news that change was an idea whose time had come.

In order to keep the local bigoted power structure off guard, I kept the pressure on them. In 1959, I mounted a political campaign for mayor of the town. In those days, it was unimaginable that an Afro-American militant would dare run for mayor of a southern town. A Reverend Chavis volunteered to serve as my campaign manager. We asserted the equal time clause and forced the local radio station to grant me time to speak.[1] My run for the town's mayor lifted the sagging spirit of the Afro-American community. We knew that the bigoted vote counters would cheat, but the object was to run and to have a platform. The local press expressed surprise that I received any votes at all, lamenting that some votes even came from all-white precincts. These votes were labeled protests against the administration. My votes were acknowledged to have been as much as 10 percent; however, it was whispered that there were many more than that.

1. The equal time clause was a federal regulation, established with the Radio Act of 1927, that required radio stations (and, later, other broadcast media) to provide competing candidates for public office the same amount of airtime, on the same terms.

CHAPTER 35

ESCALATION OF KLAN ACTIVITY AND ECONOMIC PRESSURE

The Klan started to raise its ugly hood again. It didn't dare invade our community again. Meetings were being advertised in the media that it was holding giant rallies in rural communities in the county. Isolated Blacks were still being harassed and occasionally attacked. Posters were put up everywhere that a great Klan rally was being planned for Marshville, twelve miles from Monroe, and that the Grand Dragon, a preacher called "Cat Fish" Cole, was going to speak. Five of our rifle club members armed ourselves with .30-caliber rifles and went to the meeting. We stood at the rear of the mammoth crowd. It was nearly dark where we stood. A truck was parked in an empty field along Highway 74. When we arrived, Cat Fish Cole was viciously lambasting "niggers, Jews, and Catholics." He was working the crowd up to a passion of white heat. He said, "Ava Gardner, a white girl who went to school right here in North Carolina, who attended your Sunday schools, has just left her third white husband for a one-eyed 'nigger'!" He was referring to Sammy Davis Jr. "I say, ladies and gentlemen, that we have got to move now if we want to save our white race and our God-given country!"

The crowd roared its approval. One of the security guards approached the makeshift platform, spoke to Cole, and pointed toward the darkened rear where we stood with our rifles. Cat Fish said, "They tell me that some niggers are out here. But I tell you there ain't a nigger within ten miles of here. They are at home hiding under the bed and shaking like they got the double pneumonia."

Again, the crowd up front roared with laughter and applause while those near us looked back and inched closer toward the speaker. Another hooded vigilante came back and stared at us. We did not cow, so he moved back and reported to Cat Fish.

Cat Fish again interrupted his tirade to announce over the PA system, "I understand some niggers are here. Well, that's all right; it's always good to have a few 'burr heads' around—they bring us luck!" At that the crowd snickered but made no move toward us. We had again seized the initiative and had successfully applied the element of surprise in our struggle.

A few nights later, an Afro-American trucker who was passing through town sought us out at midnight. He explained that he had read about our troubles with the Klan. He refused to state his name and said that in the future he would deny ever having seen us and that he wanted us to do likewise. He said that he had brought us a gift, compliments of the Teamsters Union. The box he gave us was a full case of dynamite.

Volunteers were beginning to show up from many unexpected places. Two white students from Davidson College came offering their services. Two soldiers—one Black, one white—came from Fort Jackson, South Carolina, offering to get us any kind of weapons we needed to fight off the Klan.

Another Klan rally was publicly announced to take place behind the Mineral Springs School, which was located six miles from Monroe. Klansmen claimed to be getting strong enough to wipe us out. We wanted to let them know that we were also preparing for defense, so a detail from our Guard volunteered to go and set off a big explosion along the road near the huge rally site.[1] It so happened that we had had a heavy rainfall the day before the event. The dynamite was dropped in a stream of water and did not explode. It had to be retrieved just before daybreak the day after the rally to avoid the danger of being discovered and traced to us.

A series of fires started to plague the town almost nightly. Sometimes the night seemed to be aglow with fires. My telephone started to ring incessantly. An unidentified white man would call after each fire alarm. His accusatory conversations would go, "Nigger, goddamn your Black soul. If we don't get rid of you soon, you going to burn this goddamn town down!"

I told him that he was a witness that I was at home, and it was a known fact that I could not be in two places at the same time. His response: "Well, goddamn it, if you ain't doing it, you're hiring it done!"

1. The Guard was the name of the paramilitary defense force of the Monroe movement. Robert Carl Cohen, *Black Crusader: A Biography of Robert Franklin Williams* (Secaucus, NJ: Lyle Stuart, 1972), 97–99.

Again, I reminded him that the whole power structure had unleashed economic pressure against me to the extent that I was hardly able to survive, and how in hell did he think I would be financially able to pay someone to burn the town down. In a rage, he would slam down the phone.

Telephone threats against my family and me started around the clock. We could not sleep through the night. We dared not take the phone off the hook, because the telephone was our lifeline of communication for our defense. Occasionally, we could hear distant gunfire in the night. These terror tactics were meant to strike fear in our hearts. The robed terrorists had to remain in the distance, using fire-and-run tactics. They did not confront us personally, but the telephoned threats intensified. The harassment was taking its toll. We got our heads together and tried to ascertain where calls might possibly originate from on a twenty-four-hour basis. We reasoned that they most likely were coming from someplace that operated around the clock. We considered the police and fire stations. If the calls were coming from there, we had no way to prove it.

It so happened that one night a Black man whom the racists trusted as a "good Negro" had gone to an all-night service station where many white men congregated late at night. As he manipulated the cigarette vending machine, he overheard one of the men making threats on the telephone while the others looked on and laughed. He immediately came to inform us as to what he had observed. Six of us got our weapons and descended on the nest of bigots. They were stunned and sat frozen and speechless as we burst into the service station. I announced to them that I was Robert Williams, that they had been making threatening calls to my house around the clock, and that if another such call should be made to my home, we would return and shoot that place all to pieces. After that confrontation, the calls ceased. It was quite a relief to be able to sleep again.

I was a member of the local Unitarian Fellowship. We had complete integration in the fellowship before the courts had mandated integration in the South. The founder of the fellowship, J. Ray Shute, who was also a businessman-developer, had attracted a textile mill from Boston, Massachusetts, to locate in Monroe. He interceded on my behalf and convinced the owner to hire and train me. The industrialist boasted that he was going to make me the first Black steam boiler engineer in the entire South. I was elated that at last I was going to have the opportunity to explore an income-producing opportunity that would help me gain some economic stability.

When the mayor of Badin, North Carolina, the town where the plant had located, came to inspect the new plant, he recognized me from photographs that had appeared in the press. That was the end of my promised career. (I learned from my FOIA files that the FBI was involved.)

The Nationwide Insurance Company agent J. L. Rabin had canceled my car insurance on grounds that I was too much of an insurance risk. Many of the local laborers, some of whom earned as little as forty dollars a week, gave me two dollars of their pay to keep me afloat economically. The local Klan-infested power structure had hoped to do economically what it had failed to do violently. Local Black farmers brought us food, and the community gave what they could in order that I could manage to stay there as their leader. When local whites failed to starve me out, they spread the rumor that I was being supported by Communists. They could never accept the fact that Blacks could ever demonstrate unity to that extent.

CHAPTER 36

CONNECTING WITH CUBA LIBRE AND RED-BAITING IN THE NAACP

In the summer of 1960, I was extended an invitation to become a founding member of the Fair Play for Cuba Committee.[1] I joined, and in late summer I was invited, along with a group of eighteen other Black people, to visit Cuba on the occasion of the first anniversary of the revolution.[2] I was the only southerner and local leader in the group. The others were writers and artists. Because I was from the South of the United States, Fidel Castro took a special interest in me. At the end of our tour, Fidel suggested that I remain in Cuba. He said

1. The Fair Play for Cuba Committee was founded by CBS newsman Robert Taber in 1960 in solidarity with the Cuban Revolution, defending Cuba from US intervention. The national organization went out of existence in the United States in 1963 due to repression sparked from the association of one of its members, Lee Harvey Oswald, believed to be the assassin of President John F. Kennedy. Louis Cassels, "Fair Play for Cuba Committee Activated," *Lodi (CA) News-Sentinel*, June 17, 1961, 11; Keith Gilyard, *John Oliver Killens: A Life of Black Literary Activism* (Athens: University of Georgia Press, 2010), 151–52; "Pro-Castro Organization Now Defunct," *Sarasota (FL) Herald-Tribune*, December 29, 1963, 20.

2. Fidel Castro had seized power on January 1, 1959. Some of the other Black activists and intellectuals on this historic trip to Cuba in 1960 included historian John Henrik Clarke, author and political organizer Leroi Jones (aka Amiri Baraka), novelist John Oliver Killens, political theorist Harold Cruse, and writer and actor Julian Mayfield. Komozi Woodard, *A Nation within a Nation: Amiri Baraka (Leroi Jones) and Black Power Politics* (Chapel Hill: University of North Carolina Press, 2005), 52–53; Gilyard, *John Oliver Killens*, 151–52.

the Cuban people liked me. I explained to him that I wanted to remain in the South; however, I could foresee the possibility of my having to leave the South eventually.

A few months later, I was back in Cuba, along with Richard Gibson and Bob Taber, to cement relations relative to the Fair Play for Cuba Committee. While there, I received a telephone call from my wife that the Klan had threatened to blow up the house and kill my family. This threat was a source of great concern to me because I was not there to defend them. I knew the Guard would go to any extent to defend them, but I had observed that the local people were much more effective and daring when I was on the scene to lead them. I decided to up the ante. I felt the need to escalate the situation to a point wherein the US government would have some special incentive to protect my family. I made a call home and discovered that the local police chief had made a joke of my wife's complaint. Accompanied by a Cuban newsman, I went to the US embassy and asked to speak with the US ambassador, Phillip Bonsul. Subsequent to the fact that I was told that the ambassador was busy and therefore unable to see me, I asked the receptionist to relay a message to him. I asked the receptionist to please inform him that my visit was urgent and that it could possibly involve a life-and-death situation for him. An instantly invigorated receptionist turned red in the face, displayed nervousness, and told me to wait. She hurried to a nearby office and came back and escorted me into the ambassador's office.

He offered me a seat, but I continued standing. I told him that I was an American visiting Cuba and that back in Monroe, North Carolina, the Ku Klux Klan had threatened to blow up my home and kill my family. He asked me when this had happened and how I had received the information. I informed him that my wife had called me by telephone and that she had taken the threat seriously. He didn't seem to give too much credence to my story until I told him that if anything should happen to my family, I would kill Americans in Havana and he would be the first one to go. His interest perked up immediately. He started asking questions, wrote down my name and the city, and promised that he would contact the US State Department immediately. He assured me that I could rely on my family being protected. He counseled me that there was no need to even think of such extreme measures. Later that night, when I called home, my wife told me that a police car was patrolling the street on which I lived. For the first time, the police displayed a protective presence.

On my first trip to Cuba, I had been given a Cuban national flag, which I flew in my backyard under the US flag. When I returned home from my second sojourn, the Cuban flag had disappeared. I learned from an eyewitness that a local young Black paratrooper had torn it down and taken it away. One night while I was talking to one of the town's tough guys, a few blocks from my home, the Black paratrooper appeared, and the tough, named Holly Shannon, struck him, knocked him down, and held him down with a knife to his throat. I pleaded with Holly not to cut his throat and to let him up. Holly said the paratrooper knew judo and if he let him up he could be hurt. I was really terrified that the paratrooper was going to be killed. To save the paratrooper's life, I pulled my pistol and promised Holly that if he let him up and the paratrooper jumped him, I would shoot the soldier. The trooper seemed greatly relieved to have survived the ordeal. Two days later the paratrooper came to my door and gave me a repaired, cleaned, starched, ironed, and neatly folded Cuban flag. He said that he was sorry for what he had done and wanted to apologize. He said he knew what he had done was wrong but that he had done it while drinking and prompted by a dare.

Relative to the series of initiatives we had taken, local bigots were inflamed to the kindling point. The only thing that kept them from waging all-out war was the realization of the terrible injury we were equipped and ready to inflict on them. Beginning late in 1959, I had begun to run articles about Cuba in *The Crusader*, extolling the effort on behalf of racial equality there. The articles seemed to have stirred up the national office of the NAACP, for Roy Wilkins sent me a letter, which included statements such as these:

> I wonder, however, whether you are fully aware of the dangers and disadvantages of the course of action you seem to favor. I have followed closely the events in Cuba in recent months and in particular, Dr. Castro's visit to the United Nations this fall. Regardless of the merits of the Cuban cause I was greatly disturbed by the frequent show of insincerity which, I believe, should give you food for thought before you find yourself used as just another pawn in the present unfortunate feud between Cuba and our country.
>
> . . . It is a callous interference in a native American problem and should be recognized as such by anyone in a responsible position of leadership in the American Negro movement.
>
> . . . The present Cuban attempts to endear themselves to American Negroes are obviously caused by ulterior motives. (Let me just ask you how the American Negro tourist would feel in Cuba at the constant chant of "Cuba sí, Yanqui no!")
>
> . . . Are you willing to forsake the important support of that section of the people who are equally opposed to suppression of Negro rights in our country?

. . . Does not the unfortunate example of the great American Negro singer, Paul Robeson, show you the dangers and mistakes of the road which you seem to be choosing? What has Paul Robeson, with all his greatness, done for the American Negro in his present struggle for equality? The answer, regrettable as it is, must be; Nothing.

In my reply to Roy Wilkins and the national office, I wrote:

Only a fool or a mercenary hypocrite could muster the gall to call a nation and its great leader insincere in dealing with the captive blacks of North America when in the course of their daily lives they display the greatest measure of racial equality and social justice in the world today. It is certainly a first magnitude truism that social justice starts at home and spreads abroad. In the past months, I have twice been to Cuba and there is nothing insincere about my being made to feel that I was a member of the human race for the first time in my life. If this is America's idea of insincerity, then heaven help this nation to become insincere like Fidel Castro and "Free Cuba" in granting persons of African descent entrance into the human race.

As for my being "used as a pawn" in the struggle of Cuba against imperialist and racist North America, I prefer to be on the side of right than on the side of Jim Crow and oppression. I prefer to be used as an instrument to convey the truth of a people who respect the rights of man rather than to be used as an Uncle Tom white-washer of black oppression and injustice and an apologist for American hypocrisy. Cuba's aversion for America's inhumanity to man is not an interference in a "native American problem." It is a common knowledge that the master race of the "free world" is out to export North American manufactured racism. Racism in the USA is as much a world problem as was Nazism. If the USA is to be the only nation exempt from the Human Rights Charter of the United Nations, then that august body is a party to the great transgressions against America's captive people. I, for one, refuse to remain silent and cooperate with the very force that is seeking after my destruction.

The racists in America are the most brutal people on earth. It is foolhardy for an oppressed Afro-American to take the attitude that we should keep this life and death struggle a family affair. We are the oppressed. It is only natural for us to air our grievances at home and abroad. This race fight in the USA is no more a fight to be fought just by Americans than is the fight for black liberation to be conducted by colored only. Any struggle for freedom in the world today affects the stability of the whole society of man. Why would you make our struggle an exception?

I am not afraid of alienating white friends of our liberation movement. If they really believe in freedom, they will not resent deviation from the old worn path that has led us in fruitless circles. If they are insincere, they are no more than Trojan horses infiltrating our ranks to strike us a treacherous, nefarious blow on behalf of those and that which they pretend to detest. For if they resent our becoming truly liberated, they will detest us for not following their misguiding and skillful subterfuge designed to prevent our arrival to the promised land. They speak much of tolerance, yet they display unlimited intolerance toward those Afro-Americans who refuse to become their puppets and yes men Uncle Toms.

It is strange that I am asked how a "Negro" American tourist would feel in Cuba hearing the constant chant of "Cuba sí, Yanqui no!" No one has bothered to ask how it feels to constantly face "White Only" signs. These signs mean white yes, colored no! No one has asked me how it feels to be marched under guard with felons along a public street to jail for sitting on a "white only" stool. On hearing "Cuba sí, Yanqui no!" and having lived all of my life under American oppression, I was emotionally moved to join the liberation chorus. I knew it didn't apply to me because the white "Christians of the free world" have excluded me from everything "Yanqui."

You make a cardinal mistake when you fail to give the great Paul Robeson credit for making a great contribution to the American "Negro Struggle." Paul Robeson is living proof that the Afro-American need not look upon the United States as "Nigger Heaven" and the last stop for us on this earth. Paul is living proof that other civilized societies honor and respect Black people for the things that "free" America curses, oppresses and starves us for. Paul has proven that all Black men are not for sale for thirty pieces of silver. He has lit a candle that many of the new generation will follow.

Yes, wherever there is oppression in the world today, it is the concern of the entire human race. My cause is the same as the Asians against the imperialist. It is the same as Cuba against the white supremacist imperialist. When I become part of the mainstream of American life, based on universal justice, then and then only can I see a possible mutual cause for unity against outside interference.

In spite of my highly charged conflict with the national office and its submissive supporters, I never wanted to create the impression that I was against the NAACP; on the contrary, I thought it to be an important weapon in our freedom struggle, and I wanted with all my heart to strengthen it. It was deeply hurtful for me to think of all that had happened to me and especially to our dehumanized race during our long ordeal in the so-called free world of the United States of America and to know that the NAACP, to which I belonged, was more concerned about denigrating and slandering victimized little Cuba than in giving aid to the besieged Black people of Monroe, North Carolina USA.

CHAPTER 37

POOL PROTEST REINITIATED, VIOLENT BACKLASH, AND FIRST ATTEMPT ON MY LIFE

We were now experiencing escalated tension. Racial hatred was no longer submerged and disguised. It was so sharp and pronounced that one could feel it in the air all over the county. By now I was being branded a Communist troublemaker and no doubt had been designated the number-one target for destruction. Threats started arriving through the mail from many parts of the South. It was more than obvious to me that to slide into inactivity at this point would cede the momentum to the racists and sign my own death warrant.

In a move that seemed to represent a cynical, provocative challenge, the swimming pool was reopened on a "for white only" basis. Relative to our complaints, the US Justice Department had informed the media that investigations in the Monroe area had turned up no violations of civil rights. We felt this to be a latent blessing for the bigots who wanted to get rid of militant Blacks. No doubt, as had been customary, relative to southern tradition, they expected us to get out of town, for our organization to fall apart, or to take the stance of a low profile, hoping the whites would allow us to stay alive.

Again, we used the element of surprise. We established another picket line at the pool. This time the bigots had become like wild, raging animals. The local media reflected the shrillness of the voices calling for violence. The crowds that assembled to intimidate and harass us grew bigger and bigger.

In the ugly face of all kinds of threats of violence, the young teenagers who had asked me to lead them there never wavered.

On Friday, June 23, 1961, I left the swimming pool and drove into Monroe to pick up a late picketer. I also checked with my wife, Mabel, and with the secretary of our branch, Mrs. Azalea Johnson, who were standing by to join us at the pool. I explained to them that the situation was getting very near the explosion point at the pool and that they would be at great risk to join us there at that time. After giving in to their insistence to join us, I gave them my pistols to carry in Mrs. Johnson's car for their protection in case of an attack.

I picked up seventeen-year-old Albert Rorie, the tardy high school picketer, and we set out for the pool where other youths were already picketing. Heading east on Highway 74, we had just reached the crest of a long hill when a large black 1955 DeSoto sedan suddenly rammed into my little Hillman, a British subcompact, from the rear. My first thought was the belief that some freak accident had befallen us. I glanced into the rearview mirror, expecting a slowdown as I applied the brakes, but instead of diminishing speed, we were moving faster. I glimpsed a big white man behind the wheel of the DeSoto, guiding it as he pushed us forward. The first impact had been of such force that the front seats of my car had jumped off the tracks. I recognized the driver of the would-be killer car as a local Pontiac dealer, one of the Griffin brothers who owned the dealership.

Every time I applied my brakes, the little Hillman would go into a skid. Fearful of losing control, I stepped on the accelerator in an effort to pull away. The bumpers were stuck together. Increasing his speed, Griffin began swerving back and forth, trying to force us off the highway at a seventy-five-foot drop down onto a rail line. The cars had reached seventy miles an hour in a forty-five-miles-per-hour zone. All of this was taking place right near and in front of a Highway Patrol station. Two state troopers were standing beside the road in the station yard witnessing the event. I started blasting on my horn to attract their attention. They looked, waved, and laughed. I became so enraged that all I can remember saying to Rorie was, "I am going to kill this one! Give me my rifle! I am going to kill this one!"

Rorie struggled and tugged feverishly at the rifle, but it was stuck under the seat. When the seat jumped the track, it had pinned the rifle to the floor of the car. At all times before this day, I had carried a Luger and a .45 in holsters and a gun belt on the seat of the car, but this day I had given the pistols to the women for their protection.

As we approached the busy US 74 and 601 intersection, the Pontiac dealer gunned his motor in another attempt to ram our car into the heavy cross-traffic. I made a final desperate effort to disengage the car bumpers by breaking and accelerating in rapid succession. I was able to create a violent, jerking motion on the Hillman. Just at the last moment, less than thirty yards from the crowded intersection, the bumpers wrenched apart. With a sudden deep turn to the right, I was able to run my car off the road and into a shallow ditch without turning it over.

As soon as I got the Hillman stopped, Roric and I pulled the broken seat off the carbine. I was still repeating, without any thought about anything else, that I was going to kill bigoted Griffin. By the time we were able to free the carbine, he had sped away. If it had been my fate to have my pistols on the seat, or if I had been able to get my rifle, I would have killed the racist for sure.

We continued our return to the swimming pool, and once there, I approached chief of police A. A. Mauney, pointed to the smashed-in rear of my car, and exclaimed, "Do you see this? This was done by Byrum Griffin, who tried to run us off the road and kill us! You saw me drive away and you know that my car was all right when I left here. I have got his license number and I want to take out a warrant for him!"

Standing a few feet from the car, with the back all smashed in and oil running out of the damaged wheels and brake drums, the police chief said, "I don't see anything, Williams; I don't see anything at all. How can I arrest a man when there is nothing wrong with your car?"

Our swimming pool picketing and the local situation surrounding it had become hot enough to attract a reporter from the *Charlotte Observer*. He had overheard the chief, and he stepped forward and volunteered, "I saw your car when you left for town a little while ago; this must have just happened."

Reacting to the statement of the reporter, Chief Mauney exclaimed, "OK Williams, come on down to the station and we'll discuss issuing a warrant."

When I arrived at the station, Chief Mauney was standing behind the counter that separated working policemen from the general public who had business to be conducted there. The judge from the Recorder's Court was occupying a swivel chair near the entrance to the work area. Mauney glanced back at the judge, then looked at me with a contemptuous grin on his sunbaked face. He was short and fat with a noticeable gap in his front teeth. His mannerism and tone of voice betrayed his feigned pretense of fulfilling the duties of an officer of the law. His deportment was typical of the standard rendition of the comic drama always available in the white man's repertoire of cruel jokes played on Black Americans desperately in pursuit of justice. Mauney told me that the man

I had named had sworn that he had been in his office all day and that he hadn't done anything to me. He said, "I can't indict a man just because you got his name and license number from somewhere. You and your witness go to his house. If you recognize him, bring him here and then I will consider issuing a warrant."

I knew the face of Byrum Griffin; I had bought a used car from him. I also knew there was no place in Union County's American justice that required a white person to respect the civil and human rights of a Black man.

"I'm no policeman; you're supposed to be the police. It's your place to round up people like that. I'm not going to his house, but I can tell you one thing—you can tell him that he is one of the luckiest men in the world. The only reason that he is still alive is because my rifle jammed under the seat. Tell him that if he tries anything against me again, one of us is going to die!"

CHAPTER 38

THE SWIMMING POOL INCIDENT

SECOND ATTEMPT ON MY LIFE

Eventually, the bigots grew tired of making cautious, unsuccessful attempts on my life. On Sunday, June 25, 1961, they made their big move. When I left home with three high school students on our way to join others who were already picketing at the swimming pool, I noticed a police car trailing us. As we approached the intersection, there were so many cars in the area that two policemen were directing traffic. Just as we entered the crossroads, an old 1949 Ford, which evidently from its appearance had been used in a car-crashing derby because it was all banged up and all glass had been removed, came backing toward my car at full throttle. Ascertaining that the driver of the old wreck had aimed at the driver's side of my already damaged Hillman, I turned sharply toward him and took the force of the collision with his front fender instead, causing both cars to end up in the ditch.[1] As the dust cleared, the crowd of angry, screaming racists surged forward. The young, violence-prone white man who had driven the Ford came toward my stricken Hillman wielding a baseball bat. His eyes were aflame with hatred, and it was more than obvious that he and his fellow bigots were planning to commit the dastardly ritual of violence and lynching that was typical

1. Williams offers a somewhat clearer explanation of what happened in his book *Negroes with Guns*: the Ford—which he refers to there as a 1955 DeSoto—came at his car from behind, and the force of the collision landed both cars in the ditch.

of their forefathers, venting savage rage against helpless and defenseless Black victims. However, today was not to be just another lynching as usual to inflate the statistics relative to the history of lynching in the "free world."

The would-be bigoted killer, who had missed in his first attempt, approached us waving the baseball bat menacingly. He shouted angrily, "What did you hit my car for, nigger?"

We sat in the car, momentarily stunned. The vast angry white mob started to roar like a stormy sea. They were cursing, screaming, and moving ever closer. I told seventeen-year-old Richard Crowder, who was sitting on the rear seat with sixteen-year-old J. D. Blount, to pass me my carbine. I gave Richard my Luger and handed Jay Van Covington, the other teenager, my army .45 pistol. I instructed the students to watch me and not to shoot unless they saw me shoot, and if I did have to shoot, they should kill as many people as possible before they killed us. Having said this, I exited the car on the driver's side and leaned back against the car. The screams and curses of the crowd grew even more ferocious. The crowd started to throw stones against the car. Someone threw a black snake at the car. I felt an urgent need to ready my carbine. I shifted the bolt to slide a round into the chamber, not knowing that Richard had already injected a round into the chamber as he had passed the rifle to me. As I pulled the bolt back, a long 8mm military cartridge ejected to the ground. Members of the angry mob looked attentively at the long bullet, looked at the rifle, and then looked at me.

I didn't say anything, I suppose my silence was even more demoralizing to them. After a vocal pause, as if by a prearranged signal, the crowd became noisy again. There were angry shouts, "The nigger is at fault! . . . We saw it! . . . The nigger ran into him! . . ." Then they started chanting: "Kill the niggers! . . . Kill the niggers! . . . Burn the niggers! . . . Pour gasoline on the niggers! . . . Burn 'em!"

The two policemen who had been directing traffic not more than feet away had previously seemed indifferent to what was going on. Suddenly, seeing the turn of events, they took note of us. One ran to the passenger side of the car. The other one headed straight for me. He confronted me. In a hostile voice he demanded, "Surrender your weapon! Surrender your weapon!"

He stretched his arms out for the rifle. I pushed the carbine broadside into his chest, forcing him backward, and then aiming it straight into his face I informed him, "This is a lynch mob! We will not surrender to a lynch mob! If you want this gun you can come to my house and get it."

The policeman on the passenger's side started to pull his revolver from the holster. It was obvious that his intent was to shoot me in the back. Before he could complete the cycle, Jay put the army .45 in his face and cocked it.[2] His hand was trembling dangerously as he told the policeman, "Put that goddamn pistol back in your holster or I'll blow your goddamn head off!"

The stunned and frightened officer fumbled as he re-holstered his gun and fell into a ditch as he backed away.

After witnessing this unique incident, an old white man started moaning, evidently full of liquor and deeply hurt from seeing the end to his way of life. He cried like a baby, "Oh my God! Oh my God! What is this goddamn country coming to? The goddamn niggers have got guns and the police can't even arrest them. Oh my God!" Still bawling, he was led away through the crowd.

I am sure that at that very moment, the old man saw his way of life slipping away right before his very eyes. The southern white man had maintained the cruel and savage white supremacy status quo through unmitigated violence, underpinned by the gun. The gun was their last great bulwark, and without its effectiveness, their way of life would collapse forever. It was gone with the wind.

Within moments, Chief Mauney drove up. A city councilman named Steve Presson was with him. Steve Presson was an avid golfer who was considered so cantankerous that none of the caddies I had caddied with in my earlier youth wanted to caddy for him. When I saw his face, which always seemed to carry a frown, I expected our predicament to worsen. Contemplating imminent bloodshed, Steve Presson told Chief Mauney, "Open up this highway and let Williams and his people out of here before somebody gets killed!"

The chief retorted, "But they've got guns!"

Councilman Presson exclaimed, "I don't give a damn what they've got, open up this road and let them out of here before somebody gets killed!"

In response to the councilman, Chief Mauney, with the other two policemen who had previously backed up the screaming mob, cleared a path for us to drive away. My car had been damaged from the impact of the demolition derby car. The crushed fender made an awful grinding noise as I drove away on the half mile to the swimming pool. Above the intense noise of the banged-up car, the mob, made up mostly of poor whites, became highly animated with angry jeers and screams of "There ain't gonna be no integration here! . . . Niggers go back to Africa! . . . We ain't gonna swim with no niggers! . . . Kill the niggers! Pour gasoline on the niggers! . . . Burn the niggers!"

2. "The cycle" refers to well-known schemes regularly used by whites and law enforcement officers to entrap and murder African Americans. These schemes often included shooting the victim in the back.

Arriving at the pool, I discovered that several youths were walking the picket line around the pool in stoic defiance of the angry, threatening mob. Some city and county officials had come on the scene. The Monroe police force and the county sheriff's department had been combined. They had twenty-three uniformed policemen on duty there, and the chief maintained they were unable to keep order. He proclaimed that the crowd was out of control and that there was nothing that he or his men could do.

It was more than obvious that the local power structure had planned a final showdown, and no doubt this was to be the final solution. On both sides of Highway 601, a screaming mob stretched for more than a mile. Someone had mobilized the entire county as it had never been mobilized before. No doubt a modern lynching had been promised, and those who didn't care to participate had come to see the great southern drama staged.

The situation was so explosive that I opted to remain near the car and my guns rather than join in the picketing. The crowd of screaming racists completely blocked Highway 601. They were tightening the ring around us, the car and the picketers. As the circle around us became smaller and smaller, Chief Mauney approached me and demanded, "Surrender your guns!"

I shouted right back, "No! These guns are legal! This is a lynch mob! We will not surrender to a mob! If you want these guns you can come to my house and get them but not here!"

He exclaimed, "Robert, goddamn it, if you hurt any of these white people, I'm going to kill you myself! Surrender your guns! Surrender your guns!" He kept repeating over and over as if he had become crazed with frustration.

The crowd roared with more sanctioned, vicious outcries of "Kill them, kill the niggers! Pour gasoline on the niggers! Burn the niggers!"

Holding my Italian carbine at high port, I told Mauney that if the crowd came any closer he would never get the chance to kill me, because if they kept coming, he was going to be the first one to go.

Councilman Steve Presson approached me again. I had resigned myself to a state of kill and be killed until the only reasonable white man returned, seeking desperately for a peaceful solution. He said, "Robert, I know y'all have a right to picket, but the situation is getting out of hand. If you're willing to call it off for today, I'll see to it that the police escort you and your people back home."

"The police?" I responded. "We might as well be escorted by the Ku Klux Klan! The only way I'll go with the police is if Mauney rides in the car with me, and if anything goes wrong, he will be the first one to go!"

Chief Mauney quickly responded, "No sir, I ain't about to ride with that crazy nigger!"

The raging crowd of hate inched closer. I explained to the chief that if they kept coming and I just got off one shot, the bullet was bound to pass through at least six people in the crowd and the blood of at least that many whites would be on his hands.

With Mauney and me contemptuously eyeballing each other and the crowd growing ever louder and wilder, Steve Presson was visibly worried and asked, "What do you want me to do, Robert?"

I suggested that since the local police would not maintain order, then he should ask the State Highway Patrol to come in. Presson seemed relieved at the suggestion and hurried off to make the call.

I anticipated the state troopers making a grand appearance with sirens wailing and lights glaring from a motorcade with an impressive number of troopers. I was both surprised and puzzled when a single state police car arrived on the scene with only two troopers inside. It was a strange sight to see, this odd couple approaching us. There was a very small man who wore corporal chevrons on his sleeve. His hair was gray, and he looked too old to be a state trooper. I had never before seen such an old person still on duty as a state trooper. A big, husky young man with a long truncheon followed closely behind him. The crusty little old trooper came straight up to me and asked if we were ready to go. The chief of police told him that we were heavily armed. The trooper paid no attention to the chief. After ascertaining that we would leave if the way was cleared and secure, he confronted the angry crowd and told them to open up the highway. The crowd paid no attention to him. He repeated the order. The twenty-three local officers looked on silently. The feisty little corporal informed the would-be lynch mob that they were blocking a state highway and demanded in a loud, clear, decisive voice, "Clear the goddamn road! I mean, move out now."

Many of the racists laughed and cursed in disbelief, no doubt feeling that there was some latent understanding that there would be no police intervention while they attacked the Blacks. The corporal turned to the big trooper with the truncheon and commanded him to open up the highway. The young trooper started swinging his club as he moved deliberately toward the crowd. Convinced that the state police were not a part of any conspiracy, the crowd moved back quickly. They opened up the highway. The state trooper told us to follow close behind his car, and he ordered the chief to drive closely behind us to prevent any problem.

With one police car in front and another in the rear, we started to drive through the mob. Blacks had never before been given such protection, and this particular sight irritated the racists to no end. Not understanding that the entire state maneuver was staged to protect them from us, rather than us from them, the crowd started angrily shouting, "Look how they are supporting those god-damn niggers! Look at the police guarding those Communist coons!" The police cars escorted our car to the front of my house. The little corporal waved and drove off into the distance. He didn't stop and ask for my guns, nor did I ever see him again.

Full of anger after being unable to get their way with us, the agitated racists resorted to the old southern custom of attacking every available and defenseless Black person within range. During the rest of the day, those unfortunate enough to drive past the crossroads had their cars stoned. One Black man was rumored to have been pulled from his car, tied to a tree, and severely beaten. I was never able to confirm this, but such is the hazard of Blacks living in America. Race hatred and violence are always just beneath the surface, and when we travel, we never know when we will run into racial trouble over which we have no control. Innocence is irrelevant when a mob becomes violent and bloodthirsty. Any Black blood will do, and that was the pattern followed that Sunday in Monroe. Scattered gunfire could be heard throughout the day and into the night. It was always in the distance because the bigots dared not invade our community again. They knew that we were willing and quite able to defend our homes and ourselves.

CHAPTER 39

REIGN OF TERROR

A POWDER KEG READY TO BLOW IN MONROE

As the heat of the summer increased, so did the incidents of violence. Blacks suffered some nasty and unprovoked attacks. The ones who were attacked were primarily the defenseless. I am sure if we had not displayed a will to fight, there would have been considerably more tragic incidents. One evening a member of our defense team, Otha Wynn, and his wife visited Hill Top Restaurant seeking food service. They were attacked by a large group of racists. He was caught outside his car because it was necessary for Afro-Americans to go up to the back window of the establishment to obtain service. Otha fought his way back to his car. His wife passed him his pistol off the seat. He shot one of his attackers in the buttocks, and the others scattered like frightened dogs. Evidently the racists were greatly embarrassed by the feat of a lone Black man routing a group of white men. We expected them to press charges, but instead, they sent an emissary to make a request for Wynn to pay the wounded man's hospital bill. Otha flatly refused to pay and told them, "The son of a bitch is lucky he didn't get killed." That incident was kept quiet because such an incident would have damaged the Klan's image.

By midsummer, racist attacks grew in number and intensity. As a result of the stepped-up incidents of terror, I made an urgent appeal for justice in *The Crusader*, which we were now publishing weekly. Our publication was catching on like wildfire. Our mailing list and correspondence had become international, and I was charging that the Monroe city officials, the local agents of the FBI in Charlotte, and the governor of North Carolina were jointly involved in a conspiracy to terrorize Afro-Americans and subjugate them to white supremacy, thus negating our constitutional rights. We had allowed our defense guard to become practically no more than a standby group, but now it had become necessary for us to prepare for combat once again.

As our story became more widely known because of *The Crusader*'s circulation, all kinds of people were offering support—though, because of our militant attitude, we were never in much favor with members of the Communist Party. They thought the philosophy of Rev. Martin Luther King to be the only acceptable way to struggle against US racism. Their theoreticians argued that my method would drive a wedge between white and Black workers. They expressed a belief that Blacks should struggle side by side with white workers for socialism. It was their belief that once the USA became a socialist country, the white workers would liberate their Black fellow workers. They claimed, contrary to what we southern Blacks knew, that socialism would eliminate racism.

Though we had our differences with the Communists, our backs were to the wall, and we sought support from all quarters. Two representatives of the US Communist Party surfaced in Monroe and at one of our greatest times of need brought us a scheme that involved Nikita Khrushchev. They presented us with a wish list that they claimed had already been approved in Moscow. We were told that Mr. K had already been apprised of our plight and was willing to help us. We were informed that if we made a worldwide appeal for humanitarian aid, the USSR could be counted on to respond favorably. We were cautioned not to make a direct appeal to the USSR alone but to the entire world.

We were told to canvass the town and county poor as to their greatest needs. It was indicated to us that the Soviets would have foodstuffs, medicines, clothing, mules, and tractors ready to send to us. We were highly elated at such an offer. This was really an effective way to light a fire under an indifferent, racist government that had refused to respond to our poignant cries to be addressed as human beings. This was planned to be a great masterstroke, initiated on behalf of suffering and dehumanized Afro-Americans. By the time that we had brought a committee together and were preparing a press release, our two Communist sponsors reappeared on the Monroe scene. We were told that Mr. K did not want to do anything now that might prove embarrassing to the USA and that could very well cast a shadow over détente. The fickleness of the Communists had dampened our hopes and left us as exposed as ever.

Although a fender had been smashed and a headlight knocked out of my small British car, I was still able to use it in making deliveries of *The Crusader*. *The Crusader* was being delivered locally on Saturdays. More and more we were being shadowed by police cars. The police were making note of who supported our publication, just as employers were watching workers to see who was sleepy on the job and thus possibly could be identified as members of our security guard.

After one of our Saturday deliveries, I was stopped by the police three blocks from my house. It so happened that I was stopped with great fanfare in front of Rev. J. J. Lomax's home. The policeman informed me that I was operating a motor vehicle without my lights being on. He said my lights were defective. He was fully aware that the mob had watched as my car had been wrecked at Hill Top on the way to the pool demonstration. Reverend Lomax was sitting in his yard under a shade tree. I loudly called out, asking him if it was night or day. He answered, "Of course, Robert, it is day! Why do you ask such an obvious question?"

I told him that this policeman was saying that it was night. He laughed and replied, "Oh no, it is definitely daylight, Robert!" The demeanor of the two policemen was hostile indignation. After some verbal exchange, I was given an option of being hauled off in their patrol car to the police station or following them in my car that they had already declared unfit to be on the road because of broken lights. I opted for driving behind them to the station. After being given an order to follow close behind them, I acceded to their flawed legality based on their propensity to harass me and to interfere with the delivery of *The Crusader* and followed the patrol car for almost two blocks. We crossed the intersection at Fairley Avenue and English Streets.

The next intersection was Fairley Avenue and Boyte Street. I lived on Boyte Street, halfway up the block. This was precisely why I had offered to follow the two policemen to the station in my own car. As they crossed over Boyte Street and as I approached it, I shifted gears, accelerated, and made a sharp left turn toward my house.

Blasting the car horn, I sped around my house and stopped near the back door. The back door was locked, as usual. The police car had turned around and at breakneck speed had followed me into my backyard. I owned a very ferocious German shepherd named Little Rock. The dog was on a chain leash. The sight of the officers invading the yard had provoked a temper tantrum on the part of the dog.

I tried to release him to ward off the police, but he was exerting so much pressure pulling on his chain toggle that I was unable to free him. My wife,

Mabel, opened the back door. She was armed with a 12-gauge shotgun. I called to my ten-year-old son, Bobby, to bring my rifle.

My wife asked the policemen what they wanted with me. They informed her that I was going to be taken in for operating a motor vehicle with defective lights. She asked them if they had a warrant for my arrest, and when they answered in the negative, she told them that they had better get out of our yard until such time that they did have one. The commotion drew a crowd of armed Black friends from the neighborhood. As the crowd swelled and surrounded the policemen, their nervousness and fear became very much obvious.

Armed with my 8mm semiautomatic Mauser rifle and surrounded by armed friends, I ordered the hate-motivated, illegal cops out of my yard. I told them that I wanted to hear their wheels spinning until they got out of the block or else I was going to blow their asses up. And if they wanted me, they had better bring a warrant.

They left so fast with their wheels spinning that the smell of burning rubber filled the air. A senior citizen neighbor, Mrs. Gregory, lived across the street from us, and next door to her lived Mrs. King, who was like a surrogate mother to my family. Mrs. Gregory called to Mrs. King, who was standing with her arms folded on her front porch watching the unfolding events.

"Lizzy, did you see that? Lord, I ain't never in my life seen a colored man talk to the police like that! They left here flying like scared dogs!"

"Yeah, I saw them leave here flying," Mrs. King replied. "These young Negroes just ain't gonna take what we took. They've been in the army, and they ain't scared of nothing."

The police failed to come back with a warrant, and nothing else was ever said about my lights, which the police had witnessed being knocked out while the chief claimed that he couldn't see any damage to my car and had refused to issue a warrant for the bigots who had wrecked the car and made an attempt on our lives.

The news was spreading that Monroe was one of the hottest spots in the USA. It was common knowledge that Union County was a powder keg waiting to explode. The situation had become so tense that one could feel the tension permeating the entire environment. I kept fighting off a feeling of impending doom and resigned myself to probable loss of life. If it was to be my fate to go, I wanted to go with a big bang, accompanied by a score of bigots. I felt the example would be worthwhile. There most certainly was a need to inspire Black youth to break out of the narrow confines of "turn-the-other-cheekism." Nonviolence, to me, was a guarantee to violent racists that they could visit all kinds of hurt upon us with complete impunity.

Mysterious fires continued to plague the town. The fires were primarily in the white section of town, and they all seemed to be industrial in nature. Suspicion became more prevalent as a bigot started spreading the word publicly that "Williams" was the arsonist. It seemed to frustrate them to no end to always find me at home during fires that flared in the night. One of the few fires that occurred in the Black community claimed a nightspot operated by a Black teacher who had written letters to the white papers asking supporters throughout the United States to stop sending us guns and other contributions. She claimed that Monroe was a peaceful town where the races had gotten along beautifully until I started stirring up trouble. A few days after her letter was published, her "juke joint" burned down.

The bigots and their fellow traveling Uncle Toms were spreading the rumor so intensively that I was behind the fires that I deemed it necessary to advise, "If any of our people are setting those fires, I don't want to know about it. An arson charge is something that we cannot handle. Arson is not our thing. The risk is too great. It is a wrong tactic for us at this time unless our situation becomes so desperate that we decide to go down and take the town with us. It may happen, but we will stick to self-defense, as long as we can."

CHAPTER 40

BROADENING THE SCOPE OF STRUGGLE

TEN-POINT PROGRAM

During the summer, many Blacks, including heads of families, were laid off so the local white high school and college students on vacation could take their jobs and earn extra spending money. With many young Blacks unemployed and milling aimlessly around the town, most Black graduates were forced to break family and neighborhood ties and migrate in quest of a more promising life.

The Union County Industrial Development Commission was following the new trend in the South. It was using public tax money to facilitate concessions offered to attract northern industry running from unionized and more costly labor in the North. Blacks were employed only in the lowest-paying and most menial positions in this industry. Actually, local bigots insisted that the incoming industries accede to the status quo and not spoil local "coloreds" by raising their expectations, thus transforming a surplus labor pool. We were being taxed the same as whites and felt we were being robbed to subsidize white employment. Being denied access to public facilities was a denial of a civil right that cut deep into our human pride, but the denial of the right of employment was tampering with our right of survival and the right to live worthwhile and productive lives in the development of our full potential. We were no longer content to live and respond as the white man's shadow, as some bigots thought we were created to be.

I had come to feel that the struggle throughout the South was too limited and much too narrow in directing most of our primary effort toward public facilities. On August 15, 1961, our NAACP branch, represented by Dr. Albert E. Perry Jr., John W. McDow, and me, presented a ten-point program to the Monroe Board of Aldermen. It read as follows:

1. Induce factories in this county to hire without discrimination.
2. Induce the local employment agency to grant non-whites the same privileges given to whites.
3. Instruct the welfare agency that non-whites are entitled to the same privileges, courtesies, and consideration given to whites.
4. Construct a swimming pool in the Winchester Avenue area of Monroe.
5. Remove all signs in the City of Monroe designating one area for colored and another for whites.
6. Instruct the superintendent of schools that he must prepare to desegregate the city schools no later than 1962.
7. Provide adequate transportation for all schoolchildren.
8. Formally request the State Medical Board to permit Dr. Albert E. Perry Jr. to practice medicine in Monroe and Union County.
9. Employ Negroes in skilled or supervisory capacities in the city government.
10. Act immediately on all of these proposals and inform the committee and the public of your actions.

/s/Robert F. Williams
Albert E. Perry, Jr., MD
John W. McDow

Some days before the presentation of our ten-point program, I met with Dr. Perry on the Mecklenburg/Union County line because, despite the fact that he had been paroled out of Caledonia Prison, he was still not allowed to cross into Union County where his wife and friends lived. "Doc," as we called him, informed me that an aide of Governor Terry Sanford had approached him. The aide was a Black man known as Dr. Larkin. He had engaged the influence of Dr. Perry to set up a discreet meeting with me. If Doc could swing the meeting, they would allow him to host the meeting at his home in Monroe. It would be his first opportunity to visit his home since his release from prison. Doc told me up front that the state had offered him some concessions if he would promise to come home and pull on my coattail. I agreed to the arrangement. We needed his medical services among our people, and we wanted him back home.

Dr. Perry called me on the appointed night to inform me that he and Dr. Larkin were already in town and at his house. I surveyed the area for a possible ambush before entering Dr. Perry's house from the darkened area. Dr. Larkin was sitting on the sofa behind a sizable coffee table. Dr. Perry introduced us, and I removed my army gun belt that holstered the army .45 and the 9mm Luger, placed the guns on the coffee table, and set my 8mm semiautomatic Mauser on the floor in front of us.

"Do you want to talk to me?" I asked.

Glancing down at the guns and displaying apprehension that he was trying hard to conceal, he informed me, "Williams, the governor has taken a great interest in you. He feels that you and your family deserve more, so he sent me to find out what he can do for you and what do you want."

"That's mighty nice of him," I said. "Tell him if he really wants to help me, I suggest he move to push through our ten-point program. Tell him I've already outlined what I want in the ten points. "

"Oh no! He doesn't mean help you that way. He wants you to withdraw the ten points. He wants to know what you want personally."

"I can't withdraw the ten points. They are not mine. They belong to the people, but anything he wants to give me in addition to the ten points, I would appreciate very much because I am a very poor man!"

"The governor also wants you to stop wearing those guns around town. He knows that you have a legal right to do what you are doing, but you are setting a bad example before other citizens."

"You tell the governor that there is a breakdown in law and order here and until such time that there is a Fourteenth Amendment to the US Constitution introduced here, I will be wearing these guns!"

The meeting ended with Dr. Larkin making a seemingly veiled threat, saying, "The governor is going to be upset when I report back to him. "

Later, however, the state did relax some of the restrictions that had been placed on Dr. Perry. They let him move home to Monroe to pull on my coattail. They partially restored his license to practice medicine. He could live in Monroe, but he could only practice medicine across the county line in Charlotte. No one had ever heard of a doctor being barred from practicing in his home county where most of his patients lived. That was the lowest form of racism. Many of our people were too poor to pay for medical attention, and Doc administered to them without remuneration. To cut medical attention off from a deprived community that experienced much illness because of a depressed standard of living was just a step away from flirting with genocide.

CHAPTER 41

NONVIOLENT TACTICS ARE ACCEPTABLE SO LONG AS THEY DON'T REQUIRE SACRIFICING OUR HUMAN DIGNITY

To all of those who were conscious of racial conflict and struggle across the land, Monroe had become synonymous with militant self-defense. Monroe represented the option to "turn-the-other-cheekism." A debate was sweeping the country, both pro and con, relative to the tactical value of armed self-defense. The lines soon became so obscured that it was no longer a matter that I had merely advocated self-defense. Self-defense in many quarters was being stigmatized as an advocacy of violence. Many frightened individuals and just plain pacifists were telephoning, telegraphing, and writing me to give up armed self-defense. Jackie Robinson, the first Black to break into Major League Baseball, wrote a special letter appealing to me to relinquish my right to self-defense.

Early in the summer of 1961 I received a phone call from Slim Brundage of the College of Complexes, a combination coffeehouse and militant open forum in Chicago, Illinois. A pacifist, Brundage had been active in raising contributions of clothing and money for Monroe's CARE (Crusaders Association for Relief and Enlightenment) organization. "I've been reading in the papers about all the trouble you've been having," he said. "Has it ever occurred to you that you might be using the wrong philosophy?"

"No!" I answered.

"Perhaps you have missed experiencing the power of nonviolence and love," Slim stated.

"I doubt it," I replied.

"Well, would you be willing to try a different approach? Would you be willing to let some people who believe in nonviolence come down there to help you and prove that nonviolence and love really work?"

I had never seen or heard anything of Slim Brundage, other than through the contributions he had been making on a regular basis to CARE. I had always exerted special effort to convince all who questioned our stance that not only were we not willing instigators of violence, but we believed in passive resistance where it was feasible and possible. My reply to Brundage was, "We are not trying to promote any special type of philosophy. We are willing to use whatever works without a sacrifice of our human dignity."

I explained that nonviolence and love can be powerful weapons when one engages a civilized foe, but when challenging an uncivilized brute, attempting to overcome him with love is an invitation to suffer the loss of life and limb. We were not mentally equipped to withstand brutish violence. I assured him that if anyone could subdue those bigoted savages with love, I would be more than willing to become a pacifist. I accepted Mr. Brundage's offer of nonviolent active support.

Within the next few days, I received telephone calls from Paul Brooks, a young minister and aide of Rev. Martin Luther King, and James Forman, who at that time was one of the leading organizers of the Student Nonviolent Coordinating Committee.[1] They were volunteering to come to Monroe and promised to solicit freedom riders, just recently released from prison in Alabama, to come also.[2]

The sit-in movement was taking North Carolina by storm.

I led our local group to what came to be known as the thirteenth town to stage publicized sit-ins. We had grown up in a Jim-Crowed town and had always experienced the hurt and shame of being denied the most basic of human rights, the right to seek service as a human being at an ordinary merchandise trade

1. James Forman was elected executive secretary of the Student Nonviolent Coordinating Committee in 1961.

2. Freedom riders, who pledged to practice nonviolent direct action against segregation, were dispatched to Monroe to prove the method of pacifist resistance could work in that southern town.

counter. Our first targets were the drugstores. Most of them had lunch counters, but even to get prescriptions filled, Black patrons had to remain standing in the rear of the building. Many Black men, acting in compliance with abject submission to white supremacy, waited with hat in hand to pay for their prescriptions being filled at the Jim-Crowed pharmacies.

In the beginning of July in 1961, we again seized the initiative. It was a balmy day. A low overhang of clouds obscured the sun when we arrived on Main Street. We had already been sitting-in and demonstrating at all of the town's drugstores, with the exception of one. We had deliberately excluded Wilson's Drugstore because a secretly sympathetic Afro-American worked there, and he was the source of overheard conversations among the whites. Also, we chose not to alienate all of the sources of medicine in case we experienced a need to have a prescription filled. William Crawford was the Afro-American who worked there, and we hoped that he would be watchful of any untoward action that might occur to our detriment. This day, we were retracing our steps to the segregated Jones Drugstore's lunch counter. When we entered the building and made our way to the lunch section, the workers did as they usually did when we appeared: they closed it. We were informed that Negroes were not served there, and we were asked to leave. We refused. The owner then asked everyone to leave and announced that the entire establishment was being closed to business. He stood at the door urging all patrons to leave. Along with the whites, we filed out. A mob of whites and some observing Blacks had gathered and started milling in front of the building. The inflamed bigots became highly vocal and started to make open threats of violence. One of the racist whites pointed a menacing finger at me and announced, "That nigger is going to get killed, you can bet on that!"

A Black man who had been silently watching and leaning against a parking meter became animated by the words of the bigot. His face bore many scars, indicating that he had been in some violent and perhaps life-threatening fights. Confronting the agitator, he declared, "You cracker motherfucker, you'd better hush before your goddamn mouth gets your ass all fucked up. You keep talking like that and you won't live long enough to see him dead! I just got back from Central Prison for killing a son of a bitch, and I'll go back again for killing your ass!"

His words and his appearance stunned the raging racist, and he backed away in total silence. It was a feeling of great elation to know that a proven killer was ready to take up our fight. Other Black bystanders gave approval to his stand. The incident added a completely new element to our determined assault on the oppressive status quo. It served notice to the segregationists that our action was solidifying all strata of the Black community.

As we were preparing to leave the downtown area, Chief Mauney and members of the local police surrounded our group. I was placed under arrest for trespassing. Out of the group, I was the only one arrested. I was taken before a judge who was sitting at the nearby courthouse. Two of Monroe's elder, prominent Black citizens, Rev. Baxter Perry and Mr. George Rushing, after being notified by the women in the phone-calling circle, rushed to the courthouse to bail me out.

The judge asked what they were doing there. In times past, such a question from a white judge would have sent Black men of that caliber into a nervous state of denial. Things had changed. They stood firm and unyielding. Reverend Perry told the judge, "We have come to go on Williams's bond!"

The judge retorted caustically, "Baxter, you and George don't want to go on this boy's bond!"

Mr. Rushing replied, "Oh yes we do, that's exactly what we are here for, Judge!"

"Well, he'll have to go to jail until we can finish drawing up the papers."

Reverend Perry and Mr. Rushing indicated that they would stay right there until I was released.

The sheriff ordered me into a lineup of eight felons. He deliberately paired me with a young Black woman who had just been convicted for murdering her father for sexual molestation. A group of deputies, armed with shotguns, marched us two blocks along city streets to the old dilapidated, segregated jail. I was in custody for about an hour and a half until they allowed the Black citizens to post my bond. The incarceration was a thing of mean spite rather than a case of legality. I submitted to the arrest because the charge was only a misdemeanor and the whole idea of the sit-in movement was to bring about constitutional test cases to strike down segregation in public places.

I was tried and convicted and sentenced to a fifty-dollar fine and thirty days on what was known as the prison chain gang. The national office of the NAACP consolidated my case with six others it had earmarked for the US Supreme Court. The NAACP assured me that the legal aspects of my case would be taken care of with the group. About ten days before our cases were to go up on appeal, I received a call from the Greensboro bureau of United Press International asking whether I had decided to serve my sentence rather than go up on appeal. When I informed the UPI reporter that I had not dropped the appeal of my sentence, I was told me that the bureau had checked the court records and there was no appeal registered for me. It was unbelievable that the national office would be so treacherous as to set me up for a chain gang sentence. Evidently, the NAACP had gone to such lengths to portray me as a violent wild man, rather than an American exercising his constitutional rights of self-defense, that it could not stomach the idea of my being entered in the historical record as one who had also utilized nonviolent methods.

Disgusted and angry at the national office for trying to deliver me up to southern tyrannical racism, I immediately called Attorney Conrad Lynn in New York. A shocked Lynn assured me that he was at that very moment going to make some calls soliciting emergency aid and would get back to me soon. He said that we could not afford to lose any time or else I would be a goner. The following day, Conrad called me with the good news that the Emergency Civil Liberties Union, a group I had never heard of, had agreed to take over my appeal. He told me that one of the top constitutional lawyers in the country, Leonard Boudin, was going to handle it and that I had nothing to worry about. Eventually, the case went to the US Supreme Court, and it was one of the seven where the court decided that segregation in public places was outlawed.[3]

3. See Williams v. North Carolina, 378 U.S. 548 (1964) (per curiam), vacating and remanding State v. Williams, 253 N.C. 804, 117 S.E.2d 824 (1961), in which Lynn and Leonard Boudin were co-counsel for Robert Williams.

CHAPTER 42

SPOTLIGHTED AGAIN

THE ORDEAL OF NONVIOLENT FREEDOM RIDERS IN MONROE

Drawn to the uniqueness of Monroe, individuals started to trek in and out. They wanted to see this cauldron wherein Blacks had raised a flag of militancy that had not been seen in modern times. Among the early visitors were Julian Mayfield, Dr. Reginald Wilson, Mae Mallory, Constance Lever, Ronald Frazier, Yoriko Nakajima, and many others. Blacks were fighting back, and persons from diverse locations wanted to see and experience this glorious spectacle with their own eyes. Blacks had been beaten down for so long, had turned the other cheek, sometimes cringing in the face of racist brutality and abdicating the responsibility of defending their homes, women, and children, that even just-minded whites gloried in our spunk. The world media was full of traumatic scenes of defenseless Blacks being set upon by vicious police dogs, water hoses, cattle prods, and policemen's billy clubs and sometimes being lynched in situations seemingly tantamount to meek lambs being led to slaughter.

On at least one occasion, the media had reported Rev. Martin Luther King praying prior to a demonstration that if any must fall that day to "let it be us." I could not see any need to appeal to God to let us fall. That had been happening since we were first taken into captivity. My secret prayer was that God would give us the strength and firepower to triumph over our oppressors if they should dare attack. Upon hearing the report of Dr. King's petition, recollections of my uncle Charlie's arguments with my mother readily filled my thoughts.

When word got out that we were willing to accept pacifists, freedom riders all over the country began discussing coming to Monroe. But Martin Luther King's associates obviously didn't seem interested in having Monroe become a focal point in the desegregation struggle. They let it be known that no funds would be made available for those who wanted to work with me. Despite this, a group of freedom riders, whites as well as Blacks just getting out of jail in Alabama, announced that they were coming to Monroe before returning to their homes in the North. Consequently, Reverend King then decided to send the Reverend Paul Brooks, his personal representative, along with instructions to work "under Williams's direction." I was informed that King himself was to come down the following week to lend his weight to a peaceful resolution to the highly explosive situation.

When word spread through north Monroe that freedom riders were coming, many Black people volunteered their homes for housing them. Many women in the neighborhood volunteered food and cooking. The entire community was aroused. Never before had the town witnessed whites living in the homes with Blacks. As much and as long as Afro-Americans had suffered at the hands of violently oppressive whites, they opened up their hearts and homes to the brave young whites who had come to lay their lives on the line in a cause to dignify a flawed and compromised American way of life.

I asked our local young freedom fighters to support the pacifists. At first, some intimated that "turn-the-other-cheekism" was against their nature. I finally convinced them that we had to give the freedom riders a chance. They acceded after my explanation that this would be the first time in the history of the civil rights movement that the philosophies of nonviolence and armed self-defense would be compared at work in the same environment. Personally, I was not convinced that violent racism could be changed by pacifism. I explained to the group that a lot of people from all over the world would be watching to see what happened here. It could not do us any harm, and just possibly it could do some good. The stage was now set.

When the pacifists arrived, there were seventeen of them, led by James Forman.[1] They joined with the local youths to establish the "Monroe Nonviolent Action Committee." Everyone involved in the desegregation struggle was asked to take an oath, swearing to adhere to pacifist principles, thus rejecting the use

1. James Forman tells his account of his experience in Monroe and with Williams in his memoir, *The Making of Black Revolutionaries* (Seattle: Open Hand, 1985), 158–211.

of any form of self-defense while taking part in demonstrations. I personally refused to make such a pledge but urged the members of our NAACP branch, our rifle club members, and citizens at large to give staunch support to those who had chosen to pursue that method.

Members of the Monroe Nonviolent Action Committee agreed to form a picket line around the Union County Courthouse in support of our ten-point program. This action was supposed to carry our previous efforts to fruition. On Monday, August 21, 1961, the demonstration began. That first day was so uneventful that it convinced some of the freedom riders that everything I had told them about the racists in Monroe had been greatly blown out of proportion. One northern white college student, returning from the picket line the first day, elatedly told me, "A policeman smiled at me while I was on the picket line."

"He was probably smiling at the thought of how he was going to have an opportunity to put a hurting on your ass," I told him.

He gave me a look of disbelief. Constance Lever, the British exchange student who was a guest observer in our home, after hearing the exchange, retorted, "Oh, I don't think these people are so bad, Rob; evidently, you don't know how to approach them."

All of my efforts to explain to the outsiders that the local bigots were only acting friendly in an effort to win over the strangers were to no avail. Southern hospitality was overriding their logic and blinding them to the tradition and history of southern white racist culture. I informed them that "the moment they realize that they can't get you to stop picketing by being polite, you're going to find out for yourselves."

Without consulting me, the freedom riders issued a press release declaring that they were in Monroe to try to bring about better race relations through strictly nonviolent means.

I told them that putting something like that in the newspapers there was a big mistake. They had served notice on the violence-prone white reactionaries that they could attack them with impunity! I told them, "For almost five years now, the racists have been afraid to attack us because they know we are armed and that we are willing to meet violence with violence. Our fight-back stance has frustrated the hell out of them. No doubt, they would like to recoup the face they lost and would like to retake the initiative. By making this kind of a public announcement, you are in effect challenging them to do something."

On the very same day that the *Monroe Enquirer* carried the press release, I received a telephone call from a bigot who claimed to represent the Ku Klux Klan. "Robert, I am calling for the Klan. We want to know if you have become one of these Martin Luther 'coon' pacifists?"

"No!" I answered.

"Well then, are you and your nigger goons participating with those damn Yankee pacifists?"

When I gave him another no answer he went on, "That's just fine. We're sure glad to know you won't be around, because we plan a hot reception for them college agitators!"

On Wednesday, the third day of demonstrations, the racist townspeople, as predicted, turned—they dropped their southern hospitality facade and reverted to their traditional meanness. Hecklers came out in strength and started taunting the protesters. When one freedom rider reacted with a smile, two women spat in his face. A policeman knocked another picket to the ground and threatened to break his camera. A third picket was arrested for protesting the lawman's action. Tension was mounting.

On Thursday, the fourth day, three white men attacked one of the white freedom riders. He didn't fight back. His nonviolence emboldened the vicious element of white supremacists. Inasmuch as the cops broke up the attack and promised to arrest his assailants, even the man who had been attacked remained convinced that the law was on the side of the demonstrators.

Despite the fact that my youngest son, John Williams, was only eleven years old, he insisted on joining the picket line. I refused despite the fact that he charged he was being discriminated against. He said that we were fighting discrimination while discriminating against him because he was little. Since the swimming pool incident, my children had only been allowed briefly to picket during the lunch counter actions. I had kept my family in the background as much as possible for their own protection. During interviews, I never revealed that I had a family. Only a few people knew their identity. Somehow, erroneously, the word got out that my sons were marching with the pacifists. Consequently, a group of white men severely beat ten-year-old Prentice Robinson on the Main Street of town. It was a serious case of mistaken identity. Despite several witnesses to the assault, which left the child seriously injured, the police took no action.

On that very same day, one of the white freedom riders was shot in the stomach by a high-powered air rifle. It occurred directly in front of the courthouse, in full view of the cops, but no arrests were made then either. That was also the day when the sanitation department had the picket line sprayed with insecticide. It was also the day that a hurried special ordinance was introduced, requiring pickets to remain at least fifteen feet apart. Relative to this ordinance, the cops formulated a special tactic. They would stop a freedom rider, engage him or her in conversation, and arrest the one who approached from the rear for violation of the "too close" ordinance.

On the morning of the fifth day, I was paid a very strange visit from an old man, Mr. Chambers, for whom I had pressured the local and reluctant white welfare agency to grant medical attention, which consisted of an operation on a tumor on his neck that was choking him to death. On one occasion, while working on his behalf, I had taken a Japanese exchange student with me to his home to visit his family. Yoriko Nakajima was a houseguest and a University of Michigan graduate student. She had been shocked at the condition of poverty in which they lived and remarked, "In Asia, we have very dire poverty, but everyone knows it. And we are doing our best to get rid of it. Here in the United States, I never imagined to see people living so badly. You Americans hide your poor from the rest of the world." She had snapped pictures to prove to her friends and colleagues in Japan that she was not anti-American and exaggerating conditions seldom seen by foreigners.

Mrs. Pauline Carelock, one of our very staunch NAACP CARE activists who lived in Marshville, related to me how the ailing Mr. Chambers had walked a great distance to her house at the break of day and pleaded with her to bring him to my house. She asked me to please humor the old man by pretending to take him seriously. She had not wanted to come because she knew how busy I was, but Mr. Chambers would not take no for an answer. The old man was sitting in the car in front of my house when I approached him. He looked up at me with a serious expression and announced authoritatively, "I brought you a charm."

Puzzled, I asked, "What kind of a charm?"

He fumbled with what appeared to be some type of greeting card on which he had scribbled what was obviously a religious incantation. As I visually scanned the decorative candle on the card, he handed it to me and admonished me to keep it on my person at all times. He proceeded to tell me that he had had a vision during the previous night, and in that vision he had seen thousands of white enemies coming to destroy me. He said that they would come within three days, and that was why he had insisted that Pauline bring him to warn me. He said that God had revealed the whole thing to him. He stressed with great emphasis, "So long as you keep this on your body, they will not be able to take or harm you! Write your name on it," he insisted.

Pauline, who was standing nearby, winked and smiled at me. "Go on and take it, Rob. He is sincere and is very much worried about you. He knows how much these people would like to get rid of you."

I accepted the charm, hurriedly scribbled my name where he indicated, thanked Mr. Chambers and Pauline, and said goodbye. As I entered the house, Mabel wanted to know what the old man wanted with me that was so important to him that he just had to come at such a hectic time.

Tossing the paper on the table, I explained to her what Mr. Chambers's visit was all about. She read the inscription and insisted that I fold it up and put it in my wallet. When I refused, she asked for my wallet. Carefully folding the paper, she placed it in my wallet and said, "It can't do you any harm to keep it. In fact, you need all the luck and blessings that you can get."

After Pauline and Mr. Chambers left and Mabel's desperation in grasping at straws, I became curious to know the content of the message scrawled on the supposed "charm." I took it out of my wallet, unfolded it, and read:

> Heavenly and Holy prophet, blow every blow and misfortune away from me.
>
> I seek refuge under the Tree of Life, which bears twelve-fold fruits.
>
> I stand behind the Holy Altar of the Christian Church.
>
> I commend myself to the Holy Trinity.
>
> I, Robert F. Williams, hide myself beneath the Holy Corpse of Jesus Christ. I commend myself unto the ruins of Jesus Christ that the hand of no man might be able to seize me, or beat me, or imprison me, or overcome me. By God that carries all power, I beseech Him to keep and be with me, to keep me in a safe place, safe from all my enemies, visible or invisible.

I smiled, refolded it, and stuck it back in my wallet.

The more the bigots harassed and unleashed violence, without any retaliation on the demonstrators' part, the more brazen they became. We had been able to stand them down for more than five years, but now they were beginning to sense the deterioration of our fighting spirit. Our sector of the demonstrators had sworn themselves to nonviolence, which was limited to the line while picketing. We had served notice on the pacifists that we still held fast to the right of self-defense in safeguarding our communities and our homes.

On the fifth day of demonstrations around the courthouse, the racists gave vent to their tempers. Seeing the viciousness of the growing mob, the freedom riders decided to walk in orderly and silent formation the mile and a half back to Boyte Street. In addition to sharing the homes with local sympathizers, we had established an office and a residence in a donated house just two doors from where I lived. Convinced the pickets were pacifists, taunting and rock-throwing whites dared to drive a motorcade into our community in pursuit of the students.

Screaming, blowing their car horns, and throwing objects from slow-moving cars, they turned Boyte Street into bedlam. Without realizing it, when they entered Boyte Street, they forfeited their right of immunity from violence.

Just as the first car of bigots passed beyond my house in the middle of the block, local demonstrators and defenders started to fight back with stones or whatever they could find to throw. In an effort to escape, some of the cars began to bump each other, resulting in a traffic jam. As a car came to a halt in front of my house, a local youth threw half a brick, striking the driver of the car on the side of his face. His face became a mass of blood. Screams went up in the crowd of angry Blacks calling for the invaders to be killed. A white freedom rider from New Jersey rushed to the window of the car and leaned backward with his arms outstretched in a protective shield on behalf of the bleeding bigot.

"Look at that son of a bitch protecting that cracker!" a voice screamed above the noise of the melee.

I called the student from New Jersey and asked him what the hell was the matter with him. I stated that he had been able to see our people brutalized and had never shielded any of our people from the racists. I warned him that if he ever did that again, I would put daylight through him.

Realizing the image his act had created, he stated that his pacifist ideals had automatically come into play, and he offered his apology. I told him that if his pacifism led him to abhor violence only against white people, then it might be better for him to leave Monroe. The next day he left.

His departure left me plagued by the question of whether there might be a latent white belief that violence was a lesser savage offense when unleashed against Afro-Americans than against whites. All my life, I had noticed that white Americans seemed impervious toward violence visited upon our people. They seemed to believe that life encased in a black skin was less sensitive to pain and insults. Perhaps they believed we were incapable of the same human emotions as the white race. Perhaps such erroneous thought is the basis of our tribulation in the white world.

On the evening of the fifth day of picketing, still unconvinced of the danger of violence on the part of violent racists, several of the freedom riders took a drive into adjacent Mecklenburg County. When they stopped at a business establishment just over the county line to get some refreshments, they were attacked by a group of Klansmen. Four freedom riders managed to make it to their car and escape. The fifth rider was left behind and fled into a nearby wooded area. Rev. Paul Brooks, who had been sent by Rev. Martin Luther King to work under my direction, keep the lid on things, and possibly pave the way for Dr. King's later entrance, desperately phoned the authorities for help. After being rejected by all local police agencies of both counties, Paul called the office of Governor Terry Sanford and pleaded with his chief aide, Hugh B. Cannon, to intervene on behalf of the lost rider. The only conversation Brooks could get from Cannon was a hostile complaint that I was a "troublemaker." Reverend Brooks proclaimed to the governor's aide, "We are nonviolent! We are pacifists!"

Cannon retorted, "If you are really a pacifist, you'd better hurry up and get the hell out of Monroe, because there's going to be plenty of violence there!"

Reverend Brooks then asked Cannon, "Since you are so concerned about Williams, do you want to talk to him?" When Cannon responded, Paul passed the phone to me and I started to speak. "Mr. Cannon, this has nothing to do with your feelings toward me. I appeal to you to send state troopers in to find that lost student before he gets lynched."

"You're getting just what you deserve, Williams. You've been flirting with violence, and now you've got it," Cannon yelled.

"But I'm not asking you to help me. The one who is lost and may be lynched is a white student," I informed him.

"I don't give a damn who he is!" Cannon stated.

While we were seriously debating possible plans for a more organized armed search for the missing student, fortunately he found his way back to the anxious fold, extremely exhausted and with tattered clothing but otherwise unhurt.

On Saturday, the sixth day, the freedom riders returned to the courthouse to picket despite the fact that I expressed disapproval. We had learned from earlier demonstrations that the weekend was a bad time to picket. It was a bad time because the blue-collar workers and farmers became vagrants looking for excitement. Intimidating Blacks was almost a sport. When I warned the pacifists that they should stay off the streets on weekends, otherwise they would be inviting attack and perhaps serious trouble, one of their leaders responded, "But that's exactly why we have to picket on the weekend. We want the working people to see us. Instead of trying to avoid them, we will endeavor to change their hearts through the example of our love and nonviolence."

"I have promised not to interfere with your tactics," I replied, "but I feel that I ought to warn you that the worst time of all is Sunday. When the ignorant whites finish their churchgoing, they beer up and go in quest of cheap fun. They leave the house of the Lord to create a living hell for Blacks and any whites who may be friendly to them. Love and nonviolence mean nothing to them. Racial hatred is so deeply embedded in their souls that they are little different from savage beasts."

When a highly intoxicated man who identified himself as a Klansman called my house on Saturday around midnight, I knew that his accusation portended war. He said, "Nigger, we've got your number. We know why you can get the niggers to fight. You brought in some Yankee white whores as a payoff for all the niggers who will demonstrate. Every red-blooded white man will rise to keep our race pure. Nigger, you will never live to see race-mixing in this county!" With that said, he slammed down the telephone receiver.

As the sun rose on the morning of Sunday, August 27, 1961, word came that the chief of police, who had allowed the Klan to recruit in the police station, had dispersed his men throughout Union County to urge whites to come into town. Klansmen and their supporters began arriving from neighboring counties, and the "Minutemen," another extreme right-wing paramilitary organization, also began sending people into the area. By noon there were literally thousands of racists moving on Monroe. Carloads of them were racing around the Black community, even up and down Boyte Street and in front of my house. Blacks, including well-dressed ones returning to their homes from Sunday church services, were indiscriminately attacked.

Early in the afternoon, I received information that the Klan was forming a motorcade around the courthouse square. All kinds of rumors were flying around the town. Though Dr. Perry was supposed to be keeping a low profile and keeping a distance between him and the freedom riders, the portentous atmosphere that pervaded the town brought him to my house. Dr. Perry suggested that we drive into town to ascertain for ourselves, personally, what was impending. We armed ourselves with two pistols and a .30-caliber semiautomatic rifle. He drove and I rode with the rifle butt on the floor of the car and the rifle between my legs. We went to town to size up the situation.

The downtown area was bustling with traffic. There were many cars with license plates as far away as Georgia and South Carolina. Noisy, menacing bigots were milling around the demonstrators as they walked the picket lines, as if they were in attendance at a circus. It was more than obvious that their intention was to wipe us out with an operation of overkill. It was an eerie and sobering sight. This was the first time in my life that I had experienced a feeling of impending doom. I felt the end was near, but I entertained the thought of a desperate option. No doubt I would die, but also I had the means to kill off the town. There was a possibility of the town dying with me. For a moment, it flashed through my mind that I must be feeling like a Japanese kamikaze pilot about to effect his last mission.

Monroe was my native home. I had always wanted it to accept me as a native son. I had fought to give it the kind of dignity that the Constitution had bequeathed it. In its cruelty, it had reduced my people to the status of subhuman. It had barred us from the human race. Not only was it now mobilizing to take my life and all that was precious to me, but it was thumbing its nose at all the world that had been led to believe that the cruel harshness of the Dark Ages had long passed. I was cornered, and I felt sadness at the thought of possibly having to do what was running through my mind.

On the north side of the courthouse, two racists stood speaking from the back seat of a convertible car. One, the Grand Wizard of the KKK, was decked out in a gold-colored Klan sheet. The car was draped with huge American and Confederate flags. I had come to know the Confederate flag as Klan colors. It always flew when the bigots were on a hate mission. To Black people, the Stars and Bars is a symbol of degradation and slavery. Those who fly it pay homage to all that sympathize with the cause of ungodly slavery. No doubt in their subconscious, they fantasized that somehow, someday, once again they could live as all-powerful gods, to do as they pleased with Black humanity. The Klan speaker was blasting hate from a bullhorn. He was working the vast white mob up into a frenzy.

On the drive back to New Town, Dr. Perry, looking weary, finally broke his silence. "What do you plan to do?" he asked, as if he too was sensing that doomsday was imminent.

"Kill all of the sons of bitches and burn the town!" I answered with anger overwhelming the sadness I had first felt. Through all the turmoil, violence, and threats, the freedom riders continued to picket. They stood their ground and lived up to their nonviolent philosophy. They were nonfighters, but they had guts.

When we returned to my house, angry Blacks were gathering there from all parts of the county. They were in a mood for war. Many of them were strangers to the Guard. Quite a large unruly group had assembled in the alley behind my house. They were demanding to be armed, and they wanted me to lead a battle march against the town. They wanted to destroy the town. They wanted to burn it down. Discipline and reason had flown. Years of bitter oppression, deprivation, and cruelty were venting an enmity in them that I had never seen before. The town toughs had gathered, and they wanted me to lead them on a desperate final crusade. Many of their relatives and friends had been wantonly and randomly attacked. They wanted vengeance and were thoughtless of the consequences. I was trapped between two forces ready to give vent to a lifetime of pent-up emotions of hatred. Now I had to play the role of pacifying them to prevent their going over the brink. I had to conceal my own anger and frustration from them. I was walking a tightrope, cognizant of the fact that their intense anger could very well turn against them. They kept screaming, "Let's march on the town! Burn it down to the ground!"

I was finally able to inveigh on them that the Klan was obviously massing for a night attack and that we would be more effective defending ourselves in the darkened environs of our own community. They became more receptive to waiting after I told them that we would distribute arms and ammunition, but we had to have discipline. The anticipation of being armed had a surprisingly calming effect on them. It was somewhat strange how the thought of being armed gave them confidence and a feeling of security. When one is subjected to violence and is too weak to counteract it, there is a tendency to have one's spirit and dignity crushed. With arms, they were going to be equal to the forces of violence and subjugation. Guns and violence on the part of the racists had been the instrument used to keep them on their knees. Now guns and violence would be the instrument that would give them the strength to stand upright. We armed them, and they were humored. They easily started to respond to instructions.

In midafternoon, a lone white state patrolman drove up and said that the presence of armed people in front of my house was blocking traffic. As he was speaking, a number of Blacks began to gather. Many held guns, and some wanted to know why that "white son of a bitch" was there. Someone shouted, "Kill him!"

The lone patrolman seemed shaken. He spoke in an unusually courteous manner. "It's all right for them to be in your front yard and in the alley behind your house, but we would sure appreciate your getting them off the street," he pleaded.

"I'll get everyone connected with our Guard out of the way, but I'm not responsible for anyone else. Some of the people here are strangers to me," I replied.

A man in a highly emotional voice screamed, "A goddamn police, his pistol don't mean shit over here now. Let's kill the son of a bitch!"

I had to give a quick and strong explanation to counteract the tendency toward violent responses. The state trooper had been sent into an environment wherein the inhabitants had been conditioned by lifelong bitter experiences to see white policemen as a cruel and violent enemy. I was finally able to convince the violence-prone element that nothing was to be gained by killing the trooper, who evidently for the first time found reason to be courteous and respectful in confronting ordinary Blacks who were willing to challenge his authority.

As the news continued to spread that Blacks were being wantonly attacked by roving white mobs in many quarters of the county, Monroe was electrified and charged up with a war fever that had not prevailed there before. Not only were rumors flying from agitators, roaming the streets all over New Town, but the flames of violent conflict were kindled even more as the broadcast media started to interrupt their regular programming to announce that the town was experiencing racial violence and was an armed camp on the verge of an explosion. The media reported that the governor of Alabama had volunteered to send his state's National Guard to help Governor Sanford suppress the "heavily armed troublemakers." While he was declaring that Alabama would not stand by and do nothing while "insurrectionists" overran the North Carolina forces, the US attorney general, Robert Kennedy, was becoming involved as well. When asked if he would send federal troops to Monroe to maintain law and order, he answered he wouldn't do so unless it became absolutely necessary. However, he did say that he was going to see to it that the persons responsible for the violence in Monroe were severely punished.

We had appealed to Washington many times for protection and had asked that the Fourteenth Amendment to the US Constitution be introduced to the bigots of Union County. Our appeals had fallen on deaf ears. Washington had insisted that our situation was a local matter that had to be handled locally. Considering the previously consistent attitude, it was clear to me that the US Justice Department was inclined to throw its awesome power behind the oppressive forces of injustice. The governor's attitude was typical of what the official attitude of governing officials had been toward Black people struggling to throw off the yoke of brutal oppression ever since our wretched souls arrived in chains to the so-called New World. There was no law. There was no government for us. There was no white conscience to appeal to. The only forces of restraint available to us were our guns. Our guns constituted power, and that power was derived from the fact that bigoted whites wanted to live as much as we did. It was a lonely feeling to know that so many lives and so much destruction rested on a decision confronting me. I remembered the arguments my mother and Uncle Charlie had had so often concerning God and the white man. My mother had always maintained that God would, at some point, intervene on our behalf. Uncle Charlie said that if God didn't soon act, we would be doomed unless we got up off our praying knees and acted to save ourselves.

At four in the evening, James Forman, one of the leaders of the freedom riders, telephoned, saying that the cops were allowing the racists to manhandle the pickets. He asked me to rush taxis to the courthouse square to bring the freedom riders back to New Town. The Black cab company dispatched the cabs but later called to inform me that the drivers were being prevented from reaching the stranded pickets by bands of white men who were blocking the entrance to the center of town. A few minutes later a report came in that the racist mob was out of control and people were beating the demonstrators at will. Shots had been fired, and the town was in the grip of a spreading riot.

Reacting to the news of indiscriminate attacks and the desperate situation confronting the pickets, armed men again started to insist, "Let's go! Let's go to town and get the freedom riders. If they don't let us through, let's blow the town away!"

"No!" I exclaimed. "The freedom riders are pacifists. They want to prove that love and nonviolence can work, even if it means getting their heads bloodied. If we march on the town, we will be leaving the Black community defenseless. The Klan is getting ready to attack us. We have to stay here and take them on when they come!"

Most of them responded positively to my admonition. A few nonmembers of our defense guard broke with our discipline and decided to go anyway. Some Guard members, along with the novelist Julian Mayfield, armed themselves and drove into town in an action to give transportation to the pickets who were stranded at the courthouse. When the racist mob saw the arms in the cars, they allowed them to proceed to the courthouse area. Arriving at the courthouse, they saw that Constance Lever, the white student from England, was encircled by a band of armed racists and was being cursed at and manhandled.

In an attempt to rescue her, a group of Blacks attempted to get Constance into their car. Up until that moment, the police had been content to stand idly by and do nothing. Now they had become energized. A policeman grabbed the English girl and bellowed, "No white woman is getting into a car full of niggers in this town!"

Unable to convince the policeman to let them take her away, as the armed mob of racists closed in threatening them, one Afro reached into the car and pulled out a shotgun.[2] Seeing this, one of the policemen angrily reacted, shouting, "Give me that gun, give me that gun!"

James Forman, the Black picket captain, rushed over and pleaded with the armed Black man, "Please don't make any trouble. You Williams people promised not to bring guns near our line. The best way you can help us is to give the gun to the officer like he wants."

When the youth surrendered the shotgun to him, the policeman handed it to a member of the racist mob, who went into a fit of rage and viciously struck James Forman in the head with it. Blood poured down Forman's face, and the members of the mob, with the cops helping them, went wild and began savagely attacking the rest of the pickets. As the Afros had been disarmed at the behest of the pacifists, the bigoted police turned their weapons over to the mob and twisted their arms behind their backs and allowed the racists to beat them. One elderly Black man, who happened to be on the scene as a spectator, was clubbed to the ground and fell in a pool of his own blood. He shouted defiance

2. Robert Williams and some others of his generation used "Afro" as slang for "Afro-American."

as the cops dragged him away to jail, along with forty-six or more of the other demonstrators.

The pickets were told that they were being taken to jail "for their own protection," but once there they were charged with such things as "disturbing the peace" and "resisting an officer." Prisoners serving sentences for common crimes were released in order to make room for the pickets. A number of the released prisoners came and told us that some of the students had been severely injured and were being jammed into cells without receiving medical attention. They claimed some were so badly hurt that there was danger that they could bleed to death.

Word was spreading in late afternoon that whites in speeding cars were racing through the Black communities, firing guns and throwing objects from car windows. Blacks had started to fight back.

Suddenly, a fourteen-year-old Black youth who had begged for a firearm all morning, but because of his young age and lack of training I had refused his request, came running up to me all out of breath.

"This thing is no damn good. I only got off one shot and it jammed! I could have wiped them cops out if you had given me an automatic!" he exclaimed, waving a snub-nosed revolver.

The gun was one that I had taken out of service because it was known to be defective during target practice. Although we had returned it to the Charlotte merchant for repairs, the fault still had not been corrected. The youth had taken the gun out of my house without permission, but he was proud that he had wounded an attacking cop. Racial oppression, hatred, and officially condoned violence had turned that youth, who was not much more than a baby, into a hardened potential killer. The police can thank their lucky stars that that kid didn't steal a machine gun to give vent to the bitter emotions that boiled over in him.

By now my telephone was ringing incessantly with calls from Black parents inquiring about the welfare of their children who had been arrested with the freedom riders. Tension mounted as angry young Blacks started stoning cars bearing whites, just as was being done by whites on the other side of town. The constant radio and TV news flashes about an impending "race war" caused Blacks from other towns in North Carolina, and even from out of state, to telephone. The text of most calls went like: "If it's true there's going to be a real war, then we want to come to Monroe and join you." I warned them against trying to do so because we had already received reports of state police roadblocks on the highways leading into Union County.

CHAPTER 43

THE SO-CALLED KIDNAPPING CASE

The propensity to march on the town had become so intense that I felt my control slipping. The idea that we were so well armed and were allowing defenseless pacifists of both sexes and races to be brutalized, injured, and thrown into jail without medical attention was becoming too much to bear. I had reached the line of forbearance. As a last resort, in order to placate those who demanded outright war, I inveighed on the angry crowd to let me call Chief Mauney and give him a chance to get medical attention for the wounded. If his response was positive, there would be no need to march on the town. With a number of angry delegates from the crowd listening in, I made the call to Chief Mauney. I issued an ultimatum on behalf of the enraged citizens of our community. "I've been told that injured freedom riders have been locked up without medical attention and that their lives are in danger. If you don't get a doctor to them in thirty minutes, we are going to have to take the jail!"

Mauney slammed down the receiver without saying anything, but in less than thirty minutes James Forman telephoned from the hospital to say that all of the injured were there receiving medical attention. The chief had allowed him to call in order to convince me that the injured pickets were being taken care of.

I was called away from the telephone by angry voices demanding that I come out of the house. As I came out into my front yard, the crowd was screaming, "We got 'em! Kill 'em, kill 'em!"

A white couple was surrounded by a crowd, angrier than I had ever seen in my entire life. Someone shouted, "They're Klan people! They were in a motorcade the other day with a big sign on their car saying, 'Open season on coons'!"

Our people were in a killing mood as their ring around the whites became ever smaller. The crowd was on verge of exploding. I knew that if just one person so much as touched either one of the whites, the crowd was going to tear them to shreds.

The white woman, who obviously detected that I had some measure of influence with the group, indignantly complained to me, "We've been kidnapped! These people have kidnapped us."

Her seeming contempt made the crowd even more angry. She apparently was either too confused to comprehend the seriousness of the situation or so unaccustomed to dealing with non-servile types that she thought she could deter them by raising her voice.

Despite the fact that the crowd had started to accuse me of taking up for the whites and some made veiled threats to me, I physically started forcing the crowd out of arm's reach of the couple. I told the woman that she was not kidnapped and that they were free to leave anytime they wanted to.

She whined, "We were just driving along and made a wrong turn. They stopped our car and made us get out. We ain't going through that mob! They'll kill us. If you're a good man you will take us outta here!"

I answered, "Lady, I didn't bring you here, and I'm not about to take you away. You know that rioting has been going on all around town, so why did you come driving into the colored part of town? These people are mad. Their sons and daughters are being beaten and thrown into jail at this very moment by your people. I'm busy. Getting out is your problem."

The crowd again started screaming wildly, "Kill them! Kill them! Kill the sons of bitches." An old man came running down the street with a hatchet, crying hysterically, "Let me kill them, let me kill them!"

Suddenly, a light plane zoomed low overhead. I had already received telephone threats that if the racists couldn't get us on the ground, they would get us from the air. As the plane circled to make a second pass, several men fired on it with .30-caliber semiautomatic rifles. At that very moment, in what appeared to be a coordinated attack, a carful of whites came roaring down Boyte Street, firing pistols from the car's window. It caught the armed Guard by surprise, but as it sped past, several Blacks took up positions in the middle of the street and opened up with pistol and rifle fire. The gunfire was so fierce that it sounded like a full-blown war was in progress. Sparks and flames flew from the rear of the speeding car as bullets struck its rear.

The white woman, seeing that the Blacks were ready to kill without hesitation, lost her arrogance and began trembling and mumbling hysterically. Her husband remained silent and kept calm. I was called to the telephone again. As I turned to go into the house, the white couple pressed against my back, fearful of the threatening crowd. Some members of the group became upset and accused me of giving help to the frightened whites. The woman, who I later learned was Mrs. Stegall, said in a tone of a request, "If you'll just escort us out of here, we'll be all right."

"Lady, I didn't bring you here, and I am not going to take you out. If I had been caught in a white community, I would be dead by now! These people have been transformed into killers by your white savages. You see, we are not half as bad and full of hate as your people!" The couple had followed me into the house. One of the guests in my house had offered them seats. After I had finished a brief telephone conversation and returned to the room where they were seated, the woman looked at me and in an obviously subdued and strained voice asked, "Are you the man they call Robert Williams?"

After I had nodded in the positive, she seemed inclined to mollify me. "Why, you don't seem to be the way everyone says you are. You seem to be a nice person. You know, my husband and I live in Marshville, not here in Monroe. We have colored working for us, and we treat them like one of us. I'm a Christian. All I want you to do is to take us outta here."

"Just be thankful you are not out there being torn apart by that angry crowd. You know, deep down in your hearts, that if I had been caught in your community, you wouldn't let me take shelter in your house. You'd be part of the Klan trying to kill me!" I told her.

I was called to the telephone again. I was surprised to learn the identity of the voice on the other end. It was an Afro-American woman who ran a restaurant catering to whites in downtown Monroe. We never thought of her as ever having any race consciousness. Now her sympathy was coming through loud and clear. She asked me if I had been watching television. When I explained that I had been too busy to do so, she informed me that it had just been announced from Raleigh that Governor Sanford was dispatching state troopers to Monroe to arrest what they referred to as "rioters."

Her cafe was in the vicinity of the jail, and she informed me that many troopers were already coming into town and were lining up at and around the jail area. She said they were heavily armed and that the word was being circulated that this was supposed to be the end of me.

Chief Mauney called, just as I finished talking with her, and his voice trembled with rage as he said, "Robert, you have caused a lotta trouble in this town, but this is the end of the line for you. State troopers are coming, and in thirty minutes you'll be hanging in the courthouse square!" He didn't wait for a response before he slammed down the receiver.

Shortly after the announcement from Raleigh, members of the Guard came to inform me that the police and state troopers, armed with machine guns, were surrounding the block where I lived and that it appeared they were mobilizing for night attack. Later, it was agreed that I should leave town for a week or two because I was the cardinal target of the racists and the state. It was felt that there was going to be great bloodshed during the night and that I was going to be blamed for anything that should happen. It was agreed that at the proper time, I should leave.

CHAPTER 44

LEAVING MONROE

THE UNDERGROUND RAILROAD FROM CANADA TO CUBA

Julian Mayfield had been staying at Dr. Perry's house but was keeping abreast of what was developing and was a part of our discussions. He called and said that it was time for us to get out and that we should meet him at the place we had determined, which was the American Legion Hut on Second Street. This was so that his car, with its New York license plates, would not be identified in the area.

After nightfall, I told Mabel, my wife, to get our sons because we were leaving. She said that the family would only slow me down and for that reason urged me to leave alone because I was the one whom they really wanted to destroy. I explained that if they should happen to fall into the hands of the racist state, they would use them to torment me. I explained that we had to leave without any of our belongings.

We left the house that my older son and I had been born in, without being able to bring a change of clothes. We had our worst clothes on because of the activity we were engaged in. As we left for the alley, in order to use the cover of darkness, a young relative who had moved in with us and had joined the pickets called me excitedly. She was informing me that Rev. Martin Luther King was on the telephone and wanted to speak to me. I told her to ask him what the hell did he want at this late date and to tell him that it was too late to talk now.

I carried my 9mm Luger and an army .45 and holstered an Italian carbine and an automatic weapon. When we reached the end of the block, police cars had the block surrounded. When Mabel asked how we were going to get out of the block, I told her that we were going to walk out. I brought the automatic to high port, and Mabel, the boys, and I crossed the street in front of a patrolling police car. The police patrol acted as if they didn't see us. We met Julian Mayfield on Second Street. Mabel, our two sons, Mae Mallory, and I all crammed into his little compact car and set out for New York.[1] I was hoping to return in a week or two, but our family was unknowingly on our way into exile, and it would be fourteen years before I would see Boyte Street again.

We traveled Highway 601, which was a back route out of Monroe. We met incoming state troopers speeding to Monroe in a convoy that appeared to stretch for at least a mile. When we arrived in New York the next morning, the Monroe incident and the fact that there was an all-points bulletin out for me was dominating the news. The bulletin stated that I was heavily armed, bore a scar on my face, and was an extremely dangerous schizophrenic. It also stated that I was traveling in the company of my family. The bulletin's wording was tantamount to a "shoot on sight" order.

Some militants were afraid to take Mabel and me into their homes; however, a white doctor and his Afro wife gave us refuge in their home on Long Island. Julian went into Harlem, informed individuals passing on the street that I was in New York in flight, and within a very short span of time returned with $400 that he had collected from them.

Our two sons were taken in by some friends of Julian who knew only that their parents were escaping from the South and they needed shelter.

The vast amount of media coverage was so intense that the thought of ever returning to Monroe instantly evaporated. A friend from Brooklyn loaned me his driver's license for identification. After two weeks on Long Island, the doctor and a friend drove Mabel and me to the Canadian border. He had brought along

1. Mae Mallory (1927–2007) was a Georgia-born New York City activist who was part of the solidarity network with the Monroe movement. She was at the Williams residence in Monroe on August 27, 1961, to support the local movement with the freedom riders in town. Along with Robert Williams and others, she was accused of kidnapping after the Stegalls left the Black section of Monroe. Mallory went to New York with the Williams household to avoid harassment and reprisal from white supremacist authorities. She ultimately sought refuge in Ohio and fought extradition to North Carolina before being returned there in 1964 to be tried for the kidnapping of the Stegalls, along with young Monroe activists Richard Crowder and Harold Reape and white freedom rider John Lowry. A comprehensive biography of Mae Mallory is in Paula Marie Seniors, *Mae Mallory, the Monroe Defense Committee, and World Revolutions* (Athens: University of Georgia Press, 2024).

his golf bags, and he and I proceeded through customs alone while Mabel and the friend walked on the US side, strolling along as if sightseeing from the bridge.

The only question I had to answer at customs was, "Where were you born?" True to my new identity, I answered, "Georgia." The doctor said that we were going over for a golf outing. We were waved on with wishes for a pleasant trip. After crossing, we went to the Canadian side of the bridge and waited for Mabel and our friend. They strolled arm in arm across the bridge and were not stopped on the other side.

We all rejoined and proceeded on to Toronto. In Toronto, we stayed in the home of some white friends, Vernal and Anne Olson. I had met the Olsons before when I was traveling and speaking for the Fair Play for Cuba Committee. They were dedicated activists in Toronto. They readily took us into their home, and we stayed for several weeks. One day, the *Toronto Globe and Mail* published a huge picture of me on its front page with an article stating that the US government had asked Canada to arrest and extradite me. A group of Canadian friends concluded that if I should be apprehended in Canada, it would be more in my favor to be taken into custody in French Canada. They were convinced that no French Canadian judge would send me back to the racist US southland.[2] Members from the Socialist Workers Party moved me to Nova Scotia, accompanied by a lawyer. Nova Scotia was an ideal location because of a sizable Black population there. I was lodged in the home of an elderly Afro-American. Mabel remained in Toronto with a Black family. We were separated because the police had been alerted to watch for a Black couple. A Black Canadian couple had been sent out to test the extent of the dragnet, and they had been stopped and interrogated a number of times. The senior citizen who took me into his home never inquired as to why I was on the run. He said that he didn't know my problem but was glad that he could help me. He said that he had a strange feeling that he was doing something very important and that my mission was important.

The next week I was told by my Canadian friends that the Cubans knew that I was there and that they were working on a plan to get me safely out and to Cuba.

During the time that I was escaping the FBI in the United States, I never felt that I would be caught. Though I was on the run, I felt a sense of inner security. It was a different story with the Royal Canadian Mounted Police. A segment of my childhood education came back to haunt me. When I was a child in elementary school, we read and were told many stories about the adventures of

2. While Williams was in exile in Canada, Quebec (aka French Canada) was in the beginning of its Quiet Revolution, a period of social and political change in the province culminating in the election of a pro-independence government in 1976. John Alexander Dickinson, *A Short History of Quebec* (Montreal: McGill-Queen's University Press, 2003), 305–44.

the Mounties in their colorful uniforms. Sounds of those distant days came out of the past like echoes. The teacher would ask, "Children, what is the motto of the Royal Canadian Mounted Police?" We would answer in unison, "We always get our man!" Our teacher would be proud that we had read our books and had retained what we had read. Yes, we had retained it more than the teacher knew. The stories were still with me in my subconscious mind. Now that I was hunted by the Mounties, the lessons resurfaced.

During this time of stress, I could appreciate the lifelong influences of early training. "We always get our man!" was like a refrain that I could not purge from my mind. If the motto was predicated on truth, then my flight was futile. How could I escape the mighty Mounties? I recalled storybook photographs of giant Saint Bernard dogs with flasks of rum dangling on their collars as they dragged half-dead fugitives from the Far North. I had an inclination to save myself some trouble by surrendering to the Mounties, but then I remembered that I had never seen the Mounties and their dogs capture a Black man. In a strange way, it dawned on me that perhaps they had no experience in catching Black men. I then became fired with the thought of what a good feeling it would be to be the first to triumph over them. I began to think that since I was not a criminal, it would be a credit to Afro-Americans to break their winning streak. Conditioning from experiences that formed my later years overrode the earlier ones. I had been in the US Marine Corps, and the refrain was "Go for broke!" The doubt vanished, and I could entertain no other thought than to go for broke.

After what seemed to me to be an eternity, word finally came to me that Cuba was ready to assist in my escape. I was to be transported to Gander in Nova Scotia. Gander was a refueling station for Eastern Bloc planes en route to Havana. The Canadian network of socialists transported me to the airport. I was anxiously waiting there when the plane made its refueling stop. Many Cubans from the flight entered the airport to await the completed servicing of the plane. The Canadian who accompanied me there told me to go to the restroom and wait until I was contacted by a Cuban from the flight. As I made my way to the toilet, all the Cubans had been counted by a security guard as they passed through the gate that regulated traffic entering the waiting room.

An Afro-Cuban approached me in the rest room and inquired, "Are you Williams?"

"Yes," I replied.

"I will remain here; you join the group for Cuba," he advised as he disappeared into a toilet booth.

As soon as I joined the crowd of waiting Cubans, a very attractive woman leaned on me and held onto my arm as if we might have been lovers. She and I walked arm in arm through the security gate as the guard recounted the number of passengers who reentered the plane. I was still experiencing a state of anxiety. The man who had exchanged places with me remained in Canada. I was told later that the woman who had assisted me was the wife of Juan Almeida, an Afro-Cuban commander of the army who had been one of Fidel's original revolutionaries.

The plane taxied to the runway and waited for clearance for what seemed like a lifetime. As soon as it became airborne, all of the passengers erupted in loud, emotional applause. I was told that Fidel had had complete faith that I would make it to Cuba and had instructed his aides to inform him the minute I reached Cuban soil.

Robert Williams (*far left*) and Fidel Castro (*center*), Havana, c. 1961.
Robert F. Williams Papers, Bentley Historical Library, University of Michigan.

CHAPTER 45

ON CUBAN SOIL

In Cuba I was lodged in a nice, spacious apartment and was furnished a bodyguard. I had made it, but my family was still in Canada. The days I spent in the apartment were lonely ones filled with anxiety concerning my family. I was plagued by an awful thought that I could possibly never see them again. Several weeks passed with no news about them. Occasionally an official would drop by to see me. Finally, I got a pleasant surprise when William Worthy, a writer for the Afro-American newspapers, paid me a visit. Worthy broke the news that I was safe in Cuba. After several weeks, I requested political asylum and was allowed to host a press conference. Now the news was confirmed that I was in Cuba.

Eventually, with the guidance of our Canadian friends and their Mexican and Cuban connections, Mabel was brought through Mexico to Cuba. That was a very happy occasion, but neither of us had seen our two sons since the day we had arrived in New York and had to be separated. We were informed that they were in Canada and being well taken care of. But we were both torn with anxiety, longing to be reunited with them.

After Mabel's arrival, we were given sightseeing tours all over the island. Everywhere we went, the Cuban people were very friendly and did everything possible to make us feel welcome. The friendly atmosphere made me feel that a terrible burden had been lifted. My life was undergoing a great transition as a result of the contrast between the new life and what I had known as a Black person growing up in the racist southland of the United States. When I had recurring thoughts of the dehumanization and oppression I had experienced back home, I entertained a burning desire to strike back at those who had driven me from my homeland for no other reason than seeking my God-given human rights. I knew that many white Americans would have fought to the death if they had been subjected to the brutal indignities that had filled my life. How could they expect me to do less?

After we had been in Cuba a few months, the Cuban officials surprised us with our sons. Our family was happily reunited, and the weight of their tenuous absence was past. With this weight lifted, as the days went by my desire became ever more intense to actively enter the fight again. The thought of what had been done to my family tortured me with an obsession to do everything I could to make my country the land that I had always dreamed that it would be.

Our pictures had been in the local newspapers following my press conference and many subsequent interviews. Ordinary Cuban citizens recognized me on sight and would introduce themselves to me and offer to help us in any way they could.

We began to forge friendships with many of them. One such friend, Carlos, worked in a printshop. When he learned that we had published our personal newsletter, *The Crusader*, when we were in the South, he went to his printshop and asked his fellow workers if they would volunteer to print a newsletter for me. With their support, he came to see me and told me that his whole shop had volunteered to print my publication, on workers' own time, if I wanted them to. I was overjoyed to learn of their offer. This was my visa to enter the fight again, and this time there would be no bigots and Klansmen free to snuff out my life.

The Crusader, published in exile, was reborn. We began publishing on a regular basis and contacted our Canadian friends the Olsons to see if they would serve as a bulk distribution point. They readily agreed, and we were back in the fray. They and our subscribers in the States kept us apprised of the activities going on through newspaper and magazine clippings and exchange publications. We could also hear the local and national news from radio stations in Florida and up the coast on the regular radio and broadcasts from all over the world on our shortwave radio.

In addition to the now ongoing newsletter, I felt a need to talk to the oppressed people of the Deep South. Subsequently, I made a request to Fidel Castro to grant me radio time to broadcast to the US South. During the interim, while I waited for a response from Fidel concerning my request for broadcast time, I made a concerted effort to become more familiar with the city of Havana. After being driven around the Havana area and observing conditions, it was more than obvious to me that many changes had taken place since my first visit there in 1960.

Cuba had now declared itself socialist. All kinds of individuals who declared themselves to be friends of the revolution were showing up in Havana. The atmosphere was charged with vitality as everyone seemed to be rushing about, experimenting with ways of building a new society. Many of the projects I had seen started the year before had now been completed. When I first went to Cuba, I saw housing and living conditions that were so wretched that it was hard to believe that such conditions could be allowed to exist just ninety miles from the USA. One community that I visited more than thirty-four years ago still haunts my memory. Though I would like to erase the image, it clings to my mind as vividly today as if it were an experience the morning of this very day.

The housing in that community, which I can't erase from my mind, consisted of clapboard shanties, thrown together with discarded sheets of tin, all forms of useful refuse, and whatever was available. The shacks had no windows, no chimneys, no floors, not even the most primitive plumbing. And food was cooked on old, discarded five-gallon cans. Open ditches flowed through the middle of the shantytown wherein young children played in water, polluted with raw sewage. An awful stench filled the air. The only running water in the community consisted of two aged faucets at either end of the shantytown. Water had to be carted, in some cases for at least half a mile. It was a crime against nature for a so-called civilized society to tolerate the fact that a segment of humanity was forced to live under conditions unfit for cattle breeding.

In the year since I had visited, that community had been abolished. Beautiful new housing, schools, and medical centers were springing up all over poor communities. I noticed that the more that life improved for the very wretched, the more the affluent lined up to go to the United States. Those who claimed to be leaving in quest of freedom and democracy had been most tolerant of the conditions of brutal dehumanization of their fellow citizens in despair. They were leaving to seek something that I had never been able to obtain in my native land. I had remained in my country and fought as long as I could to improve the quality of life for my people, but there was an exodus here wherein some individuals were seemingly seeking what they thought to be a ready-made paradise.

Cuba was more than an example of social change and revolutionary agitation; it had also become a major battleground in the struggle between the different brands of Communism. I found myself becoming entangled in the snarl of contending factions, despite my intention to limit my attention to the racial struggle in the United States.

CHAPTER 46

ANTISOCIAL INQUISITORS

After having been in Havana for three or more weeks, before the arrival of my family, I was invited to a party at the home of Cedric Belfrage. Cedric was a British subject who had lived many years in the United States, where he served as editor of the leftist weekly known as the *National Guardian*. He had been deported from the States for his Left-leaning stance. Cedric and his wife, Mary, were highly gung-ho in their support of the Cuban Revolution. Despite the fact that I was hammered with a barrage of questions concerning my escape, I found the gathering at the Belfrage home to be enjoyable and relaxing. It also afforded me an opportunity to fraternize with Cuban and foreign revolutionaries.

A few days after Cedric's party, I received a telegram from ICAP [the Cuban Institute for Friendship with the Peoples] saying that my presence was required at its office.[1] Arriving at the ICAP office, I discovered Belfrage and some others who had been in attendance at his party. They were surprised to learn that we had all received telegrams bearing like messages. Also in the waiting room was a middle-aged Puerto Rican Communist who had just recently come to Cuba. It was rumored that he had been deported from the United States. I noticed that he was holding a newspaper that he was supposed to be reading. It was held in front of his face as if it was being used to conceal his identity.

1. ICAP is the Instituto Cubano de Amistad con los Pueblos. Its role is to build solidarity with the international community for the Cuban Revolution.

After a brief wait, we were ushered into an office in which three top ICAP officials, including Raymond Cisneros, a member of Cuba's Communist Party Central Committee, were seated. One of the officials spoke up: "Information has reached us that you people are criticizing the ICAP. We want you to know that this is an agency of the government. Whoever condemns us attacks the revolution itself and risks being expelled from Cuba. If you are friends, you will say what you dislike to our faces, not whisper behind our backs as you have been doing."

I was both puzzled and irritated as I queried, "If that is the reason you have summoned these people, why was I required to come here?"

"Look, Bob," Cedric Belfrage said, "it's obvious you were asked here because of attending that party at my house. A few of the guests may have been talking, and someone seems to be trying to make a big thing of it."

Extremely annoyed by what seemed to me to be some type of inquisition, I stated, "First of all, I didn't hear one word about your organization at Cedric's party. Secondly, although there is severe repression of Blacks in the South of the USA, I wasn't afraid to say what I wanted to down there, and I am not afraid to speak my mind here in Cuba, either."

Evidently my blunt response had some disorienting effect on them. "Now, now, nobody is accusing you of anything. You are an honored guest of Cuba. We only asked you here in order to show you how ready we are to listen to criticism, that's all."

"If you want some criticism," I said, "then I'll be glad to tell you what I have heard. Even though this wasn't discussed at Cedric's house, in the short time since I've been here, several people have complained to me about ICAP. They accuse you of using the revolution's funds to invite only retired old Communists to visit Cuba, while those revolutionary activists who aren't party members are ignored. They charge that your organization has become little more than an exclusive social club for the aging party functionaries of the world."

At this moment, as though on cue, the Puerto Rican Communist stood up. "We might as well quit kidding ourselves and confess," he intoned. "The truth is that all of us are in it up to here," he said as he gestured toward his throat. It was more than obvious to me that he was the cause of our being there.

The atmosphere surrounding this sordid affair infuriated me. I jumped to my feet and declared, "Let me assure you of one thing. I haven't had any personal criticisms of ICAP until this point, and when I do, you won't have to wait for some stool pigeon to tell you. I'll shout them to your faces long before anyone overhears me at a party. If this is the way you do things in socialist Cuba, I don't belong in this place! I would rather go back to the racist United States in chains!"

My emotional reaction overwhelmed them with shock. The officials ended the meeting abruptly. The Puerto Rican left the room without raising his eyes. Whatever accusations he was ready to make failed to materialize. I knew and I am sure that the self-appointed inquisitors also knew that Fidel Castro would never back them up in such an antisocial affair. It was my introduction to one of the less inspiring aspects of the new undercurrent developing in Cuba, and I didn't like the tendency.

The need to defend Cuba against counterrevolutionists and US attempts to undo the revolution was justified, but this need seemed to be opening the door to a morbid element of mindless extremists and agents provocateurs.

The hostility of the US government forced Cuba to embrace the Soviets in a desperate effort to preserve its revolutionary gains. As Soviet aid steadily increased, so did the influence of the nomad Communists of the United States who thought of themselves as expert revolutionaries, capable of extending guidance to the fledgling consolidation of government in the new society. In order to strengthen their position, the US Communists seemed to be making it very difficult for anyone who wasn't allied with them to emigrate to Cuba. It was next to impossible for friends of mine and admirers of the Cuban Revolution to visit me in Cuba without the direct and personal intervention of Fidel.

Cedric Belfrage had been singled out as a target by several of the US Communist Party members I met in Havana. I was warned by them about being seen in Belfrage's company. I was told that he was a British intelligence agent. I later learned that he had worked as a spy, but it was against the Axis powers during World War II. Not only had Cedric publicly admitted this, but he had written a book extolling his ventures. Becoming disillusioned with Britain's cold war policies, he had resigned his post, according to his writings. I was convinced that the Communist nomads from the United States and perhaps some Britons were out to discredit him, even though he was a dedicated socialist. His independent views and outspokenness did not serve as an asset in such a charged environment.

CHAPTER 47

IDEOLOGICAL DIFFERENCES AND THE BIRTH OF *RADIO FREE DIXIE*

Although I had spoken to Fidel on several occasions during my 1960 visits, during the first few weeks of my 1961 exile, I did not see him until the day I was invited to the José Martí Airport with a group conveyed there to welcome an incoming Soviet high official. Fidel was there, and everyone was excited. He came over to me and asked how I was getting along in Cuba. "I'm getting along just fine, Fidel. I want to thank you and the Cuban people for helping my family and me!" I said.

"You don't owe us any thanks, Williams; it was our revolutionary duty," he replied.

As if having heard about the incident from Cedric's party, he turned to the blonde-headed ICAP woman, Yolanda, who stood beside me and said, "Williams is a friend of ours. We don't want him to have any problems in Cuba; do you understand?"

"We are taking good care of him, Fidel," she replied.

Directing his words to me again as the Russian looked on, puzzled, he said, "I hope you will excuse me for not seeing you before now, but I have been very busy. I've assigned Comandante Pinero to help you. Anytime you need anything or want to contact me, just give him a call."

Pinero was a heavyset, stocky man with a red beard. Though he kept a low profile and was not very well publicized, he was the assistant prime minister at the time and later became one of the three directors of the Ministry for Foreign

Relations. Like Fidel and Che Guevara, Pinero wore a military uniform. Unlike them, however, his photo was hardly ever displayed. Most people referred to him only as the "red beard." Rumor had it that he had become head of G-2.[1]

Having lived in the United States, Pinero spoke perfect English. He was quite reliable in assisting me in acquiring things for my personal use, but he showed somewhat of a negative side when it came to anything involving my struggle against US racism. One day, while puffing on his traditional long cigar, he admonished, "Williams, why don't you just relax, take it easy, and enjoy your stay in Cuba? After the workers make a socialist revolution in the United States, you'll be able to return to a people's homeland with no fear of arrest."

"No," I said, "I'm sorry to have to disagree with you, but there's no possibility of a workers' socialist revolution there. A Black uprising is more likely."

"No," Pinero declared, puffing on his cigar, "there can be no separate Black revolt. It will have to be a joint effort with the whites because they constitute the vast majority of Americans."

"But the white workers aren't that oppressed in the United States," I insisted. "So long as they have jobs and can buy available consumer goods, they will not rise up against the system. The Blacks are severely oppressed and victimized by racism, and so long as this situation exists, they are the only ones with the motivation to fight the system."

"Not being a Marxist-Leninist, you fail to understand the contradiction inherent in the US economy," the comandante insisted. As our conversation progressed, his position became more questionable to me. "Look at how the American people are rallying to Rev. Martin Luther King," he said. "Under his leadership, Blacks and whites are being united. That shows how wrong you are when you say a workers' revolution is impossible in the United States."

"Martin Luther King is attracting many white supporters because he is leading Blacks away from violence, and many whites see a great advantage in avoiding a violent explosion that could threaten their privileged way of life. US racism festers in a savage society. Violence perpetuates the status quo. Our people have been long-suffering and nonviolent, and we have never enjoyed any substantial and meaningful sympathy on the part of the white working class."

Pinero paused for a moment and then said, "You may be right, but the important thing is to organize Blacks and whites and get them working for the same goals. Once you have accomplished that, you can educate the workers and get them to join the Communist Party, which will make the revolution."

1. G-2 is a common name for the Intelligence Directorate in Cuba.

I was surprised to hear a Cuban leader pushing the same old line that I had heard and rejected on my many trips to New York. This line was also contrary to the historical tendency of the Cuban struggle. The Cuban Communist Party leadership had, in fact, criticized the revolutionary insurgency of the 26th of July Movement as "Bourgeois adventurism."[2] "The USCP [US Communist Party] is thoroughly infiltrated with the FBI and CIA. And besides, it strives to relegate our struggle to the status of an appendage to the white-dominated party. Our liberation is secondary on their agenda. For us to take on the Communist label is to fasten a millstone around our necks," I argued.

As he left, puffing on his long cigar, I told him to tell Fidel that I still had not been given the radio time that he had promised. Soon after I had arrived in Cuba, I had made a written request to Fidel to grant me radio time to supplement my newsletter, *The Crusader*. I sensed that Pinero, along with the old Communist clique, was less than enthusiastic concerning my establishment of *Radio Free Dixie* that I had proposed for broadcasting to Afro-Americans in the South of the United States.

Two weeks later I was invited for an interview by Cesar Escalante, the brother of Anibal Escalante, the chief of propaganda. Escalante, too, was weak in his interest. He had the old idea of appealing to the working class in general. As I was leaving, he told me that he would instruct the people in radio to allow me to set up a broadcast schedule.

Several weeks passed and I had not heard from the people at Radio Progreso. I soon heard from sympathetic Americans that Joseph North, the Havana correspondent of the USCP journal, *The Worker*, was trying to persuade the Cubans to deny my request for a radio program. North was supposed to be an expert on the "Negro problem," and I was told that all English-language broadcasts to the United States had to be cleared by him. Since I was Black and had been a leader in the Black struggle in the South, I assumed that North saw my presence in Cuba as a threat to his heretofore unquestioned expertise on all phases of American life. The USCP had sent down so-called technicians to help construct socialism

2. The 26th of July Movement was the revolutionary vanguard organization led by Fidel Castro that seized state power from dictator Fulgencio Batista in 1959. Its name derives from the date of an unsuccessful coup by Castro and his comrades on July 26, 1953. Castro and his comrades reorganized themselves in prison and launched a successful political and military revolutionary campaign in 1959. After seizing state power, the 26th of July Movement united with other pro-socialist organizations to form the United Party of the Cuban Socialist Revolution, ultimately assuming the name Communist Party of Cuba. Aviva Chomsky, *A History of the Cuban Revolution* (West Sussex, UK: John Wiley and Sons, 2015), 30–33; A. James McAdams, *Vanguard of the Revolution: The Global Idea of the Communist Party* (Princeton, NJ: Princeton University Press), 310–11.

in Cuba. This little clique huddled around Joseph North. They moved might and main to harness me to the catechism of international Marxism.

After weeks of stalling on the part of the propaganda clique, I sent a message to Fidel to inform him that I was not being allowed to broadcast and I thought that the time element was important to my friends who were facing court frame-ups back home. Fidel broke the tie-up by informing the radio officials that if they didn't put me on the radio, he was coming there himself to put me on.

Radio Free Dixie was born. It was mine. Fidel gave me three hours a week—an hour on Monday, an hour on Wednesday, and a third hour on Friday. The time was given without censorship. It was given as a contribution and in active support of the Afro-American struggle. It was an ecstatic experience to be given three hours to broadcast a format in a way that our people had never heard before. I used provocative music and songs that Afro-Americans could identify with. *Radio Free Dixie* utilized extensive drumming and a beat that was identified with what was commonly known as sanctified church music. Once the music had put the audience in a receptive frame of mind, a highly emotional message was given. We gleaned from the Black press the type of news very seldom published by the white press. When letters from listeners started to come in, I knew that I was being widely heard.

As *Radio Free Dixie* evolved, I started a psychological experiment. I studied the book *The Battle for the Mind* and learned that when the individual is exhausted, there is greater possibility of planting new ideas.[3] I knew that certain types of music, if followed at length, could tire the mind out. I created all the intensity possible. The purpose of *Radio Free Dixie* was not for entertainment or escapism; it was to agitate and motivate a people who had been too passive and submissive toward their oppression and dehumanization for too long.

3. William Sargant, *Battle for the Mind: A Physiology of Conversion and Brainwashing* (New York: Penguin, 1957).

CHAPTER 48

AGENTS PROVOCATEURS AND BOURGEOIS COMMUNIST CRITICS

Not only was *Radio Free Dixie* being listened to in the USA, but the jazz was also attracting Cubans. A Cuban woman told my wife that she really enjoyed the program, but she didn't understand why I was so obsessed with cats. This puzzled Mabel, and she tried to explain to her that I was not obsessed with cats and that we had never even owned a cat. The Cuban woman said that during several broadcasts I had talked about white cats and Black cats. She was slightly embarrassed but broke into laughter when it was explained to her that this was Afro-American slang referring to white men and Black men.

Radio Free Dixie soon triggered a severe reaction in the United States. A flood of speeches and newspaper editorials burst forth calling me a traitor, but I considered *Radio Free Dixie* a challenge to the First Amendment's much touted claim of free speech. I went on the air with a drive for vengeance. All of the injustice in the USA drove me with a passion. I remembered how cruelly the mournful cries of suffering Afros had been muffled since the advent of Blacks in the so-called New World. I remembered how my aptitude testing had shown that I deserved the right to be placed in information services, as I had been promised for enlisting in the US Marine Corps. They had refused to send me to study at Quantico, Virginia, simply because I was Black, and at that time Blacks were denied the opportunity to train there. But now, I had a chance, and I intended to use it to the very best of my ability. Eventually the US Navy placed an electronics ship off the coast to jam the broadcasts.

In what I considered a conspiracy, the US Marxists in the American community approached some of their Cuban counterparts to persuade them that the contents of such a program should be placed under a committee and that such power should not be given to one individual. Fidel reiterated that the time had been given as an act of solidarity with the Afro-American people and that inasmuch as I was a Black man from the South of the United States, no others in Cuba had a right to control my thought.

The subversive element in the foreign colony started a rumor campaign. Some whispered that I was a Black Muslim who hated white people. Some whispered that I was not a freedom fighter but had raped a fourteen-year-old girl and fled to Cuba. Cards, somewhat cryptic, were sent from Miami, Florida, stating that I should "be on the same beach next Friday as before." Foreigners started spreading rumors that I was an agent who had been planted in Cuba to stir up the race issue. When an American told a Cuban official that I was planted as an agent provocateur, the officer told him that I was beyond reproach, that Cuban intelligence knew perfectly well how I got there. He stated that I was the only American in Cuba that they were sure of how I got there. The American himself was unaware of the fact that the Cubans had brought me there. The American, who was an Afro from the USCP, realizing that he had put himself in jeopardy, became so frightened that he came to me and confessed that party cohorts had misinformed him and that the Cubans had the utmost confidence in me. He pleaded that as Afro-Americans, we should stick together.

I started experiencing many difficulties in Cuba, but I knew that the real revolutionaries and Fidel had great sympathy for my cause. I was aware of the fact that a counterrevolutionary current, in league with CIA cohorts, was trying to turn me and other foreigners against the revolution. The masses of Cuban people were always friendly toward my family and me.

After my complaints finally reached Fidel, the party gave me a monthly allowance, a car, and a house. The bodyguard and chauffeur were withdrawn. The party issued me a new 9mm P-38 pistol for protection, and I was told that Fidel had given instructions to leave me on my own because the Cuban people liked me and would protect me.

One day I was driving in the wrong direction down a one-way street when a police car pulled up on the side and waved me to the curb. After I had curbed the car, the policeman came to the driver's side. He recognized me. He said, "Oh, Williams, I'm sorry." He waved me on as he put his ticket book away. A crowd of Cubans had gathered along the sidewalk. I told the officer that he had to give me a ticket. He asked me why and I told him because I didn't want the onlookers to think that I expected to be exempt from Cuban law. He said, "OK, I'll give you a ticket, if that's what you want, but I'll tear it up later."

As he wrote the ticket, the onlookers started shouting unkind remarks to him. He said, "You see, Williams, the Cuban people like you. They don't want me to give you a ticket."

As time went by, more and more I was able to exercise my full ability in opposing US racism. My two sons, Robert and John, had settled down in a boarding school from which they returned on weekends. Mabel enrolled in the former Berlitz School of Languages, which was now the John Reed School. *The Crusader* was now being sent out to many parts of the world. I had started to write articles pertaining to the nature of US racism for the Cuban weekly magazine *Bohemia*.

Taking note of the fact that jazz music was coming under attack by some of the original Communist Party members, one of my first articles in *Bohemia* dealt with jazz, describing its African and slavery origins. "Jazz is the music of the Black people of America," I wrote, "and it's an insult to us to call it decadent. If you want to say it had been perverted by degenerate commercial elements, we can't object, but it's an affront to declare our music itself is bad." The article continued, "Those Cubans who are against jazz are confusing it with Swing, a musical form promoted chiefly by whites who call themselves 'jazz musicians.' Our music has a deep emotional basis like our blues, spirituals, work songs and folk songs. Jazz comes from the tragic experience of the Black man in America."

My *Bohemia* article became a source of controversy because Blas Roca, a high-ranking official of the Communist Party, had just written a piece attacking jazz. His position stressed the socialist realism line, and I felt that it was a demonstration of the fact that there was a great need for an understanding of music in the USA. The publication of two diametrically opposed points of view made the jazz question a political issue. Soon after my article appeared, a delegation of young Cuban Communists came to have me explain my position in greater detail. Subsequently, several newspaper and magazine articles were published supporting my contention.

In the wake of the articles now being published, the young Communist group arranged to sponsor a jazz concert in Havana. They asked me to speak on the Afro-American struggle during intermission. I gladly agreed, though I sincerely doubted that the party would tolerate a jazz concert staged by open-minded youth. I was wrong.

The concert came and went without repercussions. The house rocked, and I enjoyed it. Dogmatism was not there. Perhaps it was primarily in the imaginations of the anti-Communists. The large theater was filled to capacity, and it carried the party's stamp of approval. That was a good indication that the Cuban and American youth had a great deal in common and that they would be friends if Washington would give them a chance to manifest it.

Most of the international Communists whom I had come in contact with in Havana constituted a motley lot, but the USCP-ers and their fellow travelers represented the apex of pretentious smart-ass-ness. They had ready answers for almost everything but a genuine devotion almost limited to a common agenda. I soon learned that white Americans' agenda universally was the advancement of the cause of white nationalism. White nationalism in the final analysis was nothing less than white supremacy. Forces as diametrically opposite as Communism, Christianity, Judaism, and class stratification could be counted on to rally in defense of the perpetuation of white power nationalism. With but a few exceptions, I discovered that they [these different political factions] coalesced in an almost solid front to weaken my position and to curb my effectiveness against American racism. It was easy for me to discern from their reaction that they were ashamed to have US dirty linen aired abroad. Naturally, if foreigners were apprised of the savagery of bigotry back home, the question might arise why so-called revolutionaries would voluntarily become missionaries engaged in Cuban problem solving.

Once I happened, uninvited, upon a meeting at the CMA Radio station. An American named Harold Spencer was extolling the erroneous concept of universal working-class common interest. I heard him say, "The American workers and the Cuban workers have international solidarity. If Cuba should be invaded by the imperialists, all we would have to do is appeal to the US proletariat over the radio and they would pour out into the streets in solidarity with and in defense of their working-class Cuban brothers. That's why we have to be careful not to alienate them by harping on the race issue."

"Harold," I interrupted, "how can you tell these people such bullshit? Did Cuba's broadcasts during the invasion at Playa Girón bring the American workers out into the street? Did all those workers you're talking about stop the exile invasion?"

"Hell no! We stopped them with our guns!" one of the Cuban radio supervisors shouted.

After the meeting broke up, the supervisor told me, "The American workers aren't going to save us if we are attacked. We Cubans will have to rely on ourselves."

Later, I learned that a few USCP-ers supported my position relative to the US working class's possibility of coming to the aid of a Cuba in distress. They were also sympathetic toward my ideas of organizing Blacks in the United States.

When I explained the problems I was having with my critics, one apologetically stated, "We want you to know that all of us are not alike." Unfortunately, revolutionary Communists outside the clique held very little influence within the party.

Radio Free Dixie and *The Crusader* were getting more and more responses. We were receiving more and more letters, and more and more individuals were volunteering to distribute *The Crusader*. We got a big increase in record contributions. I supposed that we perhaps had the only program in the world where ordinary listeners donated the music and tapes. No other station, other than Pacifica, would dare broadcast programs like ours. We sent tapes of *Radio Free Dixie* to be rebroadcast over the New York and California stations. Based upon the anger inherent in the letters I was receiving from strangers, I felt secure in predicting that the United States was ripe for racial violence. Due to the mere fact that I dared to predict impending mass violence on the part of once meek and submissive Afros, I became the object of such ridicule in the American media, which seemed unable to comprehend the growing restlessness on the part of long-suffering Black people. US militants of both races were seeking my assistance in getting into Cuba. Some even requested that I assist them in getting military training. They were unaware that Pinero and certain CP-ers were working vigorously to frustrate my efforts to confer with US militants. In looking back, I can ascertain that in one such case, they [Pinero and his enemies in the USCP] unwittingly did me a favor. One request from an individual who claimed to be a distributor of *The Crusader* and a member of the Fair Play for Cuba Committee, of which I was a founding member, was Lee Harvey Oswald.[1]

When I first visited Cuba, a shell of a skyscraper was standing deserted. I assumed the project had run out of steam. During my exile, the structure remained unfinished; however, other projects were being completed in record time. In response to my inquiry, I was told that the building had been planned as Che Guevara's National Bank Building and that it had been sabotaged with a powerful new incendiary device. I was informed that the CIA was in possession of systems wrapped in simulated cigarette packs. These could be carried in a man's shirt pocket and passed off as packs of cigarettes. These instruments

1. Lee Harvey Oswald was determined to be the assassin of President John F. Kennedy by the Warren Commission, appointed by President Lyndon Johnson. "Investigation of Possible Conspiracy," chapter 6, *Warren Commission Report*, President John F. Kennedy Assassination Records Collection, National Archives, accessed November 3, 2024, https://www.archives.gov/research/jfk/warren-commission-report/chapter-6.html. There is evidence of Oswald's membership in the Fair Play for Cuba Committee. See "Letter from the Fair Play for Cuba Committee, May 29, 1963," Portal to Texas History, accessed May 28, 2024, https://texashistory.unt.edu/ark:/67531/metapth337534/.

burned so intensely that they burned through concrete for as many as fourteen floors and the heat warped the buildings to the extent that they became useless.

I soon learned that all the accusations that Cuba was practicing unrestricted sabotage against her enemies were pure fabrications. These lies were being circulated to lend credence to the proposed campaign to isolate and destroy the Cuban Revolution. Thinking that these systems [of explosive devices] would be ideal for Black freedom fighters, I requested that Pinero inform Fidel that we needed the ones they had captured so that Afro-American freedom fighters could use them. I suggested that inasmuch as it was an American product, Cuba could not be blamed. I was angry and felt that Blacks could wreak havoc on the most affluent American communities with such a device. I made a series of requests that were never honored. Considering what the United States had done to my people and me, I had no compunction about reacting to oppression the way the American revolutionaries had reacted to the British Crown. After all, history had taught that all forms of struggle are virtuous when brutal and dehumanizing subjugation is unrelenting on the part of an oppressor devoid of human compassion. Blacks never got the mighty secret weapon, and later the mainstay of their arsenal became the common match and bottles of gasoline. Lucky for the United States that the Cubans never really wanted to injure America. I detected a latent admiration and hoped that someday there would be a chance for reconciliation and neighborly friendship. However, I was certain, then and now, that so long as Cuba insisted on complete independence, the United States would remain hostile.

As time passed, the bourgeois Communists, along with their fellow traveling agents provocateurs, intensified their efforts to frustrate and turn me against the revolution.[2] I was severely criticized for not advocating socialism in my broadcasts. I was lambasted for not studying Spanish like most of the Americans, who had turned their backs on the growing struggle for social justice in the United States. Some "comrades" who displayed very little interest in the increasing struggle of American Blacks against racial oppression in the United States suggested

2. Robert Williams saw differences among the Communists he met in Cuba. The bourgeois Communists were those who opposed Black self-determination in the United States, believing that white workers would lead a socialist revolution. Williams believed most white workers were racists. Bourgeois Communists also thought that appealing to white Americans to engage in solidarity with Cuba should be a priority. On the other hand, Williams believed that Communists, particularly Cubans and white Americans, who supported Black revolutionary nationalism—and knew that Cubans needed to rely on their own people and resources to defend the revolution—were revolutionary Communists. See Robert Cohen, *Black Crusader: A Biography of Robert Franklin Williams* (Secaucus, NJ: Lyle Stuart, 1972), 217–22.

that I devote my time to studying Marxism as a panacea for the solution of the race problem. They claimed that a socialist society would eliminate racism. They claimed that in a socialist state, racism would no longer be needed for the sake of exploitation of the working class, that this was a truism because racism is predicated upon class exploitation. Having experienced racism in its most rancid forms, there was no way that anyone could convince me that through countless generations of practice, racial animosity had not become deeply ingrained in the sourness of a mutated humanity.

It disturbed the bourgeois US Communists to no end that I continued to insist that the US economy was so complex and interdependent that I was afraid of what would happen if some of them ever took over. It was one thing to crush the middle class in an underdeveloped nation, but if they tried in the United States, as in Russia, to replace every corporate executive and factory manager with someone whose only measure of competency was his loyalty to the Communist Party, it would not be long before things would be so badly screwed up that it would be necessary to import goods from abroad in order to feed and clothe the population. My ideas were soon being labeled as those of a naive individualist and that of a Social Democrat.

In 1962, in an effort to counteract the anti-Cuban position adopted by the Organization of American States at Punte del Este, besieged Cuba organized a Latin American Solidarity Conference in Havana. Although there were some white Americans present who had come with a group of observers from the Canadian Peace Council, I was the only US citizen invited to speak as a representative of North America.

In my speech, which was carried on Cuban radio and TV, I said, "The symbol of Americanism to me is the painful image of my brutally subjugated people, tugging at their chains of repression. Yes, I can still hear them dragging their chains across a so-called Christian nation that enriched itself on the sweat, blood, and tears of my captive people. If we had the opportunity to talk to the American Indians of yesteryear, to the great chiefs like Geronimo and Sitting Bull, I wonder what message they would have for us? They once faced a situation like the one Cuba faces today. They believed in the goodness of the American white man, in his treaties and words of deception. And we all know what happened to them. No, our only answer to Punte del Este must be to prepare our bullets and sharpen our machetes."

The conference responded with a thunderous ovation as attendees rose to their feet.

During the night after I had delivered my speech, several of the Canadian Peace Council and USCP people came to see me. "Williams," the spokesperson intoned, "you missed a great opportunity today to strike a blow for peace. Instead, all you spoke about was violence and war. All of America, both North and South, was listening. Why didn't you try to appeal to the good intentions of the American masses?"

"How could I, a Black refugee from racial tyranny, speak of something that I know nothing about?" I asked. "If the American people have such good intentions, why didn't they protest what Batista was doing to the Cuban people in the past? And what makes you think they have changed? And what makes you think they'll do anything to stop US attacks on Cuba now and in the future?"

"You don't understand!" was the response. "So long as Cuba is bulging with guns, the right-wing extremists can convince the American people that it threatens them. You should have spoken about the need for Cubans and Americans to peacefully settle their differences."

"Are you joking?" I asked. "Even the Blacks who live in the United States can't rely on the American people to protect them from being murdered by the racists. The Cubans being well armed is the only thing that has kept them from being destroyed."

CHAPTER 49

THE CUBAN MISSILE CRISIS

In October 1962, tension gripped the entire world. President Kennedy proclaimed that the Soviet Union had installed deadly long-range missiles in Cuba, and he demanded their removal. He threatened military action, "even if the victory turns to ashes in our mouths."[1] It seemed that the world was on the verge of a holocaust like the world had never seen before. An agent from G-2 came to inform me that a US invasion was imminent and that Fidel had designated a place in the country where my family and I would be taken when the conflict started. That act was the one of the greatest confirmations I could ever have that Fidel was truly a concerned friend. There was a possibility that Cuba would be invaded, and yet he was humble enough to be concerned for the welfare of a Black family from the colossal enemy nation.

I told the man from G-2 to please tell Fidel that I didn't want to be sent to safety. All I wanted him to do was to send me a machine gun. I would take my chances with the Cuban people. I had resisted in the South of the United States, and I wanted to resist some of the same people in Cuba. The man gave me a look of admiration as he said, "If you want to pack your bags, transportation is waiting to take you out of Havana."

"No thanks," I said. "The Cuban people have given shelter to my family. If they are attacked, I prefer to fight at their side." As an afterthought, I asked

1. John Fitzgerald Kennedy, "Address during the Cuban Missile Crisis," radio and television address, October 22, 1962, https://www.jfklibrary.org/learn/about-jfk/historic-speeches/address-during-the-cuban-missile-crisis.

him, "How do you know for certain that the invasion will take place in the next forty-eight hours as you say?"

"Russian intelligence told us that thousands of marines are boarding troop ships in Florida at this very moment."

"No!" I insisted. "I don't care what the Russians told you. No invasion is about to take place in that time frame."

"What do you know that keeps you from believing the invasion is coming now, Williams?"

"Because I'm an ex-marine, and I know that they would never mount an amphibious action without first softening up the area. It would be suicidal to attempt a beach landing against forces well-armed and dug in. In preparation for such an attack, they would stage an extensive sea and air bombardment. They would knock out everything they could. They would be sitting ducks sailing into a fortified area without strategic bombing and shelling. It would cost them more than they would be able to pay in human lives. Believe me, the staging and loading of troops in Florida is just a bluff. They also know that Cuba would be able to bomb southern US cities and that would create panic among the population. No, no! What Russian intelligence has told you is wrong!" I insisted as the seemingly puzzled G-2 agent left to return to his station.

In the afternoon, another man from the security police visited me and said, "There's a fellow a couple of floors down who claims you know him." He led me to a room that had an armed guard posted in front of it. Inside the room, Cedric Belfrage was sitting on the bed looking very perturbed. "Hi, Rob," he greeted me and then asked, "Will you please tell these people who I am? Mary and I hurried back from Mexico when we heard about the threat to Cuba, but G-2 claims there is no record of our being invited and are holding us here in the hotel."

"Do you know him?" the security man asked.

"Yes, he's a friend of the revolution," I stated.

I assumed that Belfrage's enemies had used the crisis situation to compromise his position with the Cubans. Soon thereafter, he and his wife left and went to live in Mexico.

I listened with disbelief to the radio broadcasting from Miami that the Soviets had agreed to pull out their missiles from Cuba. My first thought was that perhaps this was a broadcast of misinformation, designed to demoralize the Cuban people and a part of a softening-up process as preparation for an invasion. I tuned my short-wave radio to Moscow and heard the Russians boasting about how the statesmanship of Khrushchev had pulled the world back from the horror of a catastrophic nuclear holocaust. My disbelief turned to intense anger. This was the same Khrushchev who had promised to send the poverty-stricken people of Monroe a relief ship, raised our hopes, and backed down when he considered that such action might offend the US power structure.

The next morning, a delegation of bourgeois Communists visited me. These Americans were all elated and full of admiration for Khrushchev. "We have a cable we want you to sign. All Americans in Cuba are signing and pitching in to send this cable of thanks to Comrade Khrushchev," Harold Spencer said, almost in a demanding voice.

"Thanks, hell! What the hell are you thanking the pigheaded son of a bitch for?" I asked in an angry, disrespectful voice.

"You can't say that about Comrade Khrushchev. He's saved us! He got peace for Cuba!" one of the delegation proclaimed in an astonished voice.

The atmosphere was heated and strained, as if I had committed some religious heresy. As far as they were concerned, I may as well have cursed God.

"We are all grateful to Premier Khrushchev. If he hadn't agreed to pull out the missiles, there would have been an atomic war and we would have all been killed!" one of the American women said in a voice, trembling with fear.

"If you're so scared of dying, why in the hell don't you take your ass back to racist America? There is no way that I am going to add my name to anything thanking that yellow-bellied rat! He betrayed the Cuban people, and I will tell him to his face that I think he is a pigheaded son of a bitch!"

As the highly disturbed delegation rushed from the room, Spencer shouted back that he was going to report me to G-2.

That evening a representative visited me from Fidel's headquarters. He seemed nervous. After fidgeting for a while he said, "Williams, the 'Hoss' heard that you are raging something awful over here. He wants to know what your trouble is."

"I'm convinced that Khrushchev has betrayed the Cuban people, and I say he is a yellow-bellied rat and a pigheaded son of a bitch! You tell Fidel that's the way I feel, and he can shoot me if he wants to, but that's the way I feel. He has sold Cuba out behind her back!"

Fidel's man pulled himself to the edge of his chair, drew near, and looked me straight in the eye. "Do you really feel that way, Williams?" he asked in a soft voice, struggling with emotion.

"Yes, that's exactly how I feel. He has sold Cuba out behind her back!"

"You know what, Williams, I feel the same way as you do. Between us, when the 'Hoss' heard the news, he was raging more than you. He was so mad, he kicked a door all the way off its hinges." The Cuban stood up, reached to shake my hand, and left, saying, "We all feel the same way."

The streets of Havana had been plastered with posters showing Soviet soldiers, jet pilots, and tank and artillery crews, all with the caption "Cuba is not alone." Enraged Cubans ripped them down. They had been prepared to fight to the death and now had learned the cold fact that Khrushchev had caved in.

Humiliated Russian advisers who stayed at the Hotel Capri where we lived started having their meals served in their rooms. A Cuban bank clerk told me that a Russian colonel he knew had come into the bank and stood with his back to the counter, saying, "I can't face you this morning. It's too humiliating." My sons, who were attending school at Santa Maria Del Mar, related to me how US planes started flying over surface-to-air missiles and flying so low as they performed acrobatics that the pilots could be seen in the cockpits and that some Russian officers stood helplessly by with tears in their eyes. If given the order, they would have fought. The Russians had agreed to open Cuba up for inspection. Fidel refused to consent. U Thant, the secretary-general of the United Nations, came to Havana to attempt to persuade Fidel to change his mind. Fidel had the meeting with U Thant televised so that all of the people of Cuba would be apprised of what was transpiring.

"Under what authority do you come here? Do you represent the United Nations? Are you a spokesman for the USA, or is it the USSR you speak for? And would you mind telling us what international law says—that we, a sovereign nation, must open our territory to an imperialist aggressor for inspection?" Fidel asked an embarrassed, disarmed U Thant. A humbled U Thant replied, "It's not really a matter of international law. I am asking you to do this for the sake of world peace."

"If it's a matter of preserving peace, you have come to the wrong place. You should have gone to Washington to ask the United States to stop organizing attacks against us. It is the real threat to world peace. The only conditions under which we might consider permitting inspection would be if the USA allowed Cuba to inspect all of its military installations in turn."

U Thant returned to New York having suffered a diplomatic fiasco.

Relative to the missile crisis and the decline of Russian prestige, fellow traveling Americans who had been riding the old Communists' coattails experienced a decline in their clout; however, they continued their efforts to retard my activity. Early in 1963 they told anyone who would listen that I didn't represent anyone in the United States and that my efforts were directed solely at promoting my fortune in Cuba. Their efforts were soon belied by cables sent to Cuba by several militant Black organizations asking me to assume leadership of their groups. One such group that was expanding was the Revolutionary Action Movement (RAM). It consisted of the most militant elements of active civil rights fighters unified to constitute the basis for the Black Liberation Front. The idea was to accelerate the Black struggle across the nation. A great portion of RAM was to remain underground. The hysterical reaction of the US media further strengthened my position. RAM's goal was to pressure the US government to enforce the guarantee of the Bill of Rights and to bring about the end of racism and oppression in the United States by any means necessary.

The US government reacted viciously to the formation of RAM. It infiltrated the ranks with agents provocateurs and staged a number of frame-ups in an attempt to destroy the nation's most militant Black group.

CHAPTER 50

BIRMINGHAM BOMBING, MAO TSE-TUNG, AND INTERNATIONALIZING OUR STRUGGLE

In the summer of 1963, one of the most dastardly racist deeds in the annals of US history occurred. It caused my spirit to descend to the lowest depths I had experienced since my exile. Feeling that my exile rendered me incompetent, all the same I felt the need to respond. It was electrifying to learn that unconscionable bigots had bombed a church in Birmingham, Alabama, and murdered four little Black girls at prayer in a church. I was in a deep quandary as to what steps I could take. Finally, I decided that if I could get some well-known international leader to publicly condemn this heathenish act, then I would be striking a mighty blow against racism. It was a long shot, but I had to try it.

I sent a cable to Sukarno of Indonesia, Kwame Nkrumah of Ghana, Ahmed Ben Bella of Algeria, and Mao Tse-tung of China. I expected Sukarno to respond because there had already been demonstrations in his country against US racism. Most of all, I thought Nkrumah would condemn the incident and US racism because he had been a student in America and had witnessed racial discrimination firsthand. I anxiously waited for three weeks, and there was only silence from these known world leaders. Finally, I concluded that even the most despicable acts of barbarism against Black humanity in racist America was of no moment to these anti-imperialist leaders. At the very time I had given up my appeal to the international leaders as a lost cause, I received a telephone call from the Chinese embassy in Havana. The voice on the other end of the telephone asked, "Did you send a telegram to Chairman Mao?"

"Yes," I replied, greatly puzzled.

"He has sent a response to you through our embassy," he informed me in an excited voice. Chairman Mao's message was read to me over the telephone, but I was so excited that I really didn't get all of the reading. This was a high point in my life. I had played a long shot, and it had borne fruit. A miracle had transpired. When the voice from the embassy had finished reading the message, I was informed that an official from the embassy would bring a printed copy to me.

When the Chinese diplomat arrived at my house, it was early evening. He was sparkling with delightful astonishment. "Are you Mr. Williams?" he asked with a smile beaming from his face. He energetically shook my hand.

"Yes," I replied, thrilled to have him visit my home.

"How did you contact Chairman Mao?" he inquired.

"I sent him a telegram," I informed him.

He then told me that I could have sent my message through the embassy, but I felt that if I had asked the embassy to transmit such a message to Chairman Mao, it might never have been sent out. He handed me the long teletyped message and said that this was the first such statement the Chairman had issued in the past six years.

The statement read:

CHAIRMAN MAO TSE-TUNG'S STATEMENT CALLING UPON THE PEOPLE OF THE WORLD TO UNITE TO OPPOSE RACIAL DISCRIMINATION BY U.S. IMPERIALISM AND SUPPORT THE AMERICAN NEGROES IN THEIR STRUGGLE AGAINST RACIAL DISCRIMINATION

AUGUST 8, 1963

An American Negro leader now taking refuge in Cuba, Mr. Robert Williams, the former President of the Monroe, North Carolina Chapter of the National Association for the Advancement of Coloured People, has twice this year asked me for a statement in support of the American Negroes' struggle against racial discrimination. I wish to take this opportunity, on behalf of the Chinese people, to express our resolute support for the

American Negroes in their struggle against racial discrimination and for freedom and equal rights.

There are more than 19 million Negroes in the United States, or about 11 percent of the total population. Their position in society is one of enslavement, oppression and discrimination. The overwhelming majority of the Negroes are deprived of their right to vote. On the whole it is only the most back-breaking and most despised jobs are open to them. Their average wages are only from a third or a half of those of the white people. The ratio of unemployment among them is the highest. In many states they cannot to go to the same school, eat at the same table, or travel in the same section of a bus or a train with the white people. Negroes are frequently and arbitrarily arrested, beaten up and murdered by U.S. authorities at various levels and members of the Ku Klux Klan and other racists. About half of the American Negroes are concentrated in eleven states in the south of the United States. There, the discrimination and persecution they suffer are especially startling.

The American Negroes are awakening, and their resistance is growing ever stronger. In recent years the mass struggle of the American Negroes against racial discrimination and for freedom and equal rights has been constantly developing.

In 1957 the Negro people in Little Rock, Arkansas, waged a fierce struggle against the barring of their children from public schools. The authorities used armed force against them, and there resulted the Little Rock incident which shocked the world.

In 196, Negroes in more than twenty states held "sit-in" demonstrations in protest against racial segregation in local restaurants, shops and other public places.

In 1961 the Negroes launched a campaign of "freedom riders" to oppose racial segregation in transport, a campaign which rapidly extended to many states.

In 1962 the Negroes in Mississippi fought for the equal right to enroll in colleges and were greeted by the authorities with repression which culminated in a bloodbath.

This year, the struggle of the American Negroes started in early April in Birmingham, Alabama. Unarmed, bare-handed Negro masses were subjected to wholesale arrests and the most barbarous repression merely because they were holding meetings and parades against racial discrimination. On 12 June, an extreme was reached with the cruel murder of Mr. Medgar Evers, a leader of the Negro people in Mississippi. These

Negro masses, aroused to indignation and undaunted by ruthless violence, carried on their struggles even more courageously and quickly won the support of Negroes and all strata of the people throughout the United States. A gigantic and vigorous nationwide struggle is going on in nearly every state and city in the United States, and the struggle keeps mounting. American Negro organizations have decided to start a "freedom march" on Washington on 28 August, in which 250,000 people will take part.

The speedy development of the struggle of the American Negroes is a manifestation of the constant sharpening of class struggle and national struggle within the United States; it has been causing increasingly grave anxiety to the U.S. ruling clique. The Kennedy Administration has resorted to cunning two-faced tactics. On the one hand, it continues to connive at and take part in the discrimination against and persecution of Negroes; it even sends troops to suppress them. On the other hand, it is parading as an advocate of the "defence of human rights" and the "protection of the civil rights of Negroes," is calling upon the Negro people to exercise "restraint," and is proposing to Congress so-called "civil rights legislation" in an attempt to numb the fighting will of the Negro people and deceive the masses throughout the country. However, these tactics of the Kennedy Administration are being seen through by more and more of the Negroes. The fascist atrocities committed by the U.S. imperialists against the Negro people have laid bare the true nature of the so-called democracy and freedom in the United States and revealed the inner link between the reactionary policies pursued by the U.S. Government at home and its policies of aggression abroad.

I call upon the workers, peasants, revolutionary intellectuals, enlightened elements of the bourgeoisie, and other enlightened personages of all colours in the world, white, black, yellow, brown, etc., to unite to oppose the racial discrimination practiced by U.S. imperialism and to support the American Negroes in their struggle against racial discrimination. In the final analysis, a national struggle is a question of class struggle. In the United States, it is only the reactionary ruling clique among the whites which is oppressing the Negro people. They can in no way represent the workers, farmers, revolutionary intellectuals, and other enlightened persons who comprise the overwhelming majority of the white people. At present, it is the handful of imperialists, headed by the United States, and their supporters, the reactionaries in different countries, who are carrying out oppression, aggression and intimidation against the overwhelming majority of the nations and peoples of the world. They are the minority,

> and we are the majority. At most they make up less than 10 percent of the 3,000 million people of the world. I am deeply convinced that, with the support of more than 90 percent of the people of the world, the just struggle of the American Negroes will certainly be victorious. The evil system of colonialism and imperialism grew on along with the enslavement of the Negroes and the trade in Negroes; it will surely come to its end with the thorough emancipation of the black people.[1]

In response to Chairman Mao's call, mass rallies were held all over China in demonstration of China's support of the Afro-American struggle against racial discrimination. All of the top leaders of the Chinese government and people echoed the words of Mao.

Relative to my appeal and the Chairman's reaction, Mabel and I were invited to attend China's October 1 National Day Celebration.[2]

1. Mao Zedong, "Calling Upon the People of the World to Unite to Oppose Racial Discrimination by U.S. Imperialism and Support the American Negroes in Their Struggle against Racial Discrimination," August 8, 1963, as printed in *Peking Review*, August 16, 1963, https://www.marxists.org/subject/china/peking-review/1963/PR1963-33a.htm.

2. National Day celebrates the day Mao Tse-tung officially declared the establishment of the People's Republic of China on October 1, 1949.

CHAPTER 51

FIRST VISIT TO THE PEOPLE'S REPUBLIC OF CHINA

Slightly more than two years had passed since the coalition of bigots had driven my family from our homeland and the house I had been born in on Boyte Street in Monroe, North Carolina. Due to the efforts of unselfish friends in the United States, Canada, and Cuba, my family had survived. Toward the end of September 1963, Mabel and I boarded a Russian plane in Havana. The big Tu-114—the same type of plane that had brought Khrushchev to the United States and had to land in New Jersey, where a special extra-high set of steps had to be constructed to enable him to deplane—was now transporting us to China by way of Russia. I vividly remembered the notoriety surrounding the plane because of its size when it made its American flight. It was hard to believe that we were aboard the gigantic craft. As the roaring engines moved us high into the sky, I wondered what the Monroe bigots would think if they could see us now. This was quite a different fate from the one they had tried to thrust on me. It was not in their hands to deny the logic of the future, though they had driven me into exile. Those white supremacists had been cruel. Yet as cruel and life-threatening as it was, this exile was not the end that those hateful people had planned for me. For it was not in the hands of those race-crazed, would-be lynchers to determine my end.

The Soviet-built Tu-114 was spacious, but there was a constant slight vibration, and the noise of the large engines was not easily muffled. The twenty-one-hour nonstop flight to Moscow proved very tiring. It was hard to imagine being in

Robert Williams receiving a copy of the Little Red Book from Chairman Mao Zedong, 1963. Robert F. Williams Papers, Bentley Historical Library, University of Michigan.

the air for twenty-one hours without touching land. The Russian crew enjoyed practicing their English and Spanish languages with all of the passengers. They were friendly and most attentive. As we flew from morning to morning again, without seeing night, they darkened the plane by closing the window blinds and lowering the lights so that we could get some rest. Also, it seemed that we must have been on a baby-feeding schedule; just about every four hours, we were presented with large, full-course meals, some complete with black Russian caviar, which was another new experience for us.

We found the late September weather in Moscow quite a change from Havana. It was very cold to us, even though we saw Russians swimming in outdoor pools. Fortunate for us, even though Cuba, in league with the Russians, was at odds with China, it had done everything necessary to facilitate our journey to Peking. Thoughtfully, Cuban security had equipped us with heavy winter coats, which were an extreme rarity in subtropical Havana.

Our itinerary called for a layover in Moscow before going on to Peking. Embassy personnel met us at the airport and conveyed us to lodgings in the Hotel Metropole. The hotel atmosphere seemed to transport us back to the American mode of the 1930s and 40s.

At breakfast time, the dining room was bustling with foreigners. As we entered to be seated, we passed a table where English was being spoken. English being spoken abroad always attracts the attention of those who speak the common language. There were a number of whites and one Black woman seated together. As we passed the table, the Black woman smiled, nodded, and spoke to us in a warm, friendly manner. After we had been seated, she came over to our table, and we invited her to join us. She told us that because we had spoken to each other the way that we did, the whites in her group asked her if we knew each other. She had told them that we had met before and asked us that should they inquire, would we please tell them that we were acquainted?[1] I replied to her, "What you have told them is true, Sister, because all Black people, subjected to foreign isolation, have a common bond. We understand each other, and we feel a greater need to focus on our racial identity." She seemed greatly relieved. We learned that she was the lone Afro-American with a student exchange group. She invited us to her table and introduced us to her group. They all seemed excited to learn that we were en route to the People's Republic of China, which was then off-limits to Americans. The tour leader gave us literature to take to China and expressed a serious desire to expand their [institution's] outreach to China.

1. The young lady had lied to her group and wanted the Williamses to cover for her if asked.

At dinner, we sat at the next table to some young African students. One very vocal student, whom I remembered having seen in Cuba the year before, was lecturing the other young Africans on the affluence of the United States of America. The group listened to him intently. As his rhetoric became even more exaggerated, they seemed spellbound. "In America, all students have cars. You can get a good car in America for twenty-five dollars," he declared.

"Hey, Brother!" I said, interrupting his highly emotional speech. "If you know where in America one can buy a good car for twenty-five dollars, I am sure the American people would like to know where." After a quick glance, he no doubt recognized me from Cuba.

"Oh, you're from the United States, right?"

"Yes," I answered.

He quickly changed his subject and lowered his tone of voice.

The next day a diplomat from the Chinese embassy took us on a trip to Lenin's Tomb. I had not been in a line that long since I had been discharged from the military. If our host had not possessed a diplomatic pass, we would have never had access to even such a long line on such short notice. We finally descended into this spacious, dome-like tomb. It was cool and serene. Lenin's corpse was laid out as if he had just been prepared by a funeral home for burial. It seemed incredible that a body deceased for so long could be so well preserved. I thought of how wonderful it would have been if Abraham Lincoln's remains could have been so preserved for future generations to see.

We paid a visit to the huge department store known as GUM.[2] I was led to believe that it was a showplace and that other shopping centers were not so well stocked. The traders there more than welcomed dollars. Black-marketers offered all kinds of jewelry for dollars. Some offered to exchange rubles for dollars. Many asked for US cigarettes. Their craving for all things American denigrated the image I had of the Soviet Union. We were given a ride on the subway train. It was clean, modern, and filled with passengers. A Black English-speaking couple escorted by an English-speaking Chinese, evidently, was a rare spectacle and a cause for much attention to be focused on us by ordinary Russian citizens. I supposed that much of the attention resulted from the tension of the China-Soviet rift.

On our way to Peking, we stopped overnight in Irqrius (Urkurtz). The facilities there were quite a step down from Moscow. The weather was much colder than any that I had ever experienced. The frigid Siberian wind penetrated our clothing and felt like a razor blade cutting the flesh. The following morning, we took off on a Chinese turbo-prop plane. As we crossed the snow-capped mountains of

2. GUM stands for Gosudarstvenny Universalny Magazin, or "State Department Store."

Siberia, Chinese martial music and revolutionary songs blasted from the plane's speaker system. The graceful hostesses performed revolutionary skits and sang in praise of Chairman Mao. Many of the passengers joined in the singing. The high spirit was contagious. We most certainly were beginning to be exposed to an entirely different world.

Once we arrived in Peking, waiting to greet us at the airport was a large crowd, including many young people. There were quite a few other foreigners on the plane who also had been invited to the National Day Celebration. Each group of guests was welcomed by representatives of the respective agencies that had invited them. Mabel and I were met by officials of the Peace Committee, accompanied by some other government functionaries. Our arrival was covered extensively by the print and TV media. What was most impressive about our welcome was the affection displayed toward us as foreign guests. The handshakes and smiles of the adults went far beyond mere polite formalities. The well-groomed Chinese children, decked out in their Young Pioneer attire, greeted all the visitors with bouquets of flowers and gave spirited Pioneer salutes.[3] Their faces glowed with excitement. Even the workers at the airport paused and waved, with broad smiles beaming from their faces. Instantly, I felt that this was a China sure to find a place of lasting affection in my heart.

As guests of the Peace Committee, Mabel and I were accorded full VIP treatment. While awaiting claim for our luggage, we were given access to a special room at the airport where we were served fragrant tea. We were not required to go through customs or immigrations. A limousine trailed by a car with our luggage and special handlers transported us to the Peking Hotel. An interpreter and an official of the Peace Committee rode with us to the Peking Hotel and briefed us on our accommodations and proposed activity during our stay in China.

Instantly, I was struck by the fact that visitors in the hotel never locked their doors. It was indeed a different world, peopled by a society that had so little of personal possessions and yet had no overt inclination to covet and steal the property of others. I concluded that acquisition is the motive force that stokes greed and that greed feeds on itself. No doubt a consumer society has a great relationship to the ego, and the more the ego is inflated, the greater the drive toward conspicuous consumption. I mentally wrestled with the question of whether citizens inhabiting a consumer society, with all of its accompanying social ills, were afforded any more contentment. Chinese society seemed to be

3. The Young Pioneers is a Chinese Communist organization for youths ages six to fourteen. There are similar groups in most Communist states.

working off the need to avoid and escape boredom and the harsh reality of living in an imperfect world. The question uppermost in my mind was, Could China continue to repress the latent, seemingly basic animal instinct so rampant in the soul of Western man? It was obvious that progress was being made, and some of the most callous acts of the world are committed in the name of progress. Evolution to a more affluent society is very seldom a journey into a higher state of spiritual morality.

This is not to say that the Chinese rejected all creature comforts, for they had a surprisingly large quantity of consumer goods in their stores. The variety of textiles, transistor radios, wristwatches, bicycles, typewriters, and other such products available in Peking far exceeded what I had seen in Moscow. The Soviet Union had obviously concentrated an overwhelming portion of its resources and efforts on the development of heavy industry and military production at the expense of a consumer-oriented industry. It was more than obvious that the Soviet Union's obsession for rivaling the United States on the world stage for superpower status had required severe sacrifice on the part of their citizens.

On the night of September 30, Mabel and I were invited to a state banquet, held in the Great Hall of the People. A long black Chinese-made limousine drove us up to the steps of the Great Hall. As we mounted the many steps, accompanied by an interpreter and a host cadre from the Peace Committee, cars were arriving like clockwork with personages in their glowing national dress from many countries of the world. Soldiers of the People's Liberation Army stood erect and watchful beside huge columns of marble that gave the building an image of power and splendor. There was a huge crowd already present in the banquet room. Strangers were introducing themselves as they shared round tables; old acquaintances who had had occasion to meet in earlier times, before we had been introduced to the international scene, also greeted each other.

When all of the guests had been seated, the People's Liberation Army Band became animated as it started playing "The East Is Red."

Instantly, an intense wave of emotion swept the huge banquet hall. Asian and African heads of state, turbaned sheiks, Buddhist monks in saffron robes, Latin American revolutionaries, and Western European diplomats rose and applauded. The helmsman, Chairman Mao Tse-tung, had arrived.

What a change of fortune in my life. In my own country, I had been the target of racist killers who had missed their mark only by the grace of God. I had never been afforded an opportunity to lay eyes on the leader of my own country in close proximity. I had not even seen the governor of my native state, and now, here I was in the presence of one of the world's greatest revolutionaries and chairman of the world's most populous country. It was dazzling, and at the same time it was like a dream. It was strange and seemed unreal that fate had brought me to such a state. This was certainly not the destiny that the racists in North Carolina had hoped to bequeath me.

After the champagne toasts, many foreigners came to our table to greet us. Evidently word had fast spread that we were exiles from the United States now living in Cuba. It was obvious that exiles and refugees from the mighty United States were a rarity. Being Black and having to flee from the United States because we were struggling for human rights offered evidence that the so-called free world was not free for those who violently opposed racial oppression and the white supremacy status quo.

At nine the next morning, Mabel and I were taken to the top of the Tiananmen (Gate of Heavenly Peace), the main entrance to the ancient Forbidden City, once the palace of China's emperors. The National Day parade, scheduled for ten o'clock, was to involve half a million marchers.

Before the start of the parade, we were escorted to a flower-decked state reception room behind the reviewing rostrum atop the Tiananmen. We were personally received by Chairman Mao himself. During our brief conversation, the occasion developed into a photographic affair. We were also received by Premier Chou En-lai, Marshal Chu Teh, and President Liu Shao-Chi.[4]

It was an uplifting experience, being photographed while being received by such universally acknowledged liberators. A great portion of my elation grew out of the fact that the photographs represented indisputable proof that an Afro-American was so honored in a country that had been accused of pervasive xenophobia.

Two million Chinese lined the streets and filled the mammoth square. I had never seen so many people congregated in all my life. Most of the foreign guests were assigned to the regular reviewing stands, but Mabel and I were led to the main rostrum to view the procession alongside various foreign heads of state and high Chinese officials. The president of North Korea and a leader from Pakistan were among the foreign leaders flanking us.

Our first tour in China was to the first revolutionary base area, in a rugged and hostile mountainous countryside. We were accompanied on our visits by a likable cadre who was very much interested in our seeing as much of China as possible. Madam Ou was full of revolutionary zeal. I felt certain that was the very reason she was selected for the task. She went to great lengths to apprise us

4. On the spelling of Chinese names: The Chinese authorities changed from a Latin grammar and pronunciation system to the Pinyin system of transcription in 1979. Robert Williams, beginning his memoir as early as 1970, used the older spellings: thus, Chou En-lai rather than the modern Zhou Enlai.

of the history of the revolution and the culture of the region. She was also anxious to learn of the Afro-American struggle. We became exceptionally friendly toward each other. Her frank and outgoing personality belied the old Western adage that Chinese people are cold toward foreigners. About the fifth day of our travels, Madam Ou, a devoted revolutionary, informed me that I was making the mistake of thinking that all Chinese were good. She said, "Comrade Williams, we have some bad Chinese in China. We have some Chinese who want to be white, in the same sense as some of your compatriots." In somewhat of a disgusted tone, she continued, "Some Chinese have even raised the question of why China's friendship was limited to the poor peoples of the world and why there were no rich friends."

During our three-week sojourn, we traveled many miles across China. Our travels were focused primarily on minority and industrial areas. Everywhere we went, the people were hard at work constructing the new society. Hoping to paralyze the Chinese nation, the Russian technicians had pulled out, taking all the industrial blueprints with them. The vacuum created by the hostile Soviet pullout was being filled by strenuous human power. In the industrial city of Wuhan, I saw Chinese women and children pulling heavy two-wheeled carts, laden with steel, along the streets of the city. It made me feel sad to see women tugging so hard at the heavy loads that the veins expanded in their necks to such an extent that it appeared that they were in danger of exploding. Aside from the human power, there were also long convoys of animal-drawn wagons loaded to the hilt. Many of the carts had balloon tires that had been designed for trucks. Obviously, the truck factories, suffering the loss of Soviet technical aid, were undergoing a crash movement that could utilize China's greatest resource, its abundant population. On observing the primitive form of transportation so widely employed, the Western media erroneously claimed that all Chinese production had collapsed after the pullout of Soviet technicians. I noticed that many trucks had strange-looking balloon-type rubber containers mounted on their roofs. When I raised the question as to the reason for these mounts, our hosts explained that they had shifted to bottled gas because the Russians were refusing to sell them gasoline. With their voices ringing in caustic tones, they attributed much of their difficulty to "revisionist" Khrushchev. They admonished us not to worry and said that China would soon be able to revert back to gasoline.

With deep emotion, many Chinese cadres explained that American, European, and Russian oil explorers had done extensive research in China and had declared with certainty that there were no oil deposits in China. This attitude had evoked suspicion, since American oil companies had attempted to seduce China into signing contracts that would grant exclusive rights for petroleum production. What was the reason for sole rights to the oil production if there was no oil?

We were taken to a well-manicured park in Shanghai. Over the entrance was an old, weather-beaten sign. Our interpreter and traveling companion asked if we could read the sign that stood out like a sore thumb at such a beautifully kept, expansive garden. We answered no. He then proceeded to read it to us: "'No dogs or Chinese allowed.' Note that it says 'dogs' first!" His voice was filled with disdain. He noted that the British imperialists had placed the sign there. He related to us some of the trials and tribulations that the Chinese people suffered from the dehumanizing actions of the imperialists, who had sliced up a weak and backwards China into spheres of brutal domination.

Our Chinese hosts kept us on a tight, grinding schedule for nearly a month and a half. During that time, China really grew on us. We received many letters and gifts from ordinary citizens from many parts of China. One craftsman engraved the text of Chairman Mao's statement condemning racial discrimination in the United States on a piece of ivory, no bigger than an inch square. Peasants lined the streets waving and beaming with friendly emotion as our entourage passed their village streets. Because of Chairman Mao's statement and the attendant media coverage, we had become VIPs, widely known as the Black American refugees who had dared to take up the gun against racial oppression in the United States. I developed such strong emotional ties with the Chinese cause for a better and more dignified way of life that I started having some pangs of conscience about consuming the rice that I had seen Chinese women harvesting while standing in ice-cold water. Such sad sights left me with a burning desire that someday we would see a modern China—one that could liberate that portion of its humanity that labored so strenuously under conditions that paralleled those of beasts of burden.

Our stay in China seemed to pass exceedingly fast. I looked forward to our return to Cuba with mixed emotions. The rift between China and the USSR was creating tensions in Cuba. I had many close friends in Cuba, and we had had some fun times together. Cuba was more related to the type of culture that I had been accustomed to. China was more serious, hardworking, and deeply immersed in revolutionary spirit. With the polemics becoming more intense between the two Communist giants, I knew that my situation would be likened to an individual walking a tightrope.

CHAPTER 52

SINO-SOVIET SPLIT AND CHALLENGES IN CUBA

Upon our return to Havana, I wrote and broadcast my favorable views of China. This activity triggered a new rash of attacks in the US press, and the anti-Peking bourgeois Communists began to label me as a Chinese-controlled Black Nationalist. Copies of both the *Peking Review*, the official Chinese magazine, and the *Moscow Times*, its Soviet counterpart, were available at several Havana newsstands. Each contained violent criticisms of the other's policies. Until this time, the Cuban press had declined to take sides in the Sino-Soviet dispute or print the polemics of either nation. Fidel urged the socialist camp to unite and forget their differences. Despite their efforts to remain above the controversy, Cuba's economic dependence on the Soviet Union pushed the country toward the Russian camp. Even so, one could often hear Cubans reciting the refrain, "Our hearts may be in Peking, but our stomachs are in Moscow."

Through 1965 there was hardly any open expression of warmness toward China. The Soviet press and its US surrogates had openly denounced the Black Nationalist movement in the United States and reserved praise solely for the nonviolent movement around Rev. Martin Luther King. As a matter of principle, I could not bring myself to accommodate them. In spite of the fact that I was a besieged exile, I knowingly continued to run the risk involved in maintaining my Chinese connection. It was a dangerous game, but as a Black man I had always lived in the shadow of danger. If I surrendered to danger now, I would negate everything that exemplified my identity. My situation in Cuba was becoming tenuous and hectic. This situation was very hurtful to me because I really admired Cuba and her amiable people, among whom I had some very dear friends.

In 1965, my wife, my two sons, and I were invited to China for its sixteenth National Day. Despite the rift, the Cubans did everything possible to facilitate our journey. In fact, it was rumored that Fidel had taken special interest in our trip out of deference to a latent fondness toward China. My pro-China newsletter, *The Crusader*, was still being published for me by Cuban workers in Havana. As the plans were being formulated for our trip, a false copy of *The Crusader* was circulated internationally. The fake *Crusader* bore an attack on the Chinese minister of defense Lin Pio's treatise on the People's War. Rather than Lin's advocacy of encircling the cities from the countryside, it stressed that "modern" warfare had to give way to urban warfare. I never learned who was behind this dirty trick, though I felt it was the work of the CIA, done in order to scuttle militant Afro-Americans' growing contacts with China.

Our second visit to China was similar to the first with the exception of our itinerary being different. Both times we were asked what kinds of things we would like to see and what sections of the country we wanted to visit. Our itineraries catered to our requests. This allowed us to cover more and more of the vast, strange new land. We were learning more and more about the history of China, its diverse nationalities, and their cultures.

We learned from other foreigners that the Chinese on occasion would spring a culinary trick on their close friends. We were told that sometimes they prepared sumptuous meals for the banquet table. After finishing the tasty repast, the guests would be asked whether they had enjoyed the food. When they answered in the affirmative, they would then be asked whether they knew what the delicious meal consisted of. Obviously, they did not. When informed that they had feasted on cat, dog, and snake, those with frail stomachs suddenly developed nausea and made quick exits to the nearest toilet.

I fashioned a deterrent to the friendly pranks. I noticed that despite the fact that most of our friends were atheists, they showed great respect for the religious beliefs of others. I asked our Chinese friends to please pass the word that where we were from, it bordered on religious sacrilege to eat such critters. Thereafter, everywhere we went, our hosts went to great pains to catalog everything on the table.

The day we arrived in the Korean Autonomous Chou,[1] we were informed that we would be feted by the governor at an evening banquet, and we were

1. An area in northeast China with a large Korean population.

given a hotel suite in which to rest before the evening affair. As we started to relax, the surrounding quietness was broken by the obvious desperation of a dog being slaughtered. I told Mabel that the way the dog was carrying on, it had to be a life-and-death matter. She admonished me to get the matter out of my mind and stated that it might be a worthwhile experience to taste the dog. I vehemently disagreed on the grounds that some experiences I could do without.

The hotel dining room was really laid out for the banquet. At the dinner table, the governor was introduced to us and, as a dear friend, he welcomed us. Through our interpreter he asked whether I had any questions or requests to make to him. I answered, "Yes, earlier today, I heard a dog that sounded severely desperate. Could that dog happen to be on this table?"

"No," he replied. "We have received word from Peking not to give you dog, cat, or snake. We know it is a religious belief with you. The dog is on that table," he explained pointing to the next table. I later learned that such food was considered a special delicacy reserved for special occasions and special guests. It was once the fare of the nobility.

I found our Chinese hosts to be warm, friendly, and full of life. My relationship with them was enlightening to the point that I found the concept manufactured by Western propagandists—that the people of Asia were xenophobic, withdrawn, drab, and always with deadpan expressions on their faces—absurd. I found the characterization to be fallacious, racist, and unkind. Here I was, having been forced to flee from my native land simply for seeking human rights and the enforcement of the US Constitution, being treated like royalty by a people so stigmatized. Contrasting what I was seeing and what I had been officially indoctrinated with was enough to make me doubt everything that I had been exposed to in the US education system.

Ever conscious of the fact that my status in Cuba was being severely eroded, I felt it to be a godsend that China was taking us to heart. China officially offered our sons scholarships to study there. Although saddened by the thought of such a long and distant separation, we gratefully left them there. The Chinese friends provided them with special language teachers and immediately favored them with accelerated courses. Our older son, Robert, seemed a natural for the language. The younger, John, complained that he could not learn the language. The older son concurred. I explained that we were homeless and had no other place to go and that it was not a matter of what he could not do, but what he had to do. I went to great lengths explaining that they would be the first Afro-American students to study in China and that the image of the race was up to them. Though I had some doubts, I concealed them. I was certainly glad that such a task was not to be confronted by me. My greatest problem was merely staying alive and continuing the struggle. We found that our early misgivings gave way to growing pride as John, after two weeks of intense study, began to conquer the language and grow in self-esteem.

We returned to Cuba facing a highly charged anti-China atmosphere. It had been a common practice for Cuban officials and political activists to display portraits of Fidel, Che, and other leaders on the walls of their homes and offices. In order to show their sympathy with both China and Russia, they had also put up pictures of Khrushchev and Mao. When I returned to Cuba, though, Mao's pictures were conspicuously absent. They had completely disappeared from public display. Books, posters, and other articles that carried political connotations originating in China had vanished from public distribution. There was a new tendency sweeping the land, and everyone was expected to toe the line. I was caught up in a political vise. My political situation was severely sensitive and extremely dangerous. Part of my heart was in Cuba, the other part was in China; but my experience in analyzing complicated options led me to understand that my best chance to survive with my self-respect intact was to maintain my relationship with China.

Before leaving China, Chairman Mao, at my request, had autographed a photograph for me. Disregarding the prevailing tendency, I proudly hung it on our living room wall. This was a step of defiance that was bound to affect my well-being in Cuba. I owed the Cuban people and Fidel a great deal, and I will always feel grateful for their generous aid at a most crucial and dangerous time in my life. They had literally saved my life by bringing us to Cuba and giving us a home. They had given me a radio broadcast and a newsletter in exile and offered unlimited moral support for our struggle against racial segregation.

I had been there during the missile crisis and when President Kennedy was assassinated. Kennedy's assassination sent chills up and down my spine. Many were the nights I had lambasted him over *Radio Free Dixie*. I had declared that he would pay dearly for his disinterest in the plight of my family and of Blacks in general and for his seeming inclination to side with the violent bigots of Monroe. Though I had many times threatened that he was going to get it, I was as shocked as the rest of the world when it happened.

Strange things were beginning to happen to me in Havana. There had always been some underhanded negative occurrences, but now they were not so latent, and the situation was daily worsening.

The four persons who had been charged along with me in the so-called Monroe kidnapping had been found guilty in what amounted to a kangaroo court frame-up. Mrs. Mae Mallory had been sentenced to sixteen to twenty years in prison; Richard Crowder, eight to ten years; Harold Reape, five to seven; and John

Lowery (the only white among the accused), three to five years.[2] Disturbed and upset by the verdict, I felt the need to somehow mount an attack on the system. It was too much to passively accept. I decided along with help from some Cuban friends to file a petition with the United Nations Commission on Human Rights situated in Paris, France. I felt this to be one way of focusing attention on the US South's official brutalization of the Afro-American.

When I asked the Cubans to help me get signatures by circulating the petition through the trade union system, I was told that there were Cuban and American "comrades" who had offered to help with the petition and that they, the Cubans, felt that the American "comrades" should also be involved. I indicated that if the Americans wanted to be involved, I would work with them, but I didn't believe these white Americans were really interested in fighting racism in the United States.

Despite my reservations, Harold Spencer and several others became part of the committee formed for the petitions, and it wasn't long before half a million signatures had been collected. An Afro-Cuban woman trade union official was to ship the petitions to the United Nations group in Paris. She went on a short trip to Prague. After her return, I asked her when she planned to mail the signatures. Her answer was, "Oh, didn't you know? The petitions were sent by the other people on the committee some time ago. In fact, I have already received a letter in response to it, which seems a little strange."

The text of the letter read that they had received our petition and were pleased to know that we were interested in avoiding miscarriages of justice in the United States. It stated, "We, on the other hand, are interested in reestablishing justice in Cuba. We would, therefore, like to work with you in a campaign to secure the release of all political prisoners in Cuba and would appreciate your sending us a list of their names."

For a moment, I could not understand why the United Nations Commission on Human Rights would write such a letter, but when I examined the letterhead, I was shocked to see that it had not really come from Paris but rather had come from a private group of freewheelers in New York calling themselves the "United States Association for the U.N." Some of them were quite wealthy. I asked the trade union official who had mailed the petitions how they had come

2. Mallory and her codefendants were freed in 1965 after a judge overturned their conviction based on the fact that African Americans had been excluded from the jury. Ashley Farmer, *Remaking Black Power: How Women Transformed an Era* (Chapel Hill: University of North Carolina Press, 2017), 48; "Mae Mallory: Unforgettable Freedom Fighter Promoted Self-Defense," Workers World, February 26, 2009, https://www.workers.org/2009/us/mae_mallory_0305/.

up with such an address. I was shocked and even more suspicious when I was told that Harold Spencer, who was sometimes referred to by some non-Communist Americans as "the little weasel," had taken it upon himself to decide where the signatures should be sent. When confronted, Spencer claimed that he thought New York to be the proper place to send them. I was certain that he was feigning innocence. Operating in a vacuum with such a motley bunch, with all kinds of vested interests, can be a demoralizing and frustrating ordeal. It is an impossible task to discern which white American is an agent of the CIA or the Communist Party, an overzealous nut, or just a chauvinist American who believes in white American superiority and the divine right of the United States to direct the affairs of the entire world. Most white Americans abroad believe in the philosophy of America's manifest destiny. They seem to have some extra sense of perception and an inherent tendency toward the manifestation of white supremacy Americanism. Though latent, white nationalism pushed itself at every opportunity abroad. Though they may have called themselves Communists or Christians, they wittingly or unwittingly created a favorable atmosphere for agents provocateurs, subversives, and spies to do their nefarious work. The USCP offered cover and sanctuary to work from its ranks. The USCP was so infiltrated and its objectives so similar and entwined [with those of white nationalists] in counteracting the development of Afro-Americans' friendly relations with foreign governments that they [white supremacists and the USCP] became like Siamese twins. Many white Americans displayed a tendency to smart and develop goose pimples when experiencing situations exposing the true nature and brutality of US racism and the hypocrisy of the nation's claim of being an enviable democracy. Harold Spencer's feigned mistake was no mistake at all. It was a nasty act of Americanism in defense of white supremacy and an effort to frustrate the effort of a Black man acting in defense of his people who had refused to submit to diversionary white direction.

The more my efforts transpired to expose US racism universally, the more intense the white nationalists strove to counteract my endeavors. Some friendly and justice-minded white Americans had started to keep me abreast of the ever-widening campaign and the rumor mill grinding out misinformation against me. The campaign was beginning to retard my effectiveness in my fight against racial discrimination.

Whispers were being circulated that I was a counterrevolutionary. They became so pronounced that I made an appointment to confer with Blas Roca, a pre-revolution Communist official who was considered a Marxist theoretician.

Blas Roca was a heavyset, middle-aged mulatto Cuban. He wore a somewhat cold and smug look on his broad face. He greeted me formally and motioned for me to sit down in an office chair facing his paper-laden desk. I confronted him point-blank with why I had come. "I have been told that some of the Americans have been spreading the word that I am a counterrevolutionary. Since you are a longtime Marxist-Leninist and are well versed on party doctrine, I would like to know what your concept of a counterrevolutionary is."

He looked up from his desk with a stern expression on his face and replied, "A person can sometimes be a counterrevolutionary without even knowing it."

Surprised, I asked, "Oh, and how can that be?"

"I will give you a commonly experienced example," he said. "Suppose a person supports the government during the first stages of the revolution, but then the leadership decides on a radical change in policy that he refuses to agree with. That would make him a counterrevolutionary, wouldn't it?"

"Do you mean to say that he would be a counterrevolutionary, even if he didn't engage in any anti-government activities?" I asked.

"Yes," he answered. "You can be a counterrevolutionary in your thoughts, even if you engage in no physical opposition."

"In other words," I persisted, "are you saying that whoever fails to agree with the party is an enemy of the people?"

"No, I am not saying anything like that," he insisted.

"Well then, what are you saying? Are we permitted to have no different opinions? Marx was a smart man, but are we expected to accept his words as eternal truth? I don't believe the human mind has yet reached its limits. I think that mankind is still in a state of evolution and that someday, somewhere, someone will think up a system that will serve the needs of mankind in a better way. If we all must think alike, that day will never come."

In the middle of our frank exchange, Blas Roca intoned, "But Williams, why are you so critical? We have given you a house. We have given you a car. We have given you broadcast time and allowed you to publish your paper here. What more do you want? Do you expect us to bring all 20 million Black Americans to Cuba and give them houses and cars? You know we don't have those kinds of resources."

I was convinced that Roca was intent on avoiding serious discussion. It was now obvious to me that the attitudes of the white American Communists and their fellow traveling agents provocateurs were exercising some influence on the Cuban party line, and the fact that I refused to renounce my preference for the Chinese persuasion had left me highly exposed to the consequences that so often befall nonconformists in the state of radical transition of a revolutionary society.

Sadly, I now had to face the cold and severe fact that my heart was in Peking, but my meal ticket was in Havana. My position in Cuba was becoming untenable.

Only Fidel and the concern for me of the Cuban people kept the witch hunters from devouring me. The white nationalist Americans felt that I was fatally trapped and that it was just a matter of time before they would be able to bring an end to my uncompromising Negritude and independent crusade.

If God lay sleeping, as my uncle Charlie had suggested when I was growing up, there was a tendency for him to awaken between naps just in time to snatch me from the throes of impending doom. At a time when my world seemed crumbling about me and I was a de facto stateless person, the unexpected happened. Once again good fortune knocked at my door. As if by divine design, out of the clear blue Mabel and I were invited to the Vietnamese embassy in Havana. This was a strange occurrence to me because I had always been led to believe that when an individual falls from grace with one group of friendly Communists, he becomes a pariah to all the related factions. The Vietnamese had invited us for dinner, but it became instantly obvious that they wanted to talk.

Fidel had often made the statement that "not only will we give them [the Vietnamese] our sugar, but we will also give them our blood." Cuba had offered to send volunteers to Vietnam but had been turned down the same as China and others on grounds that Vietnam was not in need of manpower. White American radicals were some of the first in line to offer their services and were loudly complaining that Hanoi would not accommodate them.

The mission head leaned forward over the dinner table and in a carefully lowered voice said to me, "I have heard that you are having some difficulty stemming from the American group here."

"Yes," I replied. "The situation has become so bad that I can no longer function as an exiled Afro-American freedom fighter."

"I have noticed that you are no longer broadcasting to the Afro-American people in the United States." He then informed me that the embassy was ready to issue me a visa to go to Hanoi and that he understood that the Chinese were offering to give me an airline ticket. In fact, the Vietnamese embassy gave Mabel and me a visa that very evening. As we were leaving, our host informed us that it would be best if we did not allow the Russians to see our visa to Vietnam when we passed through Moscow.

In a few days, we were invited to the Chinese embassy and were supplied with tickets and told that the diplomats would take care of all arrangements, including the shipping of our personal belongings. The following week, we were regretfully leaving Cuba. It was a departure wrought with stress and sadness. I felt like it was a major tragedy in my life. I greatly admired Cuba and her people. There had been a very grave misunderstanding exacerbated by the CIA and its fellow traveling white nationalists. Fidel Castro was still tops in my book, but he had been insulated from the truth. I owed Cuba and Fidel a great deal. After all, they saved me from racial savagery in the USA. They took my family in when my own government elected to support the subversion of its own Constitution by the meanest of the mean dehumanizers of its Black humanity. My quest for human rights had transformed me into a hunted criminal outcast. I felt that I was in the same category as a stateless person. The belongings that we didn't take to China we gave to our Afro-Cuban friend Raul.

Raul had been great as a resource person in helping me to understand Cuban life. He was also fun to be with. He told me that he had been a construction worker and had operated a "Jo-nez" machine. He could not understand why I could not comprehend what kind of machine he was describing, since it was a popular American-made machine. One day we were passing a construction site, and he excitedly pointed out to me a machine and called it a "Jo-nez." He wanted to know why I was cracking up laughing. I told him that it was not a "Jo-nez" but a Jones and that I was indeed familiar with the name. I have never forgotten Raul and his "Jo-nez."

Raul and a group of our Cuban friends went to the airport to see us off. It was a sad occasion. I had grown very fond of Cuba and her people. It was almost the same as being exiled from home all over again. The huge Tu-114 Russian plane took off as we and our Cuban friends and Raul struggled to hold back the tears.

CHAPTER 53

POLITICAL ASYLUM IN THE THROES OF THE PROLETARIAN CULTURAL REVOLUTION

We arrived in China for the third time on July 20, 1966. This time it was an escape rather than a trip of joy. Most of the next day I spent at the "Anti-imperialist Hospital," previously called Union Hospital before the student Red Guards had changed its name, where I got my eyes examined and treated as a result of an infection that I had contracted in the Soviet Union.

We expected to end up in North Vietnam, where I was to reestablish *Radio Free Dixie*. Though the Vietnamese had invited me there to live and work, the subject never came up again once I was safely in China.

We were lodged in the refurbished old Hotel Peking. Though saddened by the break with Cuba, we had a happy reunion with our two sons and our old friends in China. The only sour note we experienced in our return to Peking was that contrary to our request, the Chinese had allowed our sons to socialize with the white American colony. Their de facto guardian was Sidney Rittenberg, in whom the Chinese had invested the utmost trust. Rittenberg was a wheeler-dealer who I felt was too active in Chinese affairs for his own good.

My experience in Cuba had conditioned me to be somewhat distrustful of Americans. As in Cuba, there was an American colony in Peking. Some of the Americans were honest and sincere and really wanted to help build a better and

Mabel and Robert Williams with Chou En-lai in China, 1963. Robert F. Williams Papers, Bentley Historical Library, University of Michigan.

Robert and Mabel Williams with food canning factory workers in Shanghai, c. 1963. Robert F. Williams Papers, Bentley Historical Library, University of Michigan.

more peaceful world. There were others who could be compared to wolves in sheep's clothing. Some wanted to rebuild the world in the image of the United States. Then there were others who, no doubt, labored for the CIA. In many instances, it was very difficult to discern who was who, but when one was in exile, having been hounded across the earth the way I had been, caution became a way of life that needed no apology.

The third day after arriving found us preparing to attend a rally. The pace of my lifestyle had most certainly quickened in the short time since leaving Cuba. As we rode to the mammoth rally at the People's Consultative Hall to demonstrate support for the people of Vietnam, who were sustaining fierce US aerial bombardment, people moved through the streets as thick as ants. Everywhere red banners fluttered in the wind as students, workers, peasants, and army men moved toward the meeting hall with a total absence of confusion. The splendid organization belied any hint of oppression or coercion and manifested a spirit of patriotic necessity.

The huge hall was overflowing. Mabel and I were ushered to a reception room of the hall to await the start of the rally. Foreign guests chatted with Chinese and Vietnamese officials, and the inevitable hot aromatic Chinese tea was served.

Soon, Foreign Minister Chen Yi arrived. He shook hands and moved around the room, chatting jovially. Premier Chou En-lai came in shortly thereafter, greeted the guests, and mingled with the group until we were called to the rally.

Chinese from all walks of life packed the hall. All branches of the military bore banners proclaiming support for the heroic Vietnamese people. The podium was decorated with Vietnamese and Chinese flags and huge portraits of Mao Tse-tung and Ho Chi Minh. I sat on the rostrum along with the Chinese and Vietnamese officials and guests from various countries. There were speeches from all strata of the Chinese people. Delegations from both North and South Vietnam, assigned to Peking, made reports. A strong resolution was unanimously passed condemning United States imperialist aggression in Vietnam and throughout the world. After the many speeches and shouted slogans, the meeting closed, and the great crowd dispersed in as orderly a fashion as it had formed.

The rest of the week of the 26th of July, 1966, which was also the National Day of Cuba, was spent in interviews with South American journalists from Chile and Peru. They were very much interested in why I had left Cuba and the situation that existed there. They were more than concerned to hear my opinion of the future direction of the Cuban Revolution and whether or not I considered Cuba to be too much in hock to the Soviet Union to steer clear of a "revisionist" course. They also had a great interest in the struggle of the Black people in the United States and my activities as a freedom fighter. By the end of the week, I could see, by the variety of persons who visited me, that living in Peking was going to enhance my opportunity for almost universal contact.

China was undergoing change. It was in the throes of the Great Proletarian Cultural Revolution.[1] Things were breaking fast in Peking now. On July 30, a day after the celebration of Army Day, from the vantage point of a window in my suite on the third floor of the Peking Hotel, I observed what appeared to be a sea of people marching in formation. They carried a battery of portraits of Mao Tse-tung as their chanting voices echoed in unison throughout the streets. A drum and bugle corps brought up the rear. What seemed like a forest of red banners waved over the great throng of people.

Occasionally, the thunderous beat of drums drowned out all other sounds throughout the community. The earth, the building, and all things therein quivered and vibrated in sympathetic response to the mammoth drums mounted on slow-moving trucks. Such a fantastic scene left me with a feeling of great foreboding. I sent my two sons, who had become quite fluent in the Chinese language, out to inquire as to the nature of this soul-shaking affair. I learned that some heads had rolled. The great masses of the people had taken to the streets in support of Chairman Mao and to demonstrate support for the dismissal of the chief of propaganda from the Cultural Revolution Committee. Though I had read the polemics of the Cultural Revolution sent out from Peking while I still resided in Havana, my understanding of what the whole thing was all about was vague, and there seemed to be a good deal of confusion and contradiction revolving around the matter. During my previous visits to Peking, I had heard some criticism and mention of revisionists who had been dismissed from the party ranks in the mid-1950s and early 1960s. My shallow background of Chinese history was insufficient for me to ascertain what was going on and how the named individuals pertained to the continued struggle of China's Cultural Revolution. I realized, however, that changes of world-shaking significance were in the making.

The year 1968 roared in like an aroused and unpredictable dragon. The spirit of the mythological dragon was everywhere. It was a schizophrenic monster sometimes bearing good and sometimes bearing evil. It was sometimes visible and at other times invisible. At times, it wore the mask of deception. The drums and gongs were still beating frantically to rid the land of its evil monsters. Foreigners, chief among them Americans, had invoked the internationalist Marxist

1. The Great Proletarian Cultural Revolution was a political social movement initiated by Mao Tse-tung in 1966, chairman of the Chinese Communist Party and head of state of the People's Republic of China, to wage ideological struggle to purge Chinese society of feudalist, capitalist, and bourgeois thinking and to advance socialist thought and practice in the country. It officially ended in 1976.

code and persisted in their right to participate the same as Chinese in the Cultural Revolution. They had won and were as busy as bees in stirring the flames of rumor, suspicion, dissension, conflict, and espionage. I held fast to my unpopular position that as a foreigner, I had no right to condemn Chinese officials and to participate in the Cultural Revolution.

The foreign compound at Drusba (Russian for "friendship"), which had once been the billet of the Soviet technicians and now housed a diverse group of foreign "experts," had become a center of intrigue, backbiting, and factionalism. Many foreigners were complaining about deteriorating living conditions at the compound. Some old acquaintances had stopped speaking to each other while still others isolated themselves in small groups as each set claimed to be the true defenders of the faith. Each appeared to be more Chinese than Mao. Some of the more affluent "experts" called Foreign Minister Chen Yi on the carpet and accused him of corrupting the "experts" by having them paid more than the Chinese workers, which they claimed set them apart from the mainstream of Chinese society. They claimed this to be uncomplementary to their high revolutionary spirit.

Among the Chinese masses, materialistic accumulation was being denounced, and the foreign expert concept placed the expatriates in a very sensitive position. Some "experts" from poorer countries, who were trying to accumulate enough money to survive in their respective countries, angrily denounced the whole affair as a CIA cabal. Some gung-ho "experts" insisted that foreigners should be paid the same salaries as the Chinese. The Chinese refused to bow to their demands. Chen Yi told them that if they insisted on not receiving the pay they had been contracted to work for, he would have it deposited in the bank and saved for them until such time when they would certainly desire it.

A Canadian Marxist who was visiting China spread the rumor that one of the military men on the Cultural Revolution Committee whom he had talked with had told him that he did not trust me because I was not a Marxist but a nationalist and that nationalists were never to be trusted. I had no way of verifying this report. If it were true, the Chinese never did anything or acted in any way to lend credence to this report. I had my doubts about it because most white foreigners seemed to begrudge my status and independence in Peking. They showed inclinations of detesting the attention being given by the Chinese to the cause of the Afro-American in the USA. In many instances, I also detected whites' contempt for the Chinese people the same as that held for the Afro-American people.

The American Marxists, most of whom had desperately tried to steer China away from the US race issue, which they found so embarrassing, appeared to be making headway. They were exerting all the influence they could to create friction between the Chinese and me. They were deviously invoking the Marxist class theory to weaken the Black Americans' struggle against racial discrimination. The tumults of the Cultural Revolution had given them great leverage. It was difficult for me to understand how politicians as experienced and astute as the Chinese could not see through these sometimes-crude machinations of white supremacy cloaked in Marxist terminology. It seemed that ordinary Chinese workers had more insight and understanding about the nature of racism than many of the leaders. More and more I was hearing the old familiar theme of Black and white working-class unity and the developing conditions for a united workers' revolution in the USA.

In 1968, the Americans in Peking became very happy about the new turn in the Cultural Revolution. Some had wormed their way into positions of power and influence in their centers of work. Many were participating in the movement on equal footing with the Chinese. Rumors were rife about some latent coup within the Cultural Revolution movement and that it was being diverted from its original goal. One British American, or American British, approached me almost in a state of dancing glee and proclaimed that "foreigners are now free and equal to Chinese in China." He said, "Old Liu Shao-chi is a nationalist who discriminated against foreigners by putting Chinese above them."[2]

Personally, I could not see this as a negative factor. I thought this to be only a natural attitude on the part of a patriot. However, I kept my thoughts to myself because I most certainly was not going to take the position of defending Liu. This phony Marxist knew that I was a nationalist; therefore, I felt that he had come to let me know that his kind was now riding high on the coattails of the Cultural Revolution. He also informed me that if I had any projects that I wanted pushed to let him know, and he and his friends could assist me on a very high level. I had great respect and admiration for and devotion to the cause of the Chinese people, but this encounter momentarily dampened my enthusiasm. I am certain that it was fabricated to do just that. The conclusion for me to draw, no doubt, was that even in China the white man was the medium through which a Black man had to work if he expected to be successful. This was quite a frustrating experience.

I valued my friendly relationship with the Chinese people so highly that I was becoming worried about possible strained relations. As a Black exile in China, I

2. Liu Shao-chi (aka Liu Shaoqi, 1898–1969) was a leader in the Chinese Communist Party and president of the People's Republic of China from 1959 to 1968. In the 1950s and early 1960s, he was considered the third most powerful man in China until he was condemned during the Cultural Revolution for being a "capitalist roader," upon which he was purged from leadership and disappeared from public life.

felt a great responsibility to represent the cause of my oppressed people in the USA. White Americans and some other foreigners were more and more pushing the class issue in a provocative way. More and more their influence was being felt. Little by little I was becoming convinced that the American Black man could best carry out his struggle from American soil. Certain aspects of dogmatic Marxism, combined with white racism, were beginning to obscure the essential issue of the Afro-American's plight in America. My experience taught me that the US racial issue was not a problem that could automatically be explained away through the class theory alone.

I felt the need to travel once again outside of China to check my bearing and to be exposed to other views concerning the growing conflict between the class struggle theory and the experience of those who were actually suffering racial oppression. I seemed in luck for timing. As if by an act of fate, I received an invitation to speak in Sweden. Lund University's forum "A Night with the Students" and a group called Verdandi asked me to come there. I agreed and discussed the affair with my Chinese hosts. The Chinese were positive and offered any assistance to consummate the preparations. I was elated at the thought of traveling to Sweden, where I hoped to meet other Blacks and to lay the preparatory groundwork for my return to the United States.

The Swedes at the embassy in Peking were pleasantly cordial and warm toward the idea of my visiting their country. They stated they were certain that their government would have no objection to my visiting there because they had diplomatic relations with China and the Swedish people had deep sympathy for the Black people in America. In fact, in order to expedite my visa, they resorted to the cable instead of the usual channel of the [diplomatic] pouch.[3] They seemed fascinated by the idea of having someone direct from China during the height of the Cultural Revolution to speak in their country. I had become so enthusiastic over the thought of making it to Europe that I decided to meet my lawyer, Conrad Lynn, in France in order to start legal processes for my return to the States. When I went to the French embassy, it was the same scene. I was assured that the government of France would not object to my visiting there. I spent the ensuing days in a state of anxiety, contemplating my trip to the outside world that I had been away from for seven years.

The drums were still feverishly beating in China, and "monsters" were being pulled down. The "Liu Shao-chi clique" was being vehemently accused of trying to lead China down the capitalist road and of abandoning the world revolution.

3. Official mail to and from an embassy is sent via a diplomatic pouch, which is not examined by customs.

He was charged with being soft on imperialism, tailing after revisionism, and admiring the monopoly capitalists of the West. The word in Peking was that now that these "revisionist monsters" and "poisonous weeds" were being weeded out, China would increase its resistance to imperialism and give more vigorous support to the struggling and oppressed peoples of the world. This new spirit in China was quite impressive.

Suddenly my dreams were shattered, as if struck by an unsuspected bolt of lightning that flashed from a cloudless day. The Swedish government had rejected my application for a visa. I cabled the students to investigate and to seek a reversal. They got a lawyer and appealed all the way up to the king. I finally learned that the Swedish security police had intervened and convinced immigration that my travel there would not be in "the best interest" of the security of the country. Offhand I could not ascertain whether the whole affair should be taken as a compliment or as a blight on my life. Before I could recover from the shock of the Swedish disappointment, the French came through on the same wavelength. I could smell the odious hands of the CIA. I wondered what such governments had to fear from me and concluded that perhaps I had been more effective in my pursuit of social justice than I had been led to realize. In the May 1968 issue of my harried newsletter, I was moved to write:

> There is hardly an Afro-American who has not been affected by the profusely disseminated evidence of the liberality of Europe. When Afro-Americans think of Europe, we like to think of a predominantly white society that sympathizes with Black America in its bitter struggle for emancipation from white slavery in the USA. We have a tendency to forget what white Europe has done to Black Africa. We have had more than enough contact with racist America to have all hopes of the possibility of receiving justice from it dashed in horrible situations of concrete actuality. In the past, we have viewed Europe's attitude towards Africa more from Negritude based on sympathetic abstraction than on concrete experiences. We have been so preoccupied with the Yankee that we have allowed our attitude towards Europe to be influenced by an imagination, fired by a desperate desire to convince ourselves that the overwhelming majority of white humanity is not motivated by white power and racism. By the same token and vice versa we have come to realize that for the same reasons and similar conditions, some of our African brothers who have suffered the yoke of European colonialism feel towards Europe what we feel towards America and towards America what we feel towards Europe.

Throughout my exile in Havana and Peking, I had developed a warm relationship with Africans. I was always an honored guest at their embassies, and we had reciprocal interest in the universal Black struggle for liberation and equality. Some Africans who had manifested some anti-Communist traits had vigorously raised the question as to why I, a Black man, had chosen a "red" country in which to take up exile. I was frequently informed that I would be warmly welcomed as a Black brother in Africa. I was told that my experience and insight into political problems would be highly treasured in Africa. From what I was being told, I reached the conclusion that Africa would be a good place for me to establish residency, and most certainly it would be the proper place for me to meet friends and attorneys in preparation for my return home. My enthusiasm rose for a trip to the mother country of all Black people. I applied for visas at the Guinean, United Arab Republic, Algerian, and Tanzanian embassies. The United Arab Republic responded favorably, but with some vague red tape. The Algerians were cool and never showed any genuine favorable response. The Guineans gave the excuse that because of problems with infiltrators, tourism was being discouraged at that time; however, I was encouraged to file my application because they thought it possible that the government would make an exception in my case. The visa was never issued. Tanzania had a liberal tourist policy, so I was granted a visa to visit the country the same as any other tourist.

My visa approval came through at a time when China was in an uproar and travel in and out of the country was at a very low level. I informed my Chinese hosts of my plans, and they reacted favorably. They graciously offered whatever assistance that the preparations for the trip would require. Everything seemed in order, and I was elated at the thought of traveling to Africa. The generosity and thoughtfulness of the Chinese further convinced me that they were the best and truest friends that the Black man had on earth. It was now April, and I would leave in May for Africa and realize a lifelong dream.

During the ensuing days, some Americans living and working in China approached me about a new statement that was supposed to be issued by Chairman Mao in support of the Afro-American struggle. After extensive discussion, I became apprised of the fact that I was primarily consulted on the matter of whether or not we should be called "Blacks" or "Afro-Americans." It seemed that the contents had already been decided unless the Americans had erroneously given the Chinese the impression that I was in approval and working closely with them in evaluating the new Black attitude. The Americans had long been out to push the class struggle at the expense of a hard universal thrust against US racism. It was obvious that their objective was to divert attention from America's embarrassing racism. They seemed more than anxious to have Mao Tse-tung issue a new statement that would undermine the growing unity with the Third World peoples and the universal understanding and sympathy for the Afro-American. To me, their newfound cause of happiness indicated cause for deep concern.

I was awakened at dawn on April 16, 1968, by the thunder of drums and shouts that caused the very building in which I slept to vibrate. I hurried to my front window and looked out down the street. In the first gray of morning, I could see an endless stream of humanity. Experience had taught me that such demonstrations heralded a major announcement in China. I scurried to the radio and awakened my two sons, who spoke fluent Chinese, in order to ascertain the nature of the latest great event. Chairman Mao had issued a new statement, his second one in support of US Blacks in our struggle against racial discrimination. Big character posters were being pasted up on walls everywhere. The drums and gongs were deafening. My family and I got dressed and joined the march to Tiananmen Square. I was interviewed by press and radio. To my regret, the new statement was somewhat weaker, along racial lines, and most definitely strengthened the position of the white supremacist and phony Marxist-Leninists.

I had the utmost faith in China. I had to have that kind of faith. It was too much to bear to even face up to the devastating possibility that there were "revisionist" forces of "poisonous weeds," of "monsters" and dragons afoot in China that could subvert the great spiritual achievements and direction of China as set forth in the works of Mao Tse-tung. The Russians had already abdicated their obligation to the oppressed and revolutionary peoples of the world. The Russians had turned soft in the process of aping and trying to curry favor with the West. The Russians appeared to be seeking détente at any cost, and most of all at the expense of the struggling people of the world. They had used the specter of nuclear war to tone down liberation struggles. They openly theorized that even a brushfire war or a revolutionary struggle might inadvertently be escalated into an international nuclear holocaust. They were preaching peaceful transition and had stopped truly encouraging violent liberation activity. The "Liu gang" in China was being accused of harboring the same outlook. I was told that the Cultural Revolution would clear the way for more solid Chinese support for the liberation movements and the oppressed peoples of the world. I assessed this to mean that the Left forces in China were going to follow a hard line in their attitude toward imperialism.

China was the last great country to serve as a base area for world revolution. If she took the capitulationist road of the Soviet Union, the hope of the world's oppressed peoples would most certainly and severely be darkened. The most laborious steps of oppressed man's slow and bloody trek along the dismal road of liberation would have to be retraced from the very painful and primitive beginning. Too much was at stake in the Cultural Revolution to feel comfortable. The Left had to win, and the dragon of subversion had to be destroyed, but the nagging question persisted in my Western brainwashed way of thinking. Who really represented the Right, and who really represented the Left? I raised the question of revisionism in telegrams to Chairman Mao and Chou En-lai. The official explanation was plausible and reassuring; however, the minister who came to explain it to me was himself "knocked down" as a monster shortly after his elucidating visit. He had been a popular figure around Chairman Mao but soon disappeared completely from the scene.

Word came out that Liu Shao-chi had made a confession but that it was only a weak attempt to save himself and that he had refused to back away from the most erroneous concepts of his position. It was said that he was trying to cover his "nefarious" tracks. His treatise *How to Be a Good Communist* was being used as an exhibit of indictment. He was bearing the blame for many things that I had always been led to believe resulted from a collective undertaking. My close reading of the works of Chairman Mao uncovered advocacy of some of the policies that Liu was now being charged with having implemented. Needless to say, I found the situation confusing. Everyone was being encouraged to examine everyone and to question everything. In short, the essence of the whole Cultural Revolution was said to boil down to the right to rebel. Strangely enough, Liu's book, while under fierce attack, was still on sale at some local bookshops. I obtained a copy in order to try to better understand the errors of this "renegade" Communist who had opposed the policies of Chairman Mao.

In reading the words of Liu Shao-chi, I found no solace. To me the situation became even more confusing. It was said that he had great talent for playing on words. In this case, it was even vain to read his words, and I wondered what had inspired him to write:

> Our Communist self-cultivation is the kind essential to proletarian revolutionaries. It must not be divorced from revolutionary practice or from the actual revolutionary movements of the laboring masses, and especially of the proletarian masses.
>
> . . . These are the reasons why Communists must undertake self-cultivation.[4]

4. Liu Shaoqi, "How to Be a Good Communist," lecture series, July 1939, Yan'an, https://www.marxists.org/reference/archive/liu-shaoqi/1939/how-to-be/ch01.htm.

Liu Shao-chi and his "revisionist clique" were now discredited and branded as being totally bad. So many changes were being leveled and some sounded so fantastic that rationalism was becoming more and more difficult to sort out. However, it was obvious that Liu's gang had erred. In my burning desire to find justification for my personal condemnation of this man, I went back to a speech that I had heard him make on July 22, 1966, as the Cultural Revolution was in its early and less tumultuous stage. After reading this speech, I was still nonplussed concerning my efforts to justify the whole situation. My difficulty in accepting indictment and conviction through mass suggestion was based on the fact that I was a Black man from the South of the USA and because I had developed great hatred for the white supremacy way of convicting Black people based on social circumstances rather than on impartial evidence gathered from both sides of the case. It is not that I thought the Chinese were being unjust, but I had to satisfy my own need to review facts to insulate my own conscience against nagging recriminations. There is always a great danger that those who have suffered great oppression may subconsciously identify with all underdogs, whether right or wrong. I also found it necessary for me to struggle against this extreme. It didn't help any when I reread statements of Chairman Liu Shao-chi.

Though I was perhaps the only friendly resident in Peking not taking an active part in the Cultural Revolution, the stress of the confusion and sometimes bitter recrimination had ushered me to the brink of debilitation. All kinds of charges were flying. Some seemed incredible. I was always conscious of the fact that my lack of knowledge of Chinese politics, prior to the Cultural Revolution, constituted a handicap in my ability to read some logic into what was going on. China shook from political tremors like a man suffering seizures from a deadly fever. By late April 1968, there occurred some brief letups in the intensity of the movement. Just when my hope was on the rise for the return of stability, the drums and the clamor on the streets dashed them again. If I could have felt certain that everything was going to turn out all right, it would have been much easier for me to adopt an indifferent attitude. But too much was at stake, and anxiety became a way of life. I desperately wanted the Mao forces to achieve a quick and clear-cut victory, but it seemed that the opposition was the most dogged of die-hards. I wanted a quick victory for Chairman Mao before irreparable damage could be done to the national unity and economy.

It appeared that a great part of the campaign that the Western world's press referred to as adulation for Mao Tse-tung was in actuality a Mark Antony–type maneuver staged by his enemies to dishonor and discredit him. The masses were genuine and honorable in their affection for the Chairman, but some bad elements were trying to undermine his natural greatness by exaggerating his human attributes. I was convinced that from a Western point of view, a more logical explanation was needed in order to bring some credence to the whole affair.

China had been rightfully closed to foreigners. Now everything was being opened up. Some revolutionary youths spent a great deal of time explaining the sinister work of Liu Shao-chi and Lo Jui-ching, former member of the Secretariat of the Central Committee of the Communist Party of China, vice premier of the State Council, and chief of the general staff of the Chinese People's Liberation Army. I was told over and over again that Lo Jui-ching had placed exaggerated stress on the technical training of thc army at the expense of political indoctrination and that this was in opposition to the teaching of Chairman Mao. He also was said to have ordered many installations constructed underground and had placed them off-limits to foreigners. All of this was said to have been done with the malicious intent of concealing from the Chinese people and foreign friends the success of Chairman Mao's policy. Though I supported the policies of Mao Tse-tung, feeling the way I did about American agents, I could not help but think that it was a wonderful thing to keep military secrets from the cognizance of so-called foreign friends.

Robert Williams in Tanzania, 1968. Robert F. Williams Papers,
Bentley Historical Library, University of Michigan.

CHAPTER 54

IN QUEST OF THE SOUL OF MY ANCESTORS

On Thursday, May 18, 1968, I left Peking for a visit to Africa. After two days in a Karachi, Pakistan, which was under martial law, I boarded a plane for the long-dreamed-of landing in Africa. My first stop on the continent was Addis Ababa, Ethiopia. I arrived in Africa at a time when disillusionment with the American way of life among Blacks was becoming more and more pronounced and an intense militancy was rising from every quarter of the Black ghetto. The African American was now rising proudly to proclaim his African heritage and identity. Oppressed Black Americans had for some time now been defiantly donning colorful African-type dress and were learning African languages, studying African history, and collecting African art, and those who possibly could were making pilgrimages to the original home of the Black man. Since my early childhood days, I, too, had longed to see the natural home of Black people, to experience a brotherhood wherein Blacks were not a despised minority. At last, I was making my first footprint on African soil. I was having a brief stopover in Addis Ababa.

My pleasant state of excitement was of short duration. My spirit was dampened by the sight of two giant US Air Force planes parked near the airport terminal. As we taxied toward the terminal, the sight of the American flag painted on the planes sent chills through my body. It had been more than seven years since I had seen such a sight, and being a "fugitive from American democracy," it was a disconcerting feeling to suddenly be reminded of the extent of US penetration. Fortunately, it appeared that my arrival was not expected. The reality of the situation brought me to awareness that China was one of the very few countries in the whole world that was completely detached from official Americanism. How tragic it was to think that a Black American could not look upon the Stars and Stripes as a symbol of protection, democracy, and citizenship but from bitter experience was forced to relate it to the inhumane condition of white supremacy, degradation, and denial.

Still hoping to see some Black control over what was thought to be the Black dominion, I proceeded on to Nairobi, Kenya, and in this Black country, home of the celebrated Mau Mau, with the exception of the airline workers, I saw very little of my Black brothers. This fact in itself all too clearly hinted at a tragic situation. Yes, I was in Africa, but not the Africa of the Black man that I had expected.

Upon my arrival in Tanzania, I saw a different picture with changed atmosphere. A few days later, after having walked over the capital city of Dar es Salaam, I still felt a pressing need to see the true Africa that I had always wanted to see. I talked with many individuals who had availed themselves of the regular tourist services and who had traveled the ordinary tourist routes. I felt this to be an insufficient means for an Afro-American freedom fighter to really get acquainted with Africa and her people. I did not want to travel as a tourist but as a brother. As an exile in the People's Republic of China, I had witnessed the mighty upsurge of the Great Proletarian Cultural Revolution and the long marches of the young Red Guards, who traversed the distant countryside to propagate the thought of Mao Tse-tung. The cross-country treks of China's youth offered an example in learning and becoming acquainted with the people. My problem in Africa, however, was the language barrier and the danger of predatory wild animals. I considered making the journey by bicycle, but this was ruled out as totally impossible under the conditions of travel. After conferring with an Afro-American teacher, Ronald Howard, and an African motorcycle salesman named Gabriel, I was convinced that a motorcycle trip was the nearest possible thing to the Red Guard way. Both Roland and Gabriel were anxious and excited about making the trip from Dar es Salaam to Zambia over the route commonly called Hell's Run. We set out on our cross-country safari fully aware of the hardships and dangers involved. This was not just a thrill adventure on motorcycles, but an educational experience of lasting value, a campaign designed to strengthen ties between emerging peoples. It was a revolutionary experiment carried out in the cause of the oppressed Black man's liberation. Our ten-day motorcycle safari took us across treacherous unpaved, dusty, and sandy roads that sometimes constituted impossible barriers for motor cars and trucks. We cycled over mountain peaks that extended into exceptionally beautiful cloud drifts and rode washboard-type roads that shook us like an electric vibrator along 700 miles of roads so dusty that we had to wear dust masks, shields, and goggles. We counted fifty heavy trucks and trailers overturned and wrecked. The truck traffic was very heavy because this was the route of the truck lift between the Dar es Salaam port and landlocked Zambia.

This was primarily a territory of heavy trucks and Land Rovers; consequently, curious but friendly observers gathered about us wherever we went. To them, it was a new scene to see Black men daring to mount such a venture. We stopped over in rural African hotels and met people who were not accustomed to meeting foreign visitors. The fact that two of us were African Americans aroused added interest. We visited homes, schools, villages, and marketplaces. To my great surprise, we found the people on the highlands very progressive in farming, cattle raising, and their world outlook. On visiting the village of Bulongwa, which is situated 8,000 feet above sea level and is next to impossible to reach, we found some villagers proudly wearing Chinese pins bearing the image of Mao Tse-tung. When they were told that I, a Black man, had lived in Peking, their faces beamed with smiles, and they spoke with deep emotion about the Chinese people's great concern for the oppressed peoples of the world and of their friendship and aid to Tanzania and the anti-imperialist forces in Africa.

The people of Bulongwa were living examples of a true African spirit of self-reliance, initiative, and resourcefulness. They had created a very effective modern school with a world outlook. While we were visiting a fourth-grade class, one alert little girl raised her hand and told the principal that she wanted to ask me a question. She wanted to know what Black people in America call themselves, Africans or Americans. After briefly expounding the shameful and brutal history of how captive Black people were kidnapped from Africa, savagely enslaved, and denied contact with their motherland, I explained that after many years of bitter struggle for human rights, those of us with race pride call ourselves Black Americans, Afro-Americans, or African Americans. The entire class seemed pleased to identify with their long-lost relatives in faraway America. They gave very enthusiastic applause.

At the Zambian border we cyclists went in separate ways with plans to rendezvous in two days on the way back to Dar es Salaam. Because of some minor difficulties, my companions failed to rendezvous, and I was stuck with a 700-mile return trip to Dar without them. I rode steadily but slowly, thinking my friends would overtake me. They never did. On three occasions, night overtook me riding in the rugged, animal-infested mountains alone.

Near Mbeya, I visited an encampment of Chinese engineers who were surveying the zone where a railroad was being constructed as Chinese aid to Tanzania and Zambia. When completed, the railroad would strengthen the transportation system between Zambia and Tanzania and ease Zambia's dependence on racist reactionary South Africa's transportation system. It was also to strengthen it against Rhodesian economic pressure. The Chinese railroad engineers, who were dedicated to the cause of liberation of the oppressed peoples and nations of the world, were working exceptionally hard under severely adverse and hazardous conditions. The African masses who had had the opportunity to observe them at work were very much impressed by their devotion to duty and personal conduct, despite a vicious campaign being waged by imperialist forces and agents to create an atmosphere of suspicion, distrust, and hatred toward Chinese Communists and Asians in general. On a number of occasions, the Tanzanian government found it necessary to use the news media to plead for general cooperation with the Chinese technicians in the Dar area. The Western- and European-educated Africans were some of the most anti-Chinese. Some of them had tried to bar Chinese surveyors from crossing their property because subversive anti-China elements had circulated rumors that the technicians were plotting the takeover of their property and nation.

One example of the malicious anti-China crusade being carried out on a personal level unfolded shortly after my arrival in Dar es Salaam. An Afro-American photographer was shooting a sequence of pictures of me on the waterfront. We were approached by a white American sea captain who had heard us speaking English. Having confirmed his assumption that we were Afro-Americans, he pointed to the outstandingly impressive Chinese ocean liner anchored in the harbor and somberly stated that he hoped the Chinese would not gain a foothold in Africa. I asked him why and he exclaimed that China wanted to colonize Africa and to "exterminate the nigras." He said that the Chinese hated all Black people, that China was overcrowded, and that they wanted the African territory for expansion.

I told him that this was a strange and erroneous opinion because I was a Black man who had resided in China and that I had been the recipient of more brotherhood there than in America or Africa.

He reeled from the shock of my disclosure. He was startled with disbelief until I finally convinced him that I was for real and that my home address was Peking, China. It took him a while to regain his composure, after which he sheepishly humbled his attitude. In an innocent, childlike manner, he confessed that he thought that what he had read in the press were lies. Then he asked that I tell him what China was "really like," him never having been there.

My African safari was a highly educational experience. It made me feel a deeper kinship with the ordinary people of Africa, and I became more cognizant of the hardships and tribulations ahead for Africa. The trip also led me to have a greater respect for the achievements of China and to appreciate the Chinese peoples' attitude toward me. Africa was undergoing painful, arduous, and protracted transition. The chains and rigors of an eon of colonialism was going to be extremely difficult to cast off. I concluded that it was most certainly in the interest of Africa to lean more toward the Chinese experience of self-reliance than that of the West.

After being informed, in a semiofficial manner, that a tourist visa could be extended for only six months and that if I were allowed to remain in Tanzania beyond that time it could possibly be construed as an "anti-American act" at a time when Africa could not afford a confrontation with the USA despite local sympathy for me, once again I turned toward China, the only place where I, a Black man, could go home.

My afterthought about Africa was that when the European- and American-minded intellectuals and bureaucrats were reformed or replaced by patriots who completely identified with and became the servants of the African people, then Africa's potential would be unlimited. Africa would raise herself to stand proudly on her own feet as undisputed master of her own soil. She would stand tall in her place in the sun.

CHAPTER 55

LAST DAYS IN CHINA

My Chinese friends had once again come through for me by helping me to return to a China still in the midst of its Great Proletarian Cultural Revolution. Future historical assessment and analysis would measure the success of China's Cultural Revolution. Mao Tse-tung's thought had already demonstrated its power up through this historical juncture. In a little more than twenty years, it transformed a primitive, feudalistic nation into a great nuclear power. During this period, China had done quite well in resource development and in restructuring her society. However, I was frequently cautioned by old-timers inside China that Chinese politics were highly erratic and enigmatic and that the true meaning of certain types of dialogue often must be lifted from beneath the surface of symbolic words. The Chinese are masters at allegorizing conversation. Outsiders who are not familiar with Chinese tradition and many China watchers who attempt to analyze strictly from a political point of view usually find themselves embarrassingly far off base in their interpretations of Chinese events and politics.

I learned not to be too sure of anything political in China, having been constantly advised by my hosts to remember that "what is a true evaluation of the situation today in China may not be accurate and acceptable six weeks from now." Though things had quieted down considerably, with my new understanding of Chinese politics I could not bring myself around to completely believing that the situation was totally stable. I desperately hoped that the roughest time was over and that China had ridden out the worst of the storm.

But wild rumors, in the form of whispers, were pervading the atmosphere of proclaimed triumph. These whispered rumors were fantastic and read like something out of a Western masterpiece of science fiction. Nevertheless, they were being heard over and over again. There were whispers to the effect that the current chairman, Mao Tse-tung, was not Mao at all but a double. Some went so far as to say that his facial features had been restructured. Old-timers who knew him from the old days spoke of his changed personality and the fact that he seemed to shy away from their presence. There were whispers that US agents may have kidnapped the real Mao and substituted an American fake. Some individuals, with what appeared to be overactive, fertile imaginations, even suggested the possibility that the entire Cultural Revolution Committee had been infected with a brain-mutating drug that had the effect of making members the complete opposite of their original intellectual beings. Though such rumors were unbelievable in their totality, it irritated me to no end to think that conditions had deteriorated to such a degree that many Chinese patriots felt the necessity to give some logical explanation for the convulsive dissension inside the party. The haunting fact remained that though the drums had almost ceased to beat, the monster, the dragon, might not have been dead. He may have gone underground to nurse his wounds and to plan new strategy. Then too, there was still a nagging possibility of a traitor running into the streets and shouting, "Stop, traitor!" There was too much at stake for all of oppressed humanity to think of this possibility. Still, the possibility remained. This possibility disturbed me to such an extent that I wrote and *Hsinhua*[1] published a statement cautioning the Chinese people of the danger of being deceived by phony revolutionaries who might direct attention away from themselves by indicting revolutionary patriots with false charges, discrediting and destroying them and in the end subverting and destroying People's China. It was such a caustic statement that I seriously doubted that it would be published, but it was.

By April 23, 1969, things were quite calm on the surface in Peking. I was primarily engaged in the preoccupation of preparing to leave China permanently. There was really no pressing need for me to leave, but I just had an inner feeling that it was time for me to go. Somehow it was strange how many letters I was receiving from the USA wherein all kinds of people were soliciting my aid in getting them admitted to China. I had been exiled for eight years, and I found nothing romantic about being exiled in a foreign country. Perhaps I could have easily been content forever as a guest, but as an exile, no. I had touched a thread of history unfolding. I had lived it. I had been there. What a strange twist of fate

1. A Chinese newspaper.

I had had as a Black freedom fighter from North Carolina. I had to take to the road of history again. There was still a dark path before me. Yes, I was going home. I was going at any cost.

My last days in Peking were very sad ones. Until now, I had felt happy at the thought of going home. Now that preparations were actually being made and the time of departure was but a short time away, my heart was melancholy and heavy. As I hurried about Peking shopping and bidding old friends goodbye, I realized more and more how much I was going to miss the sights and sounds of Peking. There was something about living in China that one just could not brush aside or shrug off with a customary goodbye. Even in social turmoil and political conflict, there was a serenity and dignity about China and the Chinese people that made one's affection for them almost irreversible.

Friends came. We exchanged opinions about the course of the Cultural Revolution. I heard more rumors and gossip. China was changing. Some revolutionaries who received great support from China were almost hysterical with fear in the face of certain indications of new change that they did not construe to be in the spirit of the China prior to 1966. At any rate, I suppose one's cause for concern and one's ability to see certain vague images of "revisionism" depended on the extent to which one relied on or needed the type of China that existed prior to 1966. As one going back to his own country, I had steadfastly refused to participate in choosing sides in the politics of my host countries.

In the evening of May Day, Mabel and I were invited to watch the traditional fireworks display from the Tiananmen with Chairman Mao and other dignitaries. While we were lounging around waiting for the festivities to start, I heard a refrain of hand-clapping and shouts of "Chairman Mao!" The Chairman was coming. To my great surprise he came over, shook our hands, and greeted us warmly. Needless to say, we were delighted that he took the time to greet us personally.

One day a week later, we went to visit Dr. Anna Louise Strong, who was in declining health in the "Anti-Imperialist Hospital," to say farewell to her.[2] We had lived upstairs in the same house as she and Rewi Ally in the Peace Compound for several years and had exchanged many political ideas over time.[3] She was greatly emaciated by her steadily deteriorating condition and struggled to restrain her emotions. She wished us well and spoke in a rambling way, giving indication that she, too, had a burning desire to see her native land once more.

2. Anna Louise Strong was an American radical activist and journalist who visited China during the revolutionary struggle and stayed on after the triumph of the revolution.

3. Rewi Ally was a writer and author from New Zealand who moved to China during its war against Japan in the 1940s.

By May 21, we had come to the end of a week of farewell banquets and parties. The National Liberation Front of Vietnam had hosted a most touching farewell dinner for our family. Premier Chou En-lai sent a car to pick us up on the evening of the twenty-first after a banquet at the Tanzanian embassy. We were driven to the Great Hall of the People for an extensive talk that lasted for more than two hours. We exchanged opinions on a variety of international subjects and inevitably got around to American affairs in their multiplicity. Without any effort, we reached a mutual conclusion that nothing progressive could be expected from the Richard Nixon regime.

I mentioned the Sino-Soviet border dispute and expressed a desire to obtain copies of a documentary film showing the Chinese side of the story. I expounded on the fact that the Soviets had diplomatic relations with the United States and that this was to their advantage in explaining their side of the conflict to the American people. I expressed a belief that such a film in the United States would be beneficial to China. Premier Chou said that he would personally see to it that special copies with English dubbed in would be given to me to take home with me. I told him that I was leaving for Africa the following day and that I hoped that this would be no barrier to my obtaining the film. He promised that the film would be sent to me in Africa.

With a pleasant but inquisitive voice and his traditional smile beaming from his seemingly timeless face, he asked why I had so much faith in the US government that I was willing to risk going home. I explained that I thought my place was among my people in the USA and that I did not have faith in the US government but in changed conditions. I further explained that I thought that times and conditions had changed to such an extent that it was now necessary for the USA to alter its conduct. He said that he thought I might be gunned down as soon as I alighted from the airplane in the United States or, failing that, the imperialists would imprison me and isolate me from my people for the rest of my life. I told him that I doubted that they would. He again asked why. I shared with him that I would, no doubt, be the only American with the type of Chinese experience that I had had and that if US officials were smart, they would be more concerned with hearing about China than in the sport of lynching a Black man. I indicated that I expected to be questioned at great length upon my arrival.

I could now see that what I proposed to do was beginning to make some sense to him, or at least he gave me that impression. He sat back in his chair, became silent for a moment, and then struck me with a great surprise when he said, "Well, since you insist on going home, you will be able to work for better understanding and peaceful relations between the American people and the Chinese people." I told him that after my return to the United States, perhaps we could invite him to visit us. He replied that perhaps in the future that would be possible, but at that time he was so busy that he could not even go out of Peking for other parts of China.

At the conclusion of our rap session, we all stood up and he said, "I will walk with you to your car." It was already past midnight and Tiananmen was all but deserted. As we stood in the night and engaged in the last-minute chatter, an occasional image of a lone cyclist or pedestrian pushed through the mist of the hazy night in what I suppose was a homeward trek. Now Peking was melancholy and quiet. I could hear no drums to kill a dragon. Silence almost prevailed. Chou embraced us in a solemn gesture of farewell as he wished us luck. We got into the car and he stood in the midnight haze, slowly waving goodbye. I looked back from the car, and for as long as I could see him, he was still waving, seemingly dwarfed by the Great Hall. For the first time, I thought I had detected a sense of loneliness about him.

I felt sad inside. I was really leaving China. I kept seeing Chou's face, and his words kept coming back to me. As I saw his long image vanish into the haze of night and of China, I wondered what China's destiny would be and how history would assess what I had lived and seen. Most of all, I wondered whether the silence of the drums signified that the modern political monsters were dead or whether they had cleverly eluded those who so frenetically beat the drums to kill dragons.

The Peace Committee made all of my travel arrangements, and a small delegation from the group, along with my family, saw me off at the airport. I knew that I was journeying to a lion's den of hatred, racism, and uncertainty, but I was driven by a deep commitment to fulfill my destiny, no matter the consequences. I had faced danger so many times and for so long that I had become somewhat phlegmatic.

CHAPTER 56

RETURN FROM EXILE

My first stop was in Dacca, East Pakistan, now called Bangladesh. The airport was crowded, and the plane took on more passengers. It seemed dangerously overloaded to me. After my arrival in West Pakistan, I was lodged for an overnight stay in a modest hotel. A very friendly tourist taxi driver joined me at dinner and asked if I would buy him a drink. He explained that it was a Muslim Holy Day and that no alcohol could be sold to a Pakistani. I ordered a drink for him and we became instant friends. He offered to take me on a tour around the city. I accepted the invitation.

The poverty and human degradation that I witnessed around the city was disconcerting. I witnessed women and children in tattered rags, scavenging among piles of rocks and rubbish, which made me despair of a humanity so insensate as to allow such conditions to prevail in any community of our commonly inhabited planet. My newfound, somewhat jovial friend took me to a fabulous mosque that lacked only finishing touches to be completed. After we removed our shoes and entered the extensively splendid edifice, a solemn transformation seemed to overwhelm him. He glowed with pride as he explained that this was the people's mosque, constructed by the government to the glory of Allah.

As I was leaving Pakistan the next day, an airport official approached me as I neared the waiting plane. He informed me that I need not be bothered with my carry-on bag. He insisted that I let him put it in the baggage compartment. I looked on as he secured it. Since there was nothing valuable or incriminating being transported by me, I relented.

Upon my arrival in Dar es Salaam, all my baggage was missing. I had witnessed the airline official placing my carry-on bag in the belly of the plane. Dar was just a stopover, and as passengers loaded and unloaded, the plane remained crowded. Because travelers claimed their luggage at planeside, I refused to leave for the terminal. I felt violated and had become exceedingly enraged. I could sense a conspiracy and the work of the CIA. An airline official insisted that my luggage had been sent to Entebbe by mistake. I knew he was lying. I instantly became resigned to the possibility that my destiny had finally caught up with me. I conceived this incident as possibly the end of the line for me. This was the straw that broke the camel's back. Perhaps, I thought, I was destined to die on the mother continent of Africa. If this was the end, I was going to go out with the biggest bang of my life. My death would not go unnoticed because I was going to take a lot of people with me.

During the heated argument, I moved nearer to the truck that was refueling the plane for its scheduled onward flight to Entebbe. I removed a small box of Chinese-made matches from my pocket and raised a match in a striking mode as instant panic gripped the faces of everyone who saw the threat. A nearby official screamed, "No! No! Brother, put that match away! Please, Brother, what is wrong?"

"My bag is missing! This is a dirty CIA plot, and before I let them do this to me, I'll blow us all to hell!" I shouted. "I'm ready to go down if necessary."

"Oh please, Brother, don't do it. Wait and I'll call the president of the airline to come out here to solve your problem," he said in a frightened tone.

"Well, he had better get out here in the next five minutes!" I demanded angrily.

Almost instantly a jeep came speeding across the airfield. A well-dressed and somewhat calmer African man jumped from the jeep and greeted me in a friendly tone. I was still holding the match in a threatening pose. The faces of the passengers, gathered at the windows of the plane, displayed a magnitude of horror.

"If you can give me a location where I can reach you, I will personally deliver your bags to you!" he promised.

"I'll be at the Afrique Hotel, and don't try to play me for a fool. I'm not an African, I'm an Afro-American freedom fighter, and you guys can't pull this kind of shit on me. I hope you understand the serious principle involved!"

"I understand your feeling, Brother, and my promise is sincere," the African stated. He offered me a ride with him to the terminal, and I accepted his offer. I checked into the hotel and began to get settled in.

After a couple of hours, at about 7:00 p.m. the phone in my room rang. The desk clerk informed me that a visitor wanted to see me in the lobby. I went down and found the president of the airline standing in the middle of the lobby, smiling broadly with my bags at his side. "You see, I told you that I would personally deliver your bags. I'm true to my word," he proclaimed as he handed over my luggage. He made an offer to take me out for a drink to show his sincerity. I declined the offer.

I had survived the first leg of my journey home. Now my big task was to obtain a US passport to enter the USA. I had never owned a US passport, and the whole time I was abroad, I traveled on Cuban and Chinese travel documents. I had enjoyed the protection of those governments, and now I was out of the range of such security. After a three-day wait, my request for an appointment with officials at the US embassy in Dar es Salaam came through. My first session was with a man named Barrens. It was rather cool and detached. My request to the embassy was for the issuance of a passport and an import license to bring my Chinese-made products into the USA. At that time, no Chinese-manufactured item could legally be brought into the USA. After being apprised of my history and situation, the embassy official informed me that since my case was a unique one, he would have to contact Washington for instructions on processing it.

On my prior trip to Tanzania, I had established a foreign bank account in US dollars. Such a bank account was to pay off in dollars upon request. I had made this arrangement hoping to withdraw US$7,000 when the time came for me to return to America. At the time I had made the deposit, I was greatly elated to see so many well-groomed young Africans apparently running such a modern enterprise as a bank. It was the first time I had had the opportunity to utilize such a service.

Now that I was back in Dar es Salaam en route home, I made application to close out my dollar account with the bank as originally planned. While I waited for business at the embassy to be resolved, I decided to take care of my personal financial concerns. In so doing, I was shocked beyond belief to be informed that if I wanted US dollars, I would have to purchase them with Tanzanian shillings at the going rate charged Tanzanians seeking foreign currency when going abroad. This was an extremely high rate of exchange, probably imposed to discourage out-migration. I fell into a state of shock and disbelief. Surely the clerks and tellers who were conferring over the paperwork were making a simple mistake that could easily be corrected. When I rejected their calculations, they became less than polite, insisting that the record was there before them and that its contents were final. After apprising them of my state of indignation and the fact that I would not hold still for robbery, I demanded to discuss my situation with the president of the bank.

I was ushered into an impressively plush office where a fat, well-dressed Black man sat behind an expensive desk, fingering through a sheaf of papers. He stood up, reached out and shook my hand, and then motioned for me to sit on a comfortable stuffed chair facing his desk. "I understand that you've got some problem, Brother. What can I do for you?" he asked in an air that fully exaggerated his authority and ability to handle my problem.

As if he had not already been made aware of the affair, I laid out my case to him. He summoned my records to be brought to his desk. After pretending to study my bank records, he looked up from the papers with his face glowing slyly and informed me that "the laws of our country require all requests for foreign currency to be bought with shillings unless deposits are made in foreign currency in a special account."

"But that is exactly what my transaction was from the very beginning. Here is my passbook with the dollar account stamped on it!" I stated as I handed the passbook to him.

"I don't know who serviced your account, but there is not enough evidence that you have a dollar account. Perhaps we can give you a special discount on your purchase of dollars!" he said.

"Unless this bank honors my dollar deposit, I am going to take this matter up with your minister of finance, even if I have to sit in at his office. I refuse to allow this bank and this office to rob me like common criminals," I declared in a passion of indignation.

Obviously, he had become convinced that I was not going to be fazed by his stonewalling. Finally, he informed me that I would have to take this matter up with a supervisor upstairs. A young, well-dressed woman escorted me, at his direction, to an upper floor. The upstairs was buzzing with activity. Much to my dismay, as I approached the supervisor's desk, a burly white man in shorts and his shirtsleeves, who struck a glaring contrast to the well-dressed Africans in their business suits, asked, "What can I do for you?"

After relating my problem to him, he informed me that he would straighten the matter out and that he would see to it that my withdrawal would be made in dollars.

While awaiting my travel document and permission to carry home my personal belongings manufactured in China, I formed the habit of going for a daily walk. It later became obvious to me that an African man was shadowing me on my walks. Each time I stopped to window-shop, he would invariably stop to window-shop nearby. After many days, one day I decided to trick him. I went around the corner of a building, stopped, turned around, and slightly bumped into him. He looked rather embarrassed and disappeared along the street. He was not seen again. There was no way of knowing whether he was called off or had invoked a more skillful tactic.

A message in my box at the hotel desk informed me that the US embassy's first secretary was back and was willing to discuss my travel problems with me. Upon my arrival at the embassy, I was informed that it was authorized to issue me a travel document restricted to travel to the USA only. I was also told that no item made in China could be brought into the United States because of the embargo. I informed the US diplomat that I had 2,000 pounds of personal items originating from China and that if I could not take them home, I would call the international press to the waterfront and dump my belongings and then strip off my clothes and travel to the United States naked because even my underwear was Chinese-made. I explained that if I were to resort to protesting in that way, it would focus worldwide attention on the petty stupidity of the US government's extent of trying to isolate China.

At this point, Mr. Barrens, the diplomat, displayed a greater interest in accommodating me. "Some of us are working to improve relations with China," he said. "If you do that, you will weaken our cause. Now, you wouldn't want to weaken our faction in the government, would you?" he asked. He then advised me to wait until he could confer with Washington concerning my special situation. I agreed to do so.

After a few days, I was summoned to the embassy again, and I was informed that President Nixon had intervened and that I had been granted the first import license to bring items manufactured in the People's Republic of China into the USA.

After receiving my US travel document, visiting the British embassy, and purchasing a $400 ticket on the United Arab Airlines, I was all set to run the risk of returning to my native land. I was aware of the fact that I faced some life-threatening challenges, but I was not a criminal and I would not be deterred from fighting for what I believed in.

I had been in exile eight years. The world had changed a great deal since I had fought the violent racists in North Carolina. According to all the information I had been privy to, North Carolina had greatly changed, too. A new wind was blowing, and I was going to take advantage of its flow. Many friends advised me not to return. They felt that I had misconceived the new tendency. They cautioned me that racism was still alive and well in the USA, but I had a gut feeling that this was the moment that would offer me the greatest leverage of survival. I could sense the approach of a time when the desire for détente would obviate the

Afro-American struggle conducted from foreign soil. More and more, America was being looked upon as the fountainhead of long-dreamed-of goodies, and most of the world was not going to allow mere principle and righteous causes to continue as a barrier to their obtaining them.

After being told by officials of the British embassy in Dar es Salaam that it was not necessary for me to obtain a visa to enter Britain because I would only be passing through, I continued my long, uncertain journey home.

The United Arab Republic plane stopped over in Cairo, Egypt, and all passengers were ordered off and were led to the airport while the craft refueled. Cairo's airport was bustling with activity. Once again, I was in a different world. It was most certainly a crossroads. It still bore evidence of poverty and antiquity in comparison to Western and Eastern standards. After an almost two-hour layover, a voice announced our flight was reboarding and that passengers on the through flight should come to the boarding gate prepared to continue their journey.

When I displayed my boarding pass to the gate attendant, I received another big shock, which now seemed to be a common occurrence. I was told that I could not board the plane. I was informed that someone else had a priority on my seat and that I would have to wait a few days for another flight. I could see the hands of the CIA again. It was attempting to thwart my return home. I remembered that I had been told at the US embassy that there were Africans who would kill me for fifteen cents. I had already received a cable that many members of the Republic of New Afrika would be waiting at the airport in Detroit for my arrival.[1] This was evidently a dirty ploy to avoid a rally and demonstration of support by my friends and followers at the Detroit Metro Airport. The specter of a Black man returning from exile and being greeted by a throng of dissatisfied and oppressed citizens denied entry into the mainstream of so-called American democracy most certainly was a cause for great embarrassment.

Along with the shock, I felt a sinking feeling deep within me. I was one lone fighter on the international scene, being attacked, ambushed, and sabotaged at almost every turn. In my long and dangerous struggle, I had learned that the most formidable weapon in my arsenal of defense and survival was to boldly react in a confrontation steeped in the element of surprise. Infected with a most severe

1. The Provisional Government of the Republic of New Afrika was formed in March 1968 when 500 Black Nationalists convened in Detroit, Michigan, and 100 of them signed a Declaration of Independence. Robert Williams was nominated president of the Provisional Government, which he accepted. Edward Onaci, *Free the Land: The Republic of New Afrika and the Pursuit of a Black Nation-State* (Chapel Hill: University of North Carolina Press, 2020), 25–30; Akinyele Omowale Umoja, *We Will Shoot Back: Armed Resistance in the Mississippi Freedom Movement* (New York: New York University Press, 2013), 186–88.

spate of anger, I returned to the Egyptian air terminal. Angrily, I demanded to know where the president of the airline's office was located. An attendant at an information desk informed me that the official office I was inquiring about was located on an upper floor. I am sure the functionary could detect that I was exceedingly angry, for he acceded to my demand by dialing the number of the airline chief and passing the telephone to me.

"I came in on the flight from Dar es Salaam, and now I am told that I cannot continue on that flight. What is the reason for this? Is Egypt a running dog for the CIA?" I asked, in a not-too-friendly tone.

"Oh no, my friend, the problem is caused by the fact that your continuing on that flight was based on the contingency that the person who had priority on the seat would not claim it. I'm sorry that you will have to stay over two or three days until we can find you a seat on another flight to London," the voice said, evidently expecting to have convinced me.

"No! I am an Afro-American leader with my friends and followers preparing to meet me at the airport upon my arrival in Detroit. No! I refuse to surrender my seat. I demand to leave on that flight!"

"I'm sorry, sir, there is nothing I can do for you," he informed me in a polite and mechanical air of finality.

While we were conversing on the telephone, suddenly the terminal became engulfed in excitement. There was a rush to all available windows and doors with a clamor for visibility beyond the loading zone. "What is all the excitement about?" I asked the attendant at the desk.

"President Nasser's motorcade is passing. He is meeting some foreign dignitaries here!"

"Well, President Nasser is going to be very much embarrassed if I am not allowed to board that plane, because I am going to buy a big bag lunch and I am going to the Presidential Palace and I am going to sit there in protest to let the world know that his government is helping US racists to frustrate Afro-American freedom fighters!"

"Oh no, Brother, don't do that. We would like to make you a guest of our government for three days and let you travel in our country, free of charge, if you will please accept," he stated in a voice half-apologizing and half-begging.

"No! I don't want to be a guest of your government. I want to go where I started. I want to go to Detroit to meet my people who are waiting there for me!" I replied as I started to move away toward the front entryway of the airport.

"Wait, Brother, let me see what I can do," he seemed to plead. After a short wait, a man approached hurriedly. He informed me that they had found a seat for me on the plane and that we had to hurry in order for me to board. It goes without saying as to how much I was relieved. As the plane took to the sky and I reviewed the incident, I was made cognizant of how much a Black American's life is beset with deliberate obstacles and how much wasted effort is expended in surviving traumatic and oftentimes life-threatening ambushes.

CHAPTER 57

IN CAPTIVITY IN LONDON

Having overcome another of the foe's inspired and crafted obstacles, I had now arrived at London's Heathrow Airport. I could now say that I was back in the Western world. The faces were whiter, less polite, and mechanical in a seemingly more gilded, affluent setting. In the fast-paced and somewhat complex mode of the West, I finally, with a measure of relief, found the correct line wherein I was to be serviced for the remainder of my homeward journey. Heathrow Airport represented a strange new world to me, and that added to the tenseness that swelled up in me as I realized what I expected to be the last leg of my long journey and exile. For the first time in eight years, I felt genuinely alone without the protection of a government. It was a lonely feeling, akin to not belonging anyplace special. It was also a feeling of not knowing, a feeling of uncertainty.

The people who formed the line where I was standing were nearly all white, looked affluent, and were devoid of the warmth I had experienced in China. This species of humanity bore the image of those I had grown up to know as despoilers, a negative force in the world of our lives. Growing up Black in America conditioned one to expect the worst from white people. The once-familiar, old feeling of apprehension swept over me, which I had not experienced in China and Cuba. It is a first-magnitude sacrilege that a society that claims itself to be a democracy, the leader of the free world, and a Christian nation, embodying the highest ideals of God-given freedoms, can violate the human spirit with impunity.

Having been conditioned from childhood and constantly admonished by my parents to be ever watchful of the white man's propensity for ambushing Blacks, just by virtue of the color of our skin, I entertained a gut feeling that some type of racially inspired evil could strike at any time.

While standing at the rear of the slow-moving line, I was approached by two uniformed men who identified themselves as airport security. They commanded me to come with them. They escorted me to a small office and informed me that I was to be searched. I was dressed in a Mao suit. The jacket had four outside pockets with two of them on my chest. It was customary in China to adorn the chest pockets with a fountain pen. I carried a Chinese ink pen and a ballpoint in mine. The largest security man reached for the pens and removed them from my pocket. In what I considered to be a stupid question, he asked me what they were. I told him that they were pens. He held the ink pen up to my face and told me that he was going to open it and that if it exploded, "You'll be the first one to go!"

"Do you think that the Chinese have refined the atom bomb to the extent that it could fit into a pen?" I asked.

He didn't answer. He slowly and cautiously unscrewed the top of the pen. He turned to his accomplice and said in a relieved voice, "It is a pen!"

"That's what I told you!" I injected in a triumphant voice.

After about half an hour they departed, leaving me in the room alone. Shortly thereafter, two more men entered the room and informed me that they were from the CID, the British equivalent to the FBI, and that they had come to search me.[1] I let them know that I had already been searched. They repeated the same operation, including the search of my carry-on bag, and again I was left alone. It was a puzzling situation that infected my mind with all kinds of horrendous thought. The two of them left, and in about ten minutes two more men came. They informed me that they were from the Metropolitan police and that they had come to search me. They performed what seemed now to be a ritual. It was a stupid repeat performance.

"I've already been searched twice," I said.

"We are aware of that," one stated in a not-so-friendly tone of voice.

"What's wrong with you people? Don't you trust each other?" I asked. Neither responded to my question.

I suppose an hour elapsed while I sat isolated in the room. All this official mystery had rendered me somewhat baffled. I was beginning to panic from the thought that this was a malicious maneuver staged to cause me to miss the plane on which I had been ticketed for Detroit. I had had an obstacle placed in my way

1. CID stands for Criminal Investigation Department.

in Cairo, and now the obstacles seemed even more formidable and complicated in London. Shortly, two plainclothes men came and told me that I had missed my flight and another one would not leave until the next day. I was notified that there was no place for me to stay at the airport. Therefore, they would have to take me into the city. They drove me all around London, explaining the historic sites that we passed. I was beginning to feel like a tourist being feted by the government of Britain. The two men and the driver of the car displayed a very friendly attitude. Finally, we approached a forlorn, weather-beaten ancient wall that seemed to surround some form of medieval castle. They drove to the gate and stopped. "What place is this?" I asked.

"This is Pentonville," I was told.

"It looks like a prison!" I exclaimed.

"It is a prison," the more mature man said, adding, "It is a hundred years old."

"It looks two hundred!" I exclaimed.

"You'll have to stay here tonight because there is no place else for you. We will pick you up here tomorrow morning in time to put you on the plane," the man who seemed to be in charge informed me in a voice obviously modulated to prevent a violent reaction on my part. The way I had been handled since my arrival in England displayed evidence that US agencies had convinced the British that I was some type of dangerous maniac.

I was ushered to an admittance room. I underwent a body search by prison guards while the warden was informing me that anything that was not registered on admittance could not be claimed upon my release. Considering the possibility of having my valuables confiscated, I removed my money belt from my waist.

"Aside from your watch, ring, and wallet, how much do you want to declare?" the warden asked in a routine, businesslike voice.

"Six hundred dollars in my wallet and six thousand dollars in my belt," I stated as I removed the crisp hundred-dollar bills from the money belt. He looked at the money, flinched, turned to his companion, and exclaimed, "This is the most money I have ever seen in one stash in my entire life."

His statement was disconcerting. I was very much aware of the fact that money could subvert the best of intentions. I knew that money could generate all kinds of evil conspiracies. I was alone and friendless in the custody of white men who looked like the ones who seemed to have a propensity for hating and abusing my people. What faith could I have in the British? After all, I had been told by their consulate in Dar es Salaam that I didn't need a visa to pass through their country in transit. But here I was, after having been pulled from a line of transients and declared a "Prohibited Immigrant." I was told that Trans World Airline (TWA) was refusing to fly me to my native land because the airline was afraid that I would hijack the plane. I was informed that TWA had taken the position that my presence constituted a danger to its passengers and plane.

This was the lamest excuse that the most asinine conspirators could ever dream up. Where in the world would I want to hijack a plane to? I had already been everywhere hijackers aspired to seek high-profile asylum. Voluntarily, I was on my way home to face up to false charges, and all kinds of obstacles were being put in my path. I protested on the grounds that British intervention was going to cause me to miss my second flight the next day. I was assured that I had about as much chance of missing a flight out of Britain as the queen.

I was forced to climb a long, winding steel stairway to a dingy cell. The prison was a circle of multistoried cells facing a deep, empty, cavern-type yard area. This deep and rather confined space served as an exercise space and social relief station from the horrible conditions of the lockups. Shockingly, the interior of the cell I was assigned was even worse than the mind could be stretched to imagine. It was unbelievable that a modern so-called democracy would confine members of the human race in dungeon prisons that should have faded with the dehumanizing savagery of the Dark Ages.

Beside the wall in the dingy cell lay a greasy mattress on broken springs. The springs rested on a bare concrete floor. A battered old bucket stood in the opposite corner. A guard who had ushered me to the cell explained that that was my toilet facilities. The odor in the cell was stifling. He informed me that my food would be passed through a slot in the door and that there would be only one serving a day. When the guard left the room, he closed the heavy steel door behind him, and it emitted a heavy metal sound that proclaimed my total isolation from the world. Everything was dark. Only a small shaft of light passed through a tiny hole in the formidable steel door.

This ordeal made me feel that my life was being snuffed out. Perhaps this was the final straw. Perhaps this time my spirit would be completely broken. I was locked in a darkened dungeon in a foreign country, and none of my relatives or friends knew that I was there. Here I was, innocent of any crime and guilty only of struggling for constitutional rights in a democratic America. The US government had chased me around the world, but the British, working in league with US racism, had snared me. As a Black man, it was terrifying to be caught in the web of a conspiracy woven by two racist nations. I was in prison with no charges and no legal rights. I could feel a depression akin to doom. Just as my spirit fell to the edge of complete defeat, anger exploded in my brain and pushed me into a defiant mode.

This was not a prison of some Third World or Communist nation; it was Britain of the so-called free world. Such prison throwbacks to the Dark Ages had been an object of ridicule and condemnation. The thought of the hypocrisy caused my blood to boil. I'd be damned if I was going to fall over dead just because my situation looked so bleak. I sat with my back against the wall anxiously anticipating the coming dawn and the possibility of catching a plane out. At least I had been told I was in Pentonville just for the night, but I had long ago learned that there was no bigger lie than an official lie.

It seemed that dawn would never come. Finally, a vague ray of light shone through the door. A guard came, opened a peephole, and called to me to prepare to leave. It seemed like a deliverance from the angels of heaven. I was escorted down the long, winding stairs to the reception room. The warden told me that I was leaving. I asked him when. "When they come to pick you up," he said.

"Unless they come soon, I'm going to miss my plane!" I complained. As I checked my personal belongings, the warden was called to the telephone. He came back and informed me that I was not leaving on the plane to Detroit and that he had been instructed to return me to the cell. As I was preparing for my re-incarceration, a Black man was being released. Judging from his accent, he was African. The guard who was returning his personal property contemptuously slammed one of the articles on the counter and shouted, "Here is your 'Little Red Mao Book.'"[2] His possession of the Mao book of quotations was a silent proclamation to me that he belonged to a universal fraternity of Third Worlders in opposition to racism and imperialism. To hear the name of Mao Tse-tung in that context was like a man dying from thirst in the desert stumbling upon an oasis.

This was the time. My only chance! I screamed out to him, "Brother, tell the Black people in London that I'm an Afro-American freedom fighter locked up in here in a racist plot!"

"OK!" he shouted back.

Two guards grabbed him, took his possessions, and forced him back into the lockup. Over the next few days, I wondered what had happened to him.

That incident was a vivid indication that high-level conspirators wanted my situation to be a top-notch secret. There could be no doubt that the British and American governments were perpetrating an illegal act, a human rights violation that could prove very embarrassing if the truth should become known.

2. Officially titled *Quotations from Chairman Mao Tse-tung*, published in 1964, contained quotes and statements from the Chinese revolutionary leader. This text was used by revolutionaries throughout the globe. See Alexander Cook, ed., *Mao's Little Red Book: A Global History* (New York: Cambridge University Press, 2014).

My right to travel was being negated without due process of law. I had been issued a US travel document, legalizing my travel to my homeland. There were no charges against me in Britain. I was merely in transit with no desire to stay in Britain, and yet I was being declared a "Prohibited Immigrant."

On the third day of my incarceration, in the early part of the night, I was again taken to prison reception. The warden informed me that I was to be returned to Cairo, Egypt. I was turned over to two policemen who escorted me to Heathrow Airport.

When I was ushered into a deserted waiting room, two attorneys, a man and a woman, were already there. They were from the British Civil Liberties Union (BCLU). There was also a man from the British Foreign Office. The BCLU attorneys argued that the British government had no legal right to commit me to a flight that was contrary to my travel destination. They informed me and insisted to the British authorities that since there was no legal violation involved on my part, I had a right to resist the intervention forcefully.

Emboldened by this legal information and support, though I was extremely weak from having refrained from accepting prison fare since my incarceration, I threw my topcoat that I was carrying onto a nearby desk and asked if they had brought the undertaker with them.

"What has an undertaker to do with this?" the man from the Foreign Office asked.

"Because he is the only one who can put me on a plane to Cairo!" I declared. Bristling for a physical confrontation, I exclaimed, "Come on if you want a fight!"

For a moment, they [the Foreign Office agent] stood stalking me. Soon another man arrived, and they moved to a corner of the room and conferred in a low voice. They confronted me again and started to interrogate me in a somewhat more serious tone.

"Do you know anyone in the Irish Republican Army, or have you had any contact with them?"

"No! What does that have to do with my situation?" I asked.

"Because a truck has damaged the plane that you were supposed to leave on. There is a possibility of sabotage!"

The whole situation was puzzling to me. The big man [the official] went in the next room, and I could see him through a glass partition making a telephone call. After a few minutes he returned and announced that the foreign minister had given orders that I be returned to Pentonville Prison. I was really undergoing the yo-yo treatment in Britain, and this was an indication that British officials, too, were becoming confused.

I was returned to the dingy dungeon cell, not knowing what to expect next. If I had been charged with an offense, my fate would have been potentially simple. I had now been held four days without ingesting food or liquids. Though I was unable to see anyone from my darkened cell, I could hear the voices of other prisoners yelling that I should write a letter to the queen. They informed me that it was a right of every prisoner with a complaint to do so. I wrote a letter to the queen and passed it through the opening in the door when someone came to remove my untouched food tray.

I suppose it was sometime before noon—one could distinguish night from day only by observing the small shaft of light that shone through a glassed peephole on the heavy steel door—when a guard opened up the cell to inform me that I was being moved to the prison hospital. Prison regulations required an inmate to be moved to the hospital when it was certain that he had not eaten food for four days. Weakened from hunger, I slowly and cautiously descended the long, winding iron steps that stretched down four tiers. The cavern yard enclave below was crowded with inmates who were taking advantage of respite from their cramped cells. A guard descended patiently in front of me as a second one trailed slowly behind. As I passed parallel to the throng of prisoners, they started to yell in unison. They let out a chant that I didn't understand. They gave clenched-fist salutes and called for me to keep up the struggle. Their display of sympathy bolstered my spirit. After four days without nourishment, though I was extremely weak, the pangs of hunger had vanished.

The prison hospital was antiseptically clean and comfortable. My ordeal of hunger and denial had more than rendered me an appreciative candidate for a bed fit for a human. Three times a day an attendant entered my locked and isolated room and placed a tray of an exceptionally artful tray of food that filled the room with an aroma probably selected to destroy one's will to abstain from fasting. Each time a tray of food was brought, the previous one was closely examined. Each item was recorded. The resentment against the injustice and oppression that I had experienced throughout my life welled up in me to such an extent that my mind summoned a will to resist that I never knew I possessed. My mind became the iron-willed master of every other function of my body.

I was examined by a medical doctor who seemed alarmed by what was taking place. He informed me that I was endangering my health and perhaps my life. He said that one could sustain fasting for extended periods provided there was some liquid intake, but because I was declining liquid intake, I was running the risk of irreversible harm to my body. He suggested that I at least take some juice. When I rejected his suggestion, he displayed a measure of hostility. He threatened me with forced feeding. I in turn threatened to resist any effort they might make to the last breath in my body. I asked him why England was so interested in my welfare and my life, since I was only passing through on my way home, and declared that they had detained me simply in support of US racism. That charge seemed to upset him. He left the room with a face that expressed vexation.

I was so filled with anger that I felt some feeble relief at the embarrassment that would befall England with a dead Afro-American who had been taken into captivity while journeying peacefully to his native land.

I was awakened at what I assumed to be very late night. I could hear the hospital door being unlocked. It was strange that someone would be entering my room at that late hour. A myriad train of thoughts flushed my mind. Perhaps my physical condition required a more extensive medical watch. Then there was the possibility that an assassination was about to befall me. At any rate, I was much too weak to muster much concern. In the low night light, a silent shadow approached my bed. "Wake up, mate! Do you hear that noise outside the gate? Man, you've got friends in England. All that commotion is the people protesting in support of you!"

I thanked him for his information and concern as he eased out of the dimly lit room. The roar of the crowd seemed far away, but I could tell that emotion was high. I was convinced more than ever now that the British government was going to find it more and more difficult to support its racist American counterpart.

Due to the stress of my ordeal, I had lost track of time. I was informed that I had a visitor. A member of the British Parliament came to interview me. His coming angered the warden, who cynically stated that if the MP showed as much interest in the prison and inmates during regular times as he was now doing in my case, many of their shortcomings might more easily be corrected. In an indifferent manner, he smiled at the warden as he left us alone. The MP stated that my case involved a racial matter and that his government had no business becoming embroiled in it.

Shortly thereafter, another person was allowed to visit me. He was an Afro-American living in England. He was Richard Gibson, whom I had known from the Fair Play for Cuba days.[3] Gibson informed me that I had nothing to fear from the British but would more than likely be killed by the Americans upon my arrival

3. Richard Gibson was a journalist, novelist, and expatriate who worked in Europe for CBS News. He was a cofounder of Fair Play for Cuba while simultaneously working for the Central Intelligence Agency, a relationship Williams was obviously unaware of. See "CIA Reveals Name of Former Spy in JFK Files—and He's Still Alive," *Newsweek*, May 15, 2018, https://www.newsweek.com/richard-gibson-cia-spies-james-baldwin-amiri-baraka-richard-wright-cuba-926428.

in the United States. He tried to dissuade me from my determination to return home. My position was that if I didn't die in Britain, they [the U.S. authorities] would have to kill me in the United States, because I was going home. It had always been my philosophy that Black men who faced death at the hands of racist mobs should not allow death to be executed secretly behind the barn but should force the issue to Main Street for all the world to witness. My position was unequivocally to never cooperate by being driven peacefully and never to go down without a fight in deference to the wishes of a mob. Whatever my enemies were going to do to me, I was going to force them to do it in America if I possibly could.

Gibson had been a longtime and dear friend, and I am sure that he harbored deep concern for my welfare. In looking back, it seems strange that at the weakest physical condition in my life, I felt the inner strength and confidence to defy the wishes of the US and British governments. I absolutely and positively had my mind set on continuing my hunger strike until victory or death.

On the third day of my commitment to the prison hospital, the chaplain paid me a visit. His name or appearance is not etched in my mind. Therefore, his identity is completely lost to me. However, our conversation shall never be forgotten. The chaplain sat in a chair parallel to my bed in the tight little room that had not-too-conspicuous bars on the window. Not that I wanted him to, but strangely, as a man of the cloth, he never offered to pray with or for me. He informed me that church people in London who had heard of my hunger strike had offered to furnish me food so that I would not have to consume prison food. I could readily see that they had missed the point of my action. Obviously, they had not realized that the core of the matter was much deeper than what appeared on the surface. From my point of view, my abuse and unjust treatment encompassed more than just the prison system. It encompassed the entire British government. It was a gesture I could appreciate on the part of a humane portion of the English public, but it was a proposition that my commitment to defiance against racial oppression and social tyranny did not allow me to accept.

The chaplain informed me that it was customary for persons fasting to at least resort to an intake of liquids in order to stave off irreparable damage to their bodies while undergoing such physical and mental stress. Despite his information, I was determined to maintain my hunger strike as an act of totality and without compromise. He seemed puzzled at my determined and uncompromising attitude. His voice fell silent for a moment. He lowered his head in a swaying side-to-side movement. It instantly became obvious that frustration had turned him from a source of advice to a seeker of information. With an inquisitive look on his face, he stated, "You must have a mighty strong conviction involving something that inspires you to a total commitment."

Though weak, with my elbows bracing my body, I raised myself as much as possible from the bed and mustered enough of my failing voice to declare, "Long ago, my forefathers were peacefully going about their business and your forefathers descended on them and took them into captivity. The fatal mistake that my forefathers made was to accept food from you while enslaved. By accepting your forefathers' food over a period of time, my forefathers began to look forward to being fed. After a while they became conditioned to life without human dignity. Thus, slavery was consummated. You may be the same as your forefathers, but I am not the same as mine. The greatest possession of my life is my freedom. That's all that England owes me. If anybody in England wants to give me anything, let them give me what is already mine, my freedom! Either England releases me, or it is going to have to deal with the body of a dead Black man as the world takes notice of a Britain that went out of its way to support US racism on behalf of the brotherhood of white supremacy!"

The chaplain looked rather pale, responded that he understood in a low, almost inaudible voice, turned, and slowly left the room without further dialogue.

The following day after the chaplain's visit, a prison official visited me and inquired of the conditions under which I would break my fast. I explained that I would eat only after my freedom had been restored. Then he asked whether I would eat on the plane if I were released and on my way to America. I told him that I would, and he then informed me that the US State Department had arranged a flight the following day. I had won, but I wondered at what price. I had taken greatly extreme measures that placed my very life at risk in deference to the pride of my manhood. I, a Black man, born into racial oppression and caught in a pincer move by two powerful governments, had not allowed myself to be reduced to a broken wimp.

The next day, I was told to prepare to leave. I asked how I was leaving and to what destination. I wanted to be sure that they were not still trying to ship me back to Egypt. I had previously been told that some captain of a ship had offered to transport me to the USA in view of the fact that all airlines had declined to fly me on a regular flight. I was told now that I was going to America on a TWA flight. I acceded. As a result of my hunger strike, I was almost too weak to walk, but the realization that I was once again about to embark on an untried course buoyed my determination. The prison officials had already prepared my personal effects, which they presented to me without comment.

In the company of two security police and a driver, I was swished away to Heathrow Airport. The guard who had been most talkative, respectful, and sympathetic informed me that there had been some discussion of possibly dispatching him to escort me to the States. He had desperately wanted to make the trip. Due to my weakened condition, it was ruled unwarranted, and the idea had been scratched. He expressed great regret at having lost the opportunity to visit America. Strangely enough, I regretted that he would be unable to make such a memorable journey.

The car avoided the waiting area of the airport and sped directly onto the runway and pulled up to the ramp of a plane. The guard informed me that this was done because the word had been leaked to protesters that I was to be shipped out of Britain quietly to avoid an airport demonstration.

A small party of low-level officials and a scattering of newsmen, who were allowed to take pictures but not to interview me, milled about near the ramp of the plane. My lawyer from the United States, Milton Henry, who had come to accompany me home, stood at the top of the ramp by the entrance of the plane, and we both gave a Black Power salute to the news photographers.[4]

I was surprised to learn that the flight was all mine. The plane carried a full crew, a vice president of the airline, my lawyer, and me. The semi-empty craft looked awfully big. I wondered whether my past history had warranted such genuine fear that it was truly thought that any passengers traveling with me would be in danger or whether this was some kind of ruse that I could not fathom. The excuse that TWA feared that I was a terrorist who might possibly hijack the plane was unbelievably lame. It was a well-known fact that I had been everywhere hijackers commandeered aircraft to go, and now I was headed home, so there was no need to fear diversion in flight. I found it hard to understand why a so-called wanted man experienced such difficulty in reaching a place in which to surrender.

I ate lightly on the plane. My stomach could not take a full-course meal. I felt somewhat dizzy and nauseated. The plane's crew accorded me the same service and attention that I would have received on a regular commercial flight with other passengers. I was flying directly into the lion's mouth without the slightest knowledge of the fate that awaited me. There were many unknown factors surrounding the potential moves of those who wanted to see me vanquished. Despite this train of thought, as in the past, I felt that I was being driven by some external force over which I had no control. That is the way it had always been. I was neither strong enough, wise enough, nor brave enough to have fashioned my life by a planned free will. I had always been willing to make daring moves and

4. Milton Henry (aka Gaidi Obadele) was a civil rights and Black Power advocate, former associate of Malcolm X, and a cofounder of the Provisional Government of the Republic of New Afrika.

take the kinds of chances others thought to be suicidal. Perhaps I had a guardian angel. I hoped that she was flying with me and not somewhere else sleeping. I kept remembering the distant words of my uncle Charlie, who often argued that if oppressed "praying niggers" had a God, he must be sleeping. Soon, once again, I would be in position to see if my end would come in the reign of evil triumphing over prayer that failed.

CHAPTER 58

BACK IN THE BELLY OF THE BEAST

As the 737 circled Detroit's Metro Airport, I became very tense. I had been out of the country for eight years. I felt like an immigrant coming to my own country. As the plane taxied to a stop, the first one aboard was a large man with mixed-gray hair. He approached the seat where I was sitting at the front of the plane and informed me that he had a warrant for my arrest. He flashed his identification and proclaimed himself to be a special agent of the FBI. He then proceeded to raise a pair of handcuffs. Attorney Milton Henry, who had made the trip all the way to London to accompany me on this special flight, asked, "What are you going to do with the handcuffs?"

"I'm going to cuff Williams. It is bureau policy to cuff all people who are taken into custody," he stated.

"No, not him, not here. Don't you see all of those Black people waiting out there for our leader? Do you want somebody to get killed? That's what will happen if you take him off this plane handcuffed!"

The special agent looked at me with a somewhat bewildered look and asked, "If I don't handcuff you, will you refrain from giving me trouble?"

"I've never given trouble, unless provoked!" I exclaimed.

We left the plane without my being handcuffed. Therefore, Milton and I were able to greet the waiting members and friends of the Republic of New Afrika with Black Power salutes, which later evoked much criticism of the FBI from rightists who vehemently opposed my return. They thought the FBI was remiss and handled me with kid gloves.

Mabel and Robert Williams and attorney Gaidi Obadele (*seated, left to right*), surrounded by Republic of North Afrika supporters, including Queen Mother Audley Moore (*directly behind Robert*) and Imari Obadele (*directly behind Gaidi Obadele*), at a press conference on Robert's arrival in Detroit from exile in China, 1969.

Robert and Mabel Williams at home in Michigan after eight years of exile, c. 1970s. Courtesy of the Williams family.

The FBI car in which I was transported traveled at the rate of eighty-five miles per hour in an effort to outdistance members of the Republic of New Afrika who had assembled at the airport to support my return. The RNA citizens arrived shortly after we did, however, and were there when I was rushed before a federal judge to absolve the charge of flight to avoid prosecution for a felony.[1] From federal court, I was whisked away to Recorder's Court and was released on my own recognizance.

A great cry went up across the nation by white racists. To them it was not a matter of guilt or innocence as charged, but I had defied the deep-seated racist customs of the land as no Black man had ever done before. Consequently, they shrilly screamed for my scalp. There was a hue and cry in Congress that I should be stripped of my citizenship.

1. Some Black Power advocates pledged their allegiance to the Provisional Government of the Republic of New Afrika and were known as RNA citizens. Edward Onaci, *Free the Land: The Republic of New Afrika and the Pursuit of a Black Nation-State* (Chapel Hill: University of North Carolina Press, 2020), 59–67.

CHAPTER 59

UP NORTH POLITICAL REPRESSION

I had been out of the country for eight years, five years in Cuba and three years in the People's Republic of China. While exiled, I had traveled to North Vietnam and East Africa. I returned to an America vastly different from what I had left. Despite the strife I knew was sure to descend on me, I was greatly impressed by the social changes that had resulted from the civil rights struggle. I felt a measure of pride in having taken the stand that I took in the face of extreme peril. Readjustment did not come easily. While exiled, I was treated as a royal hero by foreign leaders and governments. Now, from a government and white supremacy standpoint, I was without honor in my own native land.

Based in Detroit during the ensuing weeks, I had the opportunity to meet the brothers and sisters of the Republic of New Afrika. I was very much surprised and encouraged at the high caliber of young Afro-Americans who had become attracted to the organization. There was a vast and growing sympathy among nonmembers as well. Many enlightened activists and professionals concurred with the ideals and philosophy of the movement. I was greatly aware of the fact that the US government was going to move might and main to derail a fast-growing independence mobilization in its midst. While living abroad, I had observed many of the methods of the CIA and its surrogates, which were used to fracture, frustrate, and emasculate national liberation movements. In light of such vigorous subversion abroad, I realized that the effort on the home turf would be boundless.

As the speaking engagements increased, the US Justice Department asked the Michigan court to lift my bond "and take me off the street" [in other words, to incarcerate him]. The local court declined, but it did limit my travels to the state of Michigan. I completely disregarded the court's restriction. I was not a criminal, and I was absolutely not going to allow it to force me to live and act like one. Speaking primarily on the Chinese situation, I visited many campuses and organizations from coast to coast. There was something slightly eerie about my engagements and travels. I very seldom saw or had contact with Black people.

On one occasion, while speaking at a New York university to an audience of about 600, I noticed a lone Black man with a young white woman sitting at the rear of the auditorium. When I opened the meeting up for questions from those in attendance, the Black man was the first on his feet, and he was waving his hands feverishly to attract my attention. I extended him the recognition he seemed burning to acquire, and his question was, "Mr. Williams, I understand that you are under indictment for kidnapping. Since you are charged with a felony, how is it that the court has allowed you to come here from Detroit?"

He had attracted the attention of the entire audience. The auditorium fell silent and all eyes seemed to focus on me, anxious to see if I would be able to extricate myself from what was obviously a play aimed at cold and calculated embarrassment. He remained standing, obviously enjoying the attention of the crowd, aside from the fact that he seemed to want to demonstrate to the white people present that he was of my race, but not my kind.

After a short pause to allow the crowd to settle down, I responded, "Brother! I am a man; I didn't get permission from anyone to come here. I am restricted to the state of Michigan by court order; if you want to turn me in, feel free to do so.

"You know, Brother, when I saw you rise to present me with a question, I thought you were going to ask me what you could do to save me from prison, but instead you saddened me greatly. Instead of offering me assistance in overcoming a racist frame-up, you rose to ask me why I am not dead. Evidently that is what your question implied!"

After some applause from the audience, he spoke again in a different tone. He said he was sorry and asked me to forgive him. I am sure it took a lot of gall to do that, even if he had been a plant from the FBI.

On another occasion, while speaking at the Fountain Street Church in Grand Rapids, Michigan, the FBI recorded the license numbers of all vehicles parked within two blocks of the church. When I obtained my files under the Freedom of Information Act, the names and addresses that matched the plates were listed.

While speaking at a leftist conference of students at the University of Michigan, a young female student rose in the audience and asked in a loud, emotional voice, "Why did you testify in secret before the Internal Security Committee?"

She was from the Progressive Labor Party and obviously felt that she had scored a great point in the campaign of harassment and denigration. Her attempt was neutralized when I retorted, "You must have connections in Washington that others cannot claim! If I testified in secret, how did you obtain what transpired there?"

When I was given a Ford Foundation grant to write a book at the University of Michigan, the extreme Right mounted a letter-writing campaign condemning and threatening the university with a drive against contributions for having a "treasonous Communist" working on the campus. The university downgraded my status to "consultant" to the Center for Chinese Studies. The Detroit office of the FBI requested Washington to grant permission to cover all my activity on campus.

At year's end we moved to Baldwin, Michigan, and the FBI printed maps showing where we lived. After I purchased land in Canada, the Michigan State Police went into Canada and designated the wooded land by flying over and mapping it by photography. They also frightened the Canadians to the point that a second plot of land that I was in the process of obtaining was restricted from sale to me. The Canadians were told that I had planned to establish guerrilla warfare training camps to train Black revolutionaries there.

My wife and I underwent three years of auditing by the Internal Revenue Service [IRS]. The IRS wanted to tax us for all of the food, clothing, and housing that our family had been given in Cuba and China. It relented only after I applied for relief from the Washington court on grounds that I was being harassed because of my race and that I had lived in Communist countries. I maintained that the IRS's efforts were spurious. Therefore, I would request a public hearing in tax court and would demand that the agency prove its charges by getting my records from Cuba and the People's Republic of China.

A few days after my petition to the court, an individual telephoned me, saying, "Brother, if you don't want to go to court, I can take care of your tax situation!" I informed him that I intended to go to court only because I knew that what the IRS was trying to do had no basis in law. After the call, the harassment ceased.

A meeting was set up in Baldwin. The IRS requested a special agent from the FBI to accompany its auditors and sit in on the interview at the Baldwin courthouse, where the auditors had reserved a room to discuss taxes with my wife and me. Until this day, I cannot understand why they felt the necessity to have such protection and security. Thereafter, the FBI's surveillance was so intense that agents even recorded when Mabel worked in the yard cultivating her flowers. Even shopping trips to the local grocery stores were observed and recorded in the records.

On one occasion Mabel and I were on our way to New York for one of my numerous speaking engagements. We decided to travel the northern route through Canada, hoping not to arouse too much attention, because a court order supposedly restricted me to Michigan. I felt such a great distance along US freeways exposed me to too much possible harassment or worse. It was around two o'clock in the early morning when we crossed the border at Niagara Falls to reenter the United States.

At that time of morning, traffic was very light at the crossing, and the whole customs area seemed almost deserted. After asking us the routine questions, the customs officer directed me to pull the car into a designated stall for inspection. Everything was diligently unloaded from the trunk of the car. He removed a .30-caliber carbine and four banana clips of bullets from beneath clothing in the trunk. He stated that he would have to keep the gun unless I could prove that it was not of Canadian origin being imported into the USA. I explained that it was American and purchased at Kmart. He said he would have to keep it anyway until I could prove where it was purchased. I asked him if he had some place for me to sleep. He answered in the negative and sought an answer as to why I would need some place to sleep there. I, in no uncertain terms, declared that if he kept the gun, he would have to have some place for me to sleep, because I most certainly was going to stay with the gun.

A confrontation was developing. My straightforward attitude seemed to puzzle and confound him. He instructed me to wait until he made a call. I watched him through the glass panel as his drawn face expressed what was no doubt a serious conversation with someone on the other end of the line. I braced myself for trouble as he returned. To my great surprise, he returned the rifle to me and informed us that we could go. To this day, I still wonder who circumscribed the potential confrontation.

Three weeks after the Niagara Falls incident and my return to Detroit, two hefty US Marshals served me with a federal warrant and a court summons. The warrant informed me that I was under indictment as an individual charged with a felony who had transported a firearm across state lines. Aside from the kidnapping charges, for which I was fighting extradition to North Carolina, I was now facing a gun charge. It was more than obvious that the power structure was more than serious about putting me away. In addition to my growing troubles, unbeknownst to me at that time, the Michigan State Police had uncovered a plot hatched by the extreme racist Right to assassinate my lawyer, Milton Henry, and me. The state police had uncovered the plot, and yet they had declined to inform me. Obviously, they too hoped for my death. I learned of the plot much later from my FOIA files.

When I was hauled into federal court on the gun charge in what appeared to be an open-and-shut case, they [the prosecution] experienced a legal fiasco. The judge wanted to know why I insisted on my innocence when I had clearly violated the law. I explained that it was not my car and not my rifle. Anticipating possible problems, we had bought a new car in Mabel's name. I explained it was my wife's car and that she was not under indictment and therefore could transport a firearm in her car. He then asked who owned the gun. My brother had purchased the gun from Kmart, and I had a bill of sale to prove it. The judge seemed peeved and asked the marshals why they had brought me to court without the gun. He dismissed the case and left the bench. The marshals again approached me and demanded that I accompany them upstairs. When I asked them why, they informed me that I had to go to be fingerprinted. I insisted that I had already been fingerprinted. I was told that it didn't matter. I had to be fingerprinted again. I demanded to have the law shown to me that required that I be fingerprinted. The federal attorney came over and asked what the conflagration was about. One of the marshals stated, "He is refusing to be fingerprinted."

I explained to the attorney that I always tried not to violate laws and that if they would show me the law that required me to be fingerprinted a second time in another location, I would willingly submit. The court officials went into a brief huddle and subsequently decided to check with the law library. After a short span of time, the federal attorney returned looking rather somber. "There is no law requiring principals involved in dismissed cases to be fingerprinted by the marshals' office; however, it is a matter of custom that this is done," he informed me.

After having my hunch confirmed, I became even more enraged. "Custom! Custom my ass! I don't honor your custom. Southern graveyards are filled with my people who became victims of your customs!"

The attorney grudgingly ordered, "Let him go!"

My volunteer lawyer, Bernie Fieger, exclaimed that he had practiced law for eighteen years and had even argued civil rights cases in the Deep South and never knew that such court practices were not mandated by law. He confessed that he had always allowed his clients to submit to such court demands. Just from the power of sheer defiance, I had again confronted institutionalized arrogance with success.

A few months later the US government unleashed another surprise attack upon me. I received a summons to appear before the Internal Security Committee of Congress, located in Washington, DC. Attorney Roger Craig, who was a senator from the reactionary district of Dearborn, Michigan, volunteered to represent me before the committee. I was told by attorneys, nationalists, and leftists that I should ignore a subpoena from such a reactionary committee, staging a witch hunt and on a fishing expedition in an attempt to gather information on China and its relations with the Black movement in this country.

My failure to honor the congressional summons caused a vote to be brought forth, paving the way for me to be charged with contempt of Congress. After the news was publicized that the process was being formulated to cite me for contempt, there was a loud chorus of nationalists and leftists who declared that I should have known better than to ignore a congressional summons. I was beginning to learn that a lot of so-called revolutionaries in America were no more than wishy-washy puffs of fireless smoke blowing in puffs of wind. It was a rude awakening to see how fast these Fabian militants could reverse their positions in a move to promote themselves in deceptive plays for leadership.

My attorneys had to engage in some fast maneuvers in order to get the citation absolved. I acceded to the committee's summons and braced myself for the Washington inquisition. I went to Washington very much cognizant of the fact that I was going to have to tread territory fraught with pitfalls and minefields. I knew that these Washington bigots were mean-spirited and would ambush me at every opportunity in an all-out effort to discredit and dishonor me in order to isolate and destroy any image that I had that may have given inspiration and guidance to the new wave of freedom fighters.

On the day before the hearings, Jay Sourwine met Roger Craig and me at Washington National Airport.[1] He was a big, aging man who picked us up in an old Cadillac. I had for years heard a lot of negative things about him. According to reports, he was a vicious bastard, a reactionary headhunter whose tyrannical escapades dated all the way back to the McCarthy era.

Because of my past activity in Communist countries, I expected him to be exploding with hatred and contempt for me. I was truly surprised by the respect and courtesy he displayed toward me. It was obvious and puzzling that he was handling me with kid gloves. However, despite the veneer, I perceived him as a great danger. I remembered how General Goode, the base commander at Camp Pendleton, had feigned politeness in order to spring a racist trap of spite, dedicated to the preservation of white supremacy in the US Marine Corps.

1. Jay Sourwine was special counsel to the US Senate Subcommittee of the Judiciary Committee on Internal Security, which investigated subversive activity and Communism.

On February 16, 1970, I faced the inquisition panel of the US Senate's Judiciary Committee. Senator Strom Thurmond of South Carolina presided. I considered it a cruel quirk of fate that I would have my activities as a Black freedom fighter dissected by an individual whose spiteful antics as a dogmatic racist had been universally publicized since my childhood. He grilled me from my very own diaries that had been stolen from my plundered personal effects. To add insult to injury, the government goon squad leaked misinformation to the press that I had cooperated with them and had voluntarily made my diaries available to them. The government's propensity for lies and dirty tricks had become full-blown before my very eyes. It was no longer deduction and speculation but a visible, hard-core fact.

I was questioned about a letter I had written and received. I was confronted with names and incidents that had long been forgotten. I was presented with photographs of Chinese children and mothers with babies in their arms. They wanted the names, even of the Chinese babies, none of which I knew. Some of my financial entries in my diaries had been entered in code. Sometimes, I had added zeroes to hundreds and thousands. I was asked about the inflated million figures. When I explained that I had coded these figures to deceive the Cubans, Thurmond and his goon squad seemed rather satisfied. They were highly interested to know how I was treated in these Communist countries. It gave me great pleasure to inform them that as a Black man, I had been treated more humanely and accorded more dignity there than I had been in my own native land.

During the second session of March 24, 1970, Sourwine informed me that the committee were going to delay hearings for a few days because they had another individual coming in. Two days later, while looking out of my hotel window, I saw a crowd milling on the sidewalk beneath my second-floor window. I recognized Stokely Carmichael and his wife, Miriam Makeba. I went down to greet them. As soon as Stokely saw me, he said, "Man, they have been asking me about you all morning. I told them that I didn't know anything about you!"

The media ran stories stating that Carmichael had invoked the Fifth Amendment more than twenty times and had refused to cooperate, while Robert Williams had been cooperative. Using the columnist Saul Friedman as a medium, they unleashed a ream of misinformation. The Friedman article stated that it was whispered in the Black community that I had traveled abroad "for interests other than my own." Avoiding an outright accusation that he could be held accountable for, he had limited his act of subterfuge to vague hints. This vague hint was concocted to plant seeds of suspicion. It was a nasty suggestion that I possibly might be an agent.

They [the FBI] had mounted a campaign to discredit me among the Black Nationalists throughout the nation. It was obvious that the objective was to slander me and destroy my image as a leader. This tactic further enraged me, but it was far off the mark of shattering a dream they thought I had of becoming a national leader. They were unaware of the fact that I had never wanted the mantle of leadership. What role I played, I had merely been thrust into. I had always viewed leadership as carrying a heavy and painful burden.

My assessment of the situation was confirmed by the files I obtained much later, under the FOIA, wherein they openly made note of the fact that a void of leadership existed in the Black Nationalist movement and that everything possible should be done to keep me from filling that void.

The informed segment of the Black community was aware of the fact that I was the most dogged victim of private and government harassment and racial persecution alive. The white Left, who claimed to so vehemently disparage the veracity of the "establishment press," vigorously joined the vicious chorus of slander. The American white Left resented the fact that although I had been received and supported in Communist countries, I had declined to embrace Marxism.

My testimony before the Senate Judiciary ended on March 25, 1970. As my testimony was ending, a man came and invited me to the US State Department. Sourwine, seeing me speaking with him, inquired of me as to what the man wanted with me. When I replied that he had invited me to visit the State Department for an interview, Sourwine bristled and stated, "We can't tell you where to go, now that we are finished with you, but we would suggest that you not get involved with those people over there!" He informed me that two persons over there were under a cloud of suspicion. He said that they had been journalists in Vietnam and may have been responsible for some intelligence leaks. Needless to say, I went to the State Department despite Sourwine's warnings.

At the State Department, the first thing I was asked was what Sourwine had said about my possible visit there. When I told them [State Department officials] what he said, I was told that the Judiciary Committee resented the fact that they [elements of the federal government] were advocating improved relations with the People's Republic of China. It was a strange and puzzling situation. I was the one whom the power structure had gone to great effort to portray as a subversive, and yet it seemed to me that factions in the government were in conflict and harboring contempt for each other.

After my appearance before the Washington inquisitors, the contempt of Congress citation against me was withdrawn. That was just one phase of what had gone before and what was to come thereafter in my life of a long series of trials and tribulations. A major hurdle still loomed before me.

Though I was working for the normalization of relations between the US and China, I was still facing extradition to North Carolina, wherein I had never known the blessings of a color-blind justice. There was an ongoing conspiracy among elements in Washington, North Carolina, and Michigan to "take me off the streets." Despite the fact that I had come in possession of a letter from a resigned assistant attorney general of the state of Michigan, who revealed that his brief, written for the governor's extradition assessment, had been changed and his signature forged, the federal court declined to grant me a hearing.

Among the number of invitations I received to speak on China was one in Sterling Heights, Michigan. Sterling Heights was known to be extremely conservative and harbored a notable enclave of reactionary, violence-prone racists. Blacks familiar with the situation in that community found it unbelievable that there were elements liberal enough to extend me an invitation to speak there. My philosophy was to speak wherever invited. I felt that whoever was interested deserved to be enlightened concerning China, the awakening giant in the East. I was invited by a human relations group. Some Blacks around me were concerned because they could not conceive of a human relations group being in such a conservative and racist community. They warned me of a possible setup to expose me to an assassination plot. When I insisted on going, three of the most trusted and dedicated members of the Black Legion, a military arm of the Republic of New Africa, volunteered to accompany me as bodyguards. I accepted them on the condition that they would maintain strict discipline and would not resort to violence unless we were violently attacked. They were to observe my every move and to give no response to any provocation until such time that I reacted to a threat.

It was dark when we arrived at the Sterling Heights Community Center. I had not expected much of a turnout in such a place. I did not expect to find much interest in China among the people of that conservative community. I was startled to see the number of cars in the parking lot. There was a constant stream of people entering the building. Upon entering the crowded auditorium, I was informed that the liberal professor who was hosting the meeting was late. I was ushered to a seat in front of the noisy audience. A tumultuous atmosphere seemed to be building. Finally, the host came in, rushing to the point that he was short of breath.

He opened the meeting, and as soon as I started to speak, in filed a noisy group of young men in military style. They carried a huge American flag that almost reached the ceiling of the building. They were identified as Nazis. I knew that they had come for trouble. They announced that I was a Communist and that they would not allow any "Black Communist" to speak there. Their file stretched from the front of the room to the rear of the building. They screamed and yelled all kinds of racist and anti-leftist epitaphs. It was obvious that they expected me to cow in frustration and to retreat. I announced that I would resume my speech when quiet was restored. I sat down and calmly watched their antics. I dared not make any threatening move for fear that the Black Legionnaires who had accompanied me would shoot the place up.

As the situation seemed to be getting out of hand, a well-dressed middle-aged man, who had come in the company of a well-dressed woman, stood up in the middle of the audience and ordered the agitators to remove their huge flag from the building. I didn't know his identity, but he spoke with an authoritative air. The obvious leader of the rightists bristled and shouted that they were carrying an American flag in an American building and that they would not lower it for a "Black Communist."

The well-dressed man declared, "We have the US flag and the State of Michigan flag here, and that is sufficient. Some of us would like to hear what he has to say about China. If you don't want to hear him, then you leave the premises!"

"No, we are not going to leave until the damn Communist leaves!" someone shouted from the ranks of the bigots. "We are taxpayers, and we don't want our police department protecting reds!" an angry voice shouted. At this point, I realized the well-dressed man with the lady was some kind of law official. In an effort to turn the tide against us, one of the racists pointed at the Black Legion, who sat waiting loyally for instructions from me, and shouted in a shrill, provocative voice, "They are cop killers! You are protecting cop killers from the New Bethel Church shoot-out!"[2]

The lawman, who I later learned was the Sterling Heights chief of police, turned to some young men dressed in army field jackets who had taken up positions in the rear of the building and ordered them to clear the building.

2. The New Bethel incident was a gun battle between the Provisional Government of the Republic of New Afrika security and Detroit police, resulting in the death of Detroit police officer Michael Czapski. Three members of the New Afrikan security force, Chaka Fuller, Rafael Viera, and Alfred 2X Hibbits, were charged and tried with the murder of Officer Czapski but subsequently acquitted. Christian Davenport, *How Social Movements Die: Repression and Demobilization of the Republic of New Africa* (New York: Cambridge University Press, 2015), 223–26; Akinyele Umoja, "Straight Ahead: The Life of Resistance of Dr. Mutulu Shakur," *Souls* 23, no. 1–2 (2022): 4–35, 11–12; doi: 10.1080/10999949.2022.2097570.

They waded into the Nazis, seized their flag, and physically forced them from the hall. The rest of the meeting proceeded smoothly and finished with many questions being asked about China. On the whole, contrary to what I had heard, Sterling Heights turned out to be quite civilized. The chief of police arranged for police cars to escort us out of town. The following day, the local press commented favorably about our calm and collected conduct in the face of heated provocation.

CHAPTER 60

STRUGGLE CONTINUES IN IDLEWILD

We moved to the Idlewild/Baldwin area, after living in Detroit and Ann Arbor, in hopes of escaping the political intrigues and conspiracies that abounded there and with the desire to withdraw from the accumulated stress of a lifetime of struggle and tumult. Idlewild/Baldwin was basically a retirement and recreation community. Idlewild, before the advent of the civil rights movement, had been one of the most prominent playgrounds for Afro-Americans, who were unwelcome at mainstream recreational sites operated by and for white America.

It was quite a relief to freely go fishing, boating, and motorcycle riding and to enjoy the winter activities of snowmobiling and hunting. I now lived pretty much incognito.

But on October 31, 1977, a quiet and rainy night, like a bolt of lightning, trouble struck with high intensity again. At about nine o'clock in the evening, I received a telephone call from Ethel Azalea Johnson. Ethel was a veteran of the Monroe struggle who had relocated to Idlewild and had become a community activist here. In a greatly disturbed tone of voice, she informed me that a Black woman had shot the sheriff a few blocks from my home and that the police had surrounded her house. At that very moment, I realized that trouble had followed me as if it had been my shadow. The following day, I learned that the sheriff and deputies had gone to Mrs. Ruby Nelson's home on that rainy night to attempt to have her committed to a mental institution some miles away. She was a widow and the mother of three young children. Her daughter had had a problem with a white teacher at school. By marriage, the teacher was connected with personnel in the sheriff's department. The sheriff had gone to her house and had kicked down three doors after she refused to let him enter. The sheriff did not have a warrant or doctor's certificate; however, their mission was to commit her to a mental institution.

Mrs. Nelson's ten-year-old daughter was alone in the living room, standing by a heater, heating a kettle of water. She confronted the sheriff and told him that if he bothered her mother, she would scald him with the hot water. The sheriff became enraged and told her that if she did that, he would "knock her Black head off." At that moment, Ruby Nelson came out of a back room and shot the sheriff.

The sheriff stumbled backwards out of the living room onto the porch, where he fell paralyzed. The deputies ran for cover and left the sheriff where he fell. Though the house was surrounded by armed policemen, Mrs. Nelson refused to surrender to them until after the sheriff had been taken away by squad car. He refused to be transported by the only ambulance in the area, which was owned and operated by a Black woman with whom he had ongoing disputes. The local Black policeman, Delbert Dotson, from the Idlewild community, was dispatched to take her into custody after he spoke with her on the telephone. She went with him quietly.

What had been a quiet and peaceful community was now seething with racial tension and resentment. The women of the community, spurred on by Ethel, designated me to visit the jail to ascertain when and how Mrs. Nelson could receive the toilet articles they were preparing for her. They were also concerned about her medical condition, due to the fact that she was a known epileptic. I went to the jail on a Sunday morning. The deputy on duty came to the glass panel, slid it open, and in a voice devoid of any semblance of friendliness asked, "What can I do for you?"

"Do you have a prisoner here named Ruby Nelson?" I inquired, hoping not to antagonize him.

"Yes, she is here. We've got her," he informed me with a timbre of satisfaction ringing from his voice.

"The women in our community want to know whether or not she has her medication, and they would like to know what other articles she may need. They want to send them to her."

"She's got everything she needs!" he retorted in a loud, harsh, angry voice.

"But the women are concerned and want to know about her personal needs so they can buy them and send them to her," I stated again.

"Look, I've told you that she has got everything she needs, and that is all I've got to say about it!" he declared harshly, in a tone that divulged the fact that anger and contempt were coloring his attitude.

"Isn't she entitled to the same treatment and rights as any other prisoner in this jail?" I insisted.

The deputy became greatly agitated and declared, "You can't tell us how to run this jail, you understand?"

"I can't tell you how to run this jail, but I can tell you that she has the same constitutional rights as any other prisoner!" I replied.

He bristled and slammed shut the glass panel as I left.

The community had not asked for much, just that one of its members be treated as a human being. A heated, spiteful, burning desire for vengeance on the part of the authorities aborted any possibility of an amiable de-escalation.

I left the sheriff's office and jail with that old, rekindled feeling that I had grown up with in the South. The vision of chief of police Jesse Helms dragging the Black woman along the main street of Monroe returned to haunt me. It was sickening how timid Black men were then, but this was a different day and, I had hoped, a different people. Driving the three miles back to my home, I felt the same spirit rising in me that had set me on the warpath many times before. It was a dreadful feeling to know that white supremacy and the dehumanization of my race had confronted me with yet another challenge to my manhood. This meant that the peace that I had moved to this small village in quest of was eluding me. As always in the past, I found it impossible to remain immobile when a situation in an environment displayed the most debasing forms of racial and human injustice.

When I returned home, Mabel anxiously inquired, "How did it go?"

I struggled to maintain my composure as I declared, "We are at war!"

My first action was to send out a distress telephone call to friends in Detroit. Elaine Steele, who had been active with the Republic of New Afrika and remained a good friend, suggested that I call a Black attorney, who served as a "Friend of the Court." She informed me that he had at one time been jailed unjustly. He had freed himself from prison through his own legal efforts and was actively helping others. I called him, and he gave me a list of Afro-American lawyers. I called all of them, but they all had excuses as to why they could not help us. When I called back to inform him of my lack of success, he then told me that I should try to get Attorney Ernest Goodman.

After I explained the situation to Attorney Goodman, he informed me, without committing himself to taking the case, that he would come to Baldwin as soon as he cleared his desk. The Black attorney "Friend of the Court" called inquiring whether I had had any luck in securing a volunteer lawyer. When I explained that Goodman had agreed to come to investigate the case, his tone of voice gave way to elation. He informed me that if Ernest Goodman was interested, I need not look any further, because I had the best legal counsel available.

Three days after my initial contact with Attorney Goodman, he called to inform me that he was on his way to Idlewild. Detroit to the Baldwin/Idlewild area is a four-hour drive. Goodman had left Detroit before sunrise that cold, snowy November morning, and just before 10:00 a.m. he drove his little Volkswagen into the yard, steaming from the long drive. A cherubic-looking, mixed-gray-haired man bounded out of the car, came to our door, and announced, "I'm Ernie Goodman and I came here to see what it is you are talking about, but I'm not promising you anything!"

We were more than happy to have him come and hear the story. After a brief conversation, he went to the jail to visit Mrs. Ruby Nelson. He returned from his visit to the jail in a fighting mood. It was more than obvious that he had been deeply touched. He reported to us that he had never, in all his visits to prisoners in jail, witnessed such blatant neglect. He told us that he had discovered that Mrs. Nelson had been denied all the basic items of hygiene a woman would need. He said she was completely unkempt to the point that she resembled a wild woman. He had learned also that she had endured an epileptic seizure and was revived only when other prisoners threw water on her from other cells, and even after that, the authorities had not bothered to seek any kind of medical assistance for her.

During the ensuing days, Goodman never allowed us to engage him as our lawyer, but it was more than obvious that he was already at work on the case. His interest in the case aroused the entire Afro-American community to united action. We were able to conduct overflow weekly meetings. The older citizens who had lived in the area for many years marveled at the unity and spirit of resistance that they had never before experienced. Local bigots were shocked that a fighting mode had taken hold of a people so long accommodating and submissive. The incident had uncovered some of the same submerged, potentially explosive force that I had witnessed surface in Monroe, North Carolina. It was now more evident to me that the Afro-American's meek acceptance of the status quo stemmed from the lack of the adequate existence of selfless, populist leadership. There have been too many Black elitist leaders who allied themselves with self-serving manipulators of Fabian struggles.

During the trial, a friend of Attorney Goodman who owned his own plane volunteered to fly him and the state-appointed psychiatrist to the little Baldwin village airport to testify in the case. Other friends of "Ernie" came to our aid when he told them what was happening. They helped in many ways, including getting the Ruby Nelson story told. It was unheard of that a penniless Black woman could be fortunate enough to be the object of such high-caliber humanitarian concern and defense.

The arrival of the lawyer and psychiatrists by air set the stage for high drama. Goodman was instrumental in having a judge brought in from another district and had all of the personnel of the local sheriff's department barred from the courthouse grounds while the trial was in session. The state police took jurisdiction. It was the first time that local citizens were made aware that the sheriff's department was not all-powerful.

The courtroom was overflowing with senior citizens, some as old as ninety. Goodman's legal aggressiveness became a type of show that they had never before witnessed in their long-suppressed lives. The judge warned Goodman to cease pursuing his determined line of approach to the case. Goodman was relentless in his method. The judge became enraged and cited him for contempt. The courtroom, filled with seniors, exploded in an outburst of rage. There were angry cries that if Goodman was sent to jail, they would all have to be arrested. Goodman told the judge, "Let's go on with the trial. I'll take care of the contempt citation later!"

The judge called a brief recess, went to his chambers, and returned soon, more composed and courteous. After the trial was completed, the judge, in a kind gesture, announced that he was absolving Goodman's contempt citation. Goodman rose to address the bench. It was obvious that the judge was relieved and expected Goodman to apologize. Goodman looked straight at the judge and in a voice of contempt declared, "I think you ought to know that I have been practicing law for fifty-two years, and this is the first time I have ever been cited for contempt. Not even in the state of Mississippi!"

It was a glorious victory for the oppressed people of Lake County, long oppressed and dehumanized. The walls of racial injustice had been pierced, and the realm of the status quo would never be the same again. The people had learned that it is possible to struggle and win. Mrs. Ruby Nelson was acquitted of all charges. The county was ordered to provide for transporting her to Detroit for ongoing treatment for chronic epilepsy at the Lafayette Clinic, which is renowned for its treatments for epilepsy. The legend of Ernest Goodman is still remembered here. Attorney Goodman continued to visit us on occasion, to engage in fishing in the rivers and streams of Lake County. His friend Sidney Rosen also accompanied him on occasion, and we thoroughly enjoyed a lasting friendship with them.

After the "Ruby Nelson case" was over, the people rallied around our newly incorporated "People's Association for Human Rights," and they were transformed into a force of resistance. During the ensuing years, a series of serious cases arose. Other volunteer lawyers, answering our pleas, came to our rescue. Roger Wotilla from Cadillac came. Melissa El, a young Afro-American lawyer from Detroit, came, and every case supported by the People's Association was won, and the rights of Black Americans in the area were accorded much more respect.

I have witnessed the insanity of white supremacy justice all of my life, and I have fought it all of my adult life. Today, I find it still infecting American life. It is more than obvious that as long as racism permeates our society, it will remain an evil curse upon the land.

CHAPTER 61

FULL CIRCLE

TAKING UP CAUSE IN NORTH CAROLINA

Early in 1994, a woman prisoner wrote appealing to me to take interest in a North Carolina legal case. Shortly after her letter was received, another arrived from a male inmate incarcerated on death row. He was Calvin Christmas Cunningham, who had been charged with killing a white policeman in Charlotte, North Carolina. At his request, I visited Cunningham three times on death row in Raleigh, North Carolina. Cunningham maintained he was innocent and vehemently stated that he was being railroaded. I started my own inquiry into the case, and in an attempt to boost interest, I visited the North Carolina Death Row Resource Center and Attorney Tom Loftin, who was handling Cunningham's appeal to the North Carolina Supreme Court. Attorney Loftin was an excellent lawyer who displayed a serious interest in the case. He had written a brief in which he had outlined 120 errors that he had found in reviewing the case. The more I became involved in the case, the more convinced I became that Cunningham was innocent of the charges.

On August 5, 1990, at 9:45 p.m., subsequent to a domestic argument with his live-in girlfriend, Calvin C. Cunningham, a forty-six-year-old Black man, was taken into custody by Charlotte police. His girlfriend had called the police merely to have him removed from the premises. When Cunningham, who was not dressed when the police arrived, insisted that the home was his, he was allowed to dress. He was handcuffed, searched by two arresting officers, and taken into custody.

Cunningham was placed alone in the back seat of a patrol car. A lone officer, who was driving the vehicle, drove headlong into a parked truck as he was exiting the block. The white officer, named Lyles (commonly called "Cowboy" because of his conduct in the Black community), got out of the car and was shot in the head. He later died in the hospital from his injuries.

Excited police descended on the community and unleashed a reign of terror against nearby homes, including the home of the Afro-American who called 911 to report that an officer was in trouble in the street. The police conduct frightened Cunningham, still handcuffed in the back seat of the squad car, to such an extent that he somehow managed to maneuver his cuffed hands from behind him to the front. Still cuffed, he remained locked inside the police car. Although afraid and fearing for his life, he attracted the attention of the investigating officers to reveal that he was still locked inside. When the officers were unable to find and apprehend a suspect in the neighborhood, Cunningham was charged with the crime.

Though having been searched and found to have no weapon except a pocketknife, which had been taken from him, he was accused of having shot Officer Lyles twice through the back seat of the police car. He was accused of having kicked a small-caliber pistol from the floor in the back of the car to the front floor, where police claimed to have found it.

Police claimed the two shots to the back of the policeman caused him to wreck the patrol car and that the resulting confusion was the cause of his being more interested in outside damage than shots against his body armor.

No glass bearing a bullet hole was presented in court. The gun that was presented in court as the murder weapon did not bear Cunningham's fingerprints. Paraffin tests revealed no powder residue on Cunningham's hand. Cunningham was assigned two court-appointed lawyers. A lawyer he selected was denied full access to his trial. He was given a death sentence, which seemed to be based more on his early life than on the crime with which he was charged. It is commonly believed that Cunningham is innocent.

According to the Charlotte police, we were expected to believe that a policeman was shot twice through the seat of a police car, and instead of reacting by blowing Cunningham away, he supposedly stopped the vehicle to investigate a wreck and was shot through the head while out of the car. It is highly logical that if the policeman had merely thought Cunningham to be armed, his primary concern would have been to neutralize his prisoner and to survive.

Attorney Tom Loftin, the southern white lawyer from Durham, North Carolina, who had appealed Cunningham's death penalty conviction, won a new trial for him. Despite the fact that I sent out many appeals for aid for Cunningham pending his new trial, no lawyer came forward to volunteer to defend him until Melissa El from Detroit offered her services. In the spring of 1994, he received a new trial. The national office of the NAACP didn't bother to answer the letter of appeal I addressed to then executive secretary Ben Chavis.[1] It was a pitiful sight to see Cunningham trying to defend himself in a courtroom presided over by a cantankerous white woman judge. He was sentenced to prison for life. One juror held out against the death penalty in the sentencing hearing.

As I stood gazing out of the window in Mecklenburg's fourth-floor court building, all I could see was a scene of all-new, expensive buildings. This was quite a changed landscape from what I remembered in the earlier days of my life. I recalled, as a child, visiting Charlotte with my mother. We and my mother's friend and our neighbor Mrs. King often rode the train on railroad passes the twenty-five miles from Monroe for a joyride and light shopping excursion. We rode in the section of the train designated for "colored only." The train was pulled by an early boxy diesel engine that local people referred to as the "boll weevil." I never really understood the designation. Just a few blocks from where I stood was a department store known as Kresge's. To eat lunch at Kresge's was a great event that I anxiously looked forward to, despite the fact that we were segregated in a restricted area that most times necessitated our standing to eat.

I remembered the less-than-elaborate homes in a community called Second Ward. Second Ward, a "colored section" of Charlotte, was no more. It had vanished in what was thought to be the new order of progress, integration, and urban renewal. Occasionally, I could see a well-dressed Afro-American traverse the beautifully arrayed plaza. Second Ward, the bustling Black community where poor Black people used to live and play, was gone. The old segregation was gone, but it was more than obvious that justice for the Black masses had floundered. It was aborted by a deep-seated and latent racism. The mark of poverty was still vivid, relative to the general situation engulfing the local African American population.

I had wondered why local Black leaders declined to stir themselves on behalf of Cunningham. In the past, a Black community would angrily mobilize to give support to any Black person sentenced to death on such flimsy evidence. Now, I was witnessing a Black man being tried for his life without even a lawyer to

1. Ben Chavis (Muhammad) is an activist and a former political prisoner (from the Wilmington 10 case) and was executive secretary of the NAACP from April 1993 to August 1994.

defend him. It was more than obvious that the new breed of attorneys were much more self-centered than their predecessors, who, in many cases, defiantly displayed a willingness to face economic sanctions, violence, and even death in the cause of the wretched victims of racist injustice.

I shuddered from the thought of the possibility of innocent Blacks being accused of capital crimes and not being able to afford first-rate lawyers. Many of the overworked, underpaid, and understaffed court-appointed lawyers are no more than conscience-salvers for a good-old-boy network more concerned with image than with the human rights of the moneyless. It must be a blow as harsh as any that could come out of hell to be innocent and poor with no community support, facing the gas chamber, devoid of all contact with the caring sector of the world. Isolation, alone, is a devastatingly hellish experience.

CHAPTER 62

FINAL THOUGHTS

WARNING TO AMERICA

I will be seventy-one years old by the time I finish this manuscript. Being born a Black person in America, as all other Blacks born here, and surveying the situation today, I realize that my relentless pursuit of social justice and human dignity has been as fruitless as a quest to find gold at the end of a rainbow.

Upon returning to my native land in 1969, after having been exiled in Cuba and China for eight years, many positive changes were highly noticeable, and that gave me great satisfaction. Lyndon Johnson's Great Society movement had erased much of the state-sponsored institutions that blatantly dehumanized African Americans.[1] The changes brought great joy to my heart. I felt vindicated for the hard line I had taken against unconscionable racism.

But now I realize that we celebrated too soon. We had deluded ourselves into believing that America's surge toward a just and fair society for all her people was the Black man's unfulfilled perennial dream of access to the constitutional promised land. The African American's faith was misplaced because there was no understanding of the historical motive force relative to the struggle for advantage,

1. The Great Society initiative was a set of programs initiated under the administration of President Lyndon Johnson ostensibly to eliminate poverty and racial discrimination in the United States. These reforms included Medicare, Medicaid, the Economic Opportunity Act of 1964, the Civil Rights Act of 1964, and the Voting Rights Act of 1965.

Mabel and Robert Williams at the Great Wall of China, c. 1980s. Courtesy of the Williams family.

Robert Williams in retirement, Idlewild, Michigan, c. 1990s. Courtesy of the Williams family.

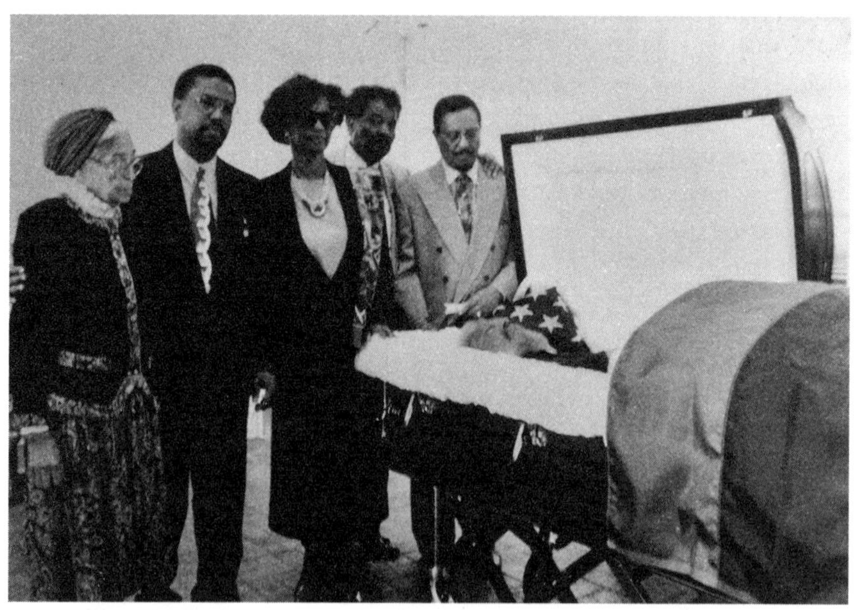

Left to right: Mrs. Rosa Parks, John C. Williams, Mabel Williams, and Robert's brothers, John H. and Edward, at Robert Williams's funeral, Monroe, North Carolina, 1996. Courtesy of the Williams family.

wealth, power, and control. This type of struggle must be continuous. The status quo is the sacred point of rally for the upper strata of society and their complement of wishful pawns. Social concessions that are given under duress must be just as vigorously defended and safeguarded after the fact with the same determination. History teaches that every revolutionary struggle is accompanied by a wake of counterrevolution. African Americans have wished for an honest white America for so long that we have forgotten the addictive nature of racism.

In the old days, when I was growing up, it was a parental ritual to condition Black offspring to know their place in racist white America. Mothers who were plagued perennially by deep-seated fears that their sons would violate the life-threatening code inherent in vicious white supremacy seldom ceased in their efforts to condition their offspring to meekly submit to such savage and blatant racism. The specter of being lynched was always hovering over the African American. The total soul and persona of the Black American was stunted and dwarfed. Whatever our potential or talent may have been, we were not allowed to develop in an atmosphere of human dignity.

In actuality, justice was just a meaningless word used as an "aka" for oppression and injustice. How can a people subjected for 300 years to the most brutal form of slavery the world has ever known, set adrift in a hostile and mean-spirited world without compensation or therapy, be expected to compete on equal terms? On the whole, Black people in America have never experienced fair play and justice. There has always been a brutal, dehumanizing, and oppressive ceiling on our lives to render us less competitive on the stage of life. I have often felt that growing up Black in America is tantamount to being forced to live in the crawlspace beneath a spacious house with no accommodation to stand or walk upright. Such conditions have taken their toll. The great sin and shame of this situation is that we have had our souls bound, like the feet of the ancient women of China, and the very ones who have done this horrible thing to us are now more than anxious to use their handiwork to argue our inferiority.

What little relief we have been given in the past few years is now being rescinded. Bigoted politicians are once again fanning the flames of racism. The white supremacy ideology is sweeping the nation like wildfire. The white populations are mobilizing for an assault on Black gains. They are being erroneously led to believe that most of the social ills and reasons for the country's decline can be traced to the presence and lifestyle of the African American. If these white supremacist agitators prevail in Washington and across the nation, America as a nation can kiss tomorrow goodbye.

The bigots cannot reinstate the old penalties on the Afro-American and unleash what is tantamount to racial tyranny without wreaking havoc on the entire nation. The old racial equation is like Humpty Dumpty—it cannot be put back together again. It behooves all factions of the country to strive for a just, wholesome, and prosperous society. The "us against them" ism is certain to make us all losers.

As one who has put his life and fortune on the line for a color-blind America, it grieves me deeply to survey the widening breach descending on the land. My grief is compounded by the sprouting of a new generation of Blacks, cast in the glow of white reactionaries. These self-centered Negroes, who have become affluent mostly as a result of the blood, sweat, and tears of their predecessors, are moving might and main to distance themselves from the suffering masses. Despite the fact that some of them owe their success to affirmative action and civil rights legislation, they now disparage governmental aid for the coming generations. They seem to have forgotten how the doors were opened for them. Some go so far in their ingratitude as to join the racist chorus in their coded anti-Afro-American litany.

One of the great tragedies of history is that America is rich enough and powerful enough to ease the burden of most of the world. Despite its ability, it is too mean-spirited to dispense social and economic justice within its own borders. Afro-Americans and some other minorities are treated like Third Worlders. There is a growing tendency for the government to favor the wealthy, and the poor be damned. This is a suicidal attitude.

In 1964, I publicly predicted that massive violence was looming just over the horizon. The ruling circles and many Black pacifists countered that it was baseless to think that the cities would explode in violence. My concern now is that the worse is yet to come. The current tendency, unless corrected, is sure to lead to a devastating explosion that will remove the mantle of world leadership from the USA. The idea that most African Americans are welfare clients and baby makers, causing deterioration of white life, is erroneous. With the white males whining about reverse discrimination and racial discrimination, animosity between the races is bound to intensify. For the white American male to whine and accuse the government of discrimination is to add insult to injury. Discrimination is the white male's creation. He has perpetuated it since he landed on these shores. Discrimination is reprehensible, no matter who is the victim. But it is first-magnitude hypocrisy when the one who cheats and steals cries foul when he starts to lose his nefarious privilege. It all comes down to whose ox is being gored.

We are traveling a path similar to Yugoslavia, and most white Americans seem not to give a damn. African Americans are the only nonnatives who did not come here seeking to enrich themselves by subjugating other people. Yes, reform is needed in many spheres of the country, but only humane and just reforms can exalt the nation. In growing up, the ceiling I experienced was concrete. It was tantamount to a crawlspace beneath a house. There was no room to stand and to grow upright. In my seventy-first year, the ceiling is glass. It is a great deal higher, but we are still stunted and forced to stand in a bent position.

I can still hear the words of my long-departed uncle Charlie declaring that "if there is a God, he must be sleeping." I can hear my mother, too, proclaiming in tones of deep faith that someday God will come, in his own time and in his own way. If he is sleeping, he will awaken someday, and woe be unto the persecutors of the poor.

Perhaps that day is nearer than we think, for what shall it profit a people to gain the wealth of a nation through greed and subterfuge and lose the entire nation and all of its ill-gotten gains? America, the sun is sinking. Put your house in order before God awakens and the curse of darkness falls.

FINIS

PART II

WE WANT TO SEE EVERYBODY RISE

MABEL R. WILLIAMS

CHAPTER 1

BEGINNINGS IN MONROE

I was born on a hot summer day, June 1, 1931, in a small shotgun house on Brickett Street in the "poor house hill" Negro section of Monroe, North Carolina. The house was located down the street from the white cemetery and down the hill from the all-white high school. My father, King David Robinson, was a driver for Dr. Belk, co-owner of the then-prosperous Belk store chain. Dr. Belk's daughter was named Mabel. My father gave me her name. When I was about two years old, my father died of a heart problem. My mother, Emma Perry Robinson, became a young widow with my sister, Elizabeth, or "Snookie"; my brother, David Jr., "June"; and me.

One of my early memories as a child is playing on a screened-in back porch, watching the dust particles ride the sunbeam over a ledge where there was a basket of bright red cherries. There was an old round dark-green icebox in one corner of the porch, with revolving shelves inside the lower section and a lift-up lid on top, where a 25-, 50-, or 100-pound block of ice could be stored. A card with those numbers hung over the icebox. The card could be placed inside the porch screen so the iceman could see from his delivery truck how much ice was wanted that day. An ice pick hung on the wall above the icebox. Through the back screen door, I could see an apple tree, a pear tree, and a much-used path that led to the house next door, where Papa Tom, his wife, Marie, and Aunt Pearl lived.

Our family was now living in the area of town called "Quality Hill." My mother had married Chalmers Barber. He worked for the railroad and was the cook for the wrecking crew whenever there was a train wreck. Our house had electricity, inside plumbing, and a bathtub with claw-like feet. We called our stepfather Daddy Barber. He was the only father I knew, and I was his baby girl.

Our house was located a few blocks away from the white elementary school, next door to my father's brother-in-law, Papa Tom Sitgraves. He was a porter on the Seaboard Railroad, assigned the route from Monroe to Atlanta, Georgia. Our cousins Sylvia, Carlton, and Ruby, Papa Tom's grandchildren, were our constant companions, playing happily for hours in our adjoining backyards. Papa Tom's daughter, Aunt Pearl, became the woman of the house after his wife, Mama Marie, passed away. As part of their extended family, we did lots of things together. Aunt Pearl, a great cook, was always baking goodies. My favorite was apple strudel, which she made with the fruit from our trees. The aromas of cinnamon and nutmeg would call us from whatever chores or play we were engaged in.

We were able to get free passes to ride the train whenever the Seaboard line ran. My mother always packed a bag or box lunch for our trips. Sometimes we went to Charlotte, which seemed very far away, with the train stopping five or six times in the small local communities. The porters would announce the names of the towns where the train would stop to pick up passengers. Their booming voices were always a delight to us as they chanted, "Peachhhh land, Polkkkk ton, Mattt thews, Stouts, Indian Trail, and Charrrr lotte!" The father of one of my friends, Mr. Walt Mosley, was the porter on the Monroe-to-Charlotte run. These trips were lots of fun.

One trip I remember quite well. We went with our mother to Southern Pines, North Carolina, to visit our brother in the tuberculosis sanatorium. June had been diagnosed with tuberculosis when he was in primary school. His favorite teacher, Mrs. Johns, had the dreaded disease, as did one of our cousins, Naomi, a junior high student, as well as others from our community. Once at the sanatorium, we were not allowed to enter the building. We were only allowed to wave to June from outside while he stood at the window of an upstairs room. I remember that my mother cried on the way there and on the way back. June had been her favorite from birth. My sister was my father's favorite, and I was Daddy Barber's favorite. Mother was given the terrible news that my brother's lung had collapsed and there was nothing further they could do for him. He was to be sent home to die.

We returned home to await my brother's arrival. He lived with us again, but now he was isolated in his own room, which had been built for him on the front porch. The only door to the room was from the porch. We handed him his meals through the living room window. When our parents were not home, we would try to get closer to our brother to play with him, but he would always caution us to stay away because he did not want us to become ill.

Tuberculosis was running rampant in our community. Our cousin Naomi, Mrs. Johns, and others we knew died of the disease during those years. June was nine years old when he died. I was six, and Snookie was thirteen. On the day of June's funeral, my mother fainted several times. I thought she was dying, too. I only realized the pain and suffering she was going through when my own son Bobby passed away at age forty-three on my sixtieth birthday in 1991.

My mother worked as a cook and a maid to help with finances as we grew up. She was always afraid that my sister and I would also contract tuberculosis. Knowing that milk was essential to our health, she was determined to provide it for us. The white milk companies did not deliver in our neighborhood, so she had the milk delivered to her white employers and brought it home when she got off work.

We walked to school each day across town to New Town, where our Black school was located. We lived and played near the two white schools in our community. This was the only area that had paved walkways where we could skate when the whites were not there. It was also a great shortcut connecting our Black communities. My lifelong best friend, Marie Williams, lived in the neighborhood where I was born. She was two months older than me, and we loved to visit and walk each other "halfway" home. Our mothers always insisted that we get back home before dark.

All of our teachers were Black. They played significant roles in our neighborhoods, serving as choir leaders and Sunday school and Vacation Bible School teachers. They did not hesitate to correct us at school, at play, or whenever they saw us engaging in unacceptable behavior. I grew up and survived those early years under the protection and watchful eyes of my parents, relatives, teachers, and other caring adults in our Black, segregated communities. We traveled through the white communities to school, to church, and in and out of the downtown area—with admonitions not to "get out of our place" and not to make trouble. I learned early on that whites posed a danger to our safety, an ever-present threat to our well-being.

One of my daily chores as a child was to make Daddy Barber's bed. There was always a large pearl-handled pistol under his pillow. The gun had to be placed in the closet each morning before my chores were complete. Even though it was available every night, the gun was fired only on New Year's Eve. The older people told me to handle it but never shoot it or put my fingers on the trigger. I understood that the gun was there because there was a threat to our lives—that some night riders might come and attack us in the middle of the night. So, I knew that there was danger.[1]

Sundays were happy times that started at the kitchen table with my mother's prayers, the smell of good food, and hot, homemade biscuits. After the meal, we dressed and walked across town to Elizabeth Baptist Church, where my mother was a member of the choir. My paternal grandmother lived with her sister in close proximity to the church. If I got there in time, I could visit them before Sunday school got started. Lots of other cousins, aunts, and uncles lived in that vicinity. We would get together after church for dinner and great times. There were two little stores on the corners next to the church. One was owned by a Black widow, Mrs. Ida Shadd, and the other by a white couple, Mr. and Mrs. Bundy. Both were open on Sundays during the short break between Sunday school and church service. I was usually given a few pennies to give to the missionary collection for the children in Monrovia, Liberia. I could spend one to buy Mary Jane or Baby Ruth candy before church service began.

One Sunday during church service, my grandma "got happy." She started crying and walking down the aisle, shouting, "I'm going home!" I am told that I jumped up and called out to her, "Wait, Grandma, I'm going with you!" I was around three or four, no doubt thinking about the candied yams that she was famous for cooking. Needless to say, the somber mood in church changed to humor at my outburst.

We would attend afternoon youth services at the African Methodist Episcopal Church, where Daddy Barber was a steward. My friend Marie and her family were members there. We both were in the very lively youth choir, directed by our second-grade teacher, whom we all loved dearly. Many of our schoolmates from all over Monroe were a part of these Sunday activities, when our Black community gathered to worship and give thanks for our blessings.

1. "The older people . . . there was danger": Mabel Williams, interview by Claude Marks and Lincoln Bergman, May 30 and 31, 2003, San Francisco, CA, Mabel and Robert F. Williams Collection, Freedom Archives, Berkeley, CA (hereinafter MRW Collection).

CHAPTER 2

TAKE ME TO THE WATER

It was a beautiful, sunshiny Saturday morning. I was dressed in one of my favorite pinafore dresses. I was as happy as could be because I was going to be baptized. At twelve years of age, I had already reached early womanhood and was about to begin a new adventure along with several of my childhood friends.

Elizabeth Baptist Church was filling with members, relatives, and friends to welcome us into the fellowship of Christian life. We girls gathered in the room leading up to the choir stand. We draped the white flowing robes over our bodies and tied them with sashes. The boys donned their robes in a room just behind the pulpit. We were all so excited that we could hardly wait for the action to start.

After what seemed forever, the door opened and we were ushered to the church vestibule, past an anxiously waiting congregation. The choir was in place, and the pianist, Mrs. Hasty, was playing some inspirational music. She was my sister's piano teacher and also the music teacher at our school. My mother and aunt were seated in the choir along with my future mother-in-law. My older sister and some cousins were seated in the pews. They waved and snickered when our eyes met as we passed their seats. We sat and waited for what seemed a long time until a woman usher, in a white uniform, came and told us to follow her slowly.

The congregation was on its feet rejoicing with "Amen, thank you, Jesus, praise the Lord," and other affirmations as we moved down the aisle to the empty pew in front of the baptismal pool. The boys were on the left, girls on the right. The pulpit platform had been moved back so that we stood facing the pastor and the top officials of the church, who were lined up in front of the pool. On the right side of the pool, my grandmother sat with the elder mothers of the church. The deacons sat on the left. The pastor, Reverend C. C. Johnson, explained what we were about to do. He questioned whether we were ready to assume responsibility for our actions. Each of us answered yes to all of his questions.

As the minister and deacons were turning to face the pool, I could hear Mrs. Boulware and my grandma Lizzie raising the hymn "Take Me to the Water." As they sang a cappella, the elderly men's group responded in cadence: "None but the righteous shall see God."

"I baptize you in the name of the Father, the Son, and the Holy Ghost," and down I went into the water and up again, sputtering and snorting and wiping my burning eyes. As I got dressed, I could hear the water splashing as the others were baptized and the singing continued. I was expecting to feel some great change that would be visible to everyone who saw me, but that was not the case. My mother and older relatives all cried as they hugged me. Mother "got happy" and had to be held until she calmed down. Then it was all over for that day.

Throughout the day, my mother's teachings, which she professed regularly, echoed in my mind. I could hear her say, "Every tub has to stand on its own bottom." "Every one of us has to meet our maker alone, face to face." I remembered her morning prayers, when she kneeled at the breakfast table. She always began with, "You know my heart and my heart's desires." She would invoke God's will to allow her to see her children grow up, ending with, "And when my time on earth is done, give me a home where I can praise Thee as I ought."

CHAPTER 3

GROWING INTO ADULTHOOD

Our town experienced big changes while I was still in elementary school. The whole school was called to the auditorium to listen to the radio when President Roosevelt announced that the Japanese had attacked the United States. As the war developed, an army base, Camp Sutton, was installed in Monroe, with a full contingent of Black soldiers and their families. The local armory was turned into a factory to support the camp. Most of the families in our community took in roomers or washed and ironed clothes for the newcomers to earn money to help with bills.

Food rationing of scarce items, such as sugar and coffee, was enforced. White margarine, which was sold with red coloring that had to be mixed in, was sold as a substitute for butter. Our school got involved by featuring entertainment by students, who performed to earn money to buy much-needed supplies for our segregated, poorly funded educational system. We were encouraged to buy and sell war savings bonds. I filled books with the ten-cent stamps I bought.

On Saturdays, we went to see movies at the segregated theater, where we were made to sit in the balcony section. I remember the smell of popcorn and seeing cowboys and Indians, the funny cartoons, and the newsreels that followed each session. The Indians and the Japanese people were always portrayed as extremely evil, while the whites were the innocent good guys. Sometimes they would show Saturday night special movies that featured Black people. Radio programs were constantly talking about the war and the threat of the "Yellow Peril."

My mother, my relatives, and other Black people were hired for work that entailed opening dirty feather pillowcases, emptying the feathers out, and then washing, ironing, and refilling them. After the cases were sewn up, the pillows would be packaged for shipping back to Camp Sutton.

Before Camp Sutton came to town, extended family members lived with us. My mother's nephew Booker T. Perry lived with us on Quality Hill until he went off to the CCC Camp.[1] My uncle Roy "Prete" Perry stayed with us while he was getting a divorce from his wife. They told us many stories about our family history and kept us laughing. Saturdays were great when we went to the segregated movie theater with Uncle Prete. When the cartoons came on, his loud, infectious laugh added a special effect to the entire outing.

In 1946, I was excited to attend my sister's graduation from Spelman College. She was soon swept off her feet by one of the local high school grads, who was already a small business owner and housepainter. They became engaged and were married within a short period of time, defying my mother's wishes that she wait a few years. I was fascinated that she followed her own mind in going ahead with marriage. She and her husband moved into a home on the route to my high school. I would stop by her house on my way home from school, and we would talk for hours. Although she was seven years older than me, we became closer than ever as I matured.

When the war ended, Camp Sutton was phased out. Most of the soldiers left. I was attending Winchester Avenue High School and was a member of the girls' basketball team. Local boys who had volunteered for military service or had been drafted were returning home. Some came back to Winchester to complete high school. Others who had graduated came back to help as volunteers at the school. One of them, John Herman Williams, became our girls' basketball team coach. Little did I know that he would become my brother-in-law.

Our team practiced after school on the grounds of our beloved Winchester School because we did not have a gymnasium. The segregated system did not provide the "colored" school that amenity. Nevertheless, our school was well known for our victories in competition with other schools. When Camp Sutton closed down, we were allowed to go there and play in one of the abandoned gyms. The trouble was that it was located over a mile away from Winchester. By the time we walked there and back, and then walked another two miles or so home, the streetlights would be on. My mother and father

1. The Civilian Conservation Corps was a federal work relief program for unmarried men, ages seventeen to twenty-eight, which lasted from 1933 to 1942.

had a strict curfew for me. I had to be home before the streetlights came on. I know now they feared for my safety, but at the time I did not understand, and I disobeyed them on numerous occasions. My last and greatest punishment from my mother was for defying her rule requiring me to get home before dark.

Mabel Williams as a teenager.
Courtesy of the Williams family.

CHAPTER 4

BEGINNING MY RE-EDUCATION

MEETING AND MARRYING ROBERT WILLIAMS

I lived with my sister, Elizabeth, for a spell when she had her first child. Robert was a good friend of my brother-in-law, Kenneth. When Robert came home on leave from the army, he visited Kenneth. That's when I remet him, or met him as a person on an equal level, more or less. We fell in love and eventually got married.[1]

Robert and Mabel were married on June 19, 1947. She was sixteen and in the eleventh grade. Robert was twenty-two.

After we married, I returned to high school and continued to play basketball. Robert didn't like that. He would say, "You don't need—a married woman don't need—to be out there playing basketball." I had to give up basketball, but I was really an all-out athletic person. And I loved school. I loved my teachers, and I loved the subjects. I was a good student as well. I think Robert might have seen some potential that I hadn't yet seen in myself.[2]

1. "I lived with . . . eventually got married": Mabel Williams, interview by Wanda Sabir, "The Political Awakening of Mabel Williams, Wife of Author of 'Negroes with Guns,'" March 17, 2004, *San Francisco Bay View National Black Newspaper*.

2. "After we married . . . seen in myself": Mabel Williams, interview by David Cecelski, August 20, 1999, Interview K-0266, Southern Oral History Program Collection (#4007), Center for the Study of the American South, Southern Historical Collection, Wilson Library,

I grew up in a family where segregation was accepted as the norm. Robert had grown up in a family where both his grandmother and grandfather came out of slavery as literate teachers. His grandmother, who had a great influence on him, encouraged him to reject anything second-class. He also had a very radical uncle, his uncle Charlie, who had influenced him when he was a young boy. From the beginning, we had two different outlooks on society as a whole. It took a long time for me to accept the fact that Robert was different, that he was going to struggle for change, and I had to struggle as well.[3]

When Robert was sixteen years old, he was given the opportunity to work in President Franklin Roosevelt's National Youth Administration program, which offered job training to youth. It was like the Community and Economic Development Agency program. He went with a group of classmates to be trained as stonemasons; but the Black boys were given the job of digging up stones, while the white boys were taught how to lay the stones. Robert saw that as an injustice—the fact that they weren't really being trained. The Black boys were given dirty eating utensils and made to drink water from buckets. So, he organized the boys to walk off the job.

Robert and Kenneth, my brother-in-law, were really close buddies growing up together. Even though Robert was involved in civil rights activities, up to the time that we left the United States, his best buddy was not involved for fear of his own parents and what they would do to him if he went afoul of the system. I didn't know anything about these past experiences, and I didn't know about the problems Robert ran into in the army until after we were married.[4] We began to talk about things then, and I began my re-education.[5]

Robert rejected the way whites treated him. He was out there trying to get employment, trying to get his GI benefits, and running into all kinds of problems. He would come home and talk about it, tell me the things that he had faced during the day, whether it had been at the veterans' office, where he was trying to get his allotment, or elsewhere. In the meantime, he was writing

---

University of North Carolina at Chapel Hill, https://dc.lib.unc.edu/cdm/compoundobject/collection/sohp/id/12844/rec/1.

3. "I grew up . . . struggle as well": Williams, interview by Sabir, "Political Awakening."

4. The US military was segregated when Williams was in the army. He challenged racism in the military and was detained for three months for insubordination. See chapters 10–13 of Robert Williams's memoir, *While God Lay Sleeping*.

5. "Even though Robert . . . began my re-education": Williams, interview by Sabir, "Political Awakening."

letters to the newspaper editor, complaining about stories he had read or about the plight of Black folks.[6]

Robert was well read. He was self-educated and knew a lot more, not just about our local society but also about the world and political issues that I had no idea about. He had a bigger library at his house than we had at our high school in Monroe.[7] We lived with his father after he was discharged from the army. One night his father said to me, "Mabel, you know Robert thinks that he ought to be president of the United States." I said, "What?" and he said, "Yes." Robert tuned in and said, "Why not? I'm a man like he is a man. Why shouldn't I want to be president? Why shouldn't I be president?" I began to realize that I had married a man who was not quite as ordinary as I thought. He was a person who could not accept being a second-class citizen.

He thought differently from everybody I knew. Most of the people that I knew were accepting the system as it existed and, as my stepfather used to say, "staying out of the way of white folks and staying in our place"—our place being the place the white folks said we needed to stay in—going to our segregated schools and churches, staying in our segregated communities, and having the least possible connection with white folks.

I was born into a segregated society, and I accepted it because that's all I knew. After we married and started trying to make a living as a family, we kept running into the barriers of segregation. We just could not make the kind of living that other young people—white people—were making. And every time we'd start to try to rise up, it seemed somebody was trying to put us back down. I didn't realize in the beginning that this was wrong, that what was happening to us was wrong. I didn't know all of the implications of segregation and what it meant for people trying to make a living.[8]

Robert and I had bumps and confrontations as we struggled against the racist system that was keeping us down—keeping all of us down. I was thinking that if he fought against the system, they would kill him or crush him as they had crushed most of our men. It was a real struggle, but thank God, we made it.[9]

6. "Robert rejected the way . . . of Black folks": Williams, interview by Cecelski.

7. "Robert was well read . . . school in Monroe": Williams, interview by Sabir, "Political Awakening."

8. "I was born . . . make a living": Mabel Williams, interview by Marks and Bergman, May 30 and 31, 2003, San Francisco, CA, MRW Collection.

9. "Robert and I . . . we made it": Williams, interview by Sabir, "Political Awakening."

CHAPTER 5

EARLY ACTIVISM

WORKING IN THE CATHOLIC CHURCH

Our early activism included my joining the Catholic Church, while Robert joined the Unitarian Fellowship Church—where he was the only Black member. I joined the Catholic Church because Robert had a dear friend, Thomas A. McAvoy, a white priest, who operated a Black mission called St. Joseph's in our community. After we were married, we began to take instructions under Father McAvoy to become Catholic. I subsequently joined the Catholic Church, but Robert never did—even though he and the priest remained friends. Father McAvoy used to tease me, saying that if I hadn't come into Robert's life, he might have gotten him to become a priest.

I started working in the church social service programs in the community—like the Clothes Closet that provided clothing to poor people for free or for a small donation. Since we were a mission, we were able to establish a day care center, which I ran. I was thoroughly involved in social programs during the time I was involved in the Catholic Church.

In addition to that, we worked with the Civic League, an organization of ministers and leaders in the Black community. They were trying to negotiate to keep good relations with the local white power structure. The Civic League was asking for streetlights, sidewalks, and paved streets in the Black community. Not only were people segregated, but the living conditions in our neighborhoods were not maintained. The sidewalks, streetlights, and paved roads would come right up to the borders of the Black community and stop there. We had no Black policemen. That was another issue that the Civic League was trying to negotiate. It's really difficult for people to understand how thoroughly life was segregated in those days.[1]

1. "In addition to . . . in those days": Mabel Williams, interview by Wanda Sabir, "The Political Awakening of Mabel Williams, Wife of Author of 'Negroes with Guns,'" March 17, 2004, *San Francisco Bay View National Black Newspaper*.

CHAPTER 6

MEDICAL GENOCIDE IN THE ELLEN FITZGERALD HOSPITAL

Most Black veterans were looking for work. Those who had finished high school were pressured by the white power structure to take the most menial jobs available, sometimes for even less than the twenty dollars a week that was promised as one of their veterans' benefits. It was very difficult for our young Black men to get good jobs—and keep their jobs, especially if they were rebellious like my husband.

I was able to get menial jobs. I worked at a segregated hospital. Black patients were assigned to the basement, which was unfinished, with exposed pipes running along the walls. The newborn babies were housed in the basement utility room, where we sterilized the instruments and emptied the bedpans. Needles were brought to the utility room to be sterilized after the doctors and nurses used them. The bedpans with waste matter were also taken into the utility room, where the Black babies were. So, babies were being exposed to life-threatening germs. That was one of the most hurtful things that I encountered. I learned a lot about segregation in the hospital—how it affected us as a people. That was a part of the beginning of my education.

I began to see the inequities. All of the supervisory nurses were white. We could hear them talking all the time about what was going on. I remember one conversation. Two nurses were talking about one of the doctors, a white doctor who had joked that he would as soon "work on a dog as work on a nigger." That stuck in my mind and heart. I still don't understand the depth of the racism and the ways we as a people were systematically mistreated medically. They didn't care whether we lived or died. I didn't realize that at the time. I didn't realize that whites were thinking of us as nonhuman. My political consciousness started to develop then. I began to realize what was actually going on—a systematic neglect of Black people. At that time, 75 percent of those babies were not surviving. How could they survive? I had my children at home. The only reason that my sister's child was born in the hospital was that he was having some complications, but most babies at the time—since Black doctors couldn't go into white hospitals—were born at home with Black doctors or midwives.[1]

The white doctors who maintained offices in Monroe had separate waiting rooms for Black people. They would tend to all their white patients before seeing us. Again, I was seeing that something was wrong. It was just so hurtful to see what was happening to our people. Nurses' aides and maids who treated Black people in the basement of the hospital were allowed to perform injections and other procedures that only licensed nurses could do for whites. What happened downstairs didn't matter. And to this day, I feel that was a form of genocide, and that mentality may still be present.[2]

I always wondered why my husband could not get and keep a job, while I could get jobs—small jobs, but jobs nonetheless. I recognize today that this, too, was a part of the system to divide Black men and Black women. Black women were given better opportunities to make a living than Black men. There was always this contention, "I can work, but you can't." I could get a job as a maid. I worked as a hotel maid. I worked in a turkey plant where we processed poultry, working in water almost up to our ankles, in rubber boots. There was a big contingent of women working in those plants but very few men. If a young Black man was not able to get a job working on the railroad, he didn't really have a chance of getting a job that would pay enough to support his family. It was a very difficult time that put pressure on marriages and families.[3]

1. "I was able to get . . . doctors or midwives": Mabel Williams, interview by Wanda Sabir, "The Political Awakening of Mabel Williams, Wife of Author of 'Negroes with Guns,'" March 17, 2004, *San Francisco Bay View National Black Newspaper*.

2. "The white doctors . . . still be present": Mabel Williams, interview by David Cecelski, August 20, 1999, Interview K-0266, Southern Oral History Program Collection (#4007), Center for the Study of the American South, Southern Historical Collection, Wilson Library, University of North Carolina at Chapel Hill, https://dc.lib.unc.edu/cdm/compoundobject/collection/sohp/id/12844/rec/1.

3. "I always wondered . . . marriages and families": Williams, interview by Sabir, "Political Awakening."

CHAPTER 7

NEGROES WITH GUNS

THE MONROE MOVEMENT

Robert attended college until his GI Bill ran out. There was an advertisement saying that if you joined the Marine Corps, the military would pay for your education. He was always writing articles in the newspaper to protest discrimination and segregation and the fact that he could not get a job. So he thought—as a lot of our young minorities do even today when they can't find any other work—well, I can go into the armed services. He decided to go into the marines, assuming that they were going to give him a free education. He thought they would train him for whatever his aptitude tests indicated, but they didn't do that, and he started having all kinds of problems. He was sent to the brig a couple of times.[1] I went out to California to visit him.

We later found out that the FBI had opened and copied pages from my diary and the letters I had written to him. The FBI was investigating him even then. The military didn't train him in a special field as he had hoped, but it did train him as a marine, militarily. His outfit was outstanding in firepower, in methods of self-defense, and in defense of democracy. He had received similar training in the army. As a result, he had been taught well how to handle arms, and he

1. The "brig" is slang for military prison.

had also been taught—and believed in—the American tradition of freedom through guns.[2]

He didn't believe in doing violence to others—except in defense of his own. I think his stance on violent self-defense did more for the civil rights movement than people want to believe, because once those evil people out there found that they couldn't do violence and remain immune, they didn't do as much violence. They assumed that nobody was going to prosecute them, that they weren't going to have to pay a price if they killed. During slavery times, there was a saying, "Kill a nigger, buy another one."[3]

When Robert came back home to Monroe, we started to organize again. He became the president of the local NAACP chapter. The Supreme Court had outlawed segregation in public schools, and we started organizing in the community, getting people together.[4]

Robert Williams began to visit households, pool halls, farms, beauty shops, and barbershops in Union County to recruit members for the local NAACP. His efforts increased the ranks of the chapter with Black working-class men and women, including Black military veterans. The Monroe NAACP began to increase its activity, including protests to desegregate a "white-only" public swimming pool.

The increased activity brought death threats and harassment from the local Ku Klux Klan to the NAACP, its leadership (particularly Williams and chapter vice president Dr. Albert Perry), and the Monroe Black community. Williams organized a Black paramilitary sentry to defend the NAACP, its leadership, and the community from white supremacist, terrorist violence. Williams's Black defense guard repelled a KKK raid on the residence of Dr. Perry on October 5, 1957.[5] The disciplined, organized resistance and firefight that ensued that evening prompted an emergency session of the Monroe City Council, which issued an ordinance to ban KKK motorcades.

Robert organized a rifle club in which we all were members. I'm still a member of the National Rifle Association, the same organization we established

2. "We later found . . . freedom through guns": Mabel Williams, interview by Claude Marks and Lincoln Bergman, May 30 and 31, 2003, San Francisco, CA, MRW Collection.

3. "He didn't believe . . . buy another one'": Mabel Williams, interview by David Cecelski, August 20, 1999, Interview K-0266, Southern Oral History Program Collection (#4007), Center for the Study of the American South, Southern Historical Collection, Wilson Library, University of North Carolina at Chapel Hill, https://dc.lib.unc.edu/cdm/compoundobject/collection/sohp/id/12844/rec/1.

4. "When Robert came . . . getting people together": Williams, interview by Marks and Bergman.

5. Timothy Tyson, *Radio Free Dixie: Robert F. Williams and the Roots of Black Power* (Chapel Hill: University of North Carolina Press, 1999), 88.

in Monroe. We ladies started training, learning how to handle weapons and how to shoot—all for the protection of our homes and ourselves whenever the Klan and other rabble-rousers decided that they wanted to invade our neighborhoods. That's how the rifle club got started, and that's how our self-defense movement began.[6]

6. "Robert organized . . . self-defense movement began": Williams, interview by Marks and Bergman.

CHAPTER 8

THE CRUSADER AND ITS INTERNATIONAL NETWORK

In 1959, we decided that we needed to have a means to tell our own story. Ethel Azalea Johnson, another one of our neighbors on Boyte Street, had become one of our close friends and collaborators. She was an active member of the NAACP, the Parent-Teacher Association, the Civic League, and many other community groups. Azalea, Robert, and I had tried out a Ditto process, where you imprinted an original document on a jelly-like pad and then pressed clean copy paper on it. Realizing that process wouldn't work, we drove up to Charlotte, North Carolina, to look for an alternative method. We had no money—other than our own meager funds, which we were prepared to invest. After exploring machines in several office supply stores, we finally decided on a hand-cranked mimeograph machine. None of us had ever operated one before, so we had to rely on instructions and suggestions from some acquaintances to get started.

The three of us discussed for weeks what we would call our newsletter and who would be responsible for what. We would each write our own articles, with Robert as the editor. Our original equipment was an old upright typewriter on which we learned to type stencils to run on the mimeograph machine. The dining room in our home on 410 Boyte Street became our office. The table served as space to create cartoons, and it accommodated the mimeograph machine, typewriter, and assembly line for stapling pages, stuffing envelopes, and mailings.

We talked about making it a personal journal but decided to make it a community journal, to foster unity within our local struggles and inform our out-of-town friends and supporters. We already had a small mailing list acquired from our travels "up North." We worked collectively to compose cartoons based on Robert's editorials and comments on the issues of the day. We had lots of fun finding, sketching, and creating the cartoons. None of us knew how to draw, but we included our crude sketches.

Our most productive time for working was usually from late afternoon into the wee hours of the morning. Robert suffered from extreme migraine headaches that would sometimes incapacitate him for days. Azalea and I would get our articles ready to run off as we waited for the editorial. Robert's editorial and the cartoon were usually the last items to be printed. Azalea and I would search for short historical items to fill blank spaces before we actually cut the stencils.

Robert used to tease Azalea about the facts in her column, "Did You Know?" She quoted J. A. Rogers quite often. One of the quotes from Rogers stated that a Black man had invented the *okum* picking machine. When Robert asked Azalea what kind of machine that was, she replied that she didn't know. We all laughed about it, only to find out years later that *okum* was the African word for the very popular southern vegetable okra.

We recruited our friends and neighbors to help us with the publishing and distribution of the paper. Once all stencils were cut and ready to be run, the volunteers would come to help. We created a party atmosphere on the day that we ran the assembly line. We ate snacks, some that we provided, some brought in by the other lady volunteers. I was responsible for attaching and inking the machine. Azalea fed the copy paper, and we all took turns at the crank. We had to spread out the pages to dry before we could print them on the reverse side. We learned through trial and error, with some of our early *Crusader* issues showing the errors of our experiments. Once we finished with the printing, we had to lay out, assemble, and staple the pages together.

When the assembly was finished, our sons and other neighborhood kids would take the papers out to sell them locally. They were instructed to leave a paper whether or not the resident could pay for it. The lady volunteers then came back and helped us fold, stuff, and address the envelopes for mailing. That's the way we got our story out to other people. We published *The Crusader* as a weekly newsletter. As a result, people in New York, California, and all around the country knew what was happening in Monroe. As Robert traveled around the country speaking, he learned of other people's struggles. He wrote about those issues as well as pending court cases. There was the "Kissing Case," which involved two little Black boys who allegedly kissed or were kissed by a little white girl. The boys were sent to a youth training center for indeterminate sentences. In addition to writing about such cases, Robert reported on the emerging struggles in Africa, South America, and Cuba.

There was a rising tide of national movements in Africa, people rising up to take control of their own destiny. There were similar movements all over South America. The Native Americans were moving. And we were uniting with all of those people. Through our *Crusader*, we were able to publish what was happening in other movements. We sent our *Crusader* to these other movements so that they could see what was happening not only with us but in uprisings going on all over the world. As a result, we were building a whole network of people who desired change, and we were internationalizing our struggle.

We began to win friends all over the country through *The Crusader* and Robert's public speaking. We developed a very close relationship with a group of activists in New York. During the course of our struggle in Monroe, they organized to support us. The group included Julian Mayfield, Mae Mallory, and many others.[1] The New York friends supported our right to bear arms. They raised money to sustain our efforts and buy rifles for our defense committee.

In the course of his traveling, Robert became acquainted with Malcolm X. Whenever we went to New York, Malcolm would either take us out to a restaurant, or he would invite Robert to speak at the mosque, Temple No. 7, where Malcolm was the minister. Robert began his relationship with Malcolm at that time. They exchanged ideas. I wasn't privy to their conversations, but Robert mentioned that they discussed what was going on in Monroe, Atlanta, all over the South, and all over the world.[2]

1. Julian Mayfield (1928–84) was a Pan-Africanist activist, writer, playwright, and actor.

2. "That's the way we got . . . over the world": Mabel Williams, interview by Claude Marks and Lincoln Bergman, May 30 and 31, 2003, San Francisco, CA, MRW Collection.

CHAPTER 9

MEETING VIOLENCE WITH VIOLENCE

The local power structure in Monroe was committed to segregation. The courts were segregated. Black people had to sit in the balcony of the courts. There were no Black judges. Most of the lawyers were white, and they were protected in the North Carolina system of segregation. Robert kept telling all of our women, "Well, we don't want to take revenge on these white Klansmen for what they're doing to our people. We need to use the legal system in order to make sure that they are brought to understand what the law is, and that they can't just take advantage of us."

There were several cases in which white men abused Black women in Monroe. In one instance, a white man kicked a Black hotel maid, complaining that she was making too much noise as he tried to sleep. He came out of his room and kicked her down the stairs. When she came to report the incident to the NAACP, Robert took it up and went to find a lawyer. We got a volunteer lawyer to come down from New York, but the judge kicked the case out, saying the abuser was not guilty. He just threw it out. Another case, in which a white man accosted a pregnant woman, was brought to us at the NAACP. Robert's response was, "We don't want to do anything. We just want to take it through the court." We took that case through the court, and the judge once again threw the case out. There were four or five similar cases, but these two involved the worst abuse. The ladies complained, "Well, you know, these folks are just gonna do whatever they want to us. If our men don't stand up, support us, and do something, it's just open season. What are you gonna do?" Rob answered, "Well, since we don't have any justice in the courts when people come and do harm to us, we will defend ourselves. We will meet their violence with our violence."

Oh, my God! The press blew that all out of proportion! They said, "Robert Williams advocates the indiscriminate slaughter of white babies in their cribs." That was one of the extreme things they said. We didn't realize at the time that the system of segregation was fighting for its life. The white power structure was going to do everything possible to crush the rising freedom movement.

Hearing all of the news releases, NAACP leaders at the national level got very upset, called Robert, and asked him to retract that statement. Their worry was that the white liberals and others who were giving money to the NAACP would stop contributing and distance themselves from the NAACP. Robert responded, "Well, I can't retract that statement, because that's really what I believe in. I don't think that we should continue to allow the Klan and other racist elements to come into our communities and terrorize our people. I think we should defend ourselves when that happens." He was not talking about aggressive violence but self-defense. However, the NAACP national leaders were so afraid that when he refused to retract his statement, they decided to suspend him as president of the Monroe branch. They suspended him for six months, or until such time as he would recant, or they would revisit the issue. After they suspended him, our local branch voted me in as president, and we just carried on as usual. The NAACP announced to the world that it had suspended Robert Williams for advocating violence. It did not add that his stance was for self-defense.

All this was happening around the time of the fiftieth anniversary of the NAACP. The organization was having a big convention in New York. I don't know how it came about that Robert was invited to New York to appeal to the NAACP to relax or terminate the suspension. Robert addressed the leaders, letting them know that he was not going to retract his statement and that he thought it was wrong of them to suspend him for advocating self-defense. They kept insisting it was a statement advocating violence. They said they would let him know their decision later.

As part of the convention, they were planning a presentation in Harlem in front of the Theresa Hotel. They had built a platform for the distinguished guests. Robert and I were supposed to leave New York that evening, but some of our friends in *The Crusader* family who had organized in New York came to tell Robert, "We don't want you to leave. The NAACP is having a presentation out in front of Hotel Theresa tomorrow, and we want you to speak." This was a group of very robust, strong young men, some from Mosque No. 7, Malcolm X's mosque. Robert asked them, "What do you mean, you want me to speak? The NAACP will not allow me to speak." They assured him, "Don't you worry 'bout that, Brother Rob. They will allow you to speak. We just want you to stay." Robert insisted, "Well, I'll stay on, but I just want you to know, they are not gonna let me speak."

As we were sitting in the crowd at the rally, people started chanting, "We want Rob!" Young people were in the front, leading the crowd in the chants. "We want Rob Williams! We want Rob Williams!" Joe Williams, the famous jazz singer, was there on the platform. In order to try to quiet the crowd, the rally organizers asked Joe to sing "The Star-Spangled Banner." As Joe started singing, the crowd started booing. It was the first time I had ever seen disrespect for the national anthem. Joe Williams, with his beautiful voice, couldn't finish singing it because the crowd was booing! Someone, I don't remember who—trying to keep the crowd under control—got up and announced, "We have a program for you, and we are going to carry it out," but the chanting started again, "We want Williams. We want Williams. We want Williams."

Gloster B. Current, director of NAACP branches at that time, got up and announced to the crowd, "Robert Williams has gone; he is not here. We can't present him to you because he is not here."[1] Then one of the young men from the *Crusader* support group said, "Oh, yes, he is! Oh, yes, he's here." And they came over to where Robert and I were standing and picked him up, physically, although he weighed about 260 pounds at that time. They put him on their shoulders and carried him to the platform. Gloster B. Current was so angry but nodded, "Rob, we gonna let you speak, but we don't want no shit outta you." The crowd heard Robert say, "Well, I didn't ask to come here. If you don't want me to speak, I will leave." The crowd shouted, "No! No!" Then Gloster said, "No, no, no. Come on. We gonna let you speak."

So, they allowed Robert to speak to the crowd out there on the streets of Harlem. He reiterated that we had a right to self-defense, we had a right to protect our homes and our children against the violence of racist offenders, and he would never denounce that right. He said we were within our constitutional rights to defend our homes and children. When he got through speaking, the crowd roared in approval. The young men again picked Rob up physically and brought him back to where I was, on the other side of the street, waiting in amazement. Gloster started calling for the next speakers. The fellas put Robert down and shouted, "No, no, no. The program's over. We heard what we want to hear." They started booing again so that the program couldn't continue.

1. Gloster Current (1913–97) was a deputy in the national leadership of the NAACP from 1946 until 1978.

That was a wonderful day! It was just so inspiring to see how those young people took charge: "This is our community, and you don't come down here and tell us anything unless we approve it." That was beautiful. There really was a growing movement, with everybody learning to work together and loving working together. The people up north—in New York especially—were anxious to see that we got support for the work that we were doing in the South. We were a part of the larger, growing movement of people becoming conscious of the need for change, who were willing to put their lives on the line to make change.[2]

Robert Williams's popularity; his stand on armed resistance, internationalism, and the significance of the Monroe movement; and the popularity of The Crusader *led to his invitation to join a delegation visiting revolutionary Cuba in 1960.*

Robert was invited to go to Cuba with ten other writers and political activists to see what the Cuban Revolution had accomplished right after Fidel Castro came to power. At that time, Cuba had not declared itself a leftist, Communist nation. The Cubans had also invited some Black scholars to come to review the important changes they had made concerning the race issue. When Robert came back, he was instrumental in establishing the Fair Play for Cuba Committee, along with Richard Gibson and some of the other leftists who had visited Cuba.[3] Robert began to travel all over the country to speak on Fair Play for Cuba, trying to get our government to recognize the Cuban government's legitimacy to exist and, hopefully, to have friendly relations with Cuba.[4]

2. "There were several cases . . . to make change": Mabel Williams, interview by Claude Marks and Lincoln Bergman, May 30 and 31, 2003, San Francisco, CA, MRW Collection.

3. The Fair Play for Cuba Committee was a US-based solidarity committee for the Cuban Revolution, established in 1960. Richard Gibson was a novelist and expatriate who worked as a correspondent for CBS News in Europe. Gibson was a cofounder of Fair Play for Cuba while simultaneously working for the Central Intelligence Agency. Robert Williams was unaware of Gibson's relationship with the CIA. See "CIA Reveals Name of Former Spy in JFK Files—and He's Still Alive," *Newsweek*, May 15, 2018, https://www.newsweek.com/richard-gibson-cia-spies-james-baldwin-amiri-baraka-richard-wright-cuba-926428.

4. Robert was invited . . . relations with Cuba": Williams, interview by Marks and Bergman.

CHAPTER 10

MY ROLE, WOMEN, AND BUILDING COMMUNITY IN MONROE

I was able to get jobs and work for a while at menial labor, which helped support the movement. I was helping to organize *The Crusader*—recruiting volunteers, interviewing people about past history, and writing articles. I was also a mother and a wife, trying to help Robert in every way I could. Often, he'd run things by me, and I would be scared to death. I would caution, "Oh, no, don't do that, don't do that;" but he usually convinced me that we had to do whatever it was. And he was usually right. I helped to recruit ladies for our rifle club and defense committee. Not every woman belonged to the rifle club, but most of the women belonged to our defense committee. When one of our men was in trouble or one of our homes was attacked or threatened, we had a telephone line call-up: I would call three people, those three people would call three people, and so on, so that we let everyone know that we had to be on guard, that we might have to meet at somebody's house to help protect their home. Or we might have to go downtown and help out if people were having problems—just show up.

I was actively involved in the struggle in just about every way imaginable. When we had the freedom riders coming in, I helped to find places for them to stay, cooked for them, and introduced them to people in the neighborhood. We were just in the thing together! For instance, there were young Black women with children who would go for help, trying to get what they called "welfare" at that time. But they couldn't get help. So they would come to the NAACP, ask Robert for help, and he would go with them. The social workers would try to embarrass him, asking, "Is this one of your family members?" "Is this your girlfriend?" "What's your interest in this?" They wanted to keep the Black ladies from getting the help to which they were entitled. Robert was able to help some of them get aid for their children. I remember one case in which he had helped out a family in that way, and the father brought us a load of vegetables from his garden at a time when we didn't know where our fresh vegetables would come from. So, we were caring for them, but they were caring for us, too. That's how we were building a sense of community.

People were beginning to care for each other, look out for each other's children, and just work together. We had volunteers who would help us crank out *The Crusader*, staple it, and distribute it. And our *Crusader* family in New York would bring used clothing down to the needy people in our community. They were looking out for the needs of the people in the Monroe community as well. Not only were they supplying guns for us and giving us money to help buy guns, but they were bringing clothes and food down to give away to people. It was just wonderful seeing that purpose and people working together for the good of each other.

A young student from London who had joined the freedom riders and was arrested with them on that Sunday when we had the big blowup,[1] said that she had traveled all over the South, but it was in Monroe that she first felt the brotherhood of human society. She said, "I didn't feel white. I didn't feel English. I just felt a part of the community of people." And that was the kind of spirit that was growing within our movement. Most of the people who joined the movement felt that spirit. They began to feel that they could help make a change by their actions. It was a wonderful feeling.

The Monroe movement had drawn national and international attention from its dynamic armed resistance against the Klan, the distribution and impact of The Crusader, *and the campaign to defend Black children in the "Kissing Case." With the growing national and international significance of the Monroe movement, there was increased collaboration among the Ku Klux Klan, local police agencies, and the FBI.*

1. See chapter 42 of Robert F. Williams, *While God Lay Sleeping* (p. 159), for the beginning of the story of "the big blowup."

CHAPTER 11

THE FBI, THE KKK, AND THE POLICE

In Monroe, the Klan was recruiting right out of the police station. The FBI was working right along with the local officials. Whenever we made a report, we'd go all the way to the FBI office in Charlotte, North Carolina. Robert would report all the illegal things that the police were doing to Black people. The FBI would come to the sheriff's department and tell the sheriff what Rob had reported but would never get back to him. Rob would call and say, "Well, I'm sure you saw in the paper that they're getting ready to have a Klan rally at such-and-such a place. The police are usually there to support the Klan." The FBI agent would answer, "Well, yeah, well, OK, thank you." We found out after we got our Freedom of Information files that the Klan was in cahoots with the chief of police.

Several attempts were made on Robert's life. In one instance, the bigots tried to run him over in his little Hillman car. One day we were on the way to the swimming pool, which we were picketing because the city would not allow access to Black children. We had to drive right by the state police post. A Klan car got between my car and the car Rob was driving, and the Klansmen tried to bump Rob off the road. This happened right in front of the state police post, with state police watching what was going on, but they never once tried to intercede. An attempt on his life, in plain view of the state police, and they did nothing! It just so happened that Rob was able to outmaneuver them. He was reaching for his rifle—which he carried all the time—but the seat had fallen down over the rifle, and he couldn't quite reach it. The Klan attackers sped off, realizing that he was reaching for his rifle. He reported the incident to the police chief, who told him, "If you go and bring him in, we'll see if we can issue a warrant for him." Obviously, there was collusion. The police were working with the Klan, and the FBI was supporting them. They were trying to preserve their system of segregation that had been enforced for so many years—but it was about to be cracked.

CHAPTER 12

THE COORDINATED ATTACK ON THE MONROE MOVEMENT

Robert Williams and The Crusader *movement served as an ideological counterpoint to the argument that nonviolence was the most important vehicle for victory of the Black freedom struggle. The nonviolent wing of the civil rights movement decided to initiate a direct-action campaign by sending "freedom riders" to Monroe to challenge segregation and to prove that passive resistance could work there.*

Freedom riders, Black and white students from all over, were sent to Monroe by Martin Luther King's organization to do nonviolent workshops and participate in our struggle. They picketed around the courthouse and called on the county and city officials to relent on their hard segregationist stand, but we were protecting our community with guns. We had an arrangement with the freedom riders that we would not take guns out of our own neighborhoods. We would practice nonviolence on the picket lines downtown, but we would not allow violent people to come into our neighborhoods, threaten us, or do harm to us. We were armed and ready to defend our community.

The city officials decided they were going to crush our movement. They sprayed the protesters from their insecticide trucks. Then the police and the white crowd beat both the students and the local picketers. Among those arrested was a young white woman student from England who had come to the United States to join the civil rights movement. It was a Sunday, and people were just getting out of church. They heard that students were being beaten and thrown in jail, and out of concern, they began to gather in our area of town. We were trying to organize our community to keep things from getting out of hand.

A white couple, Mr. and Mrs. Bruce Stegall, drove into our community as all of this was happening. A group of angry citizens advised them to get out of their car. The couple then walked up the street to our house, came into our yard, talked with Robert, and tried to get him to take them out of the community. Robert told them, "I didn't bring you in the community, and I'm not taking you out." They stayed a while and then left. Later they said that they didn't think that they had been kidnapped; they just thought that they had been mistreated. They went home and forgot about the incident; but when the police and the press got involved, the incident became a kidnapping.

Mrs. Stegall made a tape on which she stated that she and her husband didn't consider the incident a kidnapping. She said they thought they were mistreated because the people in the street made them get out of the car and walked them up to our house. She said that she thought she was being treated wrongly, but she didn't call that kidnapping. The talk of kidnapping began when the police and the press came to her house. There are so many details involved in what the officials did and how they did it to construct a kidnapping charge.

In any case, we knew that the main reason that the police had vamped on [attacked] the students that day was that they were planning to crush our movement. The Klan and the state forces from Georgia and South Carolina had told the local officials that they would come in and help to stamp out our movement. So, when the police chief phoned and threatened Robert, we made the decision to leave. We knew that they were going to come and try to kill him. In fact, he was told on the telephone, "In thirty minutes, you'll be hanging in the courthouse square." We decided to leave and come back later. We left. They surrounded the house. When they found out we were not there, they trumped up the kidnapping charge in order to have Robert brought back.

CHAPTER 13

FLIGHT

We left Monroe in the middle of the night. With the help of some of our *Crusader* family from New York and local people, we were able to escape Monroe, thinking that we would go to New York and stay there until things blew over. Robert urged me, "Get the children; we have to go." I was afraid that if the children and I went with him, we would slow him down and they might catch up with him and kill him before he could even get out of town. But he insisted, "No, you know that if you and the children stay here, I can't go in peace. They know that, and they would use you to bring me back here and get rid of me." That is what they were trying to do. He insisted that we go with him, and we did.

When we got to New York, we found out that the FBI had issued an all-points bulletin for Robert, saying he was armed and dangerous and traveling in the company of his family. It was a "shoot on sight" kind of announcement. The FBI posted his picture in the post offices as one of the "Ten Most Wanted" criminals in the United States. The criminal charge was a so-called kidnapping of the white couple who had come into our community.

Our supporters in New York went to Malcolm at the mosque and out on the Harlem streets, and in a few minutes they had raised enough money to get us out of the country and provide for us for as long as necessary. This was possible because of Malcolm's congregation and the Harlem community—particularly people who frequented Mr. Michaux's bookstore on 125th Street.[1] During his visits to New York, Robert would speak from the ladder in front of the store, and people would raise money to buy guns and help us.

We received all kinds of support from the New York community and from the organizations that had been helping us, as well as from their extended contacts. I had never thought about leaving the country. I didn't have a passport. When we left Monroe with the Klan and the state police in hot pursuit, we were thinking that once we got to New York, we would stay there until things cooled down and then come back to Monroe; but then the FBI put out the all-points bulletin for Robert, and we knew we had to get out of the country.

People that I had never seen before took us in. A couple volunteered to take our two children, who were eleven and thirteen, and I didn't see them anymore until we got to Cuba, which was months later. That's just how wonderful that network of friends and supporters was—and how it had grown simply because we had stood up and said that we wanted to make a change in the way things were. People just joined in to help us make that change.

We had supporters in Toronto who used to distribute *The Crusader* for us. They had also worked with Robert as members of the Fair Play for Cuba Committee. Some of our New York friends contacted them to let them know what was happening, and they responded immediately, "Yes, come on up." We decided to go to Canada because the Canadians had never extradited any Black people to the United States when they were engaged in human rights struggles. We thought we would go to Canada, where we would be safe, stay there until things cleared up, and then come back home.[2]

After crossing the border from New York into Canada, Robert; the medical doctor; my walking escort, Zaid; and I met friends from Toronto, Lloyd and Helen. They were waiting at a predesignated site to drive us on to Toronto. We bade our friends farewell after heartfelt tears of appreciation and were off. When we arrived in Toronto, our longtime friends and supporters Anne and Vernal Olson were waiting with open arms to greet us and receive us into their home at 21 Ellis Gardens. We sat in their living room and recounted our escape ordeal and our mutual struggles.

1. Lewis Michaux was the owner of the African National Memorial Bookstore in Harlem, an important institution in the Black Nationalist community of New York.

2. "We left Monroe . . . come back home": Mabel Williams, interview by Claude Marks and Lincoln Bergman, May 30 and 31, 2003, San Francisco, CA, MRW Collection.

Verne and Anne were political activists who had supported the Cuban government since the triumph of the revolution. After Robert visited Cuba and became one of the founding members of the Fair Play for Cuba Committee, he had spoken to a group in Toronto, which was hosted by Anne and Verne. Afterward, they stayed in touch with us and continued to distribute our *Crusader* newsletter in Toronto. They continued their unwavering friendship and support throughout our entire torturous eight-year exile—our extradition struggle and beyond. Our friendship endured through the years until they both passed away. This dedicated couple lived the doctrines that they espoused. They put their own lives and personal interests on the line to actually fight for the greater good of mankind and especially the working poor.

Historically, Canada had never returned anyone who was escaping slavery in the United States or any Black person fleeing injustice in the United States, so all of us felt quite confident that we were now "home free" from the conspirators. We proceeded to live with the Olsons in relative openness until one day the daily newspaper carried a large picture of Robert on the front page. The story stated that Rob was "armed and dangerous" and was traveling in the company of his family. The FBI had asked the Royal Canadian Mounted Police (RCMP) to help the agency apprehend and send Rob back to the United States, and the RCMP had agreed to do so. We were all shocked and horrified by this news.

The newspaper had included the photo to help the public identify Robert. Thankfully, it was an old picture, and Rob looked very different by then because I had shaved his head and his beard while we were on the run.

The Olsons went to work immediately to find a place for us to hide inside their home. Then they appealed to their network of political activist friends to help find an appropriate place for us to go before the RCMP came calling. Within a few hours, I had thrown together the few belongings that I had brought from North Carolina and was being driven to a home to stay with a West Indian family. They welcomed me at the door and showed me to a room where I would live until further arrangements could be made.

Once again, I was isolated from everyone and everything that I had known for all my life. I could have no contact with Robert, my sons, my family, or friends in Monroe—not even the Olsons. I could not call or write to them. For my own safety, I had to attempt to become a part of this wonderful host family of husband, wife, son, and daughter. I was a visiting relative.

My head was swimming, my heart breaking, and I could not control the tears. I thought I would never see my family, my hometown, or my friends again. I was debating whether I should just run away back to the United States and try to find my sons. Would we be safe, or would we be killed to make an example for others who dared to challenge the system? I wondered where Robert was and if he would be safe. If he was caught and sent back, how would I know what happened? Would I ever see him again? I prayed day and night for the protection of Robert and the boys, for our friends who were still in Monroe, and for those who had helped us to escape.

My host family was so supportive. The mother allowed me to help with the kitchen chores and preparation of the meals and tried to engage me in conversations while we worked. When the father was at home, he talked to me about things that had no relevance to my situation. The children brought out the board games they liked. They tried to interest me in playing the games I knew and in learning new games. Of course, they would beat me even in those that I knew because I had no heart for playing. Nevertheless, the games were a distraction that brought about some fun and laughter and helped relieve some of the pressure that I was feeling. Yet I am sure my presence put a strain on that family.

After what seemed an eternity, Anne Olson showed up one evening. She assured me that our boys were being cared for by a family in New York and that Robert was still safe but was now in a different city in Canada. She presented me with a letter from home. Ethel Azalea Johnson, our *Crusader* partner, had written to me under Anne's name and had mailed the letter from Philadelphia, where she had gone for refuge after our departure. She enclosed a letter from my mother and sister and reported on events that had occurred after our escape.

That visit with Anne was like a welcome rain on a summer day after a long dry spell. It brought relief from the stress of worry but also increased my longing for family, home, and friends. Anne stayed for only a short while, spoke briefly with all of us, and warned us that the FBI and the RCMP were still searching for us and that we needed to continue to live under cover while preparations were being made to get us out of Canada to Cuba.

We went to Cuba out of necessity. It was the only other place available to us. Since Robert had done speaking tours for the Fair Play for Cuba Committee and the Olsons were a part of that committee, they contacted the Cuban embassy to see if the Cuban government could help us get away. And as it turns out, we learned later that Fidel Castro had notified the Cuban embassies around the world when he found out that Robert was in trouble, instructing them that they should help him in any way they could should he show up. That's how we were able to go to Cuba.[3]

3. "We went to Cuba . . . go to Cuba": Williams, interview by Marks and Bergman.

CHAPTER 14

FROM CANADA TO MEXICO TO CUBA

I was provided an outfit of different clothing and a small suitcase of items. I was told to prepare for travel the following day and that I should not include any items that might identify me with Robert, the boys, or Monroe. That meant that I needed to destroy the precious letter that Azalea had sent me, which had been my only solace for weeks. The next morning, Anne came, presented me with a passport, and drove me to the airport. I was given a ticket to Mexico and was told that I should proceed as though I was the person on the passport. Anne told me that Lloyd, Helen, and a contingent of supporters were going to be very close by so that if I should be stopped at any time, I should start screaming, "Help!" as loud as I could. They were prepared to stage a protest on my behalf if the authorities tried to prevent me from leaving.

I was now really conflicted. I had learned that Robert was already in Cuba, the boys were in Canada, and I was on my way to Cuba. This meant that once again I was to be farther away from the boys, much farther from my family and friends in Monroe, and on my way to places I had only heard about through others. I knew that I could not continue to cry about my situation. I needed to be as calm as possible. I prayed for strength and proceeded to follow the instructions. I presented my credentials to the authorities at the airport. They simply glanced at me and the document and waved me on through without the slightest hesitation.

When I arrived in Mexico, I was warmly greeted by a woman who spoke to me in English with a heavy Spanish accent, grabbed my arm, and walked me through the airport to a waiting car. Once inside the car, she told me how relieved she was that I had arrived safely and that I would be in her home for a few days before traveling on to Cuba.

My hostess provided me with toiletries and some new clothing and showed me to a bedroom with shower and restroom. I was told to rest and that she would come and get me for dinner. In the evening, my hostess came and escorted me into a room full of guests who had come to dinner in her home. I didn't know or recognize any of them. I was introduced as a visiting teacher from Trinidad, passing through. I was left to my own thoughts as they discussed world political issues, politics in Mexico, cultural personalities, and events.

After being served a variety of wines, pastries, and cheeses by Mexican house servants, we were ushered into a huge dining area where we were seated around a dining table outfitted with ornate crystal, china, silverware, candles, and unique floral arrangements. My hostess introduced me to several Mexican dishes as they were being served throughout the multiple courses. This was my very first experience with formal dining. It ushered me into a new world of diplomacy that I had only read about in books or heard my mother describe from her work as a servant to the Belk family. In my room after the meal, I was once again immersed in thoughts of home, family, and friends. I was thankful that I was safe in Mexico, but I cried myself to sleep.

My travel on to Cuba was without incident. By then I realized that the authorities were not interested enough in a Black woman traveling alone to look twice at my documents. Robert was waiting at the airport when I arrived. He was in a car provided by the Cuban government. Our reunion was glorious, with tears flowing freely, as we held on to each other, questioned each other, and wondered about our boys.

CHAPTER 15

REFUGE IN CUBA

The Hotel Capri was to be our home for the next few months. When I arrived from the airport, the doormen opened the car doors and welcomed me to the hotel. It was a fascinating experience for me, being treated with respect and dignity. My new home away from home was beautiful. Our suite on the third floor was spacious, more than adequate for our needs. We were provided daily maid service. We ordered our meals from the menu in the main restaurant. Although the menu was limited in the variety of items available every day, our meals were healthy and substantial.

My interactions with Fidel Castro were very limited. The only time that I got a chance to say "thank you" to him was shortly after I arrived in Havana. We were sitting in the lobby of the Capri Hotel, speaking with some students from Africa and the United States. Suddenly individual soldiers arrived and walked through, intermingling with the crowd. Everyone became very quiet, and people started to whisper, "Fidel is coming." Soldiers stood at the ready in front of the casino doors and the elevators, blocking anyone else from entering the lobby.

Within a few minutes, Fidel came in with other officials, stopping to shake hands and chat briefly with people as he moved through the crowd. When he reached us, he welcomed all of us in English as he shook our hands. Robert spoke with him for a few minutes. There was a brief exchange when Fidel introduced Robert to one of the officials who was traveling with him. When Fidel got to me, I was in an emotional state, with tears flowing. I blurted out a thank-you to him for saving Robert, our boys, and me. I was told later that his reply was,

"No need to thank me. It was our duty." That whole visit in the hotel lasted less than half an hour.

After Fidel left the hotel, our dialogue with the students continued well into the evening. We all waited in quiet anticipation for the broadcast of what was to be a major policy speech. We listened to the loudspeakers in the lobby as Fidel addressed the animated crowd. He asked whether revolutionaries should continue to tolerate gambling when the country was experiencing such economic pressures. He expounded on the issue, then said finally that as of that date, Cuba's famous casinos would be closed. Soldiers stood on guard as the hotel casino doors were locked. After that meeting, I saw Fidel only from a distance—as he was passing through gatherings with his entourage or at the large rallies where he spoke.

CHAPTER 16

CRUSADER IN EXILE AND *RADIO FREE DIXIE*

Before we went to Cuba, we used to send *The Crusader* there. So many Cubans were aware of our struggle in the United States. There had been a good deal of publicity and stories in their newspapers concerning our being granted exile in Cuba. Once we were settled there and established as a family again, we met many ordinary Cubans out on the street, wherever we went. Sometimes they would pass by the hotel and notice, "Oh, there's Robert Williams!" Often, they would come over and talk. Robert was talking to one particular man about *The Crusader* and how we used to publish it in the United States. The gentleman asked, "Why don't you put it out again here?" Robert answered that he didn't think he could. The man persisted: "I work in a printshop. I'll go and see if the people will do it. I think we'll do it for nothing. We'll print it for you." Robert repeated that he didn't think that would be possible. However, the man went to his printshop and called the union folk together, and they decided they would indeed print the newsletter—free of charge. That's how *The Crusader* got started in Cuba, *The Crusader* in Exile.

We resumed publishing Robert's editorials about the struggle. We were beginning to get newspapers and clippings from our network of friends all over the United States. They would send us information—by direct mail, through Canada, and sometimes through Mexico. We also got magazines and other publications. That's how we kept up with the news. In addition to that, we listened to shortwave radio. Strangely enough, we got more information about what was going on in the US civil rights struggle from the BBC than we got from US radio. Occasionally we could get public radio as well. We also received personal journals and newsletters that were being published by movement activists; but Robert insisted that there was nothing coming out of the United States officially that was really telling Black people's story, and we needed to get that message out. So, he approached Fidel Castro with the idea of establishing a radio program. Fidel liked the idea and gave Robert permission to develop it. Rob decided to call it *Radio Free Dixie*.

It took a while for us to get the program up and running, but with Fidel's backing and his instructions to the people not to interfere with what we wanted to say, we were able to finally get *Radio Free Dixie* on the air. In the meantime, we were requesting and receiving records—jazz records, protest records—from our network of friends in the United States, Canada, Mexico, wherever. Robert wanted to include the jazz and protest music that was coming out of our struggle to attract listeners. Once we had the people's attention through the music, we would give them the message of Black people's ongoing freedom fight in the United States.

We had volunteer help from the Cubans and from some of the other exiles who were living in Cuba, but Robert wrote his own script. The editorials were his. I helped select the music, but my main jobs were reading news items concerning current affairs in the US and making announcements. We prepared a weekly program that was aired twice a week. That's how *Radio Free Dixie* was born.[1]

1. "Before we went . . . *Radio Free Dixie* was born": Mabel Williams, interview by Claude Marks and Lincoln Bergman, May 30 and 31, 2003, Baldwin, MI, MRW Collection.

CHAPTER 17

BIRMINGHAM AND MAO ZEDONG

During this time, the civil rights and student movements were heating up. White officials in the South were terrorizing protesters with dogs, spraying them with water hoses, and allowing white crowds to beat them. Then, all of a sudden, we got the news that four little Black girls had been killed while in Sunday school in a Birmingham church. The church had been blown up, the little girls killed, and others injured. Given such a horrendous act, Robert feared that if some worldwide attention were not brought to bear, there would a genocidal maneuver to crush our movement. With that in mind, he fired off telegrams to leaders all over the world. He urged leaders—presidents, prime ministers—and all to speak out against the genocidal attacks against Black people in the South. He received two responses that were noteworthy. One was from the Cambodian Chief of State [Norodom] Sihanouk of Cambodia, the other from Chairman Mao Zedong of China.

We were told that Chairman Mao's statement was the first political statement he had issued in ten years. He understood what was happening and was moved by Robert's persistence. He issued a statement calling on all the people of the world to support the American Negro in our struggle against racial discrimination in the United States. The statement endeared Chairman Mao and the Chinese people to us because they had come to our aid when we felt that if something had not been done, and the trend had continued of the church bombings, water hoses, and dogs, the genocidal attacks would have escalated, and our movement would have been wiped out. After Chairman Mao's statement, the US government started sending in troops to protect Black people and, in a limited fashion, started reining in some of the racist officials. That was what Rob had hoped—that something would happen to stop the genocidal attacks.[1]

CHAIRMAN MAO TSE-TUNG'S STATEMENT CALLING UPON THE PEOPLE OF THE WORLD TO UNITE TO OPPOSE RACIAL DISCRIMINATION BY U.S. IMPERIALISM AND SUPPORT THE AMERICAN NEGROES IN THEIR STRUGGLE AGAINST RACIAL DISCRIMINATION

AUGUST 8, 1963

An American Negro leader now taking refuge in Cuba, Mr. Robert Williams, the former President of the Monroe, North Carolina Chapter of the National Association for the Advancement of Coloured People has twice this year asked me for a statement in support of the American Negroes' struggle against racial discrimination. I wish to take this opportunity, on behalf of the Chinese people, to express our resolute support for the American Negroes in their struggle against racial discrimination and for freedom and equal rights.

There are more than 19 million Negroes in the United States, or about 11 percent of the total population. Their position in society is one of enslavement, oppression and discrimination. The overwhelming majority of the Negroes are deprived of their right to vote. On the whole it is only the most back-breaking and most despised jobs are open to them. Their average wages are only from a third or a half of those of the white people. The ratio of unemployment among them is the highest. In many states they cannot to go to the same school, eat at the same table, or travel in the same section of a bus or a train with the white people. Negroes are frequently and arbitrarily arrested, beaten up and murdered by U.S. authorities at various levels and members of the Ku Klux Klan and other racists. About half of the American Negroes are concentrated in eleven states in the south of the United States. There, the discrimination and persecution they suffer are especially startling.

The American Negroes are awakening, and their resistance is growing ever stronger. In recent years the mass struggle of the American Negroes

1. "During this time . . . the genocidal attacks": Mabel Williams, interview by Claude Marks and Lincoln Bergman, May 30 and 31, 2003, Baldwin, MI, MRW Collection.

against racial discrimination and for freedom and equal rights has been constantly developing.

In 1957 the Negro people in Little Rock, Arkansas, waged a fierce struggle against the barring of their children from public schools. The authorities used armed force against them, and there resulted the Little Rock incident which shocked the world.

In 196, Negroes in more than twenty states held "sit-in" demonstrations in protest against racial segregation in local restaurants, shops and other public places.

In 1961 the Negroes launched a campaign of "freedom riders" to oppose racial segregation in transport, a campaign which rapidly extended to many states.

In 1962 the Negroes in Mississippi fought for the equal right to enroll in colleges and were greeted by the authorities with repression which culminated in a bloodbath.

This year, the struggle of the American Negroes started in early April in Birmingham, Alabama. Unarmed, bare-handed Negro masses were subjected to wholesale arrests and the most barbarous repression merely because they were holding meetings and parades against racial discrimination. On 12 June, an extreme was reached with the cruel murder of Mr. Medgar Evers, a leader of the Negro people in Mississippi. These Negro masses, aroused to indignation and undaunted by ruthless violence, carried on their struggles even more courageously and quickly won the support of Negroes and all strata of the people throughout the United States. A gigantic and vigorous nationwide struggle is going on in nearly every state and city in the United States, and the struggle keeps mounting. American Negro organizations have decided to start a "freedom march" on Washington on 28 August, in which 250,000 people will take part.

The speedy development of the struggle of the American Negroes is a manifestation of the constant sharpening of class struggle and national struggle within the United States; it has been causing increasingly grave anxiety to the U.S. ruling clique. The Kennedy Administration has resorted to cunning two-faced tactics. On the one hand, it continues to connive at and take part in the discrimination against and persecution of Negroes; it even sends troops to suppress them. On the other hand, it is parading as an advocate of the "defence of human rights" and the "protection of the civil rights of Negroes," is calling upon the Negro people to exercise "restraint," and is proposing to Congress so-called "civil rights legislation" in an attempt to numb the fighting will of the Negro people and deceive the masses throughout the country. However, these tactics of the Kennedy Administration are being seen through by more and more of the Negroes. The fascist atrocities committed by the U.S. imperialists against the Negro people have laid bare the true nature of the so-called democracy and freedom in the United States and revealed the inner link between the reactionary policies pursued by the U.S. Government at home and its policies of aggression abroad.

I call upon the workers, peasants, revolutionary intellectuals, enlightened elements of the bourgeoisie, and other enlightened personages of all colours in the world, white, black, yellow, brown, etc., to unite to oppose the racial discrimination practiced by U.S. imperialism and to support the American Negroes in their struggle against racial discrimination. In the final analysis, a national struggle is a question of class struggle. In the United States, it is only the reactionary ruling clique among the whites which is oppressing the Negro people. They can in no way represent the workers, farmers, revolutionary intellectuals, and other enlightened persons who comprise the overwhelming majority of the white people. At present, it is the handful of imperialists, headed by the United States, and their supporters, the reactionaries in different countries, who are carrying out oppression, aggression and intimidation against the overwhelming majority of the nations and peoples of the world. They are the minority, and we are the majority. At most they make up less than 10 percent of the 3,000 million people of the world. I am deeply convinced that, with the support of more than 90 percent of the people of the world, the just struggle of the American Negroes will certainly be victorious. The evil system of colonialism and imperialism grew on along with the enslavement of the Negroes and the trade in Negroes; it will surely come to its end with the thorough emancipation of the black people.[2]

We were overjoyed by this strong statement of support from the Chinese government. We began to receive congratulations from friends in Africa, Asia, South America, and elsewhere. Most of the North American leftists in Cuba were not at all pleased about the statement. They tried to argue against it by inferring that it was racial in nature and would widen the chasm between the white and Black working-class people in the United States and weaken the white support

2. Mao Zedong, "Calling Upon the People of the World to Unite to Oppose Racial Discrimination by U.S. Imperialism and Support the American Negroes in Their Struggle Against Racial Discrimination," August 8, 1963, as printed in *Peking Review*, August 16, 1963, https://www.marxists.org/subject/china/peking-review/1963/PR1963-33a.htm.

for our struggle. The Eastern Europeans were vocally opposed as well. The Cold War was heating up, and anti-China hysteria was growing. Some of our Cuban friends who had previously been outspoken in support of the Chinese were not being as vocal as before.

Meanwhile, the US government got busy and recruited three of its approved Black "leaders" to send a letter to Chairman Mao, saying that the Negro people did not need or want the support of the Chinese people. It was signed by Roy Wilkins of the NAACP and by James Farmer and Roy Innis of CORE.

CHAPTER 18

MEETING CHAIRMAN MAO

My first visit to China was made after Chairman Mao had issued his "Statement Supporting the American Negroes in Their Just Struggle against Racial Discrimination." We were invited to attend the Chinese National Day Celebration on October 1, 1963. We were met at the airport in Beijing by a high-level delegation, welcomed to China, and escorted to the Peking Hotel, where we would be staying. We attended several pre-anniversary activities during the week, hosted by various officials. We were introduced to diplomats and other participants. The guests were representatives of revolutionary organizations from Asia, Africa, North and South America, and Europe.

There was a private gathering for these distinguished guests before the official celebration began. The top officials came in, greeted the guests, and gave a personal welcome. Some of the celebration events were held in the Great Hall of the People. It was at one of these activities that I met the Chairman for the first time.

He was, to my great surprise, warm, friendly, and outgoing. He moved around in a relaxed manner, chatted, and shook hands with the guests. He spoke through his interpreter, welcoming us to China. When he greeted me, I thanked him for lending his support to our struggle. I was so excited that I don't remember all of the details of that first meeting. The Chairman's interaction with us and the other guests was down-to-earth and a pleasure to watch. He seemed so humble. In that atmosphere, I truly began to feel that I was playing an important role in

Robert Williams welcomed at a Shanghai rally to support the African American freedom struggle, 1963. Robert F. Williams Papers, Bentley Historical Library, University of Michigan.

the international movement to make a difference in the world for our people and struggling people everywhere.

During our stay in China, we traveled all over the country. Robert was allowed to speak at colleges, high schools, primary schools, and universities. The people held rallies in support of our struggle in Shanghai, Beijing, and Guangzhou—all the major cities. The Chinese had an ongoing campaign in support of African Americans and our struggle. We were able to expand our network of international friends while we were there. We met Cambodian chief of state Sihanouk and other leaders when we attended diplomatic functions. Rob and I used to laugh about the fact that we had to leave America to be recognized as Americans. Every time we were introduced, we were introduced as "representatives of the American people." We would laugh about that.

Let me say that seeing a society in transition is a marvelous thing—from Cuba to China, even watching our society as it struggles and struggles and struggles. But seeing a society where the people are mobilized to make changes is just a marvelous experience that the Klan didn't have any idea we would have, or they wouldn't have run us out of Monroe! It was a beautiful experience, seeing a whole society trying to refocus its interest on serving the people, the little people who'd been left out and left behind.

When we first went to visit China, the people received us with open arms. We sympathized very much with the Chinese working people because we saw how hard they were working. There were women and children pulling heavy loads, pulling them in the streets. You could see the veins popping in their heads as they pulled those heavy loads of produce. They didn't have a transportation system then; but the next time we went, we saw trucks hauling the same kind of cargo. Trucks were gradually replacing the human beasts of burden. And then after the Soviet Union got angry with China and left, and the trucks were no longer operating on a regular basis, we saw the people put propane tanks on the top of the trucks to keep them operating. We could see a society in transition.[1]

1. "During our stay . . . society in transition": Mabel Williams, interview by Claude Marks and Lincoln Bergman, May 30 and 31, 2003, Baldwin, MI, MRW Collection.

CHAPTER 19

MEETING HO CHI MINH

Mabel and Robert Williams were invited to visit the Democratic Republic of Vietnam (North Vietnam) during their second visit to China, when the United States was engaged in military intervention in South Vietnam.

Robert and I traveled to Vietnam along with members of the China Peace Committee, our host agency, and a delegation of Americans who were living and working in China. We attended an international gathering in support of peace for the Vietnamese people, held November 25–29, 1965. The official name of the conference was "The International Conference for Solidarity with the People of Vietnam against US Imperialists, for the Defense of Peace." On the first or second evening of our stay in Hanoi, we were invited, along with the other American guests, to visit President Ho at the Presidential Palace.

President Ho met us at the door, welcomed us individually in English, and shook our hands vigorously. He then escorted us into a cozy room where we were invited to sit comfortably. There was a member of the South Vietnam [National] Liberation Front there as well. When an attendant brought in tea, President Ho promptly got up, took the pot, and served us himself.

In a very relaxed manner, President Ho sat down to share tea with us—but not in one of the plush chairs that we all occupied. His chair seemed lower and unpadded. He proceeded to tell us that he did not live in the palace but in a simple home in the countryside, where he had been living since their anti-colonial struggle began. He talked about the war and his life experiences growing up in the struggle. There was much animated discussion, including memories of his interaction with Black people—especially Marcus Garvey and others—in his world travels as a merchant seaman.[1] I listened intently, feeling at ease in the presence of this great world leader.

President Ho described the terrors of the ongoing war and then invited a young boy to come in to meet us. The child had burn scars all over his body from napalm bombs that had been dropped on his village. He told us about the horror that these bombs were inflicting on peasants as they tried to work in their fields. At that moment, I felt deeply that I hated war and what it did to people, especially children.

As the conversation wound down, President Ho told us that he had learned that it was the birthday of one of the guests, Anna Louise Strong.[2] To our surprise, an attendant then brought in a birthday cake with candles. President Ho presented the cake to Ms. Strong, and we all sang "Happy Birthday." As Ms. Strong cut the cake, the president helped serve a slice to each of us. We were delighted. By evening's end, I was glowing.

Rob spoke at the conference. He talked about our struggle as part of the worldwide struggle of the little people of the world who want a better life. We offered tapes from *Radio Free Dixie*, which, I am told, were used at a later broadcast. Attendance at the peace conference was the only time that we were in Vietnam.

We met with Everett Alvarez, a pilot who had been shot down over Vietnam.[3] The Vietnamese brought him to have an evening with us and offered to give him to Robert as a token of peace between our peoples. Robert responded, "I can't even go home myself; but I will see if there's anything I can do to get him released." The Vietnamese had captured only one American pilot at that point. Robert contacted all kinds of peace groups in the United States and asked them if they would intercede to bring him home, but they were too scared to take a stand. Not one peace group in the United States—among all those who were

1. Marcus Garvey (1887–1940) was a Jamaican-born Black Nationalist and Pan-Africanist who formed an international organization, the Universal Negro Improvement Association (UNIA). During a time when all of the African continent was colonized, Garvey envisioned building an independent African empire under the slogan "Africa for Africans at home and abroad." The UNIA (aka the Garvey movement) was initiated in 1914 and grew to a global organization by 1920 with membership throughout the Americas, Africa, Europe, India, and Australia.

2. Anna Louise Strong (1885–1970) was an anti-capitalist author, a journalist, and an anti-imperialist activist who worked in solidarity with the Soviet Union and the People's Republic of China. She became an expatriate in China from 1958 until her death in 1970.

3. Everett Alvarez (b. 1937) was a US Navy pilot captured by the Vietnamese in 1964 and released in 1973.

calling themselves peace groups—would say, "We will appeal to Hanoi to let us have him." I never will forget when he came to our hotel that evening to spend a few hours with us. He asked us if the government had sent us to Vietnam. "The US government?" Robert asked. "No, I came over here as a friend of the Vietnamese people. I'm opposed to the war. They sent you here to see if there was a way we can help you get out of here." That possibility fell through, to Rob's disappointment. Very little was ever said about that. The peace people talked about the Logan Act or something.[4] They were afraid that helping Alvarez might be construed as "collaborating with the enemy," or something like that. I think Alvarez remained there for nine more years. He was finally released when the war was over.[5]

4. The Logan Act was a federal law prohibiting unauthorized individuals and parties from negotiating with a state in conflict with the United States.

5. "Rob spoke at the conference . . . war was over": Mabel Williams, interview by Claude Marks and Lincoln Bergman, May 30 and 31, 2003, San Francisco, CA, MRW Collection.

CHAPTER 20

CONTRADICTIONS IN CUBA

Rob was a person with a keen political sense who could analyze situations far better than most people. While we were in Cuba, there was a worldwide political struggle going on. One of the main struggles was between the United State and the Soviet Union. Both nations were trying to win the allegiance of Third World peoples. Additionally, in the Communist world, there was a struggle going on between the Soviet Union and China. These countries were seeking to influence Third World peoples concerning how they should fight for their rights, whether through elections or proletarian revolution. When Chairman Mao came out in support of Black people against racial discrimination in the US, the US government saw a necessity to support the civil rights movement minimally.

In the meantime, the Soviet Union and China were vying for the Cuban Revolution. So, there were political struggles going on the whole time that we were there. There were elements within Cuba who wanted to follow the Soviet line, and elements that preferred the Chinese line. However, the Soviet Union was providing the most economic support, undergirding the Cuban economy. The United States had declared a boycott against Cuba, requiring the Cubans to make certain economic choices. And though it appeared that the Cubans were more spiritually in accord with the Chinese, they were economically forced to ally with the Soviets.

Those struggles filtered down to the ordinary folks like us—Rob and me, *Radio Free Dixie*, *The Crusader*, and all the things we were doing. At one point, a Cuban official came and remarked to Rob that we still had a picture of Chairman

Mao Zedong on the wall in the house that the Cuban government had provided for us. He told us, "In Cuba, we're taking down Mao's photos." Rob answered, "Yes, I understand that, but this photo was given to me and signed by Chairman Mao, autographed, and I plan to keep my photo. Chairman Mao came through as a friend of the Black people when we were struggling. So, I plan to keep my photo up." The Cuban official cautioned, "You know, those people who don't follow the line that the party establishes are considered counterrevolutionary." Rob pushed back, "Well, I know that you know that I am not a counterrevolutionary, and I hope that would never cross your mind; but I'm keeping my picture up."

Rob realized at that moment that it was not in our best interest to remain in Cuba and continue our *Radio Free Dixie* and our *Crusader*—which had been supported by a group of Cubans but had always been attacked by certain so-called members of the Communist Party. We always wondered about those members of the Communist Party from America who had come over to help Cuba. Were they working for the party or for the CIA? What were they working for? They gave us a fit from the time we arrived in Cuba. They didn't want us to go on radio in the first place. They didn't want us to publish our newsletter because they disagreed with our championing the Black people's struggle in the United States. They argued that it was not a national struggle but a class struggle. So, we had some very interesting arguments at different gatherings whenever we met as a group of exiles. They insisted, "It's a class problem, and Robert Williams and his tirade against white racists is gonna split up the working class and alienate the white workers from our struggle in the United States." Our stance was that it was a struggle to get our rights as a nation, a Black nation. Of course, the official organ of the Communist Party of the United States was supporting the civil rights struggle, but it wanted to support the safe side of the civil rights struggle, like Martin Luther King and nonviolence. They were saying that Malcolm X was a Black fascist and Rob was a Black Nationalist, and we were the kind of people who should not be supported. Robert was not a member of any political party—other than the Democrats at one point. He was not a member of the Progressive Party, though he certainly voted for Henry Wallace when he ran for president. Rob had his own political view. We were in the process of developing our own political view, not thinking that any one political party had the answer to all of the questions.

Who could tell whether it was the Communist Party members from the United States who were causing problems for us, or *Hoy*, the official organ of the Community Party of Cuba? They both publicly supported Martin Luther King and the civil rights movement, but some said that there should be no split between the Black and white workers. And they couldn't see that what was happening in the South of the United States was a race issue. They didn't want to recognize that race was a national problem that had to be addressed—and was being addressed through our movement. Robert was attempting to educate the world about our struggle and the fact that our struggle was a part of the overall struggle of people fighting for a better life, but at that particular point in history, it did not take on a class nature. He did not want to engage in a political fight in Cuba. He said to the Cubans, "My struggle is in the United States. I didn't come here to fight Cubans. As long as you support me in my struggle, that's fine. I'm not going to take sides in any internal struggle in Cuba." He maintained that position the whole time we were exiled.[1]

1. "Rob was a person . . . we were exiled": Mabel Williams, interview by Claude Marks and Lincoln Bergman, May 30 and 31, 2003, Baldwin, MI, MRW Collection.

CHAPTER 21

FROM CUBA TO CHINA

In response to the tensions created by ideological contradictions, Mabel and Robert Williams left Cuba to seek refuge in the People's Republic of China in July 1966. The Williamses joined their sons, Robert Jr. and John, who were already living in China.

The Cubans, the Chinese, and the Vietnamese were very helpful as we made the transition to China. We had already visited China twice and had left our children there on the second visit. They were already over there in school, so there was just the matter of the two of us making the adjustment. At the time, people all over the world were volunteering to help support Vietnam. I think one of the reasons that we were allowed to leave Cuba is that the Vietnamese had invited us to come and help them. We were able to tell the Cubans that the Vietnamese wanted our help, and we were willing to go. Since the Cubans were always ready to do everything they could to help Vietnam, they allowed us to leave.

We learned a lot about political struggle during the course of our travels through the different countries. Once we were out of Cuba, the Vietnamese told us, "Don't let the Russians see the visa." We never did complete that visit to Vietnam. After we went to China, we did not proceed on to Vietnam, and we never really got to help them out. We stayed in China once we got there. It was expedient for us that we left Cuba with the idea that we were going to help Vietnam.

We arrived in China when the country was in the process of developing through the Cultural Revolution. There was a lot of chaos, and it was a rough time. Yet it was a wonderful time as well, an educational time for us. We were able to put out our *Crusader* for a while with the help of some workers who volunteered their time and efforts. And at one time, we were told that we could reestablish our *Radio Free Dixie*; but Robert had the presence of mind, the good sense, not to accept that offer during a time when the Chinese were having internal struggles. There were groups of people saying that jazz was imperialist music and should not be listened to or encouraged. And there was another group saying, "Oh yes, jazz is the people's music, and yes, it would be good to have it."

When Henry Kissinger came to China, the Chinese invited us to the reception.[1] We were introduced and shook hands with Kissinger. I don't remember everything about the event, but Premier Zhou Enlai told us later that Kissinger had said that he didn't know who Robert Williams was.[2] When Kissinger indicated that he wanted Premier Zhou to do something, Premier Zhou said, "Well, what about the Robert Williams case? Maybe if you took care of this, then we could take care of that." Premier Zhou told us that Kissinger pretended he didn't know who Robert Williams was, that he'd never heard of him.[3]

1. Henry Kissinger was the national security adviser and foreign affairs consultant to Presidents Richard Nixon and Gerald Ford from 1968 to 1975.

2. On the spelling of Chinese names, see the note on p. 203.

3. "The Cubans, the Chinese . . . never heard of him": Mabel Williams, interview by Claude Marks and Lincoln Bergman, May 30 and 31, 2003, San Francisco, CA, MRW Collection.

CHAPTER 22

VISITING AFRICA

Robert and Mabel Williams traveled to East Africa in 1968. They desired to obtain asylum in an African country but were unsuccessful in securing political exile status on the continent.

My first visit to the African continent was to Tanzania by way of Kenya. I was traveling with a Chinese travel document that listed me as an American traveling under the protection of the Chinese government. I had to first embark to Kenya in order to proceed to Tanzania. When I arrived in Kenya, I was so happy to see all the African officials carrying out the duties that I had only seen whites doing in the US.

In customs, I was questioned by the authorities and passed from one to another so that I was the last passenger to go through. I was told to wait again while the agent made a phone call. After a short wait, a tall, fat white man came in. He was smoking a cigar and wearing khaki shorts. He looked in my direction and asked if I was an American. When I answered yes, he said something to the customs official under his breath, and they both laughed. He then took my document from the customs man and stamped it. He turned and went back into the office he had come out of. Needless to say, I was flabbergasted and sad. I flew on to Tanzania with no further incidents.

During my stay in Tanzania, I enjoyed the relaxed lifestyle of the people. I loved to go into the countryside and visit the villages. I enjoyed the golden beaches, the blue skies, and the natural wildlife. However, I saw that most of the tourist commerce was not being managed by native Africans. They had shops in the countryside and spread their wares for sale on blankets in the streets. They held the lower-paying jobs. I was sad to see such a starkly divided class structure.

CHAPTER 23

CULTURAL REVOLUTION, ZHOU ENLAI, AND THE DECISION TO RETURN

We really never wanted to leave the United States, and the whole time we were away, Robert kept uppermost in our minds, and we always talked about, the fact that we would come back home. So, it was not that we made a decision all of a sudden to come back, but as I mentioned before, Rob was a person who could analyze political situations quite well, and he had come to the conclusion that it was the time for us to come back.

During the course of the Cultural Revolution, there was growing pressure to choose sides among the struggling groups. Once again, Rob decided, "This is not a time for me to be involved in the internal politics of this country. My struggle is not here; my struggle is in the United States of America." He always made that clear when people tried to pressure him into taking sides with different factions.

We attended an affair at the Ghanaian embassy—perhaps it was their national celebration. Rob had already indicated through connections with the government leadership that he thought it was time for him to go back to America. So, while we were at this diplomatic affair, we got a message that Premier Zhou wanted to meet with us after the affair and that he would send a car for us. As soon as the affair was over, a car came, picked us up, and took us to the Great Hall of the People, where Premier Zhou was waiting for us. We had a discussion about our people's struggle, Chairman Mao's statement in support of the struggle, and the world situation. I guess the conversation lasted for over an hour.

Premier Zhou spoke perfect English. He had been informed that we were ready to go home. He questioned Rob, "You think they won't shoot you down when you first get off the plane? Why do you have such faith in the US government?" Rob answered, "I don't have any faith in the US government, but I think that they would want to know what I know before they shoot me down. I'm the only American who has had the experience that I have had with top leadership here in China. I think they'll want to know what I know before they shoot me down." Premier Zhou laughed about that and said, "Well, you may be right. When you go back, maybe you'll be able to help improve relations between our two countries." That was the first indication that Rob had that China was considering at least opening dialogue with the US. Rob said he would do everything he could to that end. Premier Zhou responded, "Since you're loyal, we'll do everything we can to help facilitate your return." And they did, and we did. I will never forget looking out of the back window of the car as we were driven away. Premier Zhou was standing on the steps of the Great Hall of the People, waving goodbye to us.[1]

1. "We really never . . . goodbye to us": Mabel Williams, interview by Claude Marks and Lincoln Bergman, May 30 and 31, 2003, Baldwin, MI, MRW Collection.

The Williams family (*holding flowers*) being greeted upon arrival in China, 1963. Robert F. Williams Papers, Bentley Historical Library, University of Michigan.

African American and African liberation leaders meeting in Tanzania, 1968: David Sibeko (*second from left*) of the Pan-Africanist Congress of Azania (South Africa), Monroe defendant Mae Mallory (*third from left, in white*), Robert Williams (*fourth from left*), and Williams's attorney and Republic of New Afrika cofounder Gaidi Obadele (aka Milton Henry) (*third from right*). Robert F. Williams Papers, Bentley Historical Library, University of Michigan.

CHAPTER 24

THE JOURNEY BACK

We traveled through Tanzania on our journey from China. I didn't have an American passport until I was on my way back home to the United States. I got my first passport from the US government in Tanzania, as did our two sons. They [US officials] wouldn't give Rob a passport; they gave him a travel document. We had traveled from Cuba to China when we visited, under a Cuban travel document that stated we were Americans traveling under the protection of the Cuban government. Once we moved our residence to China, we traveled with a Chinese document saying we were Americans under the protection of the Chinese government. So, we had been able to travel without American passports. Robert went ahead first to Tanzania to scout things out. He was thinking at that time that we might move to Africa. Unfamiliar with the political situation in Africa at that time, he thought that if we could not make the kind of connections we needed to move back to the United States, maybe we would just move to Africa and stay there for a while. In Tanzania, he met with Americans who came over to talk with him. By that time, he had been voted in as president-in-exile of the Republic of New Afrika.[1] While he

1. The Provisional Government of the Republic of New Afrika was formed at the Black Government Conference in Detroit, Michigan, in March 1968. At the conference, 500 Black Nationalists declared their independence from the United States, identified five Deep South states (Mississippi, Louisiana, Alabama, Georgia, and South Carolina) as their national territory, demanded reparations from the United States, and named Robert Williams their president. Edward Onaci, *Free the Land: The Republic of New Afrika and the Pursuit of a Black*

was in Tanzania, he met with officials from that organization. He met with Mae Mallory, who was there from the New York group, and Gaidi Obadele, aka Milton Henry, who became his lawyer for the return to the US.[2] He also did an interview with Bob Cohen, who was in the process of scouting out what could be done about our returning to the US.[3]

Robert went to the American embassy to see if the US government would allow him to return home. He assessed the situation with friends. Some of them wanted him to come home, and others didn't; but he had the final say and decided, "Well, if I can go home, I'm going home." After he found out that freedom fighters who had been a part of winning independence for Tanzania were under tremendous financial pressure from the US and Britain, he decided it would be better for him to concentrate on trying to return home.

The Americans hemmed and hawed. They told him that they might give him a travel document to come back home, but he couldn't bring anything with him because they had a ban on everything manufactured in China. Rob told them, "Well, that'll be all right. What I'll do, I'll come with all my stuff, and then I'll go out there on the beach and call a press conference and strip down, because even my drawers were made in China." They were really angry about that. He was back and forth between US officials in Washington and those in Tanzania. When the foreign ministry of Tanzania told him that his visa was about to run out and he had to do something, he approached the Chinese and told them, "I'm ready to go back to China." He came back to China, but he had laid the groundwork for us to return to the US.

Eventually all of us went back to Tanzania and stayed there for a while. Again, we were helped by someone who had been a *Crusader* supporter over the years. It was Bill Sullivan, a Quaker who was then living and working in Tanzania. He allowed us to live in his house while we were getting ready to come back to the United States.

We decided that the boys and I would return home first. We didn't have to get visas to go through England. As American citizens en route, we didn't have

---

Nation-State (Chapel Hill: University of North Carolina Press, 2020), 25–30; Akinyele Omowale Umoja, *We Will Shoot Back: Armed Resistance in the Mississippi Freedom Movement* (New York: New York University Press, 2013), 186–88.

2. Milton Henry (1919–2006) was an attorney, an associate and supporter of Malcolm X, and cofounder of the Provisional Government of the Republic of New Afrika.

3. Robert Carl Cohen (b. 1930) is an author and a journalist who interviewed Robert Williams in Cuba and China; he authored *Black Crusader: A Biography of Robert Williams* (Secaucus, NJ: Lyle Stuart, 1972).

to have a visa. We got a visa for passing through Egypt. So, the boys and I had absolutely no problem at all once we left Tanzania. We flew into Egypt, and from Egypt to England. We stayed overnight in England and got a chance to see some of the country. Then we came into Detroit.

We had chosen Detroit because the state of Michigan had never sent a Black person fleeing political oppression back to the South. When the boys and I arrived, we were met by guards from the Republic of New Africa. It was a beautiful meeting! They escorted us to our relatives' home, where we had a wonderful reunion with family and friends. The RNA armed guards stayed with us, and we all prepared for Robert's return.

Robert eventually booked his flight out. When he left Tanzania, he had problems in Egypt. They tried to send him back to Tanzania. They had everybody get off his plane. Then they called everybody back on, but he was told he couldn't get back on, that he had to go back to Tanzania. He had to do a lot of threatening and everything else to get back on that plane. He even threatened to blow the plane up, he was so upset. Eventually they let him on that plane, and he went to England.

When he got into England, he was interrogated by four or five different sets of people. At one point—we laughed about it later—they pulled an ink pen from in his pocket and asked, "What is this?" He told them, "It's an ink pen. What did you think it was?" The man who took it said, "I'm gonna open it now. If it blows up, you gonna die, too." Robert asked, "Do you think the Chinese have advanced so far that they have learned how to put an atomic bomb in an ink pen?" We laughed about that.

He was harassed terribly at the airport, then put in a car and driven around. These British officials were pointing out historic sites, and he thought they were just taking him on a tour of London. Then he looked up and saw these walls. He said to the man accompanying him, "This looks like a prison." He answered, "It is a prison." It was Pentonville Prison. The officials put Robert in prison, charging him with being an illegal immigrant. They were going to try to send him back to China. I don't know all of the details. Rumors have it that the CIA had the British put him off the plane in Egypt because the US intelligence didn't want him back in the United States. TWA refused to acknowledge the ticket that he had purchased to fly from London to Detroit.

As Rob was being inducted into the prison, he saw an African man who was being released. Guards were returning the man's belongings as they were taking everything away from Rob. Rob had a copy of Mao's book, the Little Red Book. The African also had a Little Red Book that he was getting back. Rob reached out to him: "Brother, you getting out? You tell the people out there that a freedom fighter from the United States is in prison. They have put me in prison as I was trying to return home." And the African told him, "I will do that." Evidently, he did so, because the Civil Liberties Union and the Jamaican West Indian group of activists in London all got involved. A political movement grew up in support of Rob and against the authorities for putting him in prison illegally.

While he was in prison, Rob went on a hunger strike. On the fourth day of his strike, guards put him in the hospital because there was a rule that if a person didn't eat by the fourth day, he had to be hospitalized. Officials tried to force him to eat. They brought in a minister from the Church of England who told him, "Williams, I know that you don't trust the jailers and so forth, and you won't eat for them, but my church will prepare food and bring it if you will eat it." Robert told him, "No, I don't want your food. I'm not going to eat." The minister insisted, but Rob kept telling him no. Then Rob told him, "You know, your forefathers came to Africa and put my forefathers in slavery. And they offered them food, and they took the food, and they lived. Now, here I am, in this age. Your people have put me in jail, and now you want to offer me food just to live. I don't know about you; you may be the same as your forefathers, but I'm not the same as mine. You cannot take away my freedom and give me food. I want none of your food, whether it's from the church or from the government. I will have none of your food. So, don't ask me again." After that, the minister went away.

Meanwhile, the political pressure was building on the outside. Rob could hear some chanting going on, and one of the prisoners told him, "Mate, you've got friends out there! They're chanting for you!" The officials took him to the airport twice. The first time, something happened, and they took him back to the prison. He learned later that one of the baggage cart trucks had run into the plane on the airfield. They suspected it was political sabotage and questioned him about his connection with the Irish Liberation Army. They didn't let him leave that day. The second time they took him to the airport, Rob commented to the guard, "Well, I guess I'll miss my plane again this time," but the guard assured him, "You stand as much chance of missing this plane as the queen of England has of missing her plane when she wants to go somewhere. You are getting outta here today!"

TWA had agreed to send a plane to pick him up.[4] He was the only passenger, other than his lawyer, who had come over to England to ride back with him

4. Trans World Airline was a major international airline that ended operations in 2001.

to Detroit. When Rob found out about those arrangements, he asked, "Why would TWA refuse to fly me home?" Someone explained that TWA was afraid he would hijack the plane. "I've been everywhere hijackers want to go. So why would I want to hijack a plane?" Rob asked. "I'm trying to go home! I'm only trying to go home. Why would I hijack a plane?"[5]

5. "We traveled through Tanzania . . . hijack a plane?": Mabel Williams, interview by Claude Marks and Lincoln Bergman, May 30 and 31, 2003, San Francisco, CA, MRW Collection.

Mabel Williams in her home office, Idlewild, Michigan, c. 1970s. Courtesy of the Williams family.

Left to right: African American liberation leaders Angela Davis, Kathleen Cleaver, and Mabel Williams, 2004. Photo by Scott Braley. Used by permission of the Freedom Archives.

Left to right: Revolutionary movement activists Yuri Kochiyama and Mabel and John Williams, 2004. Photo by Scott Braley. Used by permission of the Freedom Archives.

CHAPTER 25

BACK IN THE UNITED STATES

The Republic of New Afrika guards accompanied me to the airport to meet Rob. The officials kept us back because the FBI had to go on the plane and arrest him before he set foot on the ground. He came off the plane with a victorious Black Power salute. He was back home again, and we would be able to survive. Officials would not allow him to go home with us. They took him to federal court, where we had a battle. They tried to get him to sign some papers, and he questioned, "Is there a law that I have to sign these papers?" They answered, "No, it's just tradition." He responded that he was not going to live up to that tradition. He refused to sign the papers. It was so funny, because a lawyer who was helping Gaidi Obadele with the case told Rob afterward, "You know, I've been practicing law for many years, and I've always advised my clients to go 'head and sign those papers; but I didn't realize that they didn't have to do it. I didn't know it was just a tradition!"

The struggle continued. The government dropped the federal fugitive charges. So, the federal government was out of it. However, the Monroe kidnapping charges were still there, and North Carolina had asked Michigan for extradition. So, Robert had to fight extradition from Michigan back to North Carolina. I don't know if they [US government] let him sign on his own recognizance or if some kind of bond had to be put up so that he could finally come home; but for the next few years, he was in a legal battle, fighting extradition back to North Carolina.

That was our return to the United States. From there, we just continued to struggle—and the struggle continues on and on and on. One thing I learned from all of this: I began to see a lot of contradictions. Traveling, being in positions where I could engage with top leaders of governments all over the world, I began to see that a lot of our struggling people are misguided in taking sides—vying "isms" and so forth. They don't know how manipulated they are. For instance, once we were back in the United States, Robert was called to the State Department to talk to the people who were trying to arrange for President Nixon's visit to China. He was also called to the House Un-American Activities Committee. The people in the House Un-American Activities Committee didn't trust the people in the State Department. People in the State Department didn't trust the people in the House Un-American Activities Committee. There were elements in the US government who wanted to see better relations with China, and there were elements who didn't. So, we learned that even within our own government at the higher level, there were contradictions. I think that one of the reasons that Robert was able to survive through all of this, from the very beginning, is that he was able to see the contradictions at an early stage, both those within our government and those in the international scene, and take advantage of some of them. That's why we were able to survive, having built networks of people who really have the true interests of the people at heart. I think that there are still people out there working, and that we all constitute a real power, but we don't know it. I think that those of us who have come to this understanding, who hold this truth, need to look out for each other because we are all in this world together. We can't just be selfish and look out for self, and we can't try to push other people down. Once we join together, we can make a better world—working individually and collectively, networking with people with like minds, raising the consciousness of our young people so that they can understand this struggle, rather than seek self-gratification, which is the opposite of what we're trying to do. We want to see everybody rise and have a better life all over the world, not just here in the United States. That's my personal philosophy.[1]

1. "The Republic of New Africa . . . my personal philosophy": Mabel Williams, interview by Claude Marks and Lincoln Bergman, May 30 and 31, 2003), San Francisco, CA, MRW Collection.

CHAPTER 26

LOVE YOUR NEIGHBOR

Robert and Mabel Williams returned to Michigan, moving to Baldwin (Lake County) in 1972. Baldwin is near the unincorporated resort community of Idlewild. They became involved in grassroots activism in Lake County. They formed the People's Association for Human Rights as their vehicle to engage in local political action. Even after the death of Robert in 1996, Mrs. Williams engaged in advocacy and providing services for families, particularly senior citizens, promoted the historic preservation of Idlewild, and engaged in work as a layperson in Baldwin's St. Ann Catholic Church. Because of her work and service in Lake County, the name of the Idlewild Culture Conference Center was changed to the Mabel R. Williams Center in 2012. Mrs. Williams also served as a popular public speaker in Lake County and around the United States, sharing the history of the Monroe movement and the international experiences of her family in the fight for Black liberation and human rights.

Today is September 16, 2010. I am in East Lansing, Michigan. It is rainy and gloomy outside, which matches my mood to the utmost. I received an email today informing me that the famous Black civil rights photographer Ernest Withers was an FBI agent who spied on the movement and on Dr. Martin Luther King right up to and including the very day that he was assassinated. Sarah Palin and the Tea Party victories are being touted everywhere as the backlash of racial hatred fires up all over again.

Needless to say, the news does nothing to help me out of the dumps. What begins to help is the memory of some of my neighbors in our New Town

Left to right: John C. Williams, Mabel Williams, Robert Williams Jr. (aka Bobby), and Robert Williams with unidentified friend (*front*), c. 1970s. Courtesy of the Williams family.

Mabel Williams and John C. Williams, 2006. Photo by Scott Braley. Used by permission of the Freedom Archives.

community in Monroe, North Carolina. We had moved in with Robert's father the same night that we were married by a local minister in my Quality Hill community. I quickly became friends with the neighbors, and they accepted me as one of their own. Mr. and Mrs. Crowder lived next door. He was a retired disabled railroad worker who walked with a cane. A rather jolly person, he enjoyed sitting with my father-in-law, exchanging tales of their railroad experiences. His wife, Mrs. Bessie, had been a domestic and still took in washing and ironing to supplement her husband's meager check. In their backyard, she boiled the white clothes in a black cast-iron washpot, under which she kept a hot fire blazing. She and my mother performed this task every Monday morning. My mother bought her starch from the grocery store, but Mrs. Bessie made hers from white flour. They heated the irons on their stoves, but Mother had graduated to an electric iron by the time I left home.

Mrs. Bessie, a diabetic, had to have injections every morning before breakfast. Mr. Crowder had become shaky, and Mrs. Bessie, with only one arm—she had lost the other in a train accident years earlier—could not handle the needles. I was immediately recruited to do the job. In those days, the needles had to be boiled for sterilization, and the syringes had to be filled every day. Fortunately, I had worked in a hospital and knew how to do these things.

On the other side of us lived Mr. and Mrs. Jake Smith. He, too, was an ex–railroad worker. He had suffered a stroke that had left his vocal cords paralyzed. His speech was slow and garbled, and he would become agitated when he couldn't get his words out. Mama Smith was also diabetic. I became her nurse as well. She had worked as a seamstress in her youth.

Both these couples became our surrogate parents. They shared with us many stories of their struggles for survival in the segregated work world that they had come through. The ladies were dress-up, regular Sunday worshippers who lived out their professed Christian beliefs through their everyday care of their spouses and their neighbors. Sometimes, when I came home from work, I would find entire meals prepared and waiting for us.

Both couples treated our sons like grandchildren, but Mama and Daddy Smith were babysitters for our younger son, Johnny. They would really get upset if they heard him cry. She would come to the fence between our houses and call me to see what the problem was. One day I went over to speak with them and found Daddy Smith crying and trying to speak through his tears. He wanted to know if Johnny was all right. I immediately went back to get Johnny and brought him over. Daddy Smith took my son in his arms, hugged him, and said how much he loved him. By that time, he, Mama Smith, and I were all shedding tears, and their little dog was growling and barking, too. Mama Smith said the dog had been the first to alert them to Johnny's crying. There was always a friendly, subtle rivalry between the grandfathers—John Williams, Rob's father, and Chalmers Barber, my stepfather—for the affection of John Chalmers, their namesake. Daddy Smith was right in the middle of that rivalry.

CHAPTER 27

AM I WHITE?

The family was seated together in the family room, watching a television forum hosted by popular radio host Tom Joyner, focused on "The State of the Black Nation." Gwen Ifill had made a heart-wrenching presentation.[1] Others spoke, and then Dick Gregory was introduced.[2] He started his presentation, as they all did, from a seated position, but gradually his historic diatribe about our journey as a people brought the studio audience to its feet with applause and shouts of agreement.

My son and daughter-in-law, John and Lisa; her father; my youngest grandson, Benjamin; my five-year-old great-granddaughter, Cali June; and Lisa's two-year-old niece, Anijah, were the family unit watching the show. All the adults present were watching with excitement and reacting similarly to the studio audience, recalling issues from our own experiences. When the show broke to a commercial, Cali got off my lap and stood in front of me, cradling Anijah's Black doll in her arms. She looked me in the eyes with a sincerely puzzled expression and asked, "Great-Grandma Mabel, am I white?"

Stunned by her question, I reached out to her with open arms and finally replied, "You are a beautiful, wonderful, loving *human being*, and I love you very much." Cali snuggled closely, returned my hug, said she loved me, too; but then

1. Gwen Ifill (1955–2016) was an African American journalist and co-anchor on *PBS NewsHour*.

2. Dick Gregory (1932–2017) was an African American comedian, civil rights activist, and social critic.

Mabel and Robert Williams, c. 1980s.
Courtesy of the Williams family.

she repeated her question, "But, am I white?" Not wanting to give her a definitive answer on the spur of the movement, I repeated my answer. She drew back a little, made a gesture of drawing a line down the middle of her chest, and said, "I am this much white and this much Black." At that remark, I repeated that she was a totally whole, beautiful, lovable *human being.*

This episode, which occurred some time ago, has remained in my thoughts as current social and political events unfold. One of my close, dear friends and allies over the years, Gwendolyn Midlo Hall, just finished her memoirs.[3] She is Jewish by birth, but her children are biracial. We have shared mutual concerns over the years about our society and our kids.

My husband and I shared forty-nine years of married life, which began in the prejudiced, segregated, southern town of Monroe, North Carolina, but ended at his death in the integrated, but still prejudiced, town of Baldwin in northwestern Michigan. During the course of those years, we fought for civil and human rights and against racial discrimination among people. We lived and struggled in many societies that were in transition, interacting with people of most known ethnic groups.

As parents, we harbored only the best wishes for our children—as we had struggled to improve the lot of all children through our political efforts. We watched and counseled our two sons as they grew into maturity, from North Carolina to Cuba, to China, to Africa, and back to the United States. Our son Robert—Bobby—was thirteen years old when we left the country, and son John was eleven. Bobby had already laid claim to two of his Black female classmates as his girlfriends.

In Cuba, Bobby had girlfriends from the whole spectrum of races available there but left for China traumatized because he had to part from his Afro-Cuban girlfriend. Both our sons interacted with girls and boys from all over the world with whom they lived and studied. However, John, unlike his brother, did not form any love ties, as far as we knew.

While in China, their friends and acquaintances were again as varied ethnically as they were in Cuba. Bobby, once again, courted girls from various ethnicities and races, including African, Chinese, and white Americans. It occurred to me then that one day our family might possibly reflect ethnic diversity.

When we returned to the United States, Bobby again sought out old girlfriends and new ones among his acquaintances. Upon entering college, both sons acquired new friends. At graduation, they were closely involved with young

3. Gwendolyn Midlo Hall was a historian, an author, a revolutionary activist, and a longtime friend of Mabel Williams and the Williams family.

African American ladies from their university. John went on to law school in Indiana. Bobby stayed in Lansing, working summers for Ingham County Probate Court. He eventually became engaged to Melanie Fink, one of his white friends and coworkers.

Robert and I were both shocked and surprised when he announced that he was going to ask her to marry him. We discussed the issues of family, future children, and circumstances related to living in what we recognized as a white male–dominated, racist society. We finally met with Melanie's family. We shared our concerns but eventually gave our blessings, and the new Robert F. Williams Jr. family began.

Over the next few years, Bobby and Mel brought two sons into the family, Robby and Ben. As I approach my seventy-seventh birthday, my heart and mind still ponder the question posed by my great-granddaughter, Cali, Robby's daughter. I pause and take note that many of the political realities that guided my past actions have not changed very much in our land.

CHAPTER 28

MY MESSAGE TO FUTURE GENERATIONS

Being a high school graduate from Monroe, North Carolina, just a "nobody" from Monroe, I never thought I would end up meeting heads of state and becoming involved in world politics. We never know when we're born in this world whose life we are going to impact or who is going to impact us, and if we just live for self, we cut off all kinds of experiences. We shut out the rest of the world's people, we don't gain anything, we don't learn anything, and we don't grow. In order to grow and become a fully developed human being, you need to keep your mind open, recognizing that education is an ongoing process and that if you cloud your mind with things that satisfy only sensual pleasures, you're cutting yourself off. You're really doing yourself a disservice. People were shocked when 9/11 happened. The young people today need to know what other people are thinking about America. They may be out here trying to satisfy themselves, but as Americans, they need to know the things that their tax dollars are supporting, the things that they're voting for—if they vote—and the things that they're involved in politically as Americans. They need to know more about what other people think about them and what America is doing, and they need to have a say in what America does so that we can change things.

We don't want to be on the road to extinction as an American society. If you have any thought that we can't lose what we have, then you're very wrong. I tell the young people this all the time. We can lose what we have as Americans.

We are so fortunate and so blessed to have the highest standard of living in the world. However, we better know the decisions that our government is making so that we can have an impact on those decisions and the way they are affecting other people around the world. That would be my message to young people.[1]

Mrs. Mabel Robinson Williams joined the Ancestors on April 19, 2014. She was survived by her son John Chalmers Williams and wife, Lisa; stepson, Franklin Williams; grandsons, Robert F. Williams III and Benjamin Paul Williams; great-granddaughters, Cali and Sasha Williams; brother-in-law, John H. Williams; and a host of other relatives and friends. Mrs. Williams's story and powerful legacy, as a committed, self-determining freedom fighter working in partnership with her husband, provide compelling insights for all those engaged in contemporary liberation movements.

1. 1. "Being a high school graduate . . . to young people": Mabel Williams, interview by Claude Marks and Lincoln Bergman, May 30 and 31, 2003, San Francisco, CA, MRW Collection.

INDEX

Page numbers in italics indicate illustrations.